CONTEXTUALISM IN PHILOSOPHY
Knowledge, Meaning, and Truth

Edited by

Gerhard Preyer
  and
Georg Peter

CLARENDON PRESS · OXFORD

OXFORD
UNIVERSITY PRESS

Great Clarendon Street, Oxford OX2 6DP

Oxford University Press is a department of the University of Oxford.
It furthers the University's objective of excellence in research, scholarship,
and education by publishing worldwide in

Oxford New York

Auckland Cape Town Dar es Salaam Hong Kong Karachi
Kuala Lumpur Madrid Melbourne Mexico City Nairobi
New Delhi Shanghai Taipei Toronto

With offices in

Argentina Austria Brazil Chile Czech Republic France Greece
Guatemala Hungary Italy Japan Poland Portugal Singapore
South Korea Switzerland Thailand Turkey Ukraine Vietnam

Oxford is a registered trade mark of Oxford University Press
in the UK and in certain other countries

Published in the United States
by Oxford University Press Inc., New York

British Library Cataloguing in Publication Data
Data available

Library of Congress Cataloging in Publication Data
Data available

Typeset by SPI Publisher Services, Pondicherry, India
Printed in Great Britain
on acid-free paper by
Biddles Ltd, King's Lynn, Norfolk

ISBN 0-19-926740-5   978-0-19-926740-8
ISBN 0-19-926741-3-X(Pbk.)   978-0-19-926741-5 (Pbk.)

10 9 8 7 6 5 4 3 2 1

Contextualism in Philosophy

Contents

Contributors

Professor Kent Bach, Department of Philosophy, San Francisco State University, San Francisco, CA 94132, USA.

Professor Herman Cappelen, Department of Philosophy, Vassar College, 124 Raymond Ave, Poughkeepsie, NY 12604, USA.

Professor Andy Egan, Department of Philosophy, Australian National University, Cambarra ACT 0200, Australia.

Professor Michael Glanzberg, Department of Philosophy, University of California, Davis, 2238 Social Science and Humanities Building, Davis, CA 95616, USA.

Professor John Hawthorne, Department of Philosophy, Rutgers University, 26 Nichol Avenue, New Brunswick, NJ 08901, USA.

Professor Ernie Lepore, Center for Cognitive Science, Rutgers University, New Brunswick Psych Bldg Addition, Busch Campus, 152 Frelinghuysen Road, Piscataway, NJ 08854-8020, USA.

Professor Peter Ludlow, Department of Philosophy, University of Michigan, Ann Arbor, MI 48109-1003, USA.

Professor Peter Pagin, Department of Philosophy, Stockholm University, 106 91 Stockholm, Sweden.

Dr Georg Peter, J. W. Goethe-University, Protosociology, 60054 Frankfurt am Main, Germany.

Professor Paul M. Pietroski, Department of Philosophy, Skinner Building, College Park, MD 20742, USA.

Dr Gerhard Preyer, J. W. Goethe-University, Protosociology, 60054 Frankfurt am Main, Germany.

Professor Francois Recanati, Institut Jean-Nicod (CNRS/EHESS/ENS), 1bis, avenue de Lowendal, 75007 Paris, France.

PROFESSOR JONATHAN SCHAFFER, Department of Philosophy, University of Massachusetts-Amherst, 352 Bartlett Hall, Amherst, MA 01003, USA.

PROFESSOR JASON STANLEY, Department of Philosophy, Rutgers, The State University of New Jersey, 26 Nichol Avenue, New Brunswick, NJ 08901-1411, USA.

PROFESSOR BRIAN WEATHERSON, Department of Philosophy, Brown University, Providence, RI 02912, USA.

PROFESSOR TIMOTHY WILLIAMSON, New College, Oxford OX1 3BN, UK.

Introduction: The Limits of Contextualism

GERHARD PREYER AND GEORG PETER

In contemporary epistemology, the thesis that epistemic vocabulary is con-text-sensitive has been adopted by a number of authors. Since the thesis is a semantic claim, evaluation of its truth has interested those working in philosophy of language. In particular, serious consideration of the thesis requires some account of when a linguistic construction is context-sensitive. This book will look at contextualism in epistemology and its linguistic underpinnings, and at related general issues in the philosophy of language. The fruitful interaction between empirical questions about language and philosophical issues in epistemology that occurs in the essays in this book can perhaps be viewed a considerably more empirically grounded return to the linguistic turn in epistemology offered by Wittgenstein, Austin, and Malcolm.

The motivations of epistemic contextualism, until recently, had chiefly to do with its supposedly enabling good responses to scepticism, showing where—at least a certain form of—sceptical arguments get their seeming strength, without actually endorsing (acontextually, anyway) the conclusions thereof (see for example the work of Keith DeRose, Stewart Cohen, David Lewis). Thinking about our use of epistemic terms, DeRose advertises contextualism as at least as much motivated by a sort of 'ordinary language'. In his essay, Peter Ludlow uses the test case of contextualism to illustrate this new linguistic turn in epistemology, and raises some of the many subtle questions that we need to consider when we take up topics such as the nature of gradable predicates, the different forms that implicit arguments can take, and the way in which different definitions of contextualism will yield differ-ent predictions about bound variable anaphora in knowledge reports. He concludes that linguistic resources, handled carefully, can be a valuable tool, but that they cannot be deployed in isolation.

Contextualists try to resolve sceptical paradoxes not by refuting sceptical arguments but by confining them to contexts in which far-fetched possibilities are raised. In so doing, they assume that the conflicting intuitions that generate these paradoxes relate to the truth conditions of knowledge and are not merely vaccillating responses to sceptical considerations. Contextualists reject invariantism about knowledge attributions and claim that a given knowledge-ascribing sentence can express different propositions in different contexts, which implies that there are many knowledge relations, not just one. However, as Kent Bach argues in his essay, this thesis is not as dramatic as it sounds, for even if it were correct, those propositions themselves would not be context-bound. More importantly, the fact that it can vary from one context to another how strictly we apply 'know' does not require a contextualist explanation. It also does not require dubious warranted assertibility arguments (WAMs), whose use DeRose imputes to invariantism. The fact that people use words with varying degrees of strictness and looseness does not show that the words themselves have semantic contents that come in various degrees. It could well be, Bach suggests, that with 'know' we often attribute knowledge to people who do not have it and often resist attributing it to people who do. Sometimes we are extra cautious, and sometimes we are even taken in by seductive sceptical arguments. Either way, we cannot attribute knowledge to someone, even if he has it, when he believes something on grounds that leave us with doubts or worries about the truth of the proposition in question. We sometimes demand more from knowledge than it requires. Bach argues that contextualism does not really come to grips with scepticism or with the sceptical version of invariantism, according to which knowledge requires the highest degree of evidence, justification, and conviction.

Scepticism denies that we have knowledge by ordinary standards, and sceptical invariantism does not use WAMs to explain why we casually make the knowledge attributions that we do. In any case, these sceptical views are implausible on independent grounds. Much more plausible is a moderate, non-sceptical version of invariantism, which also can interpret contextualist data without resorting to WAMs. What vary in contexts where special concerns arise, whether sceptical or practical, are not the truth conditions of knowledge attributions but the knowledge attributions people are prepared to make. It is not the standards for the truth of knowledge attributions that go up but the attributor's threshold of confidence regarding the relevant proposition.

One element of Bach's defence of moderate invariantism is the answer to a question raised by Lewis's version of contextualism: how can a possibility that is ignored be properly ignored? He suggests that this is so to the extent that the cognitive processes whereby beliefs are formed and sustained are sensitive to realistic counterpossibilities (so-called relevant alternatives). The occurrence of the thought of a possibility contrary to a tempting proposition gives one prima-facie reason to take it seriously. And the fact that such a possibility does not come to mind is (defeasible) evidence for its irrelevance. But this fact shows evidently that one cannot explicitly consider it, since to consider it would bring that counterpossibility to mind.

Contextualism is a mild form of relativism about the truth of sentences. There is a standard form of contextualist strategy for explaining the appeal of sceptical arguments. While vagueness is not merely a case of context-dependence, it does appear to be highly conducive to context-dependence. In his essay, however, Timothy Williamson shows that context-dependence in representation causes its own problems in the retention and transmission of information, especially when language users are unaware of the context-dependence. Moreover, a contextualist treatment of certain problems of practical reason is implausible, because the agent's context seems to have primacy over the speaker's context in practical respects. This primacy is incompatible with contextualism about the relevant terms. The case of practical reasoning suggests a way in which vagueness need not induce context-dependence. Williamson draws an analogy between the case of practical reasoning and the case of epistemic appraisal to show how the vagueness of epistemological vocabulary need not make it context-dependent. The analogy is then argued to be more than an analogy, because there is a practical aspect to epistemic appraisal with respect to the formation and retention of beliefs. Therefore, Williamson concludes, something is wrong with epistemological contextualism; he suggests an alternative explanation.

Contextualists speak of the semantic value of knowledge ascriptions as somehow shifting with context. But what is it that shifts? What is the parameter that shifts with the context? What epistemic gear do the wheels of context turn? In his essay, Jonathan Schaffer considers three possible answers. What shifts might be: (T) the threshold of justification (Cohen), (S) the standard of epistemic position (DeRose), or (A) the set of epistemic alternatives (Lewis). He assesses these three answers in the light of four desiderata. The parameter of shift must be: (D1) linguistically plausible, (D2) predictively adequate, (D3) in accord with contextualist resolutions of scepticism, and (D4) connected to our practices of inquiry. He argues that

(A) fares best, by these desiderata. Both (T) and (S) fail all of (D1)–(D4) while (A) satisfies them all. Thus he concludes that what shifts is the set of epistemic alternatives. A very simple contextualistic treatment of a sentence containing an epistemic modal, for example, *a might be F*, is that it is true iff for all the contextually salient community knows, *a* is *F*. It is widely agreed that the simple theory will not work in some cases, but the counterexamples produced so far seem to be amenable to a more complicated contextualist theory. In their essay, Andy Egan, John Hawthorne, and Brian Weatherson argue, however, that no contextualist theory can capture the evaluations speakers naturally make of sentences containing epistemic modals. If we want to respect these evaluations, our best option is a *relativist* theory of epistemic modals. On a relativist theory, an utterance of *a might be F* can be true relative to one context of evaluation and false relative to another. They argue that such a theory does better than any rival approach at capturing all the behaviour of epistemic modals.

The contemporary debate on contextualism shows more than *one* view on epistemology and the philosophy of language. There are rather *two* views dealing with the role of context, both called by the same name. One clear relationship is that, if contextualism about language is true, the certain semantic arguments against contextualism in epistemology will be disarmed. So even if the essays by François Recanati and Herman Cappelen and Ernie Lepore are closely related to the semantic underpinnings of contextualism in epistemology, their central claims are within the philosophy of language.

Two traditions in the philosophy of language and semantics take effect in our understanding of language and claim to give us an answer to the question: What is the basic notion of semantic content (properties)? According to literalism, we may legitimately ascribe truth-conditional content to natural language *sentences*, quite independent of what the speaker who utters this sentence means. For the contrasting view, namely contextualism, *speech acts* are the instances of content. Therefore it can be concluded that only in the context of a speech act does a sentence express a determinate content. It follows that the same sentence may express different contents in different contexts. Context-sensitivity must be generalized, as François Recanati claims to show in his essay. First, he looks at the historical development of literalism. The extent of context-sensitivity in natural language was progressively acknowledged. Where does this tendency ultimately lead us? Recanati's answer is to contextualism. Secondly, he describes the steps which can lead from a critique of the dominant literalist position (minimalism) to contextualism. In the last sections he presents several possible arguments in favour of contextualism, corresponding to three distinct versions of contextualism. According to the first version, individual words have determinate contents but semantic composition requires going beyond that content: to determine the content of *complex* expressions (e.g. sentences) we must creatively enrich or otherwise adjust the meaning of individual words—and that cannot be done without appealing to speaker's meaning. In the second version it is not just semantic composition which requires adjustment and modulation of word meaning. Individual word meanings themselves could not go directly into the interpretation. They are either too abstract and schematic—in such a way that elaboration or fleshing out is needed to reach a determinate content—or they are too rich and must undergo 'feature-cancellation', or some other screening process through which some aspects will be backgrounded and others focused on. According to the third, even more radical version, the content which a word contributes is contextually constructed, but the construction can proceed without the help of conventional, context-independent word meanings. Recanati's turn is that the contextual sense which an expression assumes on a particular occasion of use can be computed directly on the basis of the contextual senses which that expression had on previous occasions of use.

Herman Cappelen and Ernie Lepore take a different view. The context-sensitive expressions which semantic minimalism recognizes are not only obvious, they also pass certain tests for context-sensitivity. Beyond fixing the semantic value of these obviously context-sensitive expressions, contexts of utterance have no effect on the propositions semantically expressed by the sentences we use. Cappelen and Lepore outline a defence of semantic minimalism and speech act pluralism against two common objections. In particular, it is alleged by some to follow from semantic minimalism that comparative adjectives are context-insensitive, and it also has been objected to minimalism that it postulates contents that are explanatorily idle, that play no role in an account of communication. Cappelen and Lepore defend semantic minimalism against the first objection not, as we might expect, by denying that implication, but by endorsing it. They go on to address the second objection and end with a reversal, that is, they argue that, although on their account meaning is not explanatorily idle, those who deny minimalism wind up with an account that is. In particular, they show that Recanati's view fails to satisfy his own availability principle.

The essays of Jason Stanley, Paul M. Pietroski, and Peter Pagin connect issues of context-dependence with fundamental issues in the philosophy of language: meaning and truth, and compositionality. In his essay, Jason

Stanley continues his recent project of defending the view that the intuitive truth conditions of an utterance are the result of a compositional semantic process. In particular, he argues that this view is compatible with the context-dependency of what is expressed by an utterance. Furthermore Stanley argues that many of those who proceed otherwise are unfairly saddling the position with strange theoretical commitments. Part of his goal in this essay is to elucidate the target concept of the intuitive truth conditions of an utterance, in order to better elucidate the actual commitments of the view that intuitive truth conditions are due to semantics. Along the way, he discusses the proper attitude to take when some particularly troublesome data on the semantics/pragmatics divide, such as deferred reference, are concerned.

It is widely held that, if meaning is compositional, then the meaning of a declarative sentence S determines a truth condition for S, at least relative to a contextually determined choice of semantic values for any context-sensitive expressions in S. There has been a lot of debate about what conclusions we should draw from this conditional. But following Chomsky and a few others in his essay, Paul M. Pietroski asserts that the conditional is false: the meaning of a sentence S is pretty clearly determined by the meanings of the relevant constituents. But sentences may not even have (context-sensitive) truth conditions. And as many critics of the Davidsonian programme have noted, available evidence—across a wide range of examples—suggests that truth conditions are not compositionally determined. Indeed, we should be suspicious of the very idea that in natural language names denote things that satisfy predicates. Once we make this idea clear enough to serve as the basis for a theory of meaning that can also be a theory of understanding, the idea faces huge difficulties. And we should not be impressed by the usual philosophical motivations for a truth-theoretic conception of linguistic meaning because of their descent from considerations of radical interpretation or semantic externalism. The real question is whether we can articulate an alternative conception that is more descriptively adequate while retaining the explanatory virtues of the Davidsonian programme. Leading off from remarks by Chomsky, Pietroski argues in the direction of such a conception. He shows that such a conception is required if we want to have any real account of how lexical meanings and compositional principles interact to yield the compositional meanings which are characteristic for natural language.

How is the concept of compositionality to be extended from context-invariant to context-dependent meaning? And how might the compositionality of natural language conflict with context-dependence? Several new distinctions are needed, including a distinction between a weaker (e-) and a stronger (ec-) concept of compositionality for context-dependent meaning. In his essay, Peter Pagin investigates the relations between the various notions. A claim by Jerry Fodor that there is a general conflict between context-dependence and compositionality is considered. There is in fact a possible conflict between ec-compositionality and context-dependence, but not of the kind Fodor suggests. It involves so-called unarticulated constituents, in John Perry's sense. Because of this phenomenon, some semantic accounts might have a variation in the meaning of a complex expression between contexts without any corresponding variation in the meaning of its syntactic parts. The conflict can be resolved in several ways. One way is to make the unarticulated context-dependence explicit only in the meta-language, which turns it into an unarticulated constituent account. A recent argument by Jason Stanley against such accounts is discussed. According to him, certain readings of English sentences are unavailable in these theories because they involve a binding of contextual variables. After considering a reply to Stanley by Recanati, Pagin presents an outline of a fully compositional theory—of the unarticulated constituent variety—which does deliver these readings.

Michael Glanzberg's essay addresses a more general question: what is the relation between the philosophical notion of expressing a proposition and the linguistic notion of presupposition? First, he offers an analysis of the philosophical notion of failing of expressing a proposition. Secondly, he gives an account of how failure to express a proposition may be recognized in natural language, by way of some discourse-based diagnostics which are more robust and reliable than simple truth-value judgements. Thirdly, he attempts to document what gives rise to the phenomenon of expression failure. This part of the essay involves some detailed investigation of presupposition. Glanzberg shows that some presupposition failures lead to expression failure, but some do not. He goes on to offer an analysis of elementary presuppositions which explains why presuppositions fall into these two categories. This involves a close examination of some important cases of presupposition: clefts, factive verbs, and presuppositions generated by conventional implicatures such as those of 'too' and 'even'. He ends with some speculation about the relation between conventional implicature and presupposition.

This project was initiated by Protosociology, J. W. Goethe-University, Frankfurt am Main, Germany. We would like to express our thanks to the contributors and to Ernie Lepore and Peter Momtchiloff who encouraged us to undertake the project.

Part I

Contextualism in Epistemology

2

Contextualism and the New Linguistic Turn in Epistemology

PETER LUDLOW

According to the thesis of contextualism in epistemology, many of our knowledge attributions (including self-attributions) are context sensitive. That is, a particular knowledge attribution uttered in one context might be true, while more or less the same attribution, uttered in a context with different epistemic standards, might be false. Typically, one might think of contexts with lower epistemic standards as holding in informal chats in a bar, while higher standards might hold in a court of law or a discussion of skepticism in an epistemology class.

This basic idea can be embodied in two apparently distinct formulations. On the first formulation of contextualism, advanced for example by DeRose (1999) and Cohen (1999) the verb 'know' is "gradable" like the adjectives 'flat' and 'bald'. The idea is that, just as different things can be flat to different degrees (grades), there are different degrees (grades) of knowledge, or as Cohen suggests, different degrees of justification. To illustrate, whether a particular surface counts as flat depends upon the context. While the degree of flatness of a surface might be sufficient for the surface to count as flat in the context of discussing recently plowed farmland, the same surface may not have a sufficient degree of flatness to be flat by the standards required for playing billiards. Similarly, the idea is that knowledge also comes in degrees, and whether a particular belief state also counts as a knowledge state will depend upon context. A true belief that has a degree of justification sufficient to count as knowledge in the context of a bar room chat may not have a degree of justification sufficient to count as knowledge in a court of law.

(As we will see shortly, this oversimplifies the contextualist position a bit, since contextualists do not as a rule (if ever) advocate a *single* linear graded hierarchy of standards.)

The second formulation (suggested, but not developed, by Cohen) is that the context sensitivity of knowledge claims stems from the fact that those claims have *implicit argument positions* for standards of knowledge. For example a standard contextualist analysis would offer that the logical form of (1) is something akin to (1′), where there is an implicit quantification over epistemic standards, and the implicit argument position is filled by the variable s.

(1) Chesner knows that he has feet
(1′) [∃s: epistemic-standard(s) and relevant-to(s,c′)] knows(Chesner, [he has feet], s)

As we will see in a bit, once these two formulations are clarified their apparent difference will blur, but for now we can think of them as distinct approaches.

Recently, some philosophers (including DeRose and Cohen) have explored the possibility that there might be linguistic evidence for this sort of context sensitivity. Meanwhile, Jason Stanley (2000, 2002*a*, 2002*b*, forthcoming *a*, *b*) has offered a series of arguments against both of these formulations of contextualism and has maintained that the linguistic arguments for context dependence in knowledge claims don't hold up. Work on both sides of this question can be seen as a throwback to classical work by figures like Wittgenstein (1969), Austin (1961), Malcolm (1963), and within a different tradition Vendler (1967, 1972), who held that we can gain insight into epistemological problems by investigating our linguistic practices surrounding knowledge attribution.

The new incarnation of this project—I hope it's not presumptuous to call it the new linguistic turn in epistemology—breaks with the original linguistic turn in a number of respects, but follows it in the idea that we can use features of our language of knowledge attribution to support or (as the case may be) refute certain positions in epistemology. The expected 'deliverables' from this new linguistic turn are more modest than in the previous go round. We are not looking for quick solutions to (or dissolutions of) long-standing philosophical concerns about issues like skepticism, but rather we are looking at linguistic theory to help us probe specific components of more complex and subtle epistemological theories. The scope of the project is constrained, as are the expected results. Still, in certain cases, the point under linguistic investigation may be one which serves as a linchpin in a broader epistemological project—contextualism being a fine example of a broader project with at least one linchpin under scrutiny.

But why suppose that linguistic data should be illuminating at all? While my goal in this chapter is not to argue for the relevance of linguistic data and is rather to illustrate its relevance by way of example, a couple of comments may be in order. First, and most obviously, any investigation into the nature of knowledge which did not conform to some significant degree with the semantics of the term 'knows' would simply be missing the point. For example, if someone claimed that to know that snow is white is to bake a cake and write 'snow is white' in icing on the cake, the first and most obvious objection is that the person simply doesn't know what 'knows' means. They are studying something else—cake decoration it would seem. That is an extreme case, but even in cases that are nearer to the meaning of 'knows', epistemological theories might be rejected if they are in serious conflict with the lexical semantics of 'knows'.

I've spoken of the lexical semantics of 'knows', but the conception of language being deployed here is not one in which our language is autonomous of the world. I assume that the contents of our expressions and in some sense even the form of our utterances are sensitive to the environment in which our linguistic practices are embedded. Accordingly, I am not advocating linguistic theory as a kind of first philosophy here. Nor am I entirely rejecting old fashioned conceptual analysis. What I am proposing is that lexical semantics is a kind of conceptual analysis naturalized, and that any investigation into the lexical semantics of 'knows' will have to take seriously our intuitions about the proper analysis of knowledge AND whatever constraints linguistic theory puts on the lexical semantics of the verb. Our task as investigators then is to solve a kind of complex equation in which we have partial information from linguistic theory, partial knowledge from our reflective analysis of knowledge, and we must find a way to balance the equation.

This discussion has been abstract, and there is really no way to make it more concrete other than to illustrate by way of cases, so that is what I will do in what follows. Specifically, in this chapter I will follow up previous work in the area of contextualism, but will advance two covering theses. First, I will argue that the lexical semantics of 'knows' is exceedingly complex—so complex that questions about the gradability of 'know' are unilluminating. Second, I will argue that the question of whether there are implicit arguments, hidden indexicals, etc., that can serve as place holders for standards of knowledge in the analysis of 'knows' are subtle, but that a good case can be made for their existence.

To illustrate the project entailed by the second thesis, consider examples (1) and (1′) again. If we want to take logical form like (1′) seriously, it must have some sort of linguistic reality—that is, it must in some sense constitute the actual form of (1). What does this sort of claim come to? One idea would be to borrow a leaf from contemporary generative linguistics and hold that what we informally call a "sentence" is in fact a rather complicated object consisting of several distinct levels of representation. For example in versions of generative linguistics advanced by Chomsky (1977, 1981), there were several levels of linguistic representation: D-structure, S-structure, PF, and LF. A particular sentence S, would then be identified with an ordered n-tuple of representations: $<PF_S, DS_S, SS_S, LF_S>$. Viewed in this way, the new linguistic turn would offer that an analysis such as (1′) must have some reflex in one of the levels of representation corresponding to (1)—presumably the level LF. This claim in turn would be subject to empirical confirmation, based upon whether such a proposal dovetails in a natural way with contemporary linguistics and in particular with the derivational principles and constraints that govern the well-formedness (or "legibility") of LF representations within the theory of grammar. In this way, the door is opened to a number of familiar probes from linguistic theory that are variously designed to locate implicit binding, implicit arguments, and other relevant linguistic phenomena. (More on these tests in a bit.)

1 Preliminaries

1.1 What is Contextualism?

Like most 'isms', contextualism admits of a fair bit of doctrinal variation. As a tentative and incomplete first start, we might beak the doctrine down into the following two components (here I am beginning with a formulation that follows Hawthorne (2002) more or less to the letter):

> C1. A given sentence, say 'Chesner knows that he has feet' has different semantic values relative to different contexts of utterance, (and this is due at least in part to contextual parameters connected to the verb 'know' itself). In brief, the contextualist claims that the epistemic standards required for someone to count as meriting a positive knowledge ascription varies from ascriber to ascriber, with the result that one ascriber may truly say 'He knows that he will be in Syracuse', referring to a given person at a

given time, and a different ascriber may say 'He doesn't know that he will be in Syracuse', speaking of the same person at the same time.

C2. According to standard contextualist semantics, the ascriber calls the shots, so to speak: the standards of application for the verb 'know' are determined by the ascriber and not by the subject (unless the subject happens to be identical to the ascriber).

A key idea in this formulation is the thought that the standards of knowledge have a lot more to do with the person ascribing the knowledge (possibly a third party) than with the person being reported on. That is, if I say that Smith knows something, I am saying that Smith knows it relative to my standards—indeed my standards in the context of my ascription. This much seems reasonable.

I said that this is a first approximation and that there is also a fair bit of variation in the details of how contextualist theories might be spelled out, so let me now offer a couple of variations on C2. The contextualist need not hold that there is an interesting sense in which the ascriber intentionally calls the shots (and this seems to be suggested by C2), but rather might want to hold that the ascriber's *context* is what is important. In other words, it is arguable that the ascriber has limited control over the standards of knowledge in play. This variation, if we choose to adopt it, yields the following replacement for C2.

C2*. According to contextualist semantics, the ascriber's context of utterance calls the shots, so to speak: the standards of application for the verb 'know' are determined by the context in which the ascription is made and not by the context in which subject appears (unless the subject happens to be identical to the ascriber).

A further variation—and one which also seems sensible—would allow that when not explicitly stated the standards are fixed by context, but that the ascriber can override the context of utterance (or perhaps it would be better to say 'fix the context') by explicitly stating the intended standards of knowledge (for example by explicitly stating something like 'by the standards of the court of law'). In this case, we would replace C2 with C2**.

C2**. According to contextualist semantics, the ascriber's context of utterance calls the shots, so to speak: the standards of application for the verb 'know' are either explicitly stated or are determined by the context in which the ascription is made and not by the context in which subject appears (unless the subject happens to be identical to the ascriber).

As I noted above, further variation is possible, but the alternatives given above will be sufficient to lend clarity to the considerations that follow. As we will see, there are also additional clauses which might be added to (C1) and (C2) and we will explore these a bit later as well. Finally, there is of course more to nail down than the definition of contextualism, including the notion of linguistic arguments and linguistic adjuncts. We will find it useful to take up these issues directly.

1.2 Arguments vs Adjuncts

One of the issues that has played a role in debates about hidden contextual parameters (and which will also play a role in our discussion of the gradability of 'know') has been the distinction between arguments and adjuncts. For the most part, the notion of an argument can be understood in the way familiar from predicate logic, so that a sentence like (2) might have the argument structure given in (2').

   (2) John hit Bill
   (2') hit(John, Bill)

If we suppose that there is an implicit event structure in an utterance of (2), then we might hypothesize that it has a logical form like that in (2'') where there is an implicit event quantifier and implicit event variable in the argument structure.

   (2'') ($\exists$e) hitting(e, John, Bill)

If this analysis is correct, then it turns out that a sentence like (2) in fact has three argument positions. Similarly, if we take a "ditransitive" verb such as 'give' in (3), it would have the argument position in (3'), or alternatively a four place argument structure if we assume an event-based semantics as in (3'')

   (3) John gave Bill the book
   (3') give(John, Bill, the book)
   (3'') ($\exists$e) giving(e, John, Bill, the book)

Other kinds of syntactic constituents have traditionally not been analyzed as arguments, but rather as *adjuncts*. That is to say, they are not taken to be part of the core event structure associated with the verb, but rather are something like additional event predicates. Accordingly, an adverb like 'reluctantly' in

(4) might be taken to be an additional event predicate as in (4′) and not an argument of the core event predicate.

(4) John hit Bill reluctantly
(4′) (∃e) hitting(e, John, Bill) and reluctant(e)

It is also arguable that there are cases of *implicit arguments*. These are arguments that have no explicit phonetic realization (i.e. they are not pronounced), but are understood to be present in some sense, and are taken by many linguists to have some reflex in the syntax of the language. To illustrate, consider an utterance of a sentence like (5).

(5) John ate

Does 'ate' in this sentence merely have only one argument (John)? Or does it have an "implicit" argument as well (for the stuff that John ate)? How about an argument for the instrument he used for eating (fork, fingers, etc.), manner (sloppily), etc. Whether there are implicit arguments, and if so how many, is a subject of debate that we will return to shortly.

One of the issues confounding the question of implicit arguments is the fact that recent work in event semantics seems to undermine the idea that the logical form of a sentence actually has multiple arguments in the sense just discussed. Consider (4) again. We considered the possibility that it might have the logical form given in (4′) where the verb has an adicity of three. But what should we say if we adopt the version of event semantics proposed by Castañeda (1967) and Parsons (1990), in which "arguments" are linked to the core event via *thematic relations* or *thematic roles* like *agent*, *patient*, *theme*, *path*, and *goal*, yielding the analysis in (4″)?

(4″) (∃e) (hitting(e) & agent(John, e) & patient(Bill, e) & reluctant(e))

Here the distinction between argument and adjunct appears to have broken down completely, since the core event predicate ('hitting') has only one argument position (filled by the event quantification variable) and all the other constituents are functioning as adjuncts, much as 'reluctantly' did in the case of (4′).

In the face of this break-down it is probably a mistake to put too much weight on the argument–adjunct distinction and to opt instead for an alternative notion due to Chomsky (1986). On his view, the relevant question is not whether a particular constituent is an argument, but rather whether it is *L-marked* by the verb. This is another way of saying that verbs *select for* certain phrases (and we can set aside the question of whether those phrases are arguments or adjuncts). The crucial question would be whether the lexical structure of the verb is such that it associates the verb with certain phrases that incorporate thematic roles.

1.3 Implicit L-Marked Phrases

Given this background, we can now return to the issues of *implicit* arguments, or better: implicit L-marked phrases. Larson (1988), following Bresnan (1982), argues that implicit arguments (what we are now calling L-marked phrases) include optional but non-iterable phrases such as phrases of source, path, goal, and phrases of instrumentality.
    Consider, for example, (6) and (7).

(6) John ran ($_{\text{Source}}$ from the house) ($_{\text{Goal}}$ to the store) ($_{\text{Path}}$ along the river).
(7) John cut the salami ($_{\text{Instrument}}$ with a knife).

In these cases the phrases in parentheses are L-marked phrases which are optionally uttered (in the sense that the sentences would remain grammatical if they were not uttered). The evidence that they are L-marked by the verb and not arbitrarily attached is that they cannot be iterated. In (8), for example, the sentence can only be naturally understood as a conjunction of some sort (first John cut the salami with a knife, then he cut it with a saw, and then he cut it with a piano wire). It is as if the place for a phrase having the thematic role of instrument is saturated and hence no further iteration is possible.

(8) *John cut the salami with a knife with a saw with a piano wire

On the view articulated by Bresnan and Larson, the evidence that certain modifying phrases are *not* arguments is that they *can* be iterated. Consider a case like (9) in which locative modifiers appear to be iterable without forcing the conjunction reading.

(9) John cut the salami in the house in the bathroom in the corner in the dark under the sink

Matters are more complex than this example lets on, however. One natural observation in this case is that (9) only works because in the transition from 'in the house' to 'in the bathroom' the location is being made more specific, and then a kind of comma intonation is required. If the order is reversed (in the bathroom in the house) then the comma intonation can be dropped but the second prepositional phrase now appears to be modifying the NP 'the bathroom'. In effect, even locatives cannot be iterated per se. It seems as though the verb 'cut' has one slot for location, and that the additional locatives are either added as NP internal modifiers, or as progressively more specific afterthoughts marked by comma intonation.

If this line of thinking is right (and obviously it needs to be investigated in much more detail), then the notion of an adjunct really is ephemeral. Verbs L-mark for certain arguments, and those arguments include not just agent, patient, and theme, but locative and temporal phrases as well, and perhaps surprisingly, there is only one each of each kind of L-marked phrase (only one satisfier of each thematic role).

So far I have been talking about phrases that are explicitly uttered, but what about cases like (10) in which the additional phrase for instrument is not phonologically realized?

(10) John cut the salami

Could it be that there is still some sense in which an instrument phrase (or for that matter, a locative phrase, a temporal anaphor phrase, etc.) is present, even if unpronounced? Arguably there is, although there are a number of options about how this might work. One possibility is to say that some dummy instrument phrase is always present even if unpronounced. We will get to some of these possibilities in section 3.

2 On the Lexical Semantics of 'Knows'

One way of investigating the lexical semantics of 'knows' (and in particular its argument structure) is by thinking about the kinds of modifiers that can naturally occur with it. Following are some examples that I extracted by means of a Google search on the internet (see appendix for details of the search), but additional examples are easily discovered.

known by any objective standards

known (by occidental science standards)

known by earthly standards

knowing for sure what we "know" by academic standards

know with some level of confidence

know, with some reasonable certainty

know with some, albeit imperfect, reliability

know with some degree of certainty

know with some degree of accuracy

know with some confidence

know with some precision
know with some authority
know with some probability
know with some degree of authority
know with some clarity
know with some accuracy
know with some level of confidence
know with complete certainty
know with complete certitude
really know
how well do we know
pretty well know
in effect knew
sort of in effect knew
by secular standards of knowledge
by today's standards of knowledge
by high standards of knowledge and accuracy

perceived standards of knowledge
by your own standards of knowledge
by today's standards of knowledge
previously known standards of knowledge
with general contemporary standards of knowledge
inappropriate standards of knowledge
halachic standards of certainty
legal and scientific standards of certainty
different standards of certainty are used in science and in politics
standards of certainty in law: criminal trials, civil lawsuits, government regulation, legislation

To a first approximation, it thus appears that a verb like 'knows' has an extremely rich thematic structure which encodes not just the agent and the content of the belief, but potentially argument places (L-marked positions) for standards of justification and evidence, for subjective certainty of the report, for the reporter's responsibility for having and defending the knowledge, the source of the knowledge, and the mode of presentation of the content of the knowledge report. The resulting picture of this first approximation would be along the following lines.

Know
agent: the ascribee,
theme: the propositional content of the knowledge,
standards of justification: "by legal/scientific/etc. standards we know that that..."
standards of evidence: "by the evidential standards of criminal law we know that ..."
degree of subjective certainty: "I know with confidence that..."
standards of subjective certainty: "by the standards of physics I know with confidence that..."
degree of responsibility for knowledge: "you know very well that..."

source of knowledge (in many languages with "evidentials"): "I see/know with my own eyes that..."

mode of presentation: "John knows, in effect that p, although he wouldn't agree to it in those terms"

The list can go on, depending upon one's favorite conceptual analysis of knowledge, and upon the constraints that are imposed by the empirical enterprise of lexical semantics. (As noted earlier, I tend to consider conceptual analysis and lexical semantics to be basically the same enterprise. To put it in a provocative way, I think of lexical semantics as a kind of conceptual analysis naturalized, and I think that traditional conceptual analysis—whatever its practitioners may have thought they were doing—was actually a form of lexical semantics, albeit a clumsy and not particularly self-enlightened form of the enterprise.)

My goal here is not to carry out a serious analysis of the verb 'knows' but to sketch out enough of such an analysis to see that the discussion of the gradability of 'knows' (on both sides) has been problematic, and to show that the idea of an implicit argument position for standards of knowledge is entirely reasonable. I will take up these issues in order.

3 The Gradability of 'Knows'

Stanley (forthcoming, *a*) offers that there are two linguistic tests for the gradability of a predicate and suggests that the relational predicate 'knows' flunks both of these tests. I think that Stanley is basically correct in supposing that talk of gradability is not entirely happy here, but I think he misdiagnoses the source of the problem. It will be instructive for us to walk through some of Stanley's arguments with an eye to developing a better grasp of the source of the gradability phenomenon in verbal elements.

3.1 The Argument from Gradable Adjectives

Stanley's first argument involves a standard test for gradable adjectives—to wit: they can be modified by elements like 'very' and 'really'. For example:

(11) *a.* That is very flat
     b. That is really flat
     c. John is very tall
     d. John is really tall

Stanley then goes on to observe that allegedly gradable verbs like 'know' cannot be so modified, thus they flunk the first test for gradability. To demonstrate this, Stanley asks us to consider the effects of juxtaposing 'very' with the allegedly gradable 'know'.

(12) *a.* *John very knows that penguins waddle
      b. *John knows very much that penguins waddle

Stanley is correct to assert that the modifier 'very' is indeed a test for something—the problem with his argument is that it is a test for gradable *adjectives*. It simply isn't a verbal modifier, so of course if it is juxtaposed with a verb the results will be a crashingly bad linguistic form.

To see this, we can consider what happens when 'very' co-occurs with an obviously scalar verb: 'flatten'.

(13) *John very flattened the vacant lot

'Very' just can't modify verbs, whether they are scalar or not.

One might think that one could make some headway by considering the adjectival form of 'know'—'known'. Clearly, there is something not quite right about the juxtaposition of this adjectival form with 'very'.

(14) *The proposition that Arithmetic is undecidable is very known.

Stanley correctly observes that the apparent repair of this case with 'very well' as in (15) is misleading:

(15) The proposition that Arithmetic is undecidable is very well known.

As he observes, this is not saying that the proposition is known by high standards, but rather that it is widely known (at least within some relevant circle of individuals). So if 'very' does not modify the adjectival form of 'know' isn't this evidence that 'know' is not gradable? Again matters are more complex than they appear at first glace.

First, notice that if we take the adjectival form of 'flatten' we have a similar kind of effect.

(16) The field is very well flattened

This does not say that the field is flattened by high standards of flatness, but rather that it is appropriately flattened given some fixed set of standards (like playing bocce ball or landing an airplane).

So what is going on in these cases? First and most obviously 'very' is not modifying 'flattened', but the adjective 'well'. But what kind of adjective is 'well' and what work is it doing here? One attractive idea due to Larson (1998) is that nouns and adjectives that are derived from verbs retain important structural elements of the verbs from which they are derived. So for example, a noun like 'dancer' is derived from the verb 'dance' and retains elements of the structure of that verb, including an implicit event variable. It is from this additional structural element that one derives the ambiguity in a sentence like (17).

(17) Olga is a beautiful dancer

Clearly (17) can be understood as saying either that Olga is beautiful and a dancer or beautiful for a dancer, or that she dances beautifully. The third meaning concerns us here. If Larson is correct, this meaning is derived from the case where 'beautiful' modifies the inner event variable within 'dancer'. Thus a property that 'dancer' inherits from its verbal form gives rise to one of the meanings of (17).

A similar story can be told for a derived participle, as in (18) and (19).

(18) That was beautifully danced

Here again, it appears that 'beautiful' can be understood as modifying the inner event variable that is now associated with the participle 'danced'. Notice that 'very well' can perform the same function:

(19) That was very well danced

It should be possible to see where I am going with this. Because 'known' is an adjectival form that is derived from a verb, it will inherit important properties from its verbal form. In particular, if we suppose that there is an implicit event position in the adjective, then it is that position that is being modified by 'very well'. In effect, we are saying that the event was done very well. 'Very well' and stand alone 'well' are adverbs of manner that take event variables as their arguments. They in no way modify standards; they speak to the manner in which the action was performed relative to some established standards.

None of this is to challenge Stanley's basic conclusion; these verbs are not neatly scalar in the way that many adjectives are—nor does this seem particularly surprising. But then once we come to understand why they are not scalar, we are a step closer to a fuller picture of how these verbal constructions work. Similar lessons can be extracted from the study of comparatives.

3.2 The Argument from Comparatives

According to Stanley's second argument, if predicates are gradable, then they should have a related comparative form. So, for example, the gradable predicate 'tall' has the corresponding 'taller than', and 'bald' has the corresponding 'balder than'. But it does not seem that 'know' has a corresponding comparative form (consider*'knower than' or *'John more knows than Bill that P)'. As Stanley (citing Dretske 2000) also notes, the better sounding use of the comparative in cases like 'John better knows than Bill that P' is misleading, since this does not appear to be talking about standards of knowledge but rather about "more direct or more compelling evidence" for P.

Once again, however, it is important to see that this test has more to do with the fact that 'know' is not an adjective than it has to do with its being graded. Very simply, verbs don't form comparatives—even verbs like 'flatten' that are derived from gradable adjectives (*'a is flattener than b'). Now of course these derived verbs can be converted back into adjectives (as in 'flattened'), but the attempt to now convert these adjectival forms into comparatives is not necessarily successful (*'a is flatteneder than b', for example, is horrible). It is true enough that we can get a comparative like 'a is more flattened than b', but there is an awful lot going on that needs to be sorted out before we try to extract strong conclusions here.

To begin with, keep in mind that we are now dealing with a linguistic form that began its career as an adjective ('flat'), is then converted to a verb ('flatten'), is then subsequently converted back into an adjective ('flattened'), and then is successfully converted to one comparative form ('more flattened') but not to another (*'flatteneder'). What is going on here? More urgently, what sort of conclusions can we extract from the apparent lack of a comparative form for the adjectival 'known'?

Stanley is certainly correct in thinking that verbs like 'know' do not have the same distribution with modifiers and comparatives that graded adjectival elements do, but as we have seen this has more to do with the fact that 'know' is nonadjectival, and even its deverbal adjectival forms carry the residue of their original logical forms. Still, this raises the question of what exactly philosophers have in mind when they say that 'know' is gradable. What does it mean to say that any sort of verbal element is gradable? I would suggest that if gradability is to mean anything in the context of verbal elements, it must have to do with two factors: (i) whether the verb has an L-marked position for standard of some form, and (ii) whether the standards are naturally gradable on a linear scale.

This immediately leads to the question of whether contextualism actually requires that one endorse (ii), that there be a linear hierarchy of standards. It could be, for example, that epistemic standards do not form a clean linear hierarchy but rather that standards cross-cut each other with respect to degrees or grades of knowledge. It might be, for example, that in some contexts the standards of knowledge of law are more stringent than the standards of knowledge for science, while in other cases it might be that the standards of knowledge for science are more stringent.

If this is right, then it suggests a reason why simple adjectival elements lend themselves to clean hierarchies, while verbs—even when converted to adjectives—do not. Verbs, although fundamentally predicational, tend to incorporate much more complex structure than basic adjectival elements. So, at a minimum, even a verb like 'flatten' has acquired a lexical argument structure which includes some notion of agency, some notion of instrument, some notion of theme, and some notion of manner. These are all predicates of the core event, and they may interact in subtle and complex ways, ways that will not necessarily lend themselves to a simple gradable hierarchy of standards.

Indeed, not only *could* contextualists say this, it is arguable that they always *have*, even when they are not explicit about it. For example, DeRose (1992) notes that he is glossing over the fact that there is no single graded standard of knowledge, and endorses a point made by Unger (1986) in explicating his "Cone Theory of Knowledge":

He [Unger] does, however, introduce an important complication which I have ignored in this paper, since it has little effect on the points I'm making here. Unger points out that there are many different aspects of knowledge and that in different contexts, we may have different demands regarding various of these aspects. Thus, for example, in one context we may demand a very high degree of confidence on the subject's part before we will count him as knowing while demanding *relatively* little in the way of his belief being non-accidentally true. In a different context, on the other hand, we may have very stringent standards for non-accidentally but relatively lax standards for subject confidence. As Unger points out, then, things are not as simple as I make them out to be: Our standards are not just a matter of how good an epistemic position the subject must be in, but rather of how good in which respects . . .

To give an idea of the subtlety that one might encounter in the analysis of a verb, consider the lexical semantics of the verb 'cut' as offered by Hale and Keyser (1987) and as discussed in Higginbotham (1989).

'cut' is a V that applies truly to situations e, involving a patient y and an agent x who, by means of some instrument z, effects in e a linear separation in the material integrity of y.

It is easy enough to see why trying to convert a verb into a comparative form is not happy, even if the verb is converted into an adjectival form. Exactly where is the linear scale to fall? What is it to be more cut? Does it mean that the linear separation is longer? That the act of separation endures longer? That the separation is of a greater distance? That amount of material cut is greater? There is so much going on in a simple verb like 'cut' that it is simply undetermined which scale might be at play. Is there any reason to expect different results from the even more complex verb 'knows'?

3.3 Gradability and the Definition of Contextualism

We have just seen that if 'knows' is anything like other verbs, there is little reason why it should have a single gradable hierarchy for standards of knowledge or standards of justification. Furthermore, there is nothing in the definition of contextualism that we have given via (C1) and (C2**) which requires it. Indeed, all that those clauses in our definition require is that the "epistemic standards required for someone to count as meriting a positive knowledge ascription varies from ascriber to ascriber". if we wanted to insist that there be a natural gradable hierarchy, we would have to stipulate it, as in (C3).

> C3. Not only do the epistemic standards required for someone to count as meriting a positive knowledge ascription vary from ascriber to ascriber, but as those standards vary, they do so in a linear gradable hierarchy of standards.

But this seems like an entirely arbitrary stipulation for a contextualist to make. It is certainly true that in the classic examples motivating contextualism we appeal to the fact that standards may be "higher" in some contexts than others, but this is a long way from saying that the entire class of standards is gradable on a linear scale which holds across all contexts. Indeed, as I suggested for the case of legal and scientific standards, the standards may cross-cut each other so that in some cases we might intuitively think of the scientific standards as being more stringent and in other cases we might think of the legal standards as being more stringent. If this is right, then (C3) should yield to the much more plausible and contextualism-friendly (C3*).

C3*. While the epistemic standards required for someone to count as meriting a positive knowledge ascription vary from ascriber (ascriber's context) to ascriber (ascriber's context), they do not vary in such a way that they form a linear hierarchy of standards.

Gradability simply doesn't cut one way or the other with respect to the plausibility of contextualism. There is an additional thesis that the contextualism may want to defend, however: the thesis that there is an implicit L-marked position for standards of knowledge. I will take up this issue in the next section.

4 On an Implicit Contextual Parameter in Knowledge Reports

If we are looking for linguistic evidence for the presence of a contextual parameter in knowledge claims, then what we are asking is whether the verb 'know' L-marks phrases for something like a standard of knowledge. More informally, does the verb have some property by virtue of which it likes to have exactly one L-marked phrase that supplies the standards of knowledge to a knowledge ascription? The question, even though it can be put informally, demands a response that is particularly complex, since linguistic theory is divided on the proper analysis of implicit L-marked phrases, the nature of their realization, and linguistic phenomena that they are associated with. At a minimum, there are five different ways in which a contextual parameter might be realized within the syntax of knowledge ascriptions.

4.1 Five Kinds of Contextual Involvement in Linguistic Theory

Following are some ways in which contextualism could be reflected in the grammar:

(i) The first possibility is that 'knows' is a context-sensitive predicate without an L-marked position for standard or degree of knowledge and that knowledge reports have no operators representing standards of knowledge. It could still be the case that 'knows' is a context-sensitive predicate. Here I am thinking that 'knows' could work like tense morphemes for A-theorists—they are context sensitive but there is no explicit argument place for times. See Ludlow (1999). A similar idea is advanced by Kamp (1975) who gives a theory of degree modification according to which comparative adjectives like 'tall' are sensitive to context even though they do not have argument positions for a comparison class (e.g. if I say 'That basketball player is tall', there is no implicit comparison class of basketball players such that I am saying that he is tall for a member of that class).

(ii) Second, it could be that 'knows' has an implicit argument, but is not syntactically realized apart from its occurrence in the thematic structure of the verb. Several linguists have advance a thesis like this for implicit arguments, including Williams (1985), who articulates the idea as follows.

Implicit arguments are not the mysterious shadowy presences they are sometimes made out to be. They are really nothing more than the argument slots in the argument structure.... A 'weak' θ-criterion is all that is needed to give implicit arguments, since these are nothing more than unlinked argument roles. (Williams, 1985: 314)

Jackendoff (1987: 409) offers a similar story about implicit arguments. "An implicit argument is a conceptual argument that is neither expressed syntactically nor bound to an argument that is expressed syntactically."

If this picture were applied to the case of 'knows' then the idea would be that the lexical item 'knows' encodes a slot in its thematic structure for standard of knowledge, but we would not expect the implicit thematic structure in the verb to have any sort of reflex in the syntax, and in particular we would not expect to find a syntactic position or phrase elsewhere in the sentence that is linked to the slot in the thematic structure of the verb. Natural language would be like a language which allows well formed structures in which the predicates have unsaturated argument positions. When these linguistic structures are passed off to what Chomsky (1995) calls the "conceptual-intensional component", they may then be interpreted as having implicit arguments of some form. But to repeat, these arguments would not have any reflex in the syntax of natural language.

(iii) A third possibility is that 'knows' does not L-mark a standards-of-knowledge phrase, but knowledge reports *do* have an explicitly represented position for standard or degree of knowledge. For example, Cinque (1999) has argued that lexical items project structures that have slots for various L-marked phrases, including tense and modals. If this is right, then the idea would be that a verb like 'knows' projects a template for the sentence, and that template will contain a slot for a standard of knowledge phrase. In this case, there would be a kind of syntactic realization of the thematic structure of the verb, but it would not obviously take the form of a syntactically realized L-marked phrase or even a dummy argument position, but as a kind of empty

branch in the linguistic phrase marker tree for the sentence (or LF representation of the sentence).

(iv) A fourth possibility is that 'knows' L-marks positions for standard or
degree of knowledge, and these (sometimes implicit) positions are syntactically represented, although the evidence for them does *not* include binding
facts. On this view, we should be able to deploy tests to show that there are in
fact syntactically realized argument positions for standard of knowledge, but
we could not necessarily expect the evidence to include evidence of bound
variable anaphora.

(v) Finally, it might be that 'knows' L-marks for standards of knowledge
and that the evidence for implicit positions *does* include binding facts.

As noted earlier, Stanley (forthcoming, *a*) has presented a series of arguments
intended to undermine the thesis that there is an implicit argument position
(L-marked position) for standards of knowledge. Some of these arguments
assume that the only way standards-of-knowledge parameter might be realized is via option (v)—an explicit occurrence of a bindable argument position. In my view this is only one option among many, and a rather
demanding option at that. A complete discussion of all the options would
be well beyond the scope of this chapter, but I do think it would be useful to
briefly discuss options (i–iv) and (v) separately, if only to see how subtle the
linguistic issues really are. I will conclude that, even with the extremely
demanding option (v), the case for implicit L-marked phrase for standard
of knowledge is plausibly made, and that further investigation may well
support the thesis that there are implicit phrases of this form.

4.2 Some Tests for Implicit L-Marking in Senses (i)–(iv)

A complete study would look for tests that would tease apart options (i)–(iv)
and lend support to one or another of those options. It is important to
recognize, however, that there are also varieties of evidence that are neutral as
to which of these specific options is correct, but which will lend support in
equal measure to the various formulations. In this section I canvass some of
these arguments, drawing the tentative conclusion that the evidence appears
to support some version of the implicit L-marking thesis.

4.2.1 Explicit occurrences of hedges and references to standards of knowledge

One of the most obvious tests for an implicit L-marked position would be to
determine whether the verb 'knows' sometimes takes a phrase that indicates

the standard of knowledge. Hawthorne suggests that we have few such devices:

> I want to draw attention to the fact that we have very few devices in ordinary life for implementing the clarification technique when it comes to 'knows'. (Think especially of our lack of clarificatory devices when we have previously said something positive of the form "I know that *p*") We don't have anything like the 'of F' and 'for a G' locutions available. Nor do we have anything like the hedge devices 'roughly' and 'approximately' available. As a consequence, our standard techniques for dealing with epistemic challenges that raise relatively far-fetched possibilities are concession and, more rarely, sticking to one's guns. Our epistemic practice runs smoothly not because we have clarification techniques available when responding to challenges, but because we are sparing about raising challenges in the first place. (2003: 78–9)

As per the data from the Google search already mentioned, we can see that 'knows' has a rich thematic structure which in fact incorporates a number of overlapping kinds of standards. Notice that not just 'knows' admits of standards, but also the informal use of 'certainty', which sometimes is deployed to mean subjective certainty and other times means 'justification'. The point is that these cases certainly appear to be natural examples of hedges invoking standards of justification, etc.

Hawthorne is, of course, aware that we do employ these sorts of expressions, but he believes that they do not play a role in our fending off challenges to our knowledge. That is, if someone challenges our knowledge claim, we either defend it or concede it, but we do not say something to the effect of, "well I knew it by my own standards of knowledge". Hawthorne is not correct about this however. The problem is that challenges usually come about when our knowledge claim turns out to be false, so of course pleading alternative standards of knowledge will fall on deaf ears. A compelling test would involve a case where the content of the knowledge claim was true, but the knowledge is being challenged anyway.

For example, consider a case where I am working for NASA and must act in accord with a certain set of scientific standards. In a performance review I am challenged if I really knew that certain conditions held when I performed some action, and the reviewer suggests that my action, although correct, was not an action that I *knew* to be correct under the circumstances. I think that this is a case where I might defend myself by saying that I knew the conditions held under the standards of knowledge established by NASA protocol.

Similar considerations apply to a case where I claim that I did not know something, but am later challenged on my claim of lacking knowledge.

Hawthorne suggests that in such cases I cannot defend myself by claiming that I was deploying different standards of knowledge at the time I claimed not to know something:

> If I say 'I don't know' at one time and someone later complains 'You did know', it is not common practice to reply along the following lines: 'It's true that I knew. But what I meant back then was that I didn't know for certain'. (Insofar as "I don't know for certain" plays an excusatory role, it is probably best understood along the lines of "I didn't hit him hard", where the point is not to deny that one hit). It is even more obvious that I standardly have no ready means of reconciling apparent conflict by indicating that my earlier self attached "lower standards" to 'know': if I say 'I know' at t_1 and then accept at t_2 a claim of the form 'I didn't know at t_1', there is little I can do in ordinary discourse to clarify my earlier remark so as to avoid criticism of my earlier self, especially in a situation where my current self is not willing to gloss 'I didn't know' as 'I didn't know for certain' . . . I thus have no easy means of indicating that my earlier self attached "lower standards" to know. (2004a: 105 n. 120)

Again, I don't think this is correct. Returning to the case of the NASA debriefing, it seems to me that I might defend myself against failing to report a belief as a piece of knowledge by saying "yes but by the standards of NASA protocol it did not count as knowledge and could not be reported as such". Or more simply as "I didn't know it under the relevant standards." Of course it is possible that I was in a position to report something when it fell far short of knowledge (say damage to the heat shield of the re-entry vehicle), but this is not to challenge my claim to lack knowledge, but rather my responsibility to report something which was a possible outcome, given the evidence in my possession. In such a case, no one is claiming that I *knew* there was damage.

These sorts of defenses are of course subtle, if only because a standard knowledge report encodes so much information that might be challenged or that might be hedged. But acknowledging this sort of subtlety it does seem to me that there are more options available to us than just sticking to our guns and concession when our true knowledge reports are challenged.

A more urgent question is whether it would show anything if Hawthorne were correct that we only have room to concede or stick to our guns when challenged. I'm not sure that this would illuminate anything about the truth of contextualism. At most, it would require that clause (C2**) of our definition of contextualism could not be sustained. That is, we would not be in a position to explicitly state some intended standards of knowledge, certainly not in a way that would override the operative epistemic context. But then we fall back on clause (C2*). Nothing follows about the truth of contextualism.

At most we would have evidence that when my knowledge is challenged it is the context of the challenger/ascriber that exclusively calls the shots.

4.2.2   The iteration test (Bresnan, 1982; Larson, 1986)

As I indicated in section 2, one of the standard tests for L-marked phrases in senses (i–iv) has been the iteration test due to Bresnan and Larson. The idea is that phrases with the thematic role of instrument *are* L-marked because they cannot be iterated.

(20) *John buttered the toast with a knife, with a spoon, with a fork.

If this test is reliable (and I see no reason to think that it isn't), then it provides a compelling piece of evidence for the thesis that 'know' L-marks for standards of knowledge, as the following examples show.

(21) *Chesner knows under standards s under standards s' that he has feet.
(22) *Chesner knows by the standards of science by the standards of physics that he has feet.
(23) *Chesner knows with some certainty with some assurance that he has feet.

4.2.3   The incorporation test (Ludlow, 1996)

Another test for L-marked phrases can be adapted from the "incorporation test" of Ludlow (1996) utilizing the philosopher's technique of forming complex predicates by conjoining two predicate phrases with hyphens (for example combining 'eat' and 'with a spoon' to yield the predicate 'eat-with-a-spoon'. According to that test, L-marked phrases are identifiable in that once they are incorporated into a predicate, the addition of additional phrases with the thematic role of the incorporated element is impossible.

To see how this works, consider (24), where a phrase bearing the instrumental thematic role has been incorporated. The addition of 'with a spoon' in this case results in an ungrammatical sentence, or at best it only makes sense under the reading where John waved a spoon over the toast and knife and the knife magically jumped up and started buttering the toast.

(24) *John buttered-the-toast-with-a-knife with a spoon

This interestingly contrasts with the case of (25), where a locative is appended without difficulty.

(25) John buttered-the-toast-with-a-knife in the bathroom

If this test is illuminating as to the presence of implicit L-marked phrases, and again I think that it is, then it too provides support for the thesis that 'knows' L-marks for a standard-of-knowledge phrase. Once a standard of knowledge phrase is incorporated into the verb, it appears that the addition of another standard of knowledge phrase is blocked, as (26–7) show.

(26) *Chesner knows-under-standards-s under standards s′ that he has feet.

(27) *Chesner knows-by-the-standards-of-science by the standards of physics that he has feet.

The tests we have been considering have been designed to probe whether there is evidence for L-marked phrases, realized in some form of cases (i)–(iv). I now want to take up the question of the more restrictive (v), which demands that we not only provide evidence for the existence of implicit L-marked phrases, but also the presence of a syntactic position that will admit of bound variable anaphora.

4.2.4 *Evidence for L-marked phrases in sense (v): the binding test*

Stanley (2000, 2002*a*, 2002*b*) has maintained that, if there are implicit arguments (L-marked phrases) for standards of knowledge in knowledge attributions, then it should be possible to find evidence of binding into these positions. I have already indicated that I find this demand unnecessarily onerous, but it is worth considering the question of whether the binding facts break in the way that Stanley believes. In my view, properly laid out, the facts are too subtle to extract conclusions one way or the other.

A good example of the sort of binding relation that Stanley is seeking can be found in (28). An utterance of this sentence can clearly be understood as saying that everyone x is such that x went to a bar that is local to x.

(28) Everyone went to a local bar.

Stanley thinks that the facts do not break in the same direction when we turn to a verb like 'knows'. Consider (29), for example, which does not seem to have the meaning given in (29′).

(29) Everyone knows that Chesner has feet.

(29′) *Everyone x knows by x's standards that Chesner has feet.

The problem with this example is that it is assuming a version of contextual-ism that violates clause (C2) (and its variations (C2*) and (C2**)) of our characterization of contextualism—the constraint that the context of the *ascriber* (not the persons we are attributing knowledge to) sets the standards. Why on earth would a contextualist endorsing (C1) and (C2) expect a bound variable reading in (29)?

More compelling tests would have to involve quantifying over knowledge *ascribers*, allowing that for each ascriber there could be a different standard of knowledge. Consider (30) under the intended interpretation in (30').

(30) Everyone asserted that Chesner knows he has feet.

(30') Everyone x asserted that Chesner knows (under x's standards) he has feet.

Here I think the judgments are inconclusive. It certainly does not seem outlandish to me that (30) could be understood as saying that different people employed different standards of knowledge, as in (31):

(31) Everyone asserted that Chesner knows that he has feet: A said that Chesner knows with certainty that he has feet, B asserted that Chesner knew with some assurance that he has feet, C asserted that Chesner in effect knows that he has feet, etc.

If such a reading is possible, then it seems that we have binding evidence after all.

However, even this sort of test is not necessarily decisive, given that the definition of contextualism that we provided has indicated nothing about the potential behavior of *reported* knowledge attributions. Quite simply, context-ualism as we have defined it with (C1) and (C2) is mute on whether we should expect reported knowledge ascriptions to carry the standards of the ascriber. To see this, consider (32).

(32) John attributed to Chesner the knowledge that he (Chesner) has feet.

If John was employing low standards when he made his attribution, does our report in (32) inherit those standards, or do the standards shift to those of us reporters? Nothing said thus far in our definition of contextualism settles the matter.

If we want our theory of contextualism to take a stand on the matter, then we need to augment our theory with either (C4a) or (C4b) depending upon our preferences.

C4a. In a report by R, of a knowledge attribution by A on a knower K, it is the context of the reporter R that calls the shots.

C4*b*. In a report by R, of a knowledge attribution by A on a knower K, it is
the context of the attributor A that calls the shots.

If we think that (C4*a*) is correct, then we will not expect binding facts to be
evident. If we think that (C4*b*) is correct, then we will expect binding facts to
hold in cases like (30). Personally, I think that they do hold in (30) and that
this is evidence for (C4*b*), but whichever picture is in fact correct, it sheds no
light on the plausibility of the core doctrine of contextualism as embodied in
(C1) and the various versions of (C2).

5 Some Objections to Contextualism Reconsidered

So far, I have argued for two theses regarding the language of knowledge
attribution. First, I've argued that the lexical semantics of 'knows' is complex
enough so that it does not entail a prediction about the gradability of
knowledge claims—if anything it suggests that for 'know' to be gradable in
the usual sense would be surprising indeed. Second, I've argued that it is
entirely reasonable to think that, given our lexical semantics for 'know', there
could be an implicit L-marked position for standards of knowledge in any of
the five senses surveyed.

There remain a couple of recent objections to contextualism that have been
advanced by Stanley and Hawthorne respectively, and while the considerations raised above do not defeat the objections directly, they do help prepare
the groundwork for a critical analysis of those objections. The first objection,
due to Stanley, involves issues having to do with context shift in knowledge
reports. The second objection, due to Hawthorne, has to do with the issue of
embedded knowledge reports.

5.1 The Issue of Context Shift

Contextualists like DeRose and Cohen have maintained that contextualism
escapes the "abominable conjunction" that allegedly plagues theories like the
relevant alternatives approach of Dretske. The problem for Dretske turns on
the intuition that it is odd to say, for example, that "I know I have a hand but
I don't know that I am not a brain in a vat." Contextualists have held out that
contextualism offers a handy solution to this problem: if context shift cannot
take place across discourse, then there is no way an abominable conjunction
can be true. The same standards would have to hold in each conjunct and so

of course one of the conjuncts would have to be false; contextualism explains *why* the conjunction is so abominable. But wait...

Stanley (forthcoming, *a*, *b*) contends that this claim is too strong as it stands; context shift within a discourse is certainly a possibility, as observed for example by Stanley and Szabó (2000) among others. However, context shift is not always easy, and Stanley may be too quick to reject an apparent advantage of contextualism here. For example, Partee (forthcoming) gives some examples involving ambiguity, such as 'that's funny, but it's not funny', where a shift in the sense of funny is more than a bit forced. If it is too strong for contextualist to assert that contexts shifts are not possible, it is likewise too strong for Stanley to suggest that *all forms* of context sensitive operators will allow shifts in context within a single discourse. In particular, it is too strong, given our state of understanding, to conclude that the sorts of context shifting allowed will infect knowledge reports and force abominable conjunctions upon us.

On top of everything else, there is a serious concern that many cases which are being passed off as examples of context shift are really nothing of the kind. For example, we can turn to constructions considered in Ludlow (1989) to find cases that look like context shift but which in fact are examples of multiple operators in distinct syntactic environments. Consider a sentence like (32).

(32)   That elephant is large and that flea is too.

There are certainly cases where we can say something like this, intending to say that the elephant is large by one set of standards and the flea large by another, and it is tempting to think that when we do, these are cases of context shift. However, as I argued in Ludlow (1989) the shift in comparison class in these this example has more to do with the syntax of "sloppy identity" than it does with context shift. In that paper I argued that in the comparison class (or c-class) argument position there is an empty operator in the sense of Chomsky (1986) which adjoins to the nearest N (N′ actually) and forms a restricted quantifier. In effect, a sentence like (33) has the base logical form in (33*a*), where O is an empty operator.

(33)   That elephant is large
(33*a*)   That elephant is large [for an O]

This operator raises and adjoins to the N′, in this case the noun 'elephant', and forms a restricted quantifier over comparison classes, as indicated in (33*b*), binding into a variable position e.

(33*b*)   That [Oi elephant] is large [for an ei]

While sometimes the operator might pick up some contextually salient property (I argued that it would do so in a sentence like 'John is tall'), in the case of (33) it is not extra-linguistic context that fixes the comparison class, but rather the syntactic environment. In a case like (32), involving VP ellipsis, the theory was that the empty operator is copied along with the rest of the VP (or AP, adjective phrase) '[is large O]'. Thus when one says 'that flea is too', one is in effect saying 'that flea is large O'. When the copied operator moves, it does not adjoin to the noun 'elephant' but to the nearest noun 'flea'. Space does not permit me to reproduce the argumentation for this conclusion, so readers are referred to Ludlow (1989) for details. My point here, however, is not about this analysis in particular but about the simple fact that shifts in *content*—even when involving *context* sensitive operators—cannot be assumed to be driven by context. Clearly some content shifts are due to shifts in context, but not all of them are happy, and indeed many are awkward to some degree. Accordingly, I think it is premature to dismiss the idea that contextualists can avoid the abominable conjunction.

To some extent, however, this concern is orthogonal to the central issue at stake. In my view, the support for contextualism comes from the linguistic evidence on its behalf, not the fact that it can dodge epistemological bullets that relevant alternatives theory could not. So even if contextualism was committed to abominable conjunctions of its own, this would not tell against contextualism so much as show that these conjunctions are more recalcitrant and deeper than we had supposed and, indeed, that we may have to find a way to live with them.

5.2 The Issue of Embedded Knowledge Reports

The considerations just explored in the previous section are relevant to another, fairly complex, argument against contextualism offered in Hawthorne (2004: s. 2.7). I think that if we play close attention to the actual formulation of contextualism, his argument can be defused.

Hawthorne begins by offering the following "schemas" or premises:

The True Belief schema
If x believes that P, then x's belief is true if and only if P.
The False Belief schema
If x believes that P, then x's belief is false if and only if it is not the case that P.
Disquotational Schema for 'knows'

If an English speaker x sincerely utters a sentence of the form 'I know that P' and the sentence in the that-clause means that P, then x believes that he knows that P.

In the background is the assumption (premise) that "if a speaker sincerely accepts an utterance u and u has semantic value P, then the belief manifested by his sincerely accepting that utterance is true iff the semantic value P is true".

The argument works as follows. Suppose a speaker S utters (34):

(34) I know I have feet.

According to Hawthorne, since the semantic value of that utterance is true, "the belief you manifest by sincere acceptance is a true belief. So if [the hearer H] is a (standard) contextualist [H] is committed to saying that [S's] belief is true. But the Disquotational Schema enjoins [H] to say..."

(35) You (S) believe that you know you have feet

but then, by the True Belief Schema, H deduces (36):

(36) You (S) know you have feet

"So standard contextualism, in combination with the True Belief Schema and the Disquotational Schema would have [H] conclude that [S] knows [S] has feet. But this conclusion is altogether forbidden by the standard contextualist. For were H to sincerely accept 'You (S) know you have feet', then [H] would have a false belief since, in the scenario envisaged, the semantic value of the latter sentence is false." (p. 102)

I can only ever read (36) as, roughly

(36') You know-by-my-standards you have feet

I don't think that Hawthorne's argument works, but we will have to move cautiously to see why. First, note that it incorporates an additional assumption, which I will label "The Lethal Assumption".

Lethal Assumption
"Grant with the contextualist there may be situations where you have low standards and I have high standards for the applicability of 'know' so that the semantic value of 'know' in your mouth is different to its semantic value in mine." (p. 101)

Once we are clear on the way that this assumption is working in the argument, we can begin to see the problem with Hawthorne's argument. Recall that according to (C2*) it is the context, not the speaker that fixes the standards. Context may even swamp the speaker's intentions to set standards. (Clearly true in Lewis, 1996: the mere mention of the skeptical problem jacks up the standards for all participants in the discourse. See also DeRose, 1995.)

This means that there are two possibilities; either the ascriptions by S and H are in the same context or not. Let's consider both possibilities.

Suppose they are in the same context. Then following (C2*) we simply deny that these are cases in which standards of knowledge can vary between speaker and hearer. If the context—not the speakers themselves—fixes the standards, and there is only one context, and that context fixes just one standard, then the sort of case envisioned by Hawthorne is just flat out impossible.

OK, now let's suppose that the utterances are made in different contexts. Then of course the standards can vary, since there are, in effect, different ascribers and different contexts of ascription. But then Hawthorne's argument falls apart. To see this, suppose S is in context c' and H is in context c'', but H is not aware of the exact context (I'll consider the case where H is aware in just a bit). S utters (34), which, given contextualist assumptions, will have the logical form given in (34*).

(34) I know I have feet
(34*) [∃s: relevant-to(s,c')]know(I, [I have feet], s)

H then responds by uttering (35), which has the form given in (35*).

(35) You (S) believe that you know you have feet
(35*) [∃c ∃s: epistemic-standard(s) and relevant-to(s,c)] You believe (you, [you have feet], s)

Following Hawthorne's deduction, utilizing the True Belief Schema etc., H deduces (36), which has the logical form given in (36*).

(36) You (S) know you have feet
(36*) [∃c ∃s: epistemic-standard(s) and relevant-to(s,c)] know(you, [you have feet], s)

The alleged tension is supposed to come when H utters (37).

(37) You (S) don't know you have feet.

But is there a tension between (36) and (37)? Well, given the assumptions we have been operating with, the logical form of (37) will be as in (37*).

(37*) [∃s: epistemic-standard(s) and relevant-to(s,c″)] It's not the case that know(you, [you have feet], s)

But (36*) and (37*) are not inconsistent, so the apparent problem is just that—apparent—and due to a failure to consider the logical form of these utterances under the definition of contextualism which Hawthorne himself has advocated.

The same applies if we suppose that H is aware of the context (c′) in which S makes her knowledge attribution. In that case the logical form of (37) is (37**).

(37**) [∃s: epistemic-standard(s) and relevant-to(s,c′)] It's not the case that know(you, [you have feet], s)

This still does not conflict with (36*).

6 The Moral

Any moral drawn from this discussion will have to be tentative, but it does seem safe to say that contextualism does not clash in an obvious way with what linguistic theory tells us about the structure of knowledge reports. Quite clearly, given the subtlety and complexity of the issues involved, a great deal of further investigation is called for. Is this subtlety and complexity cause for rejecting the new linguistic turn in epistemology? I wouldn't think so. Indeed I think just the opposite conclusion should be drawn.

Hawthorne (2004: 109 n. 131) draws a more pessimistic moral from *his* discussion of the role of linguistic argumentation in epistemology:

"For what its worth, one moral the contextualist should draw from all this is that, unlike syntax, the semantic working of our language may be as obscure to us as a whole range of metaphysical questions about the world itself. Philosophy of language is no first philosophy."

One problem with this statement is that syntax is not "in view" either. Furthermore, it is no part of the new linguistic turn in epistemology that there is a kind of first philosophy that proceeds from the study of language. As I said earlier, I would not want to privilege either syntactic or semantic data over more traditional methods in epistemology. Doing the semantics of constructions that attribute knowledge to agents will require great sensitivity to the philosophical analysis of knowledge, and this will have consequences for syntax as well. But by the same token, insights from syntax and semantics can illuminate the traditional enterprise of philosophical epistemology. A more appropriate moral might be that syntax, semantics, and epistemology must be done simultaneously and in concert. First philosophy was never part of the project.

APPENDIX: SOME GOOGLE SEARCHES FOR EXPLICIT STANDARDS OF KNOWLEDGE IN KNOWLEDGE ATTRIBUTIONS

*Known by * Standards*

www.macalester.edu/philosophy/warpowers98.htm

... and an "offensive military action" could not be **known by any objective standards**, the executive contended that without "judicially discoverable and manageable ... "

webpages.charter.net/jspeyrer/archiv2.htm

... the overlall psychic effects of Ibogaine are not very well **known (by occidental science standards**) but it has a long time history of use in Africa and I have ...

www.spiritualhealing.org/astral.htm

... absolute knowing that these beings possessed intelligence surpassing any **known by earthly standards**, it was also felt they possessed none of what we refer to ...

www.delmar.edu/engl/instruct/stomlin/1301int/lessons/content/authorty. htm

... write about what we know, and knowing for sure what we **"know" by academic standards** is a little tricky. Some students object to the fairly personal nature of ...

*Know with * Confidence/Certainty/Reliability/Assurance*

www.npwrc.usgs.gov/resource/2001/whabmgt/set.htm

... of a system before we attempt to manage it. That is, we should **know with some level of confidence** what consequences will ensue from a specific action. We never ...

www.network-democracy.org/social-security/nd/archive/invest/
msg00158.html

... it breaks. Everyone should care if you don't or can't **know, with some reasonable certainty**, what you and your family will receive from social security under ...

http://www.mtnmath.com/book/node40.html

We must know when and how to use it and we must **know with some, albeit imperfect, reliability** when it leads us too far afield from what is practically possible

http://www.sads.org/genetics.html

The genetic test allows you to **know with some certainty** whether or not you have the LQTS gene which runs in your family.

www.southwestpv.com/catalog/Batteries.htm

Southwest PV Systems, Inc., solar power products ... that will be encountered at the site. This means you need to **know with some degree of certainty** when the rainy season or winter months occur. Then when you ...

http://www.telegraph.co.uk/wine/main.jhtml?view=DETAILS&grid= P8
&targetRule=10&xml= %2Fwine%2F2002%2F02% 2F02%2Fedausto2.
xml

When you have a grounding in toxicology, you **know with some degree of accuracy** what will and won't be safe to eat.

www.astro.princeton.edu/~iskra/lecture1.ps

... about the mass of the galaxy and simple Newtonian dynamics. We **know with some confidence** that the galaxy is not expanding. Neither is the solar system, or the ...

www.fordham.edu/halsall/mod/1899veblen.html

... is an effective means of reputability. It is of moment to **know with some precision** what is the degree of archaism conventionally required in speaking on any ...

www.dyad.org/do4cande.htm

... if you develop your warm sensitive nature—you will be able to **know with some authority**. You will not have to "believe" you can know for yourself. (Practice ...

www.law.uh.edu/guides/modlcode.html

... where all (or nearly all) states have adopted (enacted) that uniform code, and businessmen **know with some assurance** how business is conducted in those states. ...

www.ce.chalmers.se/undergraduate/D/EDA385/lab3e.html

... to find out. As long as the top domain indicates a country (eg .se) we **know with some probability** the country but not for sure. Just as an example: most of the ...

www.iaw.on.ca/~jsek/steeles.htm

... As for the identity of our unit, the only things we **know with some degree of authority** are that the two local companies formed a (fighting) portion of the 5th ...

www.dcn.davis.ca.us/~dfamhays/news_articles/nov01tenure.htm

... P&T committee. In order to do that, of course, the faculty needs to **know with some clarity** just how the committee has been performing. We invite your response. ...

www.oxfordtoday.ox.ac.uk/archive/0001/13_3/06.shtml

... is a constant preoccupation of large investment banks, which need to **know with some accuracy** the extent of their 'exposure'. A floor of traders is very much ...

www.checkfraud.org/artcl05.htm

... ticket agent, loan or title insurance officer, new accounts representative) **know with some level of confidence** that the person before them with a legitimate ...

www.amazon.com/exec/obidos/ASIN/0312972601/

... this information so you can eliminate these critters for good, and **KNOW with complete confidence** that it's going to work Greatly. Then you can share what you ...

www.geocities.com/countercoupdallas/jwj.html

... this matter in his strong dissent: "Although we may never **know with complete certainty** the identity of the winner of this year's presidential election, the ..."

www.catholic.net/rcc/Periodicals/HPR/March%202000/editorial.html

... he has obtained God's grace" (Denzinger 1533). Likewise, no one can **know with complete certitude** that he will persevere in sanctifying grace and die in the ...

sxws.com/charis/apol15.htm

... available to anyone searching for truth, but how might Catholics **know with complete assurance** what constitutes the body of tradition used by the Magisterium to ...

Other Hedges on Knowledge: Really, Well, In Effect

www.pbs.org/wgbh/pages/frontline/shows/religion/jesus/reallyknow.html

... What can we **really know** about the life of Jesus? Are we dealing with facts here? Are we dealing with bits and shreds of evidence? Are we dealing with hypotheses ...

sciencepolicy.colorado.edu/pielke/hp_roger/class/pkspring98/class4.html

... was brought up with Kevin Trenberth the week before: **How well do we know whether** the trees cut down in deforestation have been turned into carbon in the air ...

www.christiananswers.net/q-flc/flc-f021.html

... them strict instructions to be sure this hasn't happened, then you **can pretty well know** why the line is busy if you try to call—it's the sitter talking to a ...

subscript.bna.com/SAMPLES/mcr.nsf/a190caa77300097c8525648000515ca5/30d7b61c646258b685256a02007ebd6c? OpenDocument

... lists certain symptoms that an actual patient does not exhibit, "I **can doggone well know** that whoever is reviewing that chart is going to say I'm overbilling.". ...

www.hansard.act.gov.au/hansard/2001/week10/3636.htm

... Suggestions that I had **in effect known** that there was a rollout figure of $230 million and refused to answer a question to that effect or pretend that I did ...

newswatch.sfsu.edu/qa/030501king_qa_tobar.html

... sued again and again for excessive use of force. We **sort of in effect knew**, before the Rodney King beating there were some injustices yet it took the Rodney ...

www.asc.upenn.edu/courses/comm575/090296B.TXT

... The Star to reveal a Dick Morris issue that the Washington Post **in effect knew** 2 weeks before when they reported that Ickies had rejected one of Dick Morris's ...

www.stat.wvu.edu/~mschucke/coursenotes/chap9.pdf

... In previous chapters, by knowing the entire distribution, we **in effect know** the entire population. So we could make statements (probabilistic statements) about ...

www.syr.edu/chancellor/letters/alcohol.html

... Though the faculty, staff, and administrators may seem somewhat detached from your experiences, I assure that we **know full well what**'s going on after hours on our campus. ...

Note that the nominal form—knowledge—easily allows a standards-of modification

www.amazon.com/exec/obidos/tg/feature/-/10787/ref=pd_br_soc/

... is a historical chronicle of Christians' seduction **by secular standards of knowledge**. The book draws on 17 studies of colleges and universities founded by ...

www.undelete.org/woa/woa09-17.html

... Some of the viewpoints are, of course, considered absurd **by today's standards of knowledge**, but they were far more sophisticated than we often give the people ...

www.smh.com.au/news/0106/13/text/obituaries.html

... quailing in her austere presence was daunted **by high standards of knowledge** and accuracy. I thought her occasionally restrictive and inflexible—about changes ...

www.kcl.ac.uk/kis/schools/life_sciences/life_sci/woodT.html

... The academic knowledge is determined **by perceived standards of knowledge** and by recent advances in research in the appropriate area. Consequently the students ...

www.ubfellowship.org/101-9.htm

... with their enlightenment and status of conscience. Do not make the mistake of judging another's religion **by your own standards of knowledge** and truth. ...

www.rationality.net/book.htm

... of scientific activity in cryogenics. Or take Aristotle: **By today's standards of knowledge** he was full of nonsense in what he asserted were scientific facts ...

kiro.lemontoss.com/FaithDawn.html

... had been exceptionally wonderful. Lane's mother had, **by Tyger's standards of knowledge**, spoiled her son—and for some reason that hadn't turned out bad ...

www.bwl.uni-kiel.de/Ordnung+Wettbewerbspolitik/german/papers/prosi2.htm

... new developments cannot be measured **by previously known standards of knowledge**. They are by definition "previously unknown". The breakthrough, the revolution ...

With * Standards of Knowledge

www.geocities.com/Athens/Olympus/6868/shoooob.html

... which have so far fallen "out of correspondence **with general contemporary standards of knowledge** and belief as to acquire an air of unreality." Not one of ...

home.no.net/rrpriddy/lim/2.html

... dependency on physical science has brought **with it inappropriate standards of knowledge**—and thus wrong methods and techniques—for studying man and society ...

Standards of Certainty

www.jewish.com/news/miryam.shtml

... DNA evidence. Written together with Rabbis Wozner and Karelitz, the decision asserts that "DNA does not meet the strict **halachic standards of certainty**." ...

www.riskworld.com/Profsoci/SRA/RiskScienceLawGroup/Casebook/cb0799x03.htm

... in other recent cases that distinguish between **legal and scientific standards of certainty**, such as Ferebee and Rubanick. Judge Newman's arguments are more ...

www.newsmax.com/archives/articles/2001/1/5/72826.shtml

... Project no state's voting results until all its polls have closed. Apply higher **standards of certainty** for calling close races. ...

www.eurekastreet.com.au/pages/106/106archi.html

... are, of course, two completely different worlds and clearly, different **standards of certainty** are used in science and in politics. Nowhere is this illustrated ...

home.attbi.com/~rustynet/t-f01-syllabus.htm

"... Popular epidemiology" vs. scientific inquiry. **Standards of certainty** in law: criminal trials, civil lawsuits, government regulation, legislation.

caselaw.lp.findlaw.com/cgi-bin/getcase.pl?navby=case&court=us&vol=401&invol=200

... The **standards of certainty** in statutes punishing for offenses is higher than in those depending primarily upon civil sanction for enforcement. The crime "must ..."

www.ortho.lsumc.edu/Faculty/Marino/Doe.html

... dye #2 can cause cancer, will be resolved according to the **standards of certainty** and concepts of causality that are routinely followed in the law. The law ...

www.lbyso.com/lbyso_rr13.htm

... grievance committee shall have broad discretion in deciding the **standards of certainty**, which they require to sustain the allegations. A disciplinary hearing ...

objectivism.cx/~atlantis/objtmp/msg02785.html

... back on track. Without a murderer's right to life, the **standards of certainty** required to justify execution could become the main topic. For starters on that ...

www.internationalschools.ca/letter.html

... Dear Parents, All of us as parents know at least two things for **certain. We know that** the 21st century is upon us and we know that our children are going to ...

www.dentalcomfortzone.com/archive/DentistsCommitSuicide.html

There are few things that we all know for **certain. We know that** the sun rises in the east, and sets in the west. We know that there is no escape from death and ...

REFERENCES

Austin, J. (1961). 'Other Minds', in *Philosophical Papers* (Oxford: Oxford University Press).

Bennett, M. (1974). *'Some Extensions of a Montague Fragment of English'*, PhD thesis, Department of Linguistics, UCLA.

Boguraev, B., and T. Briscoe (eds.) (1989). *Computational Lexicography for Natural Language Processing* (London: Longman).

Bresnan, J. (1982). *The Mental Representation of Grammatical Relations* (Cambridge, Mass.: MIT Press).

Castañeda, H.-N. (1967). 'Comments', in N. Rescher (ed.), *The Logic of Decision and Action* (Pittsburgh: University of Pittsburgh Press).

Chomsky, N. (1986). *Barriers* (Cambridge, Mass.: MIT Press).

Cinque, G. (1999). *Adverbs and Functional Heads. A Cross-Linguistic Perspective* (Oxford: Oxford University Press).

Cohen, S. (1991). 'Skepticism, Relevance, and Relativity', in B. McLaughlin (ed.), *Dretske and his Critics* (Oxford: Blackwell Publishing).

—— (1999). 'Contextualism, Skepticism, and the Structure of Reasons', *Philosophical Perspectives*, xii. *Epistemology* (Oxford: Blackwell Publishing), 57–89.

Davidson, D. (1967). 'The Logical Form of Action Sentences', in N. Rescher (ed.), *The Logic of Decision and Action* (Pittsburgh: University of Pittsburgh Press).

—— (1985). 'Adverbs of Action', in B. Vermazen, and M. Hintikka (eds.), *Essays on Davidson: Actions and Events* (Oxford: Oxford University Press).

DeRose, K. (1992). 'Contextualism and Knowledge Attributions', *Philosophy and Phenomenology Research*, 52: 913–29.

—— (1995). 'Solving the Skeptical Problem', *Philosophical Review*, 104: 1–52.

—— (1999). 'Contextualism: Explanation and Defense', in J. Greco and E. Sosa (eds.), *The Blackwell Guide to Epistemology* (Cambridge, Mass.: Blackwell), 187–205.

Dretske, F. (1981). *Knowledge and the Flow of Information* (Cambridge, Mass.: MIT Press).

—— (2000). 'The Pragmatic Dimension of Knowledge', in F. Dretske, *Perception, Knowledge, and Belief: Selected Issues* (Cambridge: Cambridge University Press).

Grimshaw, J. (1990). *Argument Structure* (Cambridge, Mass.: MIT Press).

Hale, K., and J. Keyser (1987). 'A View from the Middle', *Lexicon Project Working Papers*, 10 (Cambridge, Mass.: Center for Cognitive Science, MIT).

Hawthorne, J. (2002). Talk presented at Rutgers Semantics Workshop.

—— (2004). *Knowledge and Lotteries* (Oxford: Oxford University Press).

Higginbotham, J. (1989). 'Elucidations of Meaning', *Linguistics and Philosophy*, 12: 465–518.

Jackendoff, R. (1987). 'The Status of Thematic Relations in Linguistic Theory', *Linguistic Inquiry*, 18: 369–411.

Kamp, H. (1975). 'Two Theories of Adjectives', in E. Keenan (ed.), *Formal Semantics in Natural Language* (Cambridge: Cambridge University Press), 123–55.

Kennedy, C. (1999). *Projecting the Adjective: The Syntax and Semantics of Gradability and Comparison* (New York: Garland).

Larson, R. (1986). 'Implicit Arguments in Situation Semantics', *Linguistics and Philosophy*, 11: 169–201.

—— (1988). 'On the Double Object Construction', *Linguistic Inquiry*, 19: 335–91.

—— (1998). 'Events and Modification in Nominals', in D. Strolovitch and A. Lawson (eds.) *Proceedings from Semantics and Linguistic Theory (SALT) VIII* (Ithaca, NY: Cornell University Press).

Lewis, D. (1979). 'Score Keeping in a Language Game', *Journal of Philosophical Logic*, 8: 339–59.

—— (1996). 'Elusive Knowledge', *Australasian Journal of Philsophy*, 74: 549–67.

Ludlow, P. (1989). 'Implicit Comparison Classes', *Linguistics and Philosophy*, 12: 519–33.

—— (1995). 'Logical Form and the Hidden Indexical Theory: A Reply to Schiffer', *Journal of Philosophy*, 92: 102–7.

—— (1996). 'The Adicity of "Believes" and the Hidden Indexical Theory', *Analysis*, 56: 97–102.

—— (1999). *Semantics, Tense and Time: An Essay in the Metaphysics of Natural Language* (Cambridge, Mass.: MIT Press).

Malcolm, N. (1963). 'Knowledge and Belief', in *Knowledge and Certainty: Essays and Lectures* (Englewood Cliffs NJ: Prentice Hall).

Nirenberg, S., and V. Raskin (1987). 'The Subworld Concept Lexicon and the Lexicon Management System', *Computational Linguistics*, 13: 276–89.

Parsons, T. (1990). *Events in the Semantics of English* (Cambridge, Mass.: MIT Press).

Partee, B. (forthcoming). 'Comments on "On the Case for Contextualism", by Jason Stanley', *Philosophical Studies*.

Pustejovsky, J. (1995). *The Generative Lexicon* (Cambridge, Mass.: MIT Press).

—— and S. Bergler (eds.) (1991). *Lexical Semantics and Knowledge Representation* (Berlin: Springer-Verlag).

Schiffer, S. (1992). 'Belief Ascription', *Journal of Philosophy*, 89: 499–521.

—— (1996). 'The Hidden-Indexical Theory's Logical-Form Problem: A Rejoinder', *Analysis*, 56.

Shope, R. (1983). *The Analysis of Knowing* (Princeton: Princeton University Press).

Stanley, J. (2000). 'Context and Logical Form', *Linguistics and Philosophy*, 23: 391–434.

—— (2002a), 'Making it Articulated', *Mind and Language*, 17: 149–68.

—— (2002b). 'Nominal Restriction', in G. Preyer and G. Peter (eds.), *Logical Form and Language* (Oxford: Oxford University Press), 365–88.

—— (forthcoming, a). 'On the Linguistic Basis for Contextualism', *Philosophical Studies*.

—— (forthcoming, b). 'Context, Interest-Relativity, and Knowledge'.

—— and Z. Szabó (2000). 'On Quantifier Domain Restriction', *Mind and Language*, 15: 219–61.

Unger, P. (1975). *Ignorance: A Case for Skepticism* (Oxford: Oxford University Press).

—— (1984). *Philosophical Relativity* (Minneapolis: University of Minnesota Press).

Unger, P. (1986). 'The Cone Model of Knowledge', *Philosophical Topics*, 14: 125–78.

Vendler, Z. (1967). *Linguistics in Philosophy* (Ithaca, NY: Cornell University Press).

—— (1972). *Res Cogitans: An Essay in Rational Psychology* (Ithaca, NY: Cornell University Press).

Williams, E. (1985). 'PRO and the Subject of NP', *Natural Language and Linguistic Theory*, 3: 297–315.

Williamson, T. (2000). *Knowledge and Its Limits* (Oxford: Oxford University Press).

Wittgenstain, L. (1969). *On Certainty*, (New York: Harper & Row).

3

The Emperor's New 'Knows'

Kent Bach

> When I examine contextualism there is much that I can doubt.[1] I can
> doubt whether it is a cogent theory that I examining, and not a cleverly
> stated piece of whacks. I can doubt whether there is any real theory there
> at all. Perhaps what I took to be a theory was really some reflections;
> perhaps I am even the victim of some cognitive hallucination. One thing
> however I cannot doubt: that there exists a widely read pitch of a round
> and somewhat bulgy shape.
>
> *(A traditional epistemologist)*

The title of this chapter calls for it to stick to the obvious. Even if it did, it
would probably not convince the contextualist. Knowing that, I will be
comforted by the thought that whether or not 'knows' is a context-sensitive
term, at least 'obvious' and 'convincing' are. Perhaps 'context-sensitive' is
context-sensitive too.

I begin, in section I, with what contextualism says, what it doesn't say, and
what it implies about knowledge attributions. Even if contextualism is true
and, contrary to invariantism, a given knowledge-ascribing sentence can
express various propositions in various contexts, those propositions are not
themselves context-bound. This is something that contextualists do not make

---

[1] The allusion here is of course to Price (1932: 3): "When I see a tomato there is much that I
can doubt. I can doubt whether it is a tomato that I am seeing, and not a cleverly painted piece
of wax. I can doubt whether there is any material thing there at all. Perhaps what I took to be a
tomato was really a reflection; perhaps I am even the victim of some hallucination. One thing
however I cannot doubt: that there exists a red patch of a round and somewhat bulgy shape,
standing out from a background of other colour-patches, and having a certain visual depth,
and that this whole field of colour is of colour is directly present to my consciousness."

clear. In section II, I will sketch the contextualist's strategy for containing skepticism and discuss whether this strategy really explains why unsuspecting people can be duped by skeptical arguments. An alternative explanation is that the conflicting intuitions that give rise to skeptical paradoxes don't really bear on the truth conditions of knowledge attributions but are merely vacillating responses to skeptical considerations. In any case, as claimed in section III, contextualism doesn't really come to grips with skepticism. In attempting to confine the plausibility of skeptical arguments to contexts in which far-fetched skeptical possibilities are raised, it concedes both too much to the skeptic and too little. Also, as section IV points out, in arguing against invariantism contextualists have mainly focused on the skeptical variety, according to which knowledge requires the highest degree of evidence, justification, and conviction. Although the contextualist objections to skeptical invariantism are not cogent, this view is independently implausible.

Much more plausible is moderate (nonskeptical) invariantism, a version of which I will propose in section V. From its perspective, the evidence that seems to support contextualism appears in a very different light. In contexts where special concerns arise, whether skeptical or practical, what varies is not the truth conditions of knowledge attributions but the knowledge attributions people are prepared to make. It is not the standards for the truth of knowledge attributions that go up but the attributor's threshold of confidence regarding the relevant proposition. When that happens, as in the examples contextualists rely on, people require stronger evidence than is necessary for knowing. That's what it takes for them to eliminate residual doubts and to attribute knowledge to others. So my version of moderate invariantism is a kind of error theory, but not an extreme error theory like contextualism and skeptical invariantism.

Finally, as I will suggest in section VI, part of what makes a belief justified is that the cognitive processes whereby it is formed and sustained are sensitive to realistic counterpossibilities (so-called relevant alternatives). The very occurrence of the thought of a counterpossibility gives one prima-facie reason to take it seriously, and the fact that a counterpossibility does not come to mind is evidence for its irrelevance. But that fact is evidence that one cannot explicitly consider, since to do so would be to bring the counterpossibility to mind. Examining this underappreciated phenomenon will shed new light on why possibilities that are irrelevant to knowing are properly ignored.

Before we get down to business, a parable is in order. It's about the Dirtmatist and the Septic. The Dirtmatist thinks that he can keep his hands clean by washing them with a little soap and water every so often. The Septic thinks that because germs are everywhere, it is impossible to keep his hands clean. The best he can do is to scrub his hands repeatedly with industrial-strength cleaning agents and hope for the best. One day the Dirtmatist encounters the Septic near the sink in the men's room, and offers to shake hands. The Septic backs off in fear. The Dirtmatist assures him, "My hands are clean." The Septic retorts, "No they're not," and backs this up with the following argument:

Septical Argument
If your hands were clean, they would be free of contaminants.
Your hands are not free of contaminants.
So, your hands are not clean.

At least the Septic doesn't doubt the existence of the Dirtmatist's hands—it's only their dirtiness that worries him. Anyhow, the Dirtmatist doesn't buy the Septic's argument. "I've just washed my hands," he protests. Even though he's not at all naive about the microscopic world, he rejects the second premise. He just doesn't worry about germs or dirt particles too small for the eye to see. For him, it's out of sight, out of mind. For the Septic, it's out of mind, still in body.

The Dirtmatist and the Septic argue for a while, until in walks Notsick, a more sophisticated thinker. He accepts the truth of the second premise but rejects the first, which is supported by what he refers to as the Cleanser Principle. At this point the Dirtmatist and the Septic join sides (not that they shake hands), both thinking that Notsick is being too clever by half. Despite their disagreement about the second premise, they find it unpalatable to reject the Cleanser Principle. They gang up on Notsick, but he sticks to his guns. Then they get back to arguing with each other. Finally, a Cleantextualist emerges from a stall and comes to the rescue.

After washing his hands, the Cleantextualist assures the Dirtmatist that he was right when he uttered, "My hands are clean." He concedes to the Septic that, yes, there is no way to eliminate every last germ and particle of dirt. And, while acknowledging Notsick's noble antiseptic intentions, he chides him for rejecting the axiomatic Cleanser Principle. And though it might seem that the Cleantextualist all but concedes the Septical Argument, he hasn't really. He points out something overlooked all along by the others, that 'clean' is context-sensitive and that 'contaminant' is too. It turns out, much to everyone else's surprise, that what the Dirtmatist asserted is not what the Septic argued against.

I What Contextualism Says and Implies

Fred Dretske expresses the natural intuition that "factual knowledge is absolute. It is like being pregnant: an all or nothing affair" (1981: 363). One can be newly pregnant but not a little pregnant, or almost ready to deliver but not highly pregnant. Similarly, as Dretske observes, "I can have a better justification than you, but my justification cannot be more sufficient than yours." It can be more than sufficient for knowledge, but not more sufficient for knowledge. Justification (and evidence) comes in degrees, but knowledge does not. Now does contextualism conflict with any of this? Not at all. Contextualists say that what is sufficient for knowledge varies with the context in which knowledge is attributed. As we will see, however, that is not quite what they mean.

One can take a contextualist position about various expressions, such as 'obvious', 'tall', and 'good', as well as 'knows'. Contextualism about a given expression (or class of expressions) is a semantic thesis. It says that any sentence containing the expression, even if otherwise free of ambiguity, indexicality, and vagueness (or if the effects of these are kept fixed), expresses different propositions (or, if you prefer, has different truth conditions) in different contexts of utterance.[2] Here, since we are concerned solely with contextualism about 'knows' and knowledge-ascribing sentences, I will use the label 'contextualism' specifically for epistemic contextualism.

Contextualism directly concerns knowledge attributions, not knowledge. In fact, it is a thesis about the semantic contents of knowledge-ascribing

---

[2] This sort of contextualism, which concerns specific expressions, is not to be confused with the kind that prevails in some philosophy of language circles. There the term 'contextualism' is used for a rather radical family of theses about sentence meaning, such as that not just a great many but virtually all sentences do not express complete propositions, that pragmatics intrudes into semantics in the sense that "what is said" is generally determined partly by pragmatic factors, and that the meanings of a great many lexical items are semantically impoverished and require contextual enrichment. In 'Context ex Machina' (Bach 2005), I suggest that the platitudes that motivate such theses are misstated or overstated. When these phenomena are accurately characterized, by taking certain independently motivated distinctions into account, the motivation for such theses loses its force. The simplest distinction to observe is that between content being determined *by* context and content being determined *in* context (but by something else). Disregarding this distinction tends to lead contextualists, as well as many of their critics, to use phrases like 'context-dependent' and 'context-sensitive' interchangeably with 'contextually variable', and then to treat the relevant phenomena as having semantic import. Epistemic contextualists tend to do likewise.

sentences, not just what people implicate or presuppose when uttering them.³ It claims that a sentence of the form 'S knows (at t) that p' can be true as uttered in one context and false as uttered in another, depending on the epistemic standards that govern the context. The claim is not merely that people's willingness to make a given knowledge attribution depends on the standards but that the standards governing the context actually affect which proposition the knowledge-ascribing sentence expresses in that context.

It is crucial to see, although contextualists do not stress this, that context-ualism does not imply that the proposition expressed by a given knowledge-ascribing sentence in a given context can itself have different truth values in different contexts. Contextualism does not imply that somebody can know something if the attributor's standards are low and fail to know it if they are high. Nor does it imply that somebody can both know something relative to one context of attribution, and not know it relative to another. What it does imply is that a sentence of the form 'S knows (at t) that p' can be true as uttered in one context and false as uttered in another. This is not because the proposition the sentence expresses has a different truth value, but because the sentence expresses a different proposition. That is something contextualists recognize but, it seems, do not always keep in mind.⁴

Contextualists do make clear that the context they have in mind is not the epistemic context of the subject of the knowledge attribution. Everybody agrees that what it takes for George to know that he has hands or, to put it

³ On what people implicate and presuppose, see Rysiew (forthcoming). It is important to keep in mind that what have semantic contents are sentences, not utterances. That is why David Kaplan distinguishes a "sentence-in-a-context" from an utterance of the sentence (1989: 522). This distinction is essential to my formulation of the semantic–pragmatic distinction (Bach 1999). The basic idea is that information counts as pragmatic if it derives not from the content of the sentence but from the fact that the sentence is actually uttered.

⁴ As Stewart Cohen explains, "strictly speaking, instead of saying that S knows in one context [of attribution, not S's context] and fails to know in another, one should really say that 'S knows that P' is true in one context and false in the other" (1999: 65). Rather than use metalinguistic locutions, he prefers the less "stylistically cumbersome" object language but advises the reader not to be misled by this. Still, it is easy to mislead the reader, as when he says, for example, "the standards that determine how good one's reasons have to be in order to know are determined by the context of ascription" (1999: 59). Lewis (1996) makes no bones about misleading the reader. It is not until his very last paragraph, after making a brilliant series of startling and sometimes paradoxical observations and suggestions about knowledge and the knowledge-destroying effect of epistemology, that he acknowledges, "I could have said my say fair and square, breaking no rules. It would have been tiresome, but it could have been done. The secret would have been to resort to 'semantic ascent' " (1996: 566).

more accurately, for the sentence 'George knows that he has hands' to be true, can depend on George's epistemic situation. This is a matter not of setting standards but of meeting them. Obviously how hard it is to know something does not depend just on the thing to be known but also on the situation of the prospective knower. If there are considerations that need to be taken into account (one's memory has been shaky lately), possibilities to consider that ordinarily can be ignored (maybe the zoo keepers have placed a cleverly painted mule in the zebra cage), or alternatives to eliminate (a person's twin has returned), then the subject must reckon with them. This may be because of things the subject is aware of (or at least has reason to suspect) or facts about his circumstances that he needs to be aware of. If Austin (1961) was right, possibilities or alternatives are relevant only if there are special reasons to consider them. So the subject's context, in so far as it affects his epistemic position, can bear on the truth of a knowledge attribution. But contextualism concerns the attributor's context, which can vary even while the subject's epistemic position stays fixed, and claims that this context bears on the content of the attribution.[5]

How can it be that a sentence like 'George knows that he has hands', even with time and references fixed, does not have a fixed propositional content? Doesn't the verb 'knows' express an invariant two-term relation between the knower and the known?[6] Contextualists tend to be not all that clear about this. They don't claim that 'know' is ambiguous,[7] but some suggest that it is context-sensitive because it is a kind of indexical (Cohen, 1988) and others

---

[5] See Heller (1999a) for an especially clear explanation of how (from a contextualist perspective) this can be. I should add that in the case of first-person knowledge attributions, where the subject and the attributor are one and the same, it might seem puzzling (even from a contextualist perspective) how the subject's epistemic position can remain fixed while the content of a self-attribution of knowledge can vary. However, the standards for evaluating such an attribution, even if dependent, say, on the intentions of the (self-)attributor, can vary, for reasons independent of that person's, qua subject, epistemic position. Still, contextualists should not focus as much as they do on first-person cases. Focusing on cases in which attributor and subject are one and the same can only muddy the waters.

[6] The terms 'contextualism' and 'invariantism' were coined by Peter Unger (1984: 6–11). Arguing that there is a trade-off between their respective virtues and vices, he concludes that there is no fact of the matter as to whether contextualism or invariantism is correct. He adopts this position of "semantic relativity" not just on 'know' but also on gradable terms that can seem to be absolute, such as 'flat' and 'empty'.

[7] Of course it has an acquaintance sense, corresponding to the French 'connaître' and the German 'kennen' as opposed to 'savoir' and 'wissen', but we are ignoring that sense and limiting our attention to 'know' as followed by a clause.

because it is vague (Heller, 1999a).[8] Some are reluctant to commit themselves as to its semantic character (indexical, vague, or something else) and are content to say that the "standards" for knowing, or what "counts as" knowing (DeRose, 1995), depend on the context, or on what possibilities are "properly ignored" (Lewis, 1996).[9] There are some delicate issues here—these are not matters of incidental detail—but I will not be addressing them.[10]

Regardless of its detailed formulation, contextualism entails either that 'know' expresses different relations in different contexts or that it expresses a single relation that is relativized to a contextually variable epistemic standard.[11] Either way, 'know' has variable content. It is incoherent to suppose that it expresses a single, unrelativized relation and yet that identical knowledge attributions made in different contexts can differ in truth value. Contextualists cannot coherently mean, even if they often say, that the standards for knowledge or what counts as knowing can vary with the context.[12] It is

---

[8] Noting that "the penumbras of vague terms can dilate or constrict according to conversational purposes", Schiffer points out that if the context variability of 'know' consisted simply in its vagueness, this sort of variability would be "of no use to the contextualist, [because] speakers are perfectly aware of it when it's going on" (1996: 327–8).

[9] Unger (1986: 130–1) lists assorted factors, involving the subject's psychological state, his justification, and what he can rule out, as well as rationality, reliability, and possibility.

[10] Two issues are worth noting. Contextualists sometimes seem to suppose that what changes the standards is the salience of improbable or even far-fetched possibilities. However, if such a change is supposed to affect the semantic content of a 'knows'-ascription, salience cannot be what affects it. Salience is obviously a feature relevant to pragmatics, not to semantics (see Bach, 1999; 2005). It plays a role in what speakers are likely to mean when they say what they say. Rysiew (2001) develops a plausible account of its pragmatic role in knowledge attributions. Also, there are linguistic issues to contend with. As Jason Stanley (2004) argues, 'know' does not behave like ordinary indexicals ('I', 'tomorrow'), relational terms ('local', 'enemy'), or gradable adjectives ('tall', 'flat'). For a probing semantic analysis of such adjectives and comparison of relative ('tall', 'rich') with absolute adjectives ('flat', 'empty'), see Kennedy forthcoming, and for an ingenious semantic-pragmatic account of how absolute terms work see Lasersohn (1999). It is curious that Cohen, who argues that the context-sensitivity of 'knows' derives from that of 'justified', likens the relative term 'justified' to the absolute term 'flat' rather than to a relative term like 'tall'.

[11] Contextualists differ as to whether epistemic standards are a matter of degree of justification, extent of relevant alternatives, or range of possible worlds in which the truth is tracked. I'll ignore this difference here. Also, in so far as they distinguish standards simply by their strength, they implicitly and implausibly assume that standards form a linear ordering.

[12] Here are some examples of what they say: "One speaker may attribute knowledge to a subject while another speaker denies knowledge to the same subject, without contradiction" (Cohen, 1988: 97); "In some conversational situations, one's epistemic position must be

somewhat better to say what it takes for a given knowledge-ascribing sentence to be true can so vary, but this must be understood to mean that its truth value can vary only because its content can vary. The same content cannot be true in one context and false in another. Stewart Cohen is clear on this:[13]

> How from the viewpoint of formal semantics should we think of this context-sensitivity of knowledge ascriptions? We could think of it as a kind of indexicality. On this way of construing the semantics, ascriptions of knowledge involve an indexical reference to standards. So the knowledge predicate will express different relations (corresponding to different standards) in different contexts. But we could instead view the knowledge predicate as expressing the same relation in every context. On this model, we view the context as determining a standard at which the proposition involving the knowledge relation gets evaluated. So we could think of knowledge as a three-place relation between a person, a proposition, and a standard. (1999: 61)

As Cohen recognizes, "As long as we allow for contextually determined standards, it doesn't matter how formally we construe the context-sensitivity. These semantic issues, as near as I can tell, are irrelevant to the epistemological issues." Using 'D' to represent the standard determined by context, we can capture the contextualist conception of the variable content of a simple knowledge-ascribing sentence by means of a more elaborate one that makes the relevant standard explicit. We can do this in either of two ways:

> *indexed:* 'S knows$_D$ at t that p'
> *relativized:* 'S knows at t relative to D that p'.

---

stronger than in others to count as knowing" (De Rose, 1995: 30); "What counts as having this property [e.g. of knowing that grass is green] might vary from context to context" (Kompa, 2002: 88). Such ways of putting things misleadingly suggest that the truth value of a knowledge attribution can somehow vary with context while its content remains fixed.

[13] He is not so clear on his argument for contextualism: "Justification, or having good reasons, is a component of knowledge, and justification certainly comes in degrees. So context will determine how justified a belief must be in order to be justified *simpliciter*. This suggests a further argument for the truth of the contextualist's claim about knowledge. Since justification is a component of knowledge, an ascription of knowledge involves an ascription of justification" (1999: 60). This is a weak argument. As Richard Feldman points out, "from the fact that the word 'justified' displays context sensitivity, it does not follow that the necessary condition for knowledge is similarly context sensitive. . . . It could be that the degree of justification needed for knowledge is unchanging" (2001: 67). Not only is it entirely compatible with Cohen's assumptions that knowledge requires a certain fixed degree of justification, this degree could be the highest degree of justification. Stanley (2004: s. 3) offers more complicated objections to Cohen's argument.

The effect is the same either way:[14] a sentence of the form 'S knows at t that p' does not express a complete proposition except relative to a standard, and the standard is determined (somehow) by the context.[15] Either way, 'knows' does not express a fixed two-term relation. It expresses either a contextually variable two-term relation or a fixed three-term relation whose third term, the operative standard, varies with context. And, as contextualists stress, "there is no context independent correct standard" (Cohen, 1999: 59). But it must also be stressed that no matter how context "determines" the standard that figures in the content of a knowledge-ascribing sentence, the content is not hostage to the context. This content is a proposition that can be expressed in a context-independent way by means of a more elaborate knowledge-ascribing sentence that makes the relevant standard explicit, either indexed ('S knows$_D$ at t that p') or relativized ('S knows at t relative to D that p'). So even if which proposition a simple knowledge-ascribing sentence expresses depends on the context, the proposition thus expressed is context-independent.

Accordingly, in order to indicate that the word 'know' does not express a fixed two-term relation, from now on, at least in a contextualist context, I will put it in brackets and say that someone [knows] something. In such a context it would be better to call knowledge-ascribing sentences *'knows'-ascriptions* and to call assertive utterances of such a sentence *[knowledge] attributions*. *[Knowledge] denials* are assertive utterances of the negation of such a sentence ('S does not know that p').

Consider the effect for contextualism if some such device is not used. How would someone in one context report (or believe) a knowledge attribution made by someone else in another context where the prevailing standards are

---

[14] As Jonathan Schaffer has reminded me, their effects are not the same in special linguistic environments, such as in ellipsis and in focus constructions. As he argues in s. 3 of Schaffer (2004), the relativized approach is truer to the data; he concludes that 'knows' expresses a ternary relation and is not an indexical.

[15] Cohen goes on to ask, "How precisely do the standards for these predicates get determined in a particular context of ascription? This is a very difficult question to answer. But we can say this much. The standards are determined by some complicated function of speaker intentions, listener expectations, presuppositions of the conversation, salience relations, etc.— by what David Lewis calls the conversational score" (1999: 61). He does not explain how such seemingly pragmatic factors can contribute to semantic content. Nor does DeRose (2004), who takes the determination of standards to be a matter of implicit negotiation. Here he relies on a distinction between the "personally indicated" standards of the individual participants and the standards that actually contribute to the truth conditions of a knowledge attribution at a given stage in a conversation.

different? For example, if Martha said, "George knows that he has hands", and you later report this with (1),

(1) Martha said that George knows that he has hands.

then according to contextualism your use of 'knows' should be sensitive to your context, not Martha's. But this means that in uttering (1), you are not reporting what Martha said. Indeed, as Nikola Kompa (2002: 83) points out, contextualism predicts that you could say something true in uttering (2):[16]

(2) Martha said something true in uttering 'George knows that he has hands', but George does not know that he has hands.

This "unpleasant consequence" of contextualism, as Kompa calls it, can be avoided only if the relevant standards are made explicit, as in (3), or at least if there is some indication that the standards are different, as in (4):

(3) Martha said something true in uttering 'George knows [relative to D_2] that he has hands', but George does not know relative to D_1 that he has hands.
(4) Martha said something true in uttering 'George knows [relative to some standard distinct from D_1] that he has hands', but George does not know relative to D_1 that he has hands.

So the contextualist is faced with the problem of explaining how it is that we can use sentences like (1), which makes no mention of standards, to report what someone says (or thinks) someone else knows.

A contextualist would not respond by insisting that shifts in standards occur only when epistemologists raise skeptical possibilities and that otherwise epistemic standards stay fixed. As Keith DeRose explains (1999: 195), an essential part of the case for contextualism is that standards are sometimes raised in everyday contexts, not radically but still substantially. Supposedly this is what happens in DeRose's (1992: 913) and Cohen's (1999: 58) well-known Bank and Airport examples. Contextualists rely on such examples to show that "our ordinary intuitions" are responsive to alleged variations in the contents of [knowledge] attributions. So they do need to confront the problem posed by reporting on what someone says or thinks someone else knows, especially when, as illustrated by (2) above, the reporter's context is the stronger. In the case of a report of a [knowledge] denial, the problem is clearest when the reporter's context is the weaker, as in this variant of (2),

---

[16] Cappelen and Lepore (2003) thoroughly develop this very point.

"Martha said something true in uttering 'George does not know that he has hands', but George does know that he has hands."

What does contextualism predict if you encounter a [knowledge] attribution out of context? It seems to predict that you won't be in a position to grasp which proposition the sentence expresses. Suppose you eavesdrop on the middle of a conversation and hear one person say to the other, "Nixon knew that Liddy was planning the Watergate break-in." Since it is not evident to you which [knowledge] relation 'knew' expresses, you can have only a vague idea of what is being said. Lacking any specific information about the context in which the [knowledge] attribution was made, you should feel a bit uncertain as to what was said. But you won't. So far as I can tell, to avoid this difficulty the contextualist would have to show that there is some unique default [knowledge] relation that people presumptively take to be expressed by 'knows'. This approach would be implausible for 'flat' or 'tall', but maybe it could work for 'knows'.

For what it's worth, notice that explicitly relativized knowledge attributions and denials sound rather strange:

(5) ?Jack knows relative to ordinary standards that there's water at the top of the hill.

(6) ?Jill doesn't know relative to high standards that there's water at the top of the hill.

Comparative and degree-modified knowledge attributions sound strange too:

(7) ?Jack knows relative to a higher standard than Jill does that the hill is steep.

(8) ?Jill knows very highly/strongly that Jack fell down.

(9) ?Jack somewhat/nearly/barely knows that Jill tumbled down the hill.

(10) ?Jill knows to a high/some degree that she should have stayed home.

It is not clear what to make of the marginal status of such sentences.[17] Perhaps these sentences sound bad only because language users are not imbued with the insights of contextualism. If people were cognizant of the context variability of 'knows' and the various relations it expresses, or at least realized that knowledge is standards-relative, then maybe such forms would not only sound all right but would be in common use. As things are, however,

---

[17] For discussion of whether and in what ways 'knows' is gradable, see Stanley (2004: s. 2), and Ludlow (this volume). Stanley points out that a sentence like this variant of (8) is all right, 'Jill knows very well that Jack fell down', but that it doesn't mean what the contextualist needs it to mean.

"no ordinary person who utters 'I know that p', however articulate, would dream of telling you that what he meant and was implicitly stating was that he knew that p relative to such-and-such standard" (Schiffer 1996: 326–7).

As to method, when stating claims about the truth values of [knowledge] attributions made in various contexts, contextualists rely heavily on intuitions, mainly their own. Although I won't be stressing this methodological question, it is worth asking how reliable and robust such intuitions are, why we should assume that they are representative of people's intuitions in general, and why we should take them to provide evidence about the meaning of 'know' and the semantic contents of knowledge-ascribing sentences. Nichols, Stich, and Weinberg (2003), after making a series of empirical studies of people's intuitions about various epistemologists' examples, conclude that epistemic intuitions are not nearly as universal or robust as contextualists dogmatically assume. Our own experience tells us similar things. For instance, we all know people who insist that they "knew" things that they now acknowledge to be false. So does knowledge not even entail truth? There are college administrators who describe universities as repositories and transmitters of "knowledge", regardless of how much of what passes for knowledge is true (or adequately justified, for that matter). There are cognitive psychologists concerned with the "representation of knowledge", whether or not what is thus represented is true. And there are sociologists (of knowledge) who study how "knowledge" (true or not) is distributed and manipulated, and many of them don't even think there is such a thing as truth. Now contextualists, like other epistemologists, would balk at these uses of 'knowledge'. They would insist that administrators, psychologists, and sociologists use the term loosely, as if it meant 'what passes for knowledge', which it doesn't. In so doing, they would be debunking the semantic intuitions of all those who use the term 'knowledge' in this allegedly loose way. I would agree with them. But on what grounds can they, as contextualists, dismiss these intuitions? How, on contextualist grounds, are they to decide which intuitions to rely on and which to debunk?[18]

Also, it is worth keeping in mind that most of the time, outside of epistemology, when we consider whether somebody knows something, we are mainly interested in whether the person has the information, not in

[18] I am not suggesting that there is no basis, though in my view people's seemingly semantic intuitions are neither reliable nor robust. For one thing, they can be insensitive to the difference between the semantic content of an uttered sentence and what is implicit in the speaker's uttering of it (Bach, 2002) or even what the speaker implicates (Nicolle and Clark, 1999).

whether the person's belief rises to the level of knowledge. Ordinarily we do not already assume that they have a true belief and just focus on whether or not their epistemic position suffices for knowing. Similarly, when we say that someone does not know something, typically we mean that they don't have the information. So the examples contextualists use to make their case, to drive their intuitions and ours, are not representative of the knowledge attributions that people ordinarily make and the concerns people have in making them.

I will not dwell on the questions raised for contextualism in the last few paragraphs. Leaving aside the linguistic and methodological difficulties for contextualists to overcome, the real question is whether they have provided reason to suppose that there are many [knowledge] relations, each involving a different epistemic standard. So far we have seen that, even if contextualism is correct, so that which proposition a simple 'knows'-ascription expresses in a given context is determined by the operative epistemic standard, this does not mean that the other propositions it can express in other contexts somehow go away. They can be expressed in any context by more explicit knowledge-ascribing sentences, in which 'knows' is explicitly indexed or relativized. This point will be relevant to assessing the contextualist strategy for resolving skeptical paradoxes.

II The Contextualist Strategy

Contextualists suppose that the epistemic standard operative in a given context affects people's intuitions regarding the truth or falsity of a simple 'knows'-ascription as uttered in that context. They think this alleged empirical fact can be explained by the semantic fact (if it is a fact) that a given 'knows'-ascription can express different propositions in different contexts. It would help explain the psychological fact (if it is a fact) that different propositions expressible by the same sentence come to mind in different contexts. Of course the truth value of these propositions, each of which is expressible (by an elaborated 'knows'-ascription) in any context, is another matter. In this section I will consider how contextualists deploy their thesis to neutralize skeptical arguments.

Contextualists try to resolve skeptical paradoxes by reconciling the immovability of common sense with the irresistibility of skeptical arguments. Part of their strategy is to explain why these arguments are so seductive. However, their aim is not to refute such arguments but merely to contain them. Different contextualists consider slightly different skeptical arguments, but let's focus on just one of them. It is as representative as any. Suppose we make the naive statement that a certain George knows that he has hands. Neither he nor we have considered the possibility that he's a BBIV, a bodiless brain in a vat (one with a body might have hands), but then a skeptic presents us with an argument:

Skeptical Argument
If George knows that he has hands, then George knows that he isn't a BBIV.
George doesn't know that he isn't a BBIV.
So, George doesn't know that he has hands.

Contextualists don't rebut the argument directly, by denying its validity or rejecting a premise. Their strategy is more subtle, to expose a sneaky kind of equivocation. The equivocation is not within one Skeptical Argument but across arguments. That is, the form of what appears to be a single Skeptical Argument masks a multitude of distinct arguments. These arguments are all valid, the contextualist grants, but none of them has drastic skeptical consequences. In most cases the argument is unsound; it is sound only in the extreme case, but there it is of little consequence. Specifically, the sentence comprising the second premise expresses different propositions in different contexts, and it is false in most of them.[19] It is true only in what I'll call a skepistemic context, where skeptical standards prevail.[20] So the contextualist concedes that the argument is sound, but only in a skepistemic context, where far-fetched possibilities run rampant, possibilities that ordinarily may be ignored.[21]

[19] Contextualists generally agree that the first premise, though it too expresses different propositions in different contexts, is true in all contexts. Heller (1999*b*) is an exception—he rejects relativized closure. However, it should be noted that although the Skeptical Argument is generally assumed to rely on closure, that is not quite accurate. For one could defend the first premise not by applying a closure principle but by arguing that knowledge requires that one's evidence eliminate all alternatives. Also, as Harman and Sherman (2004) have argued, the intuitions that seem to support closure really support only the weaker claim that knowing requires justifiably and truly taking for granted that no counterpossibilities obtain.
[20] I use the neologism 'skepistemic' rather than 'skeptical' to avoid any appearance of endorsing the Skeptical Argument, even in respect to a so-called skeptical context. It would be inaccurate to call them 'epistemological' contexts, since there are plenty of epistemological contexts that don't concern skepticism.
[21] Whether a skeptical argument actually creates a skepistemic context is another matter. As DeRose points out, "a contextualist can provisionally assume a skeptic-friendly version of

OK, we make an ordinary statement in an ordinary context by saying, "George knows that he has hands" (actually, this common example is a bit far-fetched, since it is not the sort of statement we would ordinarily make—almost everybody who has hands knows that). Then a skeptic confronts us with the Skeptical Argument. Contextualists contend that as soon as he does that, he has sneaked in a change of context. Since the first premise is true in both ordinary and skepistemic contexts (not that its content is the same in both), this happens when he asserts the second premise. So, by the time we get to the conclusion, the skeptic has presented us with a compelling argument, indeed a sound one in that context. But we don't realize that he has shifted the context on us. So we don't realize that what he has argued for does not conflict with what we initially asserted. Indeed, the skeptic does not realize this either, since he thinks that he has refuted what we said, not changed the subject. It is only after we (and he) receive the contextualist revelation that we can appreciate that a change of context has occurred. At that point we are no longer seduced by the Skeptical Argument: we can concede its soundness in skepistemic contexts without losing confidence in the [knowledge] attributions we make in ordinary contexts.

It is easy for contextualists to misrepresent what they are claiming about the Skeptical Argument. For example, look at how David Lewis describes the situation:

When we do epistemology, we make knowledge vanish. First we do know, then we do not. But I had been doing epistemology when I said that. The uneliminated possibilities were not being ignored—not just then. So by what right did I say even that we used to know? In trying to thread a course between the rock of fallibilism and the whirlpool of scepticism, it may well seem as if I have fallen victim to both at once. For do I not say that there are all those uneliminated possibilities of error? Yet do I not claim that we know a lot? Yet do I not claim that knowledge is, by definition, infallible knowledge? I did claim all three things. But not all at once! (1996: 566)

Here and throughout his paper, except at the very end (see n. 4 above), Lewis commits some intentional use–mention conflations ("to get my message across I bent the rules"). Semantic ascent would have prevented that, but then he would have not been able to get his message across. In any case, knowledge doesn't vanish on account of epistemology. As Mark Heller clearly

contextualism, leaving it an open question whether and under which conditions the skeptic actually succeeds at raising the standards" (1995: 6). This does not question the soundness of the skeptic's argument *if* the skeptic succeeds at raising the standards.

explains, when unelimated possibilities are brought up and the standards are raised, "It is misleading to describe this as a loss of knowledge. Even after the skeptic changes the standards on us, S still has the property that she had before the change of standards. There is no property that she loses" (1999a: 121). Certain knowledge-ascribing sentences go from being true to being false, but only because they express different propositions from one context to another. For Lewis this a matter of which possibilities are "properly ignored", and that can vary with the context.

DeRose recognizes that the contextualist account of how this can be "involves the standards for knowledge being changed in a conversation" (1995: 6). So he rightly raises the question of why the Skeptical Argument "can be so appealing when considering it in solitude, with nothing being said". In this situation there is no one else to raise the standards, and no context other than the context of one's thinking. Even so, DeRose suggests that "there is a rule for the changing of the standards for knowledge that governs the truth conditions of our thoughts regarding what is and is not known that mirrors the [one] for what is said" (1995: 7). It is hard to see how this could be so, for in one's thinking one could perfectly well entertain thoughts that explicitly represent the strength of standard that indexes or relativizes 'know'. One could explicitly think thoughts with the contents of ordinary [knowledge] attributions or, just as easily, explicitly think ones with the contents of skepistemic [knowledge] attributions. One's context does not prevent one from doing both. Of course, contextualists are not suggesting that ordinary folk are contextualists. So it wouldn't occur to people to think these things explicitly. Even so, the relevant thoughts people can think are explicitly expressible by means of elaborated (indexed or relativized) 'knows'-ascriptions.

So the contextualist diagnosis of how skeptical arguments fool us does not apply when these arguments are framed in terms of elaborated (indexed or relativized) 'knows'-ascriptions. To be deceptive, these arguments have to involve simple 'knows'-ascriptions, such as 'George knows/doesn't know that he has hands'. Only then could it be easy, due to an implicit shift in standards (on the contextualist diagnosis), to conflate the contents of different attributions made with the exact same words.

Contextualism is clearly an error theory. As Stephen Schiffer explains, skeptical puzzles arise because "people uttering certain knowledge sentences in certain contexts systematically confound the propositions that their utterances express with the propositions that they would express by uttering those sentences in certain other contexts" (1996: 325). Schiffer finds this implausible (whether the claim is that 'know' is ambiguous, indexical, relative, or vague) because, for example, a Moorean and a skeptic can understand each other's utterances (and indeed their own utterances). So they should be able to recognize any shift in the content of the same sentence (or its negation) as uttered before and after the change in standard.[22] But, according to contextualism, they don't, at least not prior to hearing about contextualism. For example, if a Moorean dogmatically utters 'George knows that he has hands' and a skeptic springs the Skeptical Argument on him, the Moorean doesn't recognize that the skeptic isn't really contradicting him, and the skeptic doesn't either. Neither recognizes that the skeptic has changed the subject. Not only does the Moorean not realize he's being duped, the skeptic doesn't realize he's duping him.[23]

The contextualist story is that people get fooled because they don't notice when the bar gets raised. However, as we saw in the previous section, we ought to be able to make explicit what the different propositions are which, according to contextualism, can get expressed by the same simple 'knows'-ascription as used in different contexts. And once we do that, there is nothing to get fooled about. As we will see next, there is more to skeptical arguments than meets the contextualist's eye.

III Contextualism and Skepticism

Contextualists aim to diagnose and relieve the intuitive tension generated by the clash between the deliverances of common sense and the seductiveness of

---

[22] The situation would be like what happens when someone in one time zone asks or tells another what time it is. One could imagine a similar conversation about weight between an earthbound person and a man on the moon. For discussion of Schiffer's objection and how the contextualist might reply, see Hofweber (1999).

[23] In response to Schiffer's argument, Cohen (2001) contends that contextualism is an error theory only with regard to "meta-judgments" that different utterances of the same [knowledge] attributing sentence have the same contents. But surely, if people fail to recognize a shift in content between two utterances of the same sentence, or mistakenly detect a contradiction when 'not' is included in one, they've got the content one of the utterances wrong. For example, the Moorean either misunderstands what the skeptic says or misunderstands what he himself said. Ram Neta (2003), who recognizes that Cohen's attempt to kick Schiffer's objection upstairs is unsuccessful, urges the contextualist "to develop a version of contextualism that helps us to appreciate the semantically relevant difference between the context in which Moorean anti-skepticism is false and the context in which it is true, and thereby frees us from puzzlement". Our devices of explicit indexing and explicit relativization do just that.

skeptical arguments. As Cohen makes clear, contextualists do not intend their efforts at resolving skeptical paradoxes to be taken as refutations of skeptical *arguments* (1999: 69). DeRose acknowledges that "in claiming that my belief that I have hands is sensitive, I betray my conviction that I am not a BIV in this world or in nearby worlds" (1995: 50). So there is no point in accusing contextualists of begging the question against skepticism.[24] Still, many philosophers have complained that contextualists do not really come to grips with the force and content of skeptical arguments (see Feldman, 1999, 2001; Klein, 2000; Kornblith, 2000; Sosa, 2000). The complaint is simple: the contextualist's attempt to marginalize skeptical arguments by restricting them to skepistemic contexts ignores the fact that skepticism denies that we have knowledge even by ordinary standards. As Richard Feldman writes,

> The question skepticism raises is about whether our evidence really is good enough to satisfy the standards for knowledge. One can think that the familiar skeptical possibilities introduce grounds for doubt that defeat our evidence for our ordinary beliefs. One can think that we have no evidence at all that favors our ordinary beliefs rather than their skeptical rivals. Either way, there's reason to wonder whether we really do satisfy the ordinary standards. The debate about skepticism is thus seen not as a debate in which the quality of our evidence is agreed to and the debate results from differing views about what the standards for knowledge are. Instead, it is a debate about how good our evidence is. Understood that way, it's difficult to see the epistemological significance of decisions about which standards are associated with the word "knows" in any particular context. (2004: 33)

Feldman's point, then, is that when a skeptic brings up far-fetched possibilities and argues that we can't rule them out, he is not raising the standards for what it takes to belong to the extension of the word 'knowledge'. Rather, he is using these possibilities to show that it is much tougher than we realize for a belief to qualify as knowledge at all, even by the normal standards governing ordinary contexts, that is, to have the property that the word 'knowledge' actually and ordinarily expresses. So contextualists haven't really addressed what Kornblith calls "full-blooded" skepticism.

Skeptics are not proposing to reform the meaning of the term 'knowledge'. They are recommending that we use it to mean what it ordinarily means but use it much more carefully, even if it turns out rarely to apply. So it is wrong

---

[24] Contextualists do think that because, as Heller proclaims, "it is a completely convincing response to the skeptic" to point out that "even after the skeptic changes the standards on us, [the subject] still has the property that she had before the change of standards" (Heller 1999*a*: 121).

to charge them with proposing that the word 'knowledge' be used so that it expresses a property that is much more difficult for a belief to have than the property that term actually expresses. This would be the tired complaint of an ordinary-language philosopher who, preferring to speak with the vulgar, would accuse the skeptic of inventing a special, philosophical sense of 'know'. Rather, the skeptic is suggesting that we make a much more serious effort than we ordinarily do at ascribing that property accurately and let the chips fall where they may.

Just imagine that there were lots of fool's gold around and that people commonly described it as 'gold' simply because it looked and felt like gold. An auric skeptic, someone who doubted that most of the stuff that passes for gold really is, might advise us to be much more careful about what we count as gold ("All that glitters is not gold"). In a way, he would be suggesting a reform in our use of the term 'gold', but this would concern how we go about applying the term, not what the term actually applies to. He would be advising us to make sure to apply it only to samples of gold. The skeptic is offering similar advice about using the word 'knowledge'. He is not recommending that we use it to express a more precious property but that we be much more careful about what we take to possess the precious property that 'knowledge' actually expresses. He is concerned with knowledge, not 'knowledge'.

Now there is a relevant difference between the auric skeptic and the epistemic skeptic. In the above scenario the auric skeptic would not be unduly demanding—he would be right. However, the epistemic skeptic is wrong, or so we non-skeptics believe. He is wrong to suppose that knowledge is limited to beliefs that are justified to the highest degree, beliefs the evidence for which eliminates all counterpossibilities, however far-fetched. That is why we think the epistemic skeptic is being too demanding. Even so, as he see things, our situation is analogous to that of the auric skeptic in the above scenario. To appreciate this, change that scenario and suppose that we are in fact very good at identifying samples of gold as gold and at not mistaking fool's gold for the real thing. And suppose there's very little fool's gold around. Our auric skeptic would still insist that we be much more careful about what we deem to be gold, but in this case he would be too demanding. He could raise the possibility of widespread fool's gold, but in so doing he would not be alerting us to a real possibility. In letting his fantasies rip, he would be much like the epistemic skeptic.[25]

---

[25] In this paragraph I am ignoring another relevant difference between the auric skeptic and the epistemic skeptic. The epistemic skeptic's general principles always take precedence over

Contextualists grant that we can't rule out, and that our evidence doesn't eliminate, global skeptical possibilities (dreaming, demon, BBIV, Matrix, etc.), and they concede that this makes it impossible or at least very difficult for us to [know], relative to skepistemic contexts, what ordinarily we take to be everyday empirical facts. Nevertheless, they have no qualms about assuming that people easily [know], relative to ordinary contexts, those very same facts—even though our evidence regarding skeptical possibilities is the same.[26] It's just that ordinary standards don't require that we rule out or that our evidence eliminate such "irrelevant" possibilities. Relative to those standards we can [know] that such possibilities don't obtain even though our evidence doesn't rule them out. However, no self-respecting skeptic is going to concede that there is any context relative to which ordinary [knowledge] attributions can be true even though the subject's evidence does not rule them out. Indeed, he has no reason to concede that it rules out any counter-possibilities if it doesn't rule out the skeptical ones.

What would the skeptic be willing to concede regarding knowledge attributions made when less demanding standards are operative? He might concede, hypothetically, that if someone knew that no skeptical possibilities obtain, he *would* know ordinary empirical propositions to be true.[27] Since we ordinarily presuppose these things, we think that the knowledge attributions we make according to less demanding standards are often true. However, that does not make them true, even relative to those standards. The skeptic does not buy the contextualist's claim that [knowledge] attributions are true by ordinary standards. The mere fact that people's willingness to make and accept knowledge attributions is governed by their application of ordinary epistemic standards does not mean that these knowledge attributions are generally true.

Not only do contextualists not acknowledge the full force of skepticism, they also concede too much to skepticism when they suggest that skeptical

paradigm applications of the word 'knowledge', but not because it is a clear case of a natural kind term. Whereas the auric skeptic takes for granted that there is an objective, uncontroversial standard for gold, there is no such standard for knowledge, even assuming that invariantism is correct.

[26] Heller (1999*b*) is the one exception I know of. He does have qualms—he rejects closure.

[27] As Jonathan Schaffer has pointed out to me, noting that contrapossible counterfactuals are hard to evaluate, this would be an odd concession for the skeptic to make, since he denies that there is any possible world in which one could know, or even or correctly and justifiably take for granted (see n. 19), that no skeptical possibility obtains.

arguments are seductive because of a subtle shift to a very high standards context. Here's an alternative explanation, from the standpoint of moderate (nonskeptical) invariantism (to be defended in section V), of why skeptical arguments are seductive. When we are presented with a skeptical argument and confronted with what we ordinarily take to be far-fetched sources of error, in effect we are asked to imagine ourselves, with our current experiences, (apparent) memories, and beliefs, plunked into a world of we know not what sort. It could be a dream world or a demon world, a BBIV or a Matrix world, or any of a whole host of others. Or it could be a world of just the sort we think we're in. But we're not supposed to have any prejudices about which sort of world we're being plunked into. Since each of the possible worlds is consistent with our having the perceptual and memory experiences and beliefs we have, there is nothing to make the world as we commonly conceive of it epistemically special in any way. It's just one of those countless sorts of worlds any one of which we could be plunked into. So of course we can't tell that we're in any one of them, in particular, the world as we commonly conceive of it.

This explains why skeptical arguments, as inspired by Descartes's systematic doubt, are so seductive, but it doesn't show that they are any good. Yes, it's true that if we were suddenly plunked into a world, we wouldn't be able to tell what sort of world we were in. But that's not our situation. To know in this world, it is not necessary to be able to discriminate between the different possible worlds we might be in. It is not necessary to know that we're not in a world where we would be chronically prone to uncorrectable and undetectable error, at least not if knowing this requires going out and verifying that we're not in such a world (it would be impossible to verify that). True, a skeptical scenario would seem no less absurd if one were in it than it does in fact, but that doesn't show that it is not in fact absurd. The fact that there are possible worlds in which we would know very little does not show, or even suggest, that we are in such a world. Knowledge may not be as easy to come by as people casually suppose, but to be in a world which is stable in various fundamental respects, with which we informationally interact in clearly explicable ways, and in which we communicatively interact to transmit information successfully, is to be in a world in which there is plenty of knowledge to be had.

I don't know how well this rebuts skeptical arguments (for example, it dogmatically rejects internalism about knowledge and epistemic justification), but at least it doesn't change the subject by accusing the skeptic of changing the subject.

IV Contextualism and Skeptical Invariantism

Not surprisingly, contextualists try to bolster their case by arguing against invariantism. Unfortunately, they tend to limit their attention to *skeptical* invariantism. No doubt influenced by how Unger introduced the contrast between contextualism and invariantism (1984: 6–11), they follow him in likening the invariantist view of 'knows' (the view of Unger 1971, 1975) to his invariantist view of 'flat'. On that view, if something is flat, nothing can be flatter than it. So the only flat things there are are absolutely flat, as flat as flat can be. Anything less flat than that can only be somewhat flat, relatively flat (as compared with something else), rather flat, or even very flat, but not really flat. It must be perfectly flat for that. So when we describe things as flat, we are not speaking truly but only truly enough for practical purposes. Similarly, on the skeptical invariantist view of 'knows', you can know that p only if you are as well-positioned as possible about p as you could be about anything, for example, that you exist. Given such a demanding view, empirical knowledge is very hard to come by.

In challenging this very demanding view, DeRose points out that "Unger did admit that varying standards for knowledge govern our use of sentences of the form 'S knows at t that p', but did not endorse contextualism because [he] claimed that these varying standards were only standards for whether it was *appropriate* to *say* that S knows" (1999: 192). DeRose describes this as a "warranted assertibility maneuver", or WAM.[28] Although he recognizes that WAMs can be legitimate, he rejects their application to knowledge attributions (1999: 196–203; 2002: 191–4). He thinks these are as "lame" as the claim that 'bachelor' means man and that saying that someone is a bachelor merely implicates that he's not married. DeRose gives various plausible reasons for doubting the skeptical invariantist contention that ordinary knowledge attributions are generally not true but merely appropriate to make and in that sense warrantedly assertible.

DeRose is not entirely fair to Unger, who was offering not a WAM but a kind of error theory about how people use knowledge-ascribing sentences. Consider that there are two rather different ways in which a sentence can be warrantedly assertible without being true: (*a*) what is said, that S knows that p, is not true but, because it is close enough to being true, can be warrantedly

---

[28] DeRose does not use 'warranted assertibility' to mean what it usually means in philosophy, especially in discussions of anti-realism, namely a kind of metaphysical or epistemological surrogate for truth.

asserted anyway, or (*b*) in saying falsely that S knows that p, the speaker implicates something else which is true. Unfortunately, DeRose does not explicitly distinguish the two. This is unfortunate because Unger, at least if he meant anything of the sort, meant (*a*), and what DeRose argues against is (*b*). DeRose finds it highly implausible that when people make ordinary knowledge attributions and say such things as that George knows that he has hands, they are really implicating or otherwise pragmatically conveying something else instead. He goes to great lengths to show how implausible this is, but this is not Unger's view. Unger held that we often speak loosely and casually, as when we use an "absolute" term like 'flat' or 'empty' and describe a surface as flat or a container as empty. This does not imply that in so speaking, we mean something else that we are not fully spelling out. Rather, we mean just what we are saying but are construing it loosely. The flatness and emptiness attributions we ordinarily make pass as true but are not really true. To borrow a favorite contextualist phrase (but to use it differently), they "count as true". They're true enough for practical purposes, and that's good enough for us.

However, it is not clear that Unger thought of knowledge attributions as even warrantedly assertible in this way (in sense (*a*) above). Unger was not using a WAM to explain why people make literally false knowledge attributions because only the weakest sort of epistemic skepticism would concede that they are very close to being true. And he certainly was not claiming that they are warrantedly assertible in sense (*b*). He was not suggesting that attributors, in saying something literally false, implicate or otherwise convey something true. After all, ordinary folk are not privy to skeptical arguments and do not make their knowledge attributions in defiance of such arguments. Their loose use of 'know' is hardly self-conscious or sophisticated enough for them to intend their simple, unqualified knowledge attributions to be taken loosely or for them to recognize knowledge attributions made by others as intended to be taken loosely. Unger's explanation of why people make simple unqualified knowledge attributions is nothing like a Gricean or pragmatic account of how people can say one thing and mean something else instead.

Recently DeRose (2002) has offered a new argument for contextualism, which is notable for its unwitting use of a different notion of warranted assertibility. This notion is more epistemological than pragmatic. Here he does not mean that a sentence, even if false, is warrantedly assertible if uttering it implicates something true and nothing false (this is a kind of conversational appropriateness). He means something quite different, as is clear when he sums up his new argument:

The knowledge account of assertion provides a powerful argument for contextualism: If the standards for when one is in a position to warrantedly assert that P are the same as those that comprise a truth-condition for 'I know that P', then if the former vary with context, so do the latter. In short: The knowledge account of assertion together with the context-sensitivity of assertability yields contextualism about knowledge. (2002: 171)

Here he must mean that what makes 'P' warrantedly assertible is that one knows that P, since that is the truth condition for one's utterance of 'I know that P'. And, needless to say, 'P' can be warrantedly assertible in this sense without being so in the other (and conversely). Also, notice that this "powerful argument for contextualism" applies only to first-person cases, in which attributor and subject are the same (almost all of DeRose's examples are of this sort). Obviously, however, what makes 'P' warrantedly assertible by the attributor, that the attributor knows that P, is not the truth condition for his utterance of 'S know that P', where S is somebody else.

In this section, we have seen that, contrary to what DeRose contends, the skeptical invariantist, as exemplified by Unger, does not, and need not, resort to a WAM to make his case. However, I am not suggesting that his case is a good one. Skeptical invariantism relies on skeptical arguments, but these are epistemological, not semantic. If any such argument is sound, then our ordinary knowledge claims are false. But this is a thesis about knowledge, not a form of invariantism about 'knows'. To claim that the extension of the word 'know' is very small is just a roundabout metalinguistic way of claiming that knowledge is very hard to come by. Moderate invariantism, at least as I will defend it, does assume that skepticism is false, but it does not rely on any substantive epistemological arguments to make its claim that the semantics of 'know' is invariant.

V The Obvious Alternative to Contextualism: Moderate Invariantism

Nonskeptical or moderate invariantism is defined by DeRose as "invariantism that keeps the standards governing the truth-conditions of knowledge attributions constant, but meetably low" (1999: 192). This leaves open just how demanding these standards are, and for present purposes I will keep it open. I'll just assume that, whether or not most of our ordinary knowledge attributions are true, a good many of them are, far more than even the weakest form of epistemic skepticism could allow. This leaves open that plenty of them are false by almost any philosopher's standards and that plenty of them are debatable. No doubt we often credit people with knowledge when we shouldn't, but then we speak casually about a lot of things (Bach, 2001). Still, I will assume that much of what passes for knowledge really is, including perceptual knowledge, such as that you are sitting and that there are lines of print in front of you, and knowledge about simple facts, for example, that California is a state and that chickens lay eggs.

DeRose assumes that the moderate invariantist, like the skeptical one, has to "chalk it all up to pragmatics" (2002: 194) and rely on a WAM to make his case. However, whereas the skeptical invariantist claims that with an ordinary knowledge attribution "we mistake the warranted assertibility of the claim for truth", for the moderate invariantist the situation is reversed: "it's the denial of knowledge in the high standards case that's false but appropriate: Due to the high standards for the warranted assertibility of knowledge in place there, a positive claim that the subject knows would be unwarranted (though true), and it's the denial of knowledge that is appropriate (though false)" (2002: 171).[29] This applies not just to skeptical cases but to more down-to-earth yet high-standards versions of more pedestrian cases. Compare this with what contextualism says about these cases, such as the high-standards versions of the Bank and the Airport cases. Even though the subject's epistemic position is the same, according to DeRose and Cohen when the stakes go up, the standards go up, and when the standards go up, [knowledge] attributions that would normally be true are not true, and the corresponding [knowledge] denials are true.[30] The moderate invariantist has to say that when the stakes go up, the [knowledge] attributions are still true and the corresponding [knowledge] denials are still false. But he has to say more than that, as DeRose rightly insists, for there is a "glaring difference between 'I don't know P' (which often becomes assertable when the standards go up) and 'not-P' (which doesn't)" (2002: 191).

---

[29] Unfortunately (see n. 5), DeRose's own discussion here is marred by the fact that he focuses entirely on first-person [knowledge] denials, as when he stresses the "glaring difference between 'I don't know P' (which often becomes assertible when the standards go up) and 'not-P' (which doesn't)" (2002: 191).

[30] For the sake of discussion, I'm assuming that in the low-standards versions of these cases, the relevant attributions are true. You don't have to be a skeptic to think that these standards are too low and that the subject does not [know] even without the standards being raised. If you think that, then pick a different example, such as one involving ordinary perceptual identification or recollection of a simple fact.

As we will see, the contextualist account of such examples, cases in which standards on [knowledge] attributions are allegedly raised, ignores two complementary facts: that attributing to someone knowledge that p involves (confidently) believing that p yourself; and that denying knowledge of someone who has the same evidence you have involves being at least somewhat doubtful about p.[31] So I would not accept DeRose's stipulation regarding the high-standards version of his Bank case, according to which the attributor denies knowledge while "remaining as confident as [he] was before that the bank will be open tomorrow" and yet concedes that he'd "better go in and make sure" (1992: 913). It seems to me that unless he's trying to placate his wife, his belief would have to be shaken at least somewhat.

Consider the contextualist characterization of the high-standards Airport case, in which Mary is unwilling to assert that Smith [knows] that the plane will stop in Chicago. Given how important this question is to Mary, not only does she refrain from attributing [knowledge] to Smith but, unwilling to take Smith's word as based on his itinerary, she goes so far as to deny that he [knows] that the plane will stop in Chicago. According to the contextualist, that's because it isn't true that he [knows] this. But the moderate invariantist has to say that if Smith knows in the normal, low-standards case, he knows in the high-standards case too, even if Mary is not prepared to say that he does. So, does the moderate invariantist need to rely on a WAM to explain this? Should he argue that since Smith is well enough positioned for an utterance in an ordinary context of "Smith knows that the plane will stop in Chicago" to be true, then when Mary asserts its negation in a context of heightened interest, she must be saying something false and pragmatically conveying something true?

No! Mary is making a mistake, albeit a very understandable one. Mary does not say "Smith knows that the plane will stop in Chicago" and goes so far as to assert its negation because of her own doxastic situation. Because she is not sure Smith's itinerary is reliable, she herself is not confident that the plane will stop in Chicago. So she can't coherently attribute knowledge of it

---

[31] It is interesting to note that when introducing skeptical invariantism, Unger (1971) focused not on the strength of the subject's epistemic position but on the strength of the subject's belief. He did not stress the ultra-high standards which, according to contextualists, the Skeptical Argument purports to demand. Rather, he stressed the strength of the doxastic condition on knowledge, arguing that it requires "absence of doubt or doubtfulness". One could take a less demanding position but still insist that the doxastic condition on knowledge requires more than mere belief. There is also the question of how much conviction belief itself requires.

to Smith, not if knowledge implies truth. In general, you can't coherently assert that someone else knows that p if you are not confident that p and think that it still needs to be verified. That is why Mary can't very well assert that Smith knows that the plane will stop in Chicago. Not only that, she has to deny that she knows it, since she thinks it is not yet established. And, since Smith has no evidence that she doesn't have, she must deny that he knows it either.

What is decisive here is not the attributor's lack of belief but her raised threshold for (confidently) believing.[32] By this I mean that before believing the proposition in question, at least with the confidence and freedom from doubt necessary for knowing (see n. 31), the attributor demands more evidence than knowledge requires. So, in the high-standards version of the Airport case, what happens when Mary double- and triple-checks and confirms to her satisfaction (in the Airport case) that the plane will stop in Chicago? She will then be confident that it will stop there and will think that she knows this. However, she still won't concede that Smith knows this and indeed will still deny that he does, given that his epistemic position is no better than hers was. Now the explanation for her denial is not that she doesn't confidently believe it herself but, rather, that her threshold of confidence has gone up.

One's threshold for (confidently) believing a proposition is a matter of what one implicitly takes to be sufficient reason to believe it (again, if believing is compatible with residual doubtfulness, I mean the sort of confident belief required for knowing). I say "implicitly" because people generally do not reflect on such things. Even if in fact one is in a position to know something, thinking one is not in a position to know it is enough to keep one from believing it (at least not without reservations) and to lead one, if it matters enough, to look into it further. When one does look further and verifies the proposition to one's satisfaction, one implicitly takes oneself now to be in a position to know it and continues to regard one's prior, weaker position as inadequate. So one cannot consistently take someone else, who was in and still is in that weaker position, to know it. In consistency, one must regard him as not knowing it.

It might seem that I have merely described in different terms what the contextualist describes as raising the standards on a [knowledge] attribution. However, what I have described is what it takes for an attributor coherently to

[32] Thanks to Jessica Brown, John MacFarlane, and Jonathan Schaffer for urging me to spell this out.

make a knowledge attribution to someone else who has certain evidence, given the attributor's doxastic stance relative to the same evidence. Here's a way to put the difference between the contextualist view and my own. Remember that attributing knowledge that p requires believing that p. So, I am suggesting, willingness to attribute knowledge does not track the standards on the truth of a [knowledge] attribution; rather, it tracks one's threshold of doxastic confidence. In the so-called high-standards cases, the attributor's doxastic threshold goes up to the point that without additional evidence she implicitly, but mistakenly, thinks she is not in a position to know. This makes my account a kind of error theory, but only minimally. It has people sometimes denying knowledge of people who have it, but it does not have them generally confused about knowledge or 'knowledge'. In high-standards Airport and Bank cases, a special practical interest gives the attributor reservations about the truth of the proposition in question and, accordingly, raises her bar for attributing knowledge to someone else. Even so, the subject knows.

Now let us consider what happens when a skeptical possibility is raised. It could be a general skeptical possibility, such as victimization by an Evil Demon, or one specific to the case, say an imagined rumor that disgruntled travel agents are distributing inaccurate itineraries. However, merely raising such a possibility, without making it plausible, does not turn a true knowledge attribution into a false one. Making it salient is not enough. That, as Patrick Rysiew (2001) has shown, affects at most the assertibility of the knowledge attribution, because making the attribution pragmatically conveys that a newly raised possibility has been ruled out.[33] Raising plausible possibilities, on the other hand, indicates real doubts on the part of the attributor and, if taken seriously, lowers the doxastic state of his audience. Moreover, if these plausible possibilities are objective possibilities, ones that bear on the subject's epistemic position, and if the subject's epistemic position is not strong enough to rule them out, then the subject does not know that p, quite independently of the attributor's context. In no case, then, is the truth

---

[33] As Jessica Brown (forthcoming) points out, before drawing conclusions from their examples contextualists need to control separately for salience and for practical interest. She argues that salience alone does not raise the standards, at least not in the clear way that practical interest does, and she uses this observation to develop a non-skeptical version of invariantism. Her version is a modification of Patrick Rysiew's (2001), who thinks it is salience which affects the knowledge attributions people are willing to make and which bears not on the truth or falsity of the attributions but on what they pragmatically convey. Brown, like Rysiew, employs sophisticated WAMs, not lame ones of the sort that DeRose thinks moderate invariantism is stuck with. My version of moderate invariantism does not rely on WAMs at all.

condition or truth value of a knowledge attribution affected by the epistemic standards that prevail in the context of attribution. All that is affected is the attributor's willingness to make it and the audience's willingness to accept it, by way of raising their threshold for (confidently) believing.

We are now in a good epistemic position to reply to DeRose's contention that moderate as well as skeptical invariantism requires the use of WAMs in order to explain intuitions about ordinary and high standards [knowledge] attributions. He writes,

Invariantists do not begin with a good candidate for WAMing, and they have to explain away as misleading intuitions of truth as well as intuitions of falsehood. For in the "low standards" contexts, it seems appropriate and it seems true to say that certain subjects know and it would seem wrong and false to deny that they know, while in the "high standards" context [as in the Bank case], it seems appropriate and true to say that similarly situated subjects don't know and it seems inappropriate and false to say they do know. Thus, whichever set of appearances the invariantist seeks to discredit—whether she says we're mistaken about the "high" or the "low" contexts—she'll have to explain away both an appearance of falsity and (much more problematically) an appearance of truth. (DeRose, 2002: 193)

The problem is that DeRose accepts the appearances at face value.[34] Moderate invariantists should accept intuitions about ordinary [knowledge] attributions at face value but should reject DeRose's intuitions about the "high standards" Bank case (where the cost is high of the bank not being open on Saturday). The attributor's high stakes (on Friday) when asserting or accepting as true 'Keith knows that the bank is open on Saturday' do not translate into higher standards for its truth. Rather, she has good practical reason, because of the cost of him being wrong, not to take Keith's word for whether the bank is open on Saturday. Given that, she doesn't accept his statement as true without checking further. So she can't consistently accept or assert 'Keith knows that the bank is open on Saturday' as true.

Moderate invariantists should also reject the intuition that [knowledge] denials involving skeptical possibilities are true. To repeat the anti-internalist sentiments expressed at the end of section III, I think the moderate invariantist should not concede that there is something right about the intuition that George does not know he is not a BBIV and that an utterance of 'George does not know that he is not a BBIV' is true, at least in a skepistemic context. Rather, he should insist that George does know he is not a BBIV and that the intuition

---

[34] As mentioned earlier, Nichols, Stich, and Weinberg (2003) have shown that epistemic intuitions are not nearly as universal or robust as contextualists dogmatically assume.

that he doesn't is based on the false assumption that in a skeptical scenario George's epistemic situation would be no different. To be sure (pace Williamson, 2000), George does not have evidence that he would not have if he were a BBIV, but that doesn't matter. The intuition that some people have that it does matter seems to be based on a leap, from the obvious truth that George, if he were a BBIV, wouldn't know it and would still believe that he is not a BBIV, to the conclusion that in fact he doesn't know he's not a BBIV.[35] If he were a BBIV, there would be lots of things he wouldn't know, even if the world were otherwise as much as possible like the actual world, and certainly if it were vastly different. His beliefs are insensitive to the difference. But he can be in a position to know things about the actual world, such as that he has hands and that he is not a BBIV, even if, were the world quite different (or if the causes of his beliefs were quite different, as in a benign-demon world), he wouldn't know very much about it. Only certain sorts of worlds and relations to the world are such that one can know things about that world. The prevalence of massive error in some possible worlds, especially in worlds remote from this one, does not show the real possibility of massive error in the actual world.

Skeptical invariantism is admittedly an error theory, and contextualism is clearly an error theory too. Is my version of moderate invariantism also an error theory? It is, but only in a minimal way. According to skeptical invariantism, people commonly make false knowledge attributions. According to contextualism, people commonly fail to recognize shifts in the contents of 'knows'-ascriptions and thereby sense contradictions that are not there. It implies that people are frequently unaware of differences in the contents of [knowledge] attributions. The only sort of error that my version of moderate invariantism attributes to people, other than the error of being temporarily taken in by skeptical arguments (attributing this error is not specific to moderate invariantism), is one of excessive caution when it comes to believing things with confidence.

VI Ignoring as Evidence

There is more to be said about the interaction between one's doxastic state and one's epistemic position and about the implications of that for what one

---

[35] Here I am ignoring possible content-externalist differences in his beliefs, hence in what he represents his evidence to be. It is an interesting question whether issues concerning content internalism and externalism have any bearing on the debate between epistemic internalists and externalists.

is prepared to say about someone else's epistemic position. Pretty much everyone, contextualist and invariantist alike, agrees that knowing that p requires that one's experience/evidence/justification rule out counterpossibilities (alternatives to p, threats to the basis for one's belief that p). There is plenty of disagreement about how best to formulate this, especially if one rejects the skeptic's contention that knowing requires ruling out all such possibilities. It is common to limit the requirement to ruling out relevant alternatives, and there are different variations on this approach. Typical internal problems for such an approach include spelling out what it is to rule out an alternative, whether it is the subject or his evidence that does this, and, of course, what it is for an alternative to be relevant. It will be instructive to focus on David Lewis's account.

Lewis exhorts you to "do some epistemology [and] let your paranoid fantasies rip!" (1996: 559). OK, let 'em rip. That's what Descartes did with his Evil Demon fantasy, and the BBIV (or the "Matrix") scenario is just a high-tech version of that. But imagining yourself in such a scenario is not to take seriously the possibility that you're in one. These so-called skeptical "hypotheses" are just fantasies. Getting yourself and your conversational partner to entertain such fantasies may change the context but it doesn't turn them into real possibilities. It would seem, then, that they can be safely ignored. But for Lewis things are not so simple: "Our definition of knowledge requires a sotto voce provision. S knows that P iff S's evidence eliminates every possibility in which not-P—Psst!—except for those possibilities that we are properly ignoring" (1996: 554).[36] Any possibility compatible with the experience (with its having the content that it has) is not eliminated.[37] But there will always be skeptical possibilities, as many and varied as you can dream up, that are compatible with your experience. So if skepticism is to be avoided, they can't count against the truth of ordinary [knowledge] attributions. This is possible only if they can be properly ignored without having to

[36] Right before giving this definition, Lewis remarks that "an idiom of quantification, like 'every', is normally restricted [semantically?] to some limited domain" (1996: 553), so that 'every possibility in which not-P' does not include those that are being ignored. "They are outside the domain, they are irrelevant to the truth of what is said." But at the very least (never mind whether this restriction is semantic—see Bach, 2000), being ignored, which suffices for being outside the domain, can't be irrelevant to the truth of what is said. These possibilities must be properly ignored, as required by the definition of knowledge.

[37] Here, an experience or memory that P "eliminates W iff W is a possibility in which the subject's experience or memory has content different from P" (1996: 553). Notice that on Lewis's conception of elimination, it is the experience, not the person having it, that eliminates a possibility.

be eliminated. However, by Lewis's Rule of Attention, "a possibility not ignored at all is ipso facto not properly ignored" (1996: 559). So a skeptical possibility once presented cannot properly be ignored. Because it is not eliminated by one's experience, according to Lewis it inevitably "destroys knowledge". As even Lewis's fellow contextualists acknowledge, this require-ment makes it too easy for the skeptic: he can prevail just by mentioning far-fetched possibilities. But there is more to the Rule of Attention than this.

Suppose that it is not an experience but the person having it that eliminates a possibility (this will simplify our description of the situation). In that case, if the thought of some possibility occurs to you, you have to rule it out—you can't just disregard it. On the other hand, it would seem that you can't rule out a possibility if the thought of it doesn't occur to you. If it doesn't occur to you that there might be cleverly painted mules in the vicinity, you can't very well rule that out. Now could this keep you from being in a position to know you're looking at a zebra? Ordinarily you don't have to rule out such a possibility—you have no reason to and there is nothing about your environ-ment that requires you to—and the thought of it doesn't even occur to you. But what if the thought of such a possibility did occur to you? If it is as far-fetched as this one, and you have no reason to think it isn't, can't you just dismiss it? The mere fact that the thought of it occurs to you shouldn't make any difference. Or should it?

Offhand, it might seem that whether or not the thought of a certain possibility occurs to us has no epistemic significance and that what matters is what we do. Possibilities just occur to us, and we should take realistic ones seriously and do what it takes to rule them out. We can just dismiss the far-fetched ones if and when they occur to us. Thinking of them would be a distraction and, if chronic, a nuisance, but that would be all. In fact, however, possibilities don't just occur to us at random. In so far as our cognitive processes work efficiently and effectively toward our cognitive goals, the fact that a possibility occurs to us provides evidence that it is worth consider-ing. Not only that, the fact that a possibility does not occur to us provides evidence that it isn't worth considering (such evidence is highly defeasible, since it may be our ignorance that keeps the thought of a relevant possibility from occurring to us). In this way, we can safely jump to conclusions without having to verify the countless implicit assumptions that we make in our everyday reasoning.[38]

---

[38] I defended this conception of default reasoning in Bach (1984) and used it to defend a form of reliabilism about justified belief in Bach (1985).

If our cognitive processes are operating well, generally the thought of a possibility contrary to something we're inclined to take as fact occurs to us only if it is a realistic possibility, not a far-fetched one. We can always conjure up wild possibilities, as in flights of skeptical or paranoid fantasy, but when we're engaged in normal inquiry or just trying to identify what we're perceiving or remember some bit of information, we take into account only those counterpossibilities that sometimes arise in situations of the sort we're concerned with. So it is the very occurrence of the thought that gives us a reason for considering the possibility being thought of. No wonder, then, that "a possibility not ignored at all is ipso facto not properly ignored"! Of course, should it occur to us we may find reason to dismiss it.

Here's a simple example of how the unbidden thought of a possibility can undermine one's knowledge by shaking one's belief. Someone once asked me to name the capital of Kentucky and I immediately thought, "I know that. It's Frankfort." But then it occurred to me that, well, maybe it's Lexington. This put doubt in my mind, and I was more inclined to say, "I'm pretty sure it's Frankfort, but it might be Lexington." If asked to choose, I would have said it's Frankfort, but the very occurrence of the thought that it might be Lexington undermined my knowledge, at least temporarily, by shaking my belief. Second thoughts rightly yield doubt, but most of the time we simply rely on the reliability of our memory (or our eyesight or whatever) and don't have second thoughts.

We rely on our reliability at thinking of counterpossibilities when they are worthy of consideration and at knowing when to look further before settling into a belief. Also, if the relevant cognitive processes are functioning well, the *nonoccurrence* of the thought of a certain counterpossibility provides evidence, albeit highly defeasible, that this counterpossibility is *not* worth considering. However, we cannot explicitly *take* the nonoccurrence of the thought as the evidence that it is, for that would entail thinking of the counterpossibility in question. We cannot explicitly weigh the evidence that the nonoccurrence of the thought provides, at least not at the time (in retrospect we may reason that if something was a realistic possibility, it would have occurred to us).

Suppose, contrary to the above picture, that possibilities contrary to something one is otherwise disposed to believe came to mind independently of any evidence one has for their actually obtaining. If our minds worked that way, then the occurrence of the thought of a counterpossibility would just be a nuisance. It would be like random, unbidden thoughts that one has left the front door unlocked or the headlights on. One caters to such thoughts and one checks, even if it is inconvenient to do so, in order to make the thought go away. So it would be with random, unwarranted thoughts of counter-possibilities to something one is otherwise disposed to believe. But this is not how our minds generally work. Thoughts of counterpossibilities occur to us generally because there is reason to consider them, hence a need to rule them out. We need not have specific, articulable evidence, but somehow, at least to some extent, our belief-forming processes are tuned into plausible sources of error. If something like this picture is correct, then the nonoccurrence of the thought of a counterpossibility is evidence that the counterpossibility does not obtain, but it is not evidence we can directly consider. Instead, we rely on the reliability of our tendency to think of counterpossibilities when and only when they're worth considering.

Now what does this suggest about knowledge attributions and the possibilities that come to mind or get brought up in a context of attribution? Let's say that a scenario is epistemically irrelevant to a knowledge attribution if the mere possibility of its obtaining does not affect the truth of that attribution. A scenario can be epistemically irrelevant because it is just a wild skeptical fantasy, whether global or specific to the case, or because, despite the fact that it is something the attributor needs to rule out for practical reasons or for bad skeptical reasons, it has no bearing on the truth of the knowledge attribution. However, considering what is in fact an epistemically irrelevant scenario gives the attributor reservations about believing the proposition in question and puts the attributor in the position of having to deny that she knows. And, as we saw in the previous section, this is enough to put her in the position of refraining from asserting that the subject knows and even of falsely denying that she knows. What does this, we can now see, is the consideration of a possibility that epistemically is not worth considering. That is enough to keep one from settling into a belief one would ordinary adopt. Ordinarily, when the thought of such a possibility does not occur, one would confidently form the belief on the basis of the evidence one already has.

VII Summing Up

Contextualism is the thesis that a sentence of the simple form 'S knows at t that p' can be true as uttered in one context and false as uttered in another, depending on the epistemic standards that govern the context. The standards governing the context help determine which knowledge-attributing proposition the sentence expresses in that context. This means that there is no one knowledge relation and that the different propositions expressible by such a sentence involve different [knowledge] relations. Given this understanding of what contextualism says, I have argued for several things.

1. Even if contextualism is true, so that a simple knowledge-ascribing sentence can express different propositions in different contexts, those different propositions are not themselves context-bound. Each such proposition can be expressed by a more elaborate knowledge-ascribing sentence in which 'knows' is either indexed to or relativized to an epistemic standard. So each such proposition is expressible and evaluable in any context.

2. Contextualism's strategy for explaining the lure of skeptical arguments and resolving skeptical paradoxes requires that epistemologists not be cognizant of the previous point. If the relevant propositions are spelled out, then there is nothing to be confused about. And contextualism also imputes confusion to ordinary knowledge attributors: they implicitly take the standards for knowledge to vary with context and yet unwittingly take it to be one and the same thing, knowledge, that is at issue from context to context. So contextualism is a strong error theory.

3. The contextualist strategy does not do justice to skeptical arguments. However cogent or fallacious such arguments may be, they purport to show that *ordinary* knowledge attributions are generally false. Skeptics argue not merely that we don't have empirical knowledge by the highest standards but that we don't have it at all (or at least not very much of it), even by ordinary standards. How assiduously people *apply* epistemic standards may vary from context to context, but the skeptic denies that the standards themselves come in various strengths. However loosely people ordinarily apply them, they are always highly demanding.

4. In relying on skeptical arguments, skeptical invariantism implausibly attempts to draw semantic conclusions from epistemological considerations. Whatever the merits of these arguments, however, skeptical invariantism need not, and Unger's version of it does not, rely on warranted assertibility maneuvers, lame or sophisticated. It stands or falls on the strength of skeptical arguments themselves. In my view it falls.

5. Moderate invariantism also does not have to rely on warranted assertibility maneuvers. The distinction between truth conditions and warranted assertibility conditions is a red herring, for the examples that contextualists use to motivate their thesis do not really provide evidence that 'know' is context-sensitive and that the truth conditions of knowledge-ascribing sentences can vary with the context in which they are uttered. What varies, rather, is the attributor's threshold of confidence. In the problem cases, either

a practical consideration or an overly demanding epistemic reason raises that threshold and leads the attributor to demand more evidence than knowledge requires.

6. Contextualists agree, despite differences in formulations, that the varying standards governing [knowledge] attributions reflect what sorts of counterpossibilities need to be considered and eliminated. I suggest an entirely different way in which the consideration or non-consideration of counterpossibilities is relevant to having knowledge. In forming beliefs and seeking knowledge, we rely on our reliability to think of and thereby consider such possibilities when and only when they are worth considering. To the extent that we can trust our ability to know when there are no further counterpossibilities epistemically worth considering, we don't have to consider additional ones in order to be justified in treating them as not worth considering. This applies equally when we attribute knowledge to someone else.

Nobody disputes that how strictly we apply 'know', like a whole host of other words, varies with the context. But the way in which this is indisputable does not help the contextualist. As everyone knows, people use words with varying degrees of strictness and looseness, as I just did with 'everyone'. However, the fact that people do this does not show that the words themselves have semantic contents that come in various degrees. That may be true in the case of vague terms, but most contextualists do not claim that 'know' or 'knowledge' is vague. For all that the data about knowledge attributions show, it could well be that we often attribute knowledge to people who don't have it and often resist attributing it to people who do have it. Sometimes we speak casually, for example, because we're interested in the answer to a certain question, hence in who has the answer, rather than in whether their true belief about the answer qualifies as knowledge. And sometimes we're extra cautious, say because of the stakes, and thus don't make up our own minds about the answer until we have obtained a second opinion, checked out possible sources of error, or otherwise confirmed the answer to our satisfaction. We can't attribute knowledge to someone, even if they have it, when we ourselves have doubts or worries about the truth of the proposition in question. Either for practical reasons or on dubious skeptical grounds, we sometimes demand more of knowledge than it requires.[39]

[39] Many thanks to Jessica Brown, Ray Elugardo, John MacFarlane, Patrick Rysiew, and Jonathan Schaffer for very helpful comments and suggestions, which helped me forestall certain misunderstandings and meet certain objections.

REFERENCES

Austin, J. L. (1961). 'Other Minds', ch. 3 *of Philosophical Papers* (Oxford: Oxford University Press), 44–84.

Bach, Kent (1984). 'Default Reasoning: Jumping to Conclusions and Knowing When to Think Twice', *Pacific Philosophical Quarterly*, 65: 37–58.

—— (1985). 'A Rationale for Reliabilism', *The Monist*, 62: 248–63. Repr in F. Dretske and Sven Bernecker (eds.), *Knowledge* (Oxford: Oxford University Press 2000), 199–213.

—— (1999). 'The Semantics–Pragmatics Distinction: What it is and Why it Matters', in Ken Turner (ed.), *The Semantics–Pragmatics Interface from Different Points of View* (Oxford: Elsevier), 65–84.

—— (2000). 'Quantification, Qualification, and Context', *Mind and Language*, 15: 262–83

—— (2001). 'Speaking Loosely: Sentence Nonliterality', in P. French and H. Wettstein (eds.), *Midwest Studies in Philosophy*, xxv. *Figurative Language* (Oxford: Blackwell), 249–63.

—— (2002). 'Seemingly Semantic Intuitions', in J. Keim Campbell, M. O'Rourke, and D. Shier (eds.), *Meaning and Truth* (New York: Seven Bridges Press), 21–33.

—— (2005). 'Context *ex Machina*', in Z. Szabo (ed.), *Semantics vs Pragmatics* (Oxford: Oxford University Press), 15–44.

Brown, Jessica (forthcoming). 'Contextualism and Warranted Assertibility Manœuvres'.

Cappelen, Herman, and Ernest Lepore (2003). 'Context-Shifting Arguments', *Philosophical Perspectives*, 17: 25–50.

Cohen, Stewart (1988). 'How to be a Fallibilist', *Philosophical Perspectives*, 2: 91–123.

—— (1999). 'Contextualism, Skepticism, and the Structure of Reasons', *Philosophical Perspectives*, 13: 57–89.

—— (2001). 'Contextualism Defended: Comments on Richard Feldman's "Skeptical Problems, Contextualist Solutions" ', *Philosophical Studies*, 103: 87–98.

DeRose, Keith (1992). 'Contextualism and Knowledge Attributions', *Philosophy and Phenomenological Research*, 52: 913–29.

—— (1995). 'Solving the Skeptical Problem', *Philosophical Review*, 104: 1–52.

—— (1999). 'Contextualism: An Explanation and Defense', in J. Greco and E. Sosa (eds.), *The Blackwell Guide to Epistemology* (Oxford: Blackwell), 187–205.

—— (2000). 'Now you Know it, Now you Don't', *Proceedings of the Twentieth World Congress of Philosophy*, v. *Epistemology* (Bowling Green, Ohio: Philosophy Documentation Center), 91–106.

—— (2002). 'Assertion, Knowledge and Context', *Philosophical Review*, 111: 167–203.

—— (2004). 'Single Scoreboard Semantics', *Philosophical Studies*, 119: 1–21.

Dretske, Fred (1981). 'The Pragmatic Dimension of Knowledge', *Philosophical Studies*, 40: 363–78.

Feldman, Richard (1999). 'Contextualism and Skepticism', *Philosophical Perspectives*, 13: 91–114.

—— (2001). 'Skeptical Problems, Contextualist Solutions', *Philosophical Studies*, 103: 61–85.

—— (2004). 'Reply to DeRose's "Single Scoreboard Semantics" ', *Philosophical Studies*, 119: 23–33.

Goldman, Alvin (1976). 'Discrimination and Perceptual Knowledge', *Journal of Philosophy*, 73: 771–91.

Harman, Gilbert, and Brett Sherman (2004). 'Knowledge, Assumptions and Lotteries', *Philosophical Issues*, 14: 492–500.

Hawthorne, John (2004). *Knowledge and Lotteries* (Oxford: Oxford University Press).

Heller, Mark (1999a). 'The Proper Role of Contextualism in Anti-Luck Epistemology', *Philosophical Perspectives*, 13: 115–29.

—— (1999b). 'Relevant Alternatives and Closure', *Australasian Journal of Philosophy*, 77: 196–208.

Hofweber, Thomas (1999). 'Contextualism and the Meaning–Intention Problem', in K. Korta, E. Sosa, and J. Arrazola (eds.), *Cognition, Agency and Rationality* (Dordrecht: Kluwer), 93–104.

Kaplan, David (1989). 'Demonstratives', in J. Almog, J. Perry, and H. Wettstein (eds.), *Themes from Kaplan* (Oxford: Oxford University Press), 481–563.

Kennedy, Christopher (forthcoming). 'Towards a Grammar of Vagueness'.

Klein, Peter (2000). 'Contextualism and the Real Nature of Academic Skepticism', *Philosophical Issues*, 10: 108–16.

Kompa, Nikola (2002). 'The Context Sensitivity of Knowledge Ascriptions', *Grazer Philosophische Studien*, 64: 1–18.

Kornblith, Hilary (2000). 'The Contextualist Evasion of Epistemology', *Philosophical Issues*, 10: 24–32.

Lasersohn, Peter (1999). 'Pragmatic Halos', *Language*, 75: 522–51.

Lewis, David (1996). 'Elusive Knowledge', *Australasian Journal of Philosophy*, 74: 549–67.

Neta, Ram (2003). 'Skepticism, Contextualism, and Semantic Self-Knowledge', *Philosophy and Phenomenological Research*, 67: 396–411.

Nichols, Shaun, Stephen Stich, and Jonathan Weinberg (2003), 'Meta-Skepticism: Meditations on Ethno-Epistemology', in S. Luper (ed.), *The Skeptics* (Aldershot: Ashgate Publishing), 227–47.

Nicolle, Steve, and Billy Clark (1999). 'Experimental Pragmatics and What is Said: A Response to Gibbs and Moise', *Cognition*, 69: 337–54.

Price, H. H. (1932). *Perception* (London: Methuen).

Rysiew, Patrick (2001). 'The Context-Sensitivity of Knowledge Attributions', *Noûs*, 35: 477–514.

—— (forthcoming). 'Speaking of Knowing'.

Schaffer, Jonathan (2004). 'From Contextualism to Contrastivism in Epistemology', *Philosophical Studies*, 119: 73–103.

Schiffer, Stephen (1996). 'Contextualist Solutions to Scepticism', *Proceedings of the Aristotelian Society*, 96: 317–33.

Sosa, Ernest (2000). 'Skepticism and Contextualism', *Philosophical Issues*, 10: 1–18.

Stanley, Jason (2004). 'On the Linguistic Basis for Contextualism', *Philosophical Studies*, 119: 119–46.

Unger, Peter (1971). 'A Defense of Skepticism', *Philosophical Review*, 80: 198–218.

—— (1975). *Ignorance: A Case for Scepticism* (Oxford: Clarendon Press).

—— (1984). *Philosophical Relativity* (Minneapolis: University of Minnesota Press).

—— (1986). 'The Cone Model of Knowledge', *Philosophical Topics*, 14: 125–78.

Williamson, Timothy (2000). 'Scepticism and Evidence', *Philosophy and Phenomenological Research*, 60: 613–28.

4

Knowledge, Context, and the Agent's Point of View

Timothy Williamson

1. Contextualism and Relativism

Contextualism is relativism tamed.

Relativism about truth is usually motivated by the idea of no-fault disagreement. Imagine two parties: one (she) says 'P'; the other (he) says 'Not P'.[1] Apparently, if P then 'P' is true and 'Not P' false, so she is right and he is wrong; if not P then 'P' is false and 'Not P' true, so he is right and she is wrong. In both cases, there is an asymmetry between the two parties. Since P or not P (by the law of excluded middle), there is indeed an asymmetry between them, one way or the other. Yet the two parties may strike a neutral observer as on a par, equally intelligent, informed, perceptive, and alert. Relativists about truth strive to dissolve the unpleasant asymmetry: ' "P" is true for her; "Not P" is true for him'. Trouble starts when we ask what the relativists mean by 'for' in the construction 'true for X'. If to call something true 'for' X is just to say that X believes that it is true, then the attempted dissolution amounts to this: 'She believes that "P" is true; he believes that "Not P" is true'. But that is to add no more than that both parties believe that they are right; it does nothing to undermine the argument for an asymmetry between them. Relativists had better mean something else by 'true for X'. When asked to explain what else they mean, wild relativists bluster incoherently.

[1] Despite the conveniently gendered pronouns, the parties to the disputes may be social or intellectual groups rather than single individuals.

Contextualists, by contrast, have a clear answer. A sentence is true for X if and only if it is true as uttered by X, true relative to a context in which X is the speaker. Such relativism is tame because the relativity to context in the truth-value of a sentence allows for absoluteness in the truth-value of what the sentence is used to say in a given context. When she says 'P', she speaks truly: not just truly for her, but absolutely truly. When he says 'Not P', he too speaks truly: not just truly for him, but absolutely truly. The argument for asymmetry assumes that, when she says 'P', she speaks truly if and only if P, and when he says 'Not P', he speaks truly if and only if not P. But that assumption is only as good as the assumption that, when she says 'P', she says that P, and when he says 'Not P', he says that not P. Contextualism denies that assumption in the cases at issue. If I report a speaker who utters the sentence 'P' as having said that P, in effect I assume, contrary to contextualism, that she said in her context what I would have said in my context by uttering the same words.

One great strength of contextualism is that it is uncontroversially correct about some cases. If she says 'I am a woman' while he says 'I am not a woman', it would not normally occur to us even for a moment to think of them as thereby disagreeing, although verbally his sentence is the negation of hers. We automatically apply the rule that 'I' as used in a given context refers to the speaker of that context: when she uses 'I', it refers to her; when he uses 'I', it refers to him. The disquotational clause that I am the referent of 'I' as used by him or her has no allure. Thus when she says 'I am a woman', she says that she is a woman; consequently, she speaks truly if and only if she is a woman; she does not say (falsely) that I am a woman. When he says 'I am not a woman', he says that he is not a woman; consequently, he speaks truly if and only if he is not a woman; he does not say that I am not a woman. In reporting their speech correctly, we make the possibility manifest that both parties spoke truly. It should be manifest even to the parties themselves. Although they can and will disquote on 'I' in reporting their own speech, they cannot and will not do so in reporting the speech of the other.

When the context-relativity is less clearly rule-governed, we may still adjust to it equally smoothly. In the sentence 'It is one of them', the pronouns can refer to almost anything, but usually no confusion results. Sometimes we make allowances for less obvious context-relativity. If she says 'Jan is tall' in a conversation about jockeys while he says 'Jan is not tall' (speaking of the same person at the same time) in a conversation about basketball players, we may allow that both parties spoke truly. Disquotation in reporting their speech is initially somewhat more tempting than in the previous cases. I might report her as having said that Jan is tall and him as having said that Jan is not tall. On reflection, however, I had better not stick to both reports in a single context. For if she said that Jan is tall, then she spoke truly if and only if Jan is tall, and if he said that Jan is not tall, then he spoke truly if and only if Jan is not tall. Therefore, if she said that Jan is tall and he said that Jan is not tall, they did not both speak truly (assume that I am not myself shifting contexts in mid-sentence). Our difficulty in reporting them is that we lack other words to express in our context what the word 'tall' expresses in contexts with other standards, in which 'tall' does not express what it expresses in our context. Nevertheless, we can describe what seems to be going on clearly enough in schematic terms. In her context, the word 'tall' expresses the property of being tall(hers) (tall for a jockey); in saying 'Jan is tall', she says that Jan is tall(hers). In his context, 'tall' expresses the property of being tall(his) (tall for a basketball player); in saying 'Jan is not tall', he says that Jan is not tall(his). Being tall(hers) and being tall(his) are different properties, for although whatever is tall(his) is tall(hers), some things are tall(hers) without being tall(his). Thus it may be that both parties are speaking truly.

Contextualists can elucidate their point by talking of propositions. In that framework, if p is the proposition that P, uttering a sentence in a context in which it expresses p with the appropriate declarative force is necessary and sufficient for saying that P. The contextualist claim about a given sentence is that it expresses different propositions as uttered in some different contexts. As uttered by her, the sentence 'I am a woman' expresses the true proposition that she is a woman, so its negation expresses the false proposition that she is not a woman; as uttered by him, 'I am a woman' expresses the false proposition that he is a woman, so its negation expresses the true proposition that he is not a woman. The difference between the two contexts in the reference of 'I' makes a difference between them in what proposition is expressed. In all this, the linguistic meaning of the sentence and its constituent words is held fixed: both speakers are using the word 'I' with its standard English meaning; one rule determines the contextual variation in reference. A dictionary of English does not need separate entries for 'I' as used by different speakers. Understanding the word 'I' requires mastering this contextual variation, in order not to misinterpret other speakers. Contextualism does not concern the trivial point that physically indistinguishable words in different languages may have different meanings (the Italian word 'burro' means *butter*; the Spanish word 'burro' means *donkey*).

If the sentence s as uttered in a context c expresses the proposition that P, then s is true in c if and only if P, and false in c if and only if not P. As uttered in the present context, the sentence 'P' expresses the proposition that P; thus

'P' is true in the present context if and only if P, and false if and only if not P. As uttered in some other context, 'P' expresses some other proposition, that Q; thus 'P' is true in that other context if and only if Q. Since a sentence may be true in one context and false in another, truth and falsity for sentences are relative to a context. At least some apparent disagreements dissolve if the parties speak in different contexts. But truth and falsity for propositions are as absolute as you like. If 'P' expresses the proposition that P(hers) as uttered in her context and the distinct proposition that P(his) as uttered in his context, then P(hers) may be absolutely true while P(his) is absolutely false, independently of context, because P(hers) does not entail P(his). When he says 'Not P', he expresses the absolutely true proposition that not P(his). Although the sentence that he utters is the negation of the sentence that she utters, the proposition that he expresses is not the negation of the proposition that she expresses. They are talking past each other. In this tame way, contextualists restore the two parties to parity.

Normally, a difference between the propositions that a particular sentence expresses in different contexts can be traced to a difference between the contributions that a particular constituent word such as 'I' or 'tall' makes in those contexts to what proposition the sentence expresses. Sometimes, as with 'I', it is a blatant difference in reference. In other cases, the difference must be inferred from a difference in the truth-value of the whole sentence, which involves eliminating other subsentential constituents as the source of the contextual variation.

The notion of a difference in the truth-value of a sentence must be applied with care. The sentence 'Descartes died in 1650' expresses a truth as uttered in the actual world; it expresses a falsehood as uttered in a counterfactual world in which Descartes died in 1651. But such a difference in truth-value does not imply any contextual variation in the relevant sense in 'Descartes died in 1650'. As uttered in the counterfactual world, the sentence expresses the very same proposition that it expresses as uttered in the actual world, the proposition that Descartes died in 1650. If Descartes had died in 1651, someone who said 'Descartes died in 1650' (meaning by the words what they actually mean in English) would still have said that Descartes died in 1650. The difference is that the proposition that Descartes died in 1650 is actually true but would have been false if Descartes had died in 1651, because Descartes died in 1650 in the actual world but in 1651 in the counterfactual world. The truth-value of the proposition is not an essential property. In the terminology of David Kaplan (1989), we have varied not only the context of utterance (in particular, the world in which a proposition is relevantly expressed) but also the circumstance of evaluation (in particular, the world in which the proposition is relevantly true or false). For variation in the truth-value of a sentence as uttered in different contexts to constitute a genuinely contextual effect, the sentence must be evaluated with respect to a fixed circumstance. Unless the circumstances agree on whether P, the sentence 'P' may express the proposition that P in both cases and differ in truth-value in a non-contextualist way.

The criteria just sketched for isolating contextualist phenomena are not always straightforward to apply, even when we are clear about the truth-values of the sentences at issue as uttered in the relevant contexts. The temporal dimension is particularly tricky. On the majority view, defended by Frege, propositions cannot change in truth-value; since the sentence 'It is Monday' expresses a truth as uttered on Monday and a falsehood as uttered on Tuesday, it expresses different propositions as uttered on different days. More generally, any significant use of tenses creates a genuinely contextualist effect. By contrast, on a minority view, defended by Prior, propositions can change in truth-value; the sentence 'It is Monday' expresses a single proposition, that it is Monday, which is true on Monday and false on Tuesday. That would no more be a contextualist effect than is the contingency in truth-value of 'Descartes died in 1650'. Fortunately, we need not decide the proper treatment of tenses for the purposes of this chapter, although we must be circumspect in applying the framework to diachronic cases.

2. The Contextualist Strategy

According to contextualists, many philosophical problems result from subtly concealed forms of context-relativity. The mark of paradox is that apparently obvious claims are apparently jointly inconsistent. On the contextualist diagnosis, the inconsistency is really only between the sentences that express those claims, which we accept in different contexts: each sentence expresses a true proposition as uttered in the context in which we accept it, but in no single context do they all express true propositions, or do we accept them all; what varies is not the truth-value of any given proposition (the circumstance of evaluation is fixed), but rather which proposition a given sentence expresses. The contextualist resolution of apparent conflicts has become one of the most fashionable strategies in contemporary philosophy, not least through its systematic application and advocacy by David Lewis.[2]

[2] Lewis (1979) expounds his general contextualist approach.

The classic example is contextualism about the word 'know'. Many epistemologists find each claim in triplets such as the following highly plausible:

(1) Mary knows that she had her purse yesterday morning.
(2) If Mary knows that she had her purse yesterday morning, then Mary knows that the universe was not created an hour ago (with misleading apparent traces of millions of years of past history...).
(3) Mary does not know that the universe was not created an hour ago (with misleading apparent traces of millions of years of past history...).

For (1) seems to report a typical case of ordinary common sense knowledge; (2) seems to register Mary's capacity to extend her knowledge by deductive reasoning, for we may assume that she believes the conclusion that the earth was not created an hour ago on the basis of competent deduction from the premise that she had her purse yesterday morning (and perhaps on many other equally good bases too); (3) seems to record her inability to rule out possibilities to which her methods of belief formation are wholly insensitive. Yet the sentences (1)–(3) constitute an inconsistent triad of the form {'P', 'If P then Q', 'Not Q'}. To resolve the difficulty, contextualists distinguish between an ordinary context, in which we use the word 'know' in speaking of everyday concerns, according to comparatively low standards for its correct application, and an extraordinary epistemological context, in which we use the word 'know' to obsess about sceptical scenarios, according to much higher standards for its correct application.[3]

In the ordinary context, 'know' expresses a relation of know(low)ing. One can know(low) that P even though one has no way of persuading a sceptic that one is not in an apt sceptical scenario in which one falsely believes that P, for such sceptical scenarios are in some sense irrelevant to the ordinary context. Mary know(low)s that she had her purse yesterday morning. Moreover, deduction is a way of extending know(low)ledge; if one believes the conclusion that Q on the basis of competent deduction from the premise that P (and perhaps some other premises too), and one know(low)s that P (and those other premises too, if any), then one know(low)s that Q. Thus if Mary know(low)s that she had her purse yesterday morning then she know(low)s that the universe was not created an hour ago. Therefore, she know(low)s that the universe was not created an hour ago.

[3] Seminal (noncontextualist) discussions of the nonclosure problem are Dretske (1970) and Nozick (1981). Important examples of contextualist approaches include Cohen (1987, 1988, 1999), DeRose (1992, 1995, 2004), Lewis (1996), Stine (1976), and Unger (1986).

In the epistemological context, 'know' expresses a relation of know(high)-ing. One cannot know(high) that P if one has no way of persuading a sceptic that one is not in an apt sceptical scenario in which one falsely believes that P, for such sceptical scenarios are in some sense relevant to the epistemological context. Mary does not know(high) that the universe was not created an hour ago. Equally, she does not know(high) that she had her purse yesterday morning. Therefore, on a truth-functional reading of the conditional, if Mary know(high)s that she had her purse yesterday morning then she know-(high)s that the universe was not created an hour ago. More generally, deduction is a way of extending know(high)ledge, given that we are not here concerned with scepticism about the validity of the deductive reasoning itself. If one believes the conclusion that Q on the basis of competent deduction from the premise that P (and perhaps some other premises too), and one know-(high)s that P (and those other premises too, if any), then one know(high)s that Q. Thus, again, if Mary know(high)s that she had her purse yesterday morning then she know(high)s that the universe was not created an hour ago.

In the ordinary context, sentences (1) and (2) express truths while (3) expresses a falsehood. In the epistemological context, (2) and (3) express truths while (1) expresses a falsehood. Since (1)–(3) are jointly inconsistent, in no context do they all express truths. When we initially consider (1), we tend to remain in an ordinary context, for no sceptical scenario has been mentioned. But (2) and (3) advert to a sceptical scenario in which the universe was created an hour ago with misleading apparent traces of millions of years of past history. Thus considering (2) and (3) tends to put us into the epistemological context, and merely reconsidering (1) is not enough to get us out again: we may simply become more doubtful of (1). It takes less to summon up an evil demon than to exorcize him.

Different contextualists postulate different context-shifting mechanisms, although most of them make some play with the idea of change in the contextual relevance of various possibilities of error. This chapter prescinds from the details of particular contextualist accounts in order to investigate more general theoretical issues about epistemological contextualism as such.

It is important to check whether specifically contextualist ideas are crucial to the resolution of the paradox. Contextualism about 'know' does not follow merely from this possibility: when Mary is in a police station at noon, reporting the theft of her purse, it is true to say 'Mary knows that she had her purse yesterday morning', but when she is in an epistemology seminar that afternoon, discussing scepticism, it is true to say 'Mary does not know that she had her purse yesterday morning'. For we can make sense of that story by assuming that 'know' stands for a single temporary relation which a subject may have to a truth at one time and not at another, as in learning and forgetting, although here what makes the difference is her conversational situation (if she continues to believe even in the seminar that she had her purse yesterday morning).[4] Even if that is not the best treatment of the present tense in 'knows', the upshot would be at most a quite general form of contextualism about tenses, not anything specific to 'know': that is not epistemological contextualism. Similarly, one cannot argue for contextualism about 'tall' merely by pointing out that the sentence 'Michael is tall' may express a truth when Michael is an adult and a falsehood when he is a little boy. For genuine contextualism about 'know', we must keep the time and world of evaluation fixed. But contextualists argue that we can do so. Even if Mary herself is in an ordinary context at the relevant time, worrying about the loss of her purse rather than sceptical scenarios, contextualists will still ascribe truth to both 'Mary knows that she had her purse yesterday morning' as uttered in the ordinary context of a conversation about Mary's loss and 'Mary does not know that she had her purse yesterday morning' as uttered simultaneously in the epistemological context of a seminar about scepticism. It is not a question of her knowing something at one time and not at another, or in one world and not in another. Saving the truth of the two simultaneous and apparently contradictory assertions is a specifically contextualist move.

Sceptical arguments have a pull on our assent that cries out for explanation. Their power is felt immediately by a high proportion of those who are willing to listen to them carefully. Contextualists can explain this power by conceding a semantics for 'know' on which sceptics speak truly, for example in uttering (3) and the negation of (1). But this is not total capitulation to scepticism, for contextualists can also explain the pull that common sense has on our assent, for on their semantics we also speak truly when we make 'knowledge'-ascriptions in ordinary contexts, for example in uttering (1).[5] Sceptics speak truly only by creating contexts with extraordinarily high standards for the correct application of 'know', in which their favourite sentences express truths.

Contextualist explanations of the power of scepticism need not be *ad hoc*, for they may appeal to independently testable generalizations about all

---

[4] Hawthorne (2003) and Jason Stanley (forthcoming) develop such an alternative to contextualism. The main arguments of this chapter do not tell against it (except for a potential threat suggested by the final paragraph). For a line of criticism that does apply to both contextualism and such alternatives to it see Williamson (2005).

[5] See Williamson (2001) in this connection for a way in which contextualism comes closer to scepticism than is often realized.

contexts of utterance, not just those at issue in sceptical problems. For example, such generalizations may also predict a rise in standards for the correct application of epistemic terms when more is at stake practically. 'The man in the information booth knows that no train is coming this afternoon' may be true as uttered by the disappointed trainspotter on the platform, false as uttered simultaneously by the sleepy sunbather on the line. The predictions may also cover many terms of epistemic appraisal beyond 'know', such as 'justified'. These predictions may seem to be verified.

3. Contextualism, Vagueness, and the Transmission of Information

One feature of many philosophically significant terms that apparently pre-disposes them to contextualist treatment is their *vagueness*. We understand them not by learning precise definitions but by extrapolating from examples which leave their application to ranges of borderline cases unclear. In many contexts, speakers find it convenient to resolve some of this vagueness in one way or another, according to their practical purposes. Naturally, they will sometimes find it convenient to resolve the vagueness in opposite ways in different contexts. One local stipulation about the extension of 'red' makes it include x; elsewhere, another local stipulation about the extension of 'red' makes it exclude x. Vague terms appear not to cut nature at the joints, not to pick up hidden but sharp and uniquely natural divisions into kinds that might stabilize their reference: on the epistemicist view, a vague term has hidden sharp boundaries as used in a given context, but that does not stop it from having different hidden sharp boundaries as used in another context. Of course, context-relativity is not the very same phenomenon as vagueness: that 'I' refers to John as uttered by John and to Mary as uttered by Mary is an example of context-relativity without being an example of vagueness. Never-theless, one might think that the vagueness of a term makes contextual variation in its reference practically irresistible (even though it also makes the variation hard to measure). In this light, it looks as though it would be an amazing coincidence if a vague term did have exactly the same reference in all contexts.[6]

---

[6] A pioneering attempt to use sorites paradoxes to link vagueness and context-dependence is Kamp (1981); many authors have subsequently argued for similar claims. For a critique of such views see Stanley (2003).

Epistemic terms such as 'know' and 'justified' are surely at least somewhat vague; it seems obvious that they are not perfectly precise. Between the clear cases of their application and the clear cases of their non-application, they seem to have a range of borderline cases, just as one might expect. If that gives us independent reason to predict their context-relativity, then surely it is a natural strategy to put that context-relativity to work in epistemologically significant ways, as contextualists try to do.

It is beginning to look as though context-relativity must be virtually ubiquitous in natural languages, just as vagueness is. However, it comes at a cost, as we can see by considering the preservation of information in memory and its transmission by testimony.[7] Let the sentence 'P' as uttered in different contexts express different propositions, some true, some false. Suppose that in a context c you acquire an item of information, expressed by 'P' as uttered in c. You could store the sentence 'P' in your memory. But when the time comes to retrieve the information, for guiding action or passing on to someone else, you will be in a new context c^*; even if 'P' expresses a truth as uttered in c, it need not express a truth as uttered in c^*. If in c^* you remember that you acquired 'P' in c, and what c was like, you might be able to construct another sentence 'P*' that as uttered in c^* expresses the very truth that 'P' expresses as uttered in c. But that procedure imposes a heavy burden on memory. Most people cannot remember where they got much of the information on which they rely. Alternatively, when you first acquire the information, in c, you could seek another sentence 'Q' that expresses independently of context the same proposition that 'P' expresses in c; you could then store the sentence 'Q' in your memory. But if such an eternal sentence 'Q' were readily available for the occasion sentence 'P' on each occasion, then the context-relativity of 'P' would be, if not idle, at least underemployed.

One obvious problem is that you might not always know the value of some contextual parameters that affect the reference of terms in 'P'. If you do not know where you are, how can you replace 'here' by a context-insensitive designation of the place? If you do not know what time it is, how can you replace 'now' by a context-insensitive designation of the time? You could use 'there' and 'then' as memory demonstratives, but that requires preserving some memory of the incident. You could existentially quantify out by using 'somewhere' and 'sometime', but the resort to such generality involves significant loss of information. Obviously, these problems do not show that we would be better off without 'here' and 'now'; they even illustrate the utility of

---

[7] See also Hawthorne (2003: 109–10).

the words. But they also illustrate their limitations when information is to be preserved and transmitted.

The reference of paradigm indexicals such as 'here' and 'now' varies with easily isolated parameters of context, such as place and time, whose values we at least often know enough to designate non-indexically. I know that in my current context 'here' corefers with 'Room 2, Staircase 10, Old Buildings, New College, Oxford OX1 3BN, UK' and 'now' corefers with '11.23 a.m., 9 December 2003' (give or take a little specificity). But contextualism makes the reference of epistemic terms such as 'know' and 'justified' vary with a more elusive parameter, epistemic standards. We have no received scale for conveniently specifying epistemic standards in terms that contextualists would regard as context-insensitive. Phrases such as 'high standards' and 'low standards' are themselves context-sensitive, and in any case far too vague and unspecific for identifying location on a continuum of standards. In answer to the questions 'How high?' and 'How low?', one finds oneself giving a detailed account of who said what. One could try a description such as 'The epistemic standards in force in Room 2, Staircase 10, Old Buildings, New College, Oxford OX1 3BN, UK at 11.23 a.m., 9 December 2003', but such a description would clearly be of little use to those who did not know what was going on at that place at that time. If I simply store the sentence 'At 11.23 a.m., 9 December 2003, I did not know whether I had my wallet the previous morning', it may express a falsehood the next time I produce it, owing to a change of epistemic standards. If I store the sentence 'At 11.23 a.m., 9 December 2003, I did not have the relation then expressed in my context by the word "know" to whether I had my wallet the previous morning', it will do me little good the next time I produce it if I cannot remember enough about the past context to have much idea of what relation the word 'know' then expressed. Evidently, the more extensively 'know' varies in reference with context, the worse the problems of using it to preserve and transmit information will be. Yet 'know' does not seem to be designed like 'here' and 'now' primarily for immediate consumption; we need to preserve and transmit information about who has what kind of knowledge, or who knew what when.

Epistemological contextualism has been criticized for postulating contextual variation of which ordinary speakers are unaware (Schiffer, 1996). Normal competence with paradigm indexicals and demonstratives such as 'I', 'you', 'here', 'there', 'now', 'then', 'he', 'she', 'it', 'this', 'that', and 'these' makes their context-sensitivity manifest to one; no philosophical argument is needed to persuade one of its existence. The hypothesis of hidden context-sensitivity is therefore taken to be implausible: if our word 'know' is context-sensitive, why is that not obvious to us? Whatever one thinks of that argument, the use of 'know' in preserving and transmitting information is even more problematic if it is context-sensitive in ways of which ordinary speakers are unaware. For will they not be liable to store information in the shape of sentences involving the word 'know' and produce those sentences again in new contexts in which they no longer express truths? The same point applies to other philosophically contentious contextualist claims. For their very contentiousness suggests that the context-sensitivity is not manifest to ordinary speakers, who are therefore liable to run afoul of it in attempting to preserve and transmit information.

The practical difficulties in using context-sensitive terms of epistemic appraisal do not constitute a decisive argument against contextualism (Hofweber (1999) and Rysiew (2001) argue for similar conclusions). To some extent as speakers we could work round them in various *ad hoc* ways, especially if the contextual variation is not too extensive. Even if it is hard for us to become consciously aware of the contextual variation, we might somehow unconsciously adjust to it in preserving and transmitting information: much of native speakers' competence with a natural language is not open to their view. Nevertheless, the practical difficulties show that context-sensitivity carries significant disadvantages; if one were designing a language, one would not want too much of it. But the previous consideration of vagueness suggested that context-sensitivity might be unavoidable in virtually all terms of interest.

The aim of the second half of this chapter is to develop a model that makes terms such as 'know' and 'justified' context-invariant without requiring them to be precise. The next section explores a related issue in practical affairs. Section 5 applies its moral to contextualism in epistemology.

4. Contextualism and Practical Reason

Imagine that Clare faces a difficult practical decision: whether to resign her good job tomorrow for reasons of principle. She thinks 'If it would be wrong for me not to resign, I will resign; if it would not be wrong for me not to resign, I will not resign. But would it be wrong for me not to resign?'[8] The

---

[8] The sentence 'It would not be wrong for me not to resign' is treated as the negation of 'It would be wrong for me not to resign' in order to avoid the clumsy 'It is not the case that it would be wrong for me not to resign'.

relevant considerations are complex. Some tell in favour of the conclusion that it would be wrong for her not to resign; others tell against it. She is unsure what relative weights to assign the conflicting factors. When the considerations in favour of resigning are more salient to her, she is disposed to judge that it would be wrong for her not to resign; when the considerations against resigning are more salient to her, she is disposed to judge that it would not be wrong for her not to resign. As the moment for decision approaches, she oscillates, agonizing, between the opposed views.

Suddenly, a contextualist appears and says to Clare:

> Do not worry. You are mistaken in supposing that there is a disagreement between what you think when you think 'It would be wrong for me not to resign' and what you think when you think 'It would not be wrong for me not to resign'. Both thoughts are true.[9] The sentence 'It would be wrong for me not to resign' expresses different propositions as uttered in different contexts. Sometimes, the considerations in favour of resigning are more salient to you; that creates a context in which 'It would be wrong for me not to resign' expresses a truth, to which you are disposed to assent. At other times, the considerations against resigning are more salient to you; that creates a context in which 'It would not be wrong for me not to resign' expresses a truth, to which you are also disposed to assent. You have no need to reject one of the two thoughts.

This contextualist resolution of Clare's problem is liable to strike us as glib and shallow. When the moment for action comes, Clare must either resign or not resign. Given her intention expressed in the words 'I will resign if and only if it would be wrong not to do so', by resigning she goes only with the thought 'It would be wrong for me not to resign', and by not resigning she goes only with the thought 'It would not be wrong for me not to resign'. She cannot have it both ways.

Of course, context-sensitive elements occur in the sentence 'It would be wrong for me not to resign': for example, the first person pronoun and the tense of the finite verb. But no variation in their reference explains Clare's

---

[9] The ascription of truth to sentences involving moral terms such as 'wrong' is notoriously controversial but will not be defended here. No metaphysical account of truth is being assumed. Although contextualists about 'wrong' must reject a disquotational account of truth for sentences involving the word 'wrong', they can still accept that if one says that it would be wrong for Clare not to resign, one speaks truly if and only if it would be wrong for Clare not to resign, and falsely if and only if it would not be wrong for Clare not to resign (since 'wrong' is used rather than mentioned in such indirect speech reports). See Feldman (2001: 72–3) for a similar example to illustrate the implausibility of a contextualist treatment of 'wrong'. Cohen (2001) replies to Feldman.

oscillation. Throughout, 'me' refers to Clare, the time reference is to the time (which we may assume to be fixed) when she must resign if she is to do so at all, and so on.

Equally unappealing would be a contextualist resolution of the apparent disagreement between two commentators, one saying 'It would be wrong for Clare not to resign' while the other says simultaneously 'It would not be wrong for Clare not to resign'.

Can we go any deeper in explaining why the contextualist resolution misses the point of Clare's problem? In cases of decision-making, one context is distinguished above all others: that of the agent at the moment of action. The primary question is whether the sentence 'It would be wrong for me not to resign' expresses a truth as uttered in the context in which the speaker is Clare and the time is that for resigning if she is to do so at all.[10] Call that context the *agent's context*, and the proposition which the relevant first person present tense sentence (such as 'It would be wrong for me not to resign') expresses in it the *agent's proposition*. If at some point in her agonizing Clare uses the sentence to express a proposition other than the agent's proposition, which might fail to match the agent's proposition in truth-value, she is no longer concentrating on the relevant practical problem. Similarly, an external commentator who uses the sentence 'It would be wrong for Clare not to resign' to express a proposition other than the agent's proposition is no longer concentrating on the relevant practical problem for Clare.[11] But if the sentence expresses the agent's proposition in all the contexts at issue, then it expresses the *same* proposition in all those contexts, and contextualism fails for this case.

Where contextualism applies, the speaker's context is *autonomous* with respect to the agent's context in determining what propositions the relevant sentences express: the speaker's proposition need not be the agent's proposition. We have seen reason to suspect that, in practical matters, the speaker's context lacks such autonomy. The lack of autonomy would not be epistemic: for all that it implies, the speaker (a disinterested observer, or the agent herself

---

[10] We can consider such a context even if Clare does not in fact utter the sentence at that time. The convenient simplifying assumptions that Clare is a normal English speaker and that there is only one time when the action can be taken are not essential to the argument.

[11] For convenience, the individuation of propositions is assumed to be coarse-grained, so that any difference in sense between 'me' (as used by Clare) and 'Clare' makes no difference to the propositions expressed by containing sentences. Since contextualism is supposed to resolve apparent disagreements by making a difference at the level of reference and truth-value, ignoring finer-grained distinctions is harmless for present purposes.

in a cooler hour, or . . .) may be in a better position than the agent at the time of action to know what is right or wrong. That Clare is the one who stands to lose her job does not necessarily help her to know whether it would be wrong for her not to resign. The speaker's context lacks autonomy only in setting the content of the practical question. In some sense 'Would it be wrong?' is above all a question *for* the agent, in the context of agency (which is not to deny that the agent may fail to raise it); it is a question for others, or for the agent in other contexts, *because* it is a question for the agent in the context of agency. Of course, others can ask the question for some instrumental reason, for example in making predictions about the agent's behaviour in other situations. But the true answer to a question is not always the same as the most useful answer for some immediate practical purpose. To think of the true answer to the moral question about a fixed action as oscillating with the practical purposes of the questioner seems to lose sight of the meaning of the question. Plausibly, therefore, shifting from the context of agency to other contexts does not shift the content of the question.

If the contextualist misdescribes the practical case, and Clare's utterances of 'It would be wrong for me not to resign' and 'It would not be wrong for me not to resign' express genuinely incompatible contents, then for part of her deliberations Clare is disposed to misjudge whether it would be wrong for her not to resign. The contextualist might challenge us to explain why Clare would commit such an error. But an explanation is not far to seek. For, as the case was originally described, there were complex, conflicting considerations for and against resigning, with no obviously correct standard for weighting them against each other. One would expect Clare to assign more weight to considerations when they are psychologically salient to her than when they are not. As she goes through the considerations in her mind, one after another, naturally they fluctuate in salience to her. In the circumstances, it would be astonishing if her judgement did *not* fluctuate too. No special semantic hypothesis is needed to explain such a familiar psychological phenomenon.

The argument has evidently done nothing to show that, unexpectedly, 'wrong' is precise. The point is rather that, however vague the term, its meaning does not permit variation in content across contexts. In that respect we might compare 'wrong' with a proper name. The nature of a proper name is to have a constant character in Kaplan's sense: in each context it has the same content (it refers to the same object). In this sense, proper names which differ in reference are different names, even if they look and sound the same ('John Smith' and 'John Smith'). But it does not follow that proper names are perfectly precise.

The argument does not imply that the orthographic type 'wrong' is always used in English with the same sense. It may well have distinct moral and nonmoral readings in the sentence 'It is wrong to answer "Thirteen" to the question "What is the sum of seven and five?" ', with a corresponding difference in truth-value. But that is ambiguity, as in 'bank', not indexicality. It is a given sense of an expression that is indexical; one must be sensitive to the indexicality in order to understand the expression with that sense. An ambiguous orthographic type has several senses, understanding it with any one of which does not imply understanding it with any other (it may be best to regard distinct senses as marking out distinct but orthographically coincident expressions). Contextualists allege indexicality rather than ambiguity: for example, a contextualist understanding of 'know' requires sensitivity to the contextual variation in its reference. On the account just sketched, the orthographic type 'wrong' has at least one non-indexical sense, for which contextualism fails.

The argument is suggestive rather than irresistible. Nevertheless, let us see what happens when we try to develop a similar account for the word 'know'.

5. Practical Epistemic Evaluation

According to contextualism about 'know', a sentence of the form 'S knows at t that P' may be true as uttered in a context c yet false as uttered in another context c^*, even though in both contexts 'S' refers to the same subject, S, 't' refers to the same time, t, and 'P' expresses the same proposition, that P: what differs is the referent of 'know'.[12] In this case the agent's context, the context being spoken about, is the context of S as agent at time t.[13] Then at least one of c and c^* differs from the agent's context in the referent of 'know', since otherwise they would not differ from each other in that respect. Similarly, the present-tensed 'I know that P' in the agent's context differs in truth-value from 'S knows at t that P' in one of c and c^*, otherwise c and c^* would not differ from each other in the truth-value of the latter sentence. Given that

---

[12] Bound variables or complex expressions containing bound variables may replace any of 'S', 't', and 'P' to handle sentences such as 'The ancient Egypyians knew many truths of mathematics'. In that case, consider c and c^* relative to the same assignment of values to variables.

[13] Sentences are being evaluated with respect to the same possible world, the world of c, c^*, and the agent's context.

'S knows at *t* that P' expresses different propositions in *c* and *c**, at least one of those propositions differs from the agent's proposition, the proposition that 'I know that P' expresses in the agent's context. Contrapositively, if the speaker's context lacks autonomy in ascriptions involving 'know', in the sense that 'know' must have the reference in the speaker's context that it has in the agent's context, then contextualism fails for 'know'.

Even in the epistemic case, the lack of autonomy of the speaker's context would be non-epistemic in the same sense as in the practical case: for all that it implies, the speaker (an external observer, or S herself at a time other than *t*, or ...) may be in a better position than the agent S at *t* to know whether S knows at *t* that P. S may think that she knows that the animal in the cage is a zebra, while the zoo keeper knows that S does not know that it is a zebra, because he knows that it is a cleverly disguised mule. The speaker's context would lack autonomy only in setting the content of the epistemic question. In some sense 'Does S know at *t* that P?' is above all a question *for* the agent S, at time *t* (which is not to deny that S may fail to ask the question); it is a question for others, or for S at other times, *because* it is a question for S at *t*. Of course, others can ask the question for some instrumental reason, for example in deciding whether to rely on S's testimony. But the true answer to a question is not always the same as the most useful answer for some immediate practical purpose. To think of the true answer to the epistemological question as oscillating with the practical purposes of the questioner risks losing sight of the meaning of the question. Shifting from the context of agency to other contexts may not shift the content of the question.

The hypothesis that the speaker's context lacks autonomy in 'know'-ascriptions already explains how 'know' could work in a non-contextualist way without being precise. No amazing coincidence in reference is required: just a primary role for the agent's context that cannot be trumped by the speaker's context.

If there is any reason for the speaker's context to lack autonomy in 'know'-ascriptions, then epistemological contextualism may well fail non-miraculously. But is there any reason for the speaker's context to lack autonomy in 'know'-ascriptions? Traditional epistemology has concentrated on the first-person present tense question 'What do I know?', as if the agent's context had primacy (Descartes is the prime example). One might expect that primacy to deprive the speaker's context of autonomy. But the tradition is far from obviously warranted in treating the first person present tense question as the key to epistemology. For example, Edward Craig (1990) has argued that the primary point of the concept of knowledge is in distinguishing between reliable and unreliable informants. On his view, the third person question 'What do they know?' takes precedence over the first person 'What do I know?', so one might expect the speaker's context to be autonomous in relation to the agent's context. More generally, many epistemological externalists emphasize the significance for knowing of reliable causal or counterfactual connections between belief states and states of the external environment, irrespective of the subject's access to those connections; such externalism is naturally regarded as a third person approach to epistemology.[14] Speakers, in their own contexts for their own purposes, classify others as 'knowing' or as 'not knowing'; why should they defer to those others for the content of their classification?

Such defences of the autonomy of the speaker's context in 'know'-ascriptions are not decisive. After all, a politician might classify the actions available to his more scrupulous opponents as 'right' or 'wrong', merely in order to predict their behaviour; that would not make his context as speaker autonomous in relation to their contexts as agents.[15] However different his interests are from theirs, a sense seems to remain in which whether their potential actions are to be classified as 'right' or 'wrong' is a question for him because it is a question for them (even if they fail to raise it).

The epistemic case may be closer to the practical case than might initially be expected. For if one knows that P, then one can hardly be wrong to believe that P; conversely, given that one does not know that P, it arguably is wrong to believe that P. 'Believe' here is used in the sense of outright belief; assigning a high subjective probability (short of 1) to the proposition that P does not suffice for believing that P. For example, in believing on statistical grounds that my ticket has a chance of 0.9999 of not winning the lottery, and consequently assigning a subjective probability of 0.9999 to the proposition that my ticket will not win, I do not have the outright belief that my ticket will not win, for that would involve outright belief in the crucial premise of an argument for not buying the ticket in the first place (however large the prize). Let us probe the hypothesis that what it is wrong to believe goes with what one fails to know.

---

[14] Classic examples of epistemological externalism include Armstrong (1973), Dretske (1981), Goldman (1986), and Nozick (1981).

[15] For the sake of the example, we may assume that the politician is not using 'It would be wrong for S to do A' as equivalent to 'S would call doing A "wrong" '. No single meta-linguistic reading will make adequate sense of cases in which he must take into account various opponents' evaluations of another's actions. In any case, the meta-linguistic reading involves an extreme lack of autonomy for the speaker's context.

Suppose that the animal in the cage is a cleverly disguised mule, and John is in no position to distinguish his state from one of knowing by sight that it is a zebra. Since it is not a zebra, he does not know that it is a zebra. Is he wrong to believe that it is a zebra? The answer 'No' might be defended on the grounds that John is justified on his evidence in believing that it is a zebra. We may grant straight away that on John's evidence it is highly probable that the animal is a zebra. That is at least some *excuse* for believing it to be a zebra, although by itself it is consistent with knowing that he does not know that it is a zebra (consider the lottery case). A better excuse is that he is not in a position to know that he does not know that it is a zebra. Indeed, on John's evidence, it is highly probable that he knows that it is a zebra. But why regard any of that as more than an excuse? Excuses are offered in mitigation of an offence; they do not make the offending act not wrong. If it had not been wrong, no excuse would have been needed. In particular, if John had known that it was a zebra, he would have needed no excuse for believing that it was a zebra.

To vary the example, suppose that the animal in the cage really is a zebra, although to save money most of the other animals in the zoo have (unbeknownst to John) been replaced by cleverly disguised farm animals; he is again in no position to distinguish his state from one of knowing by sight that it is a zebra. On the usual view, he still does not know that it is a zebra.[16] He has the same excuses as before for believing it to be a zebra. On his evidence, it is highly probable that he knows that the animal is a zebra. Given that he does not in fact know that it is a zebra, he still seems to need some excuse for believing that it is a zebra, in which case it is wrong for him to believe that it is a zebra. That contrasts with knowing that it is a zebra, which is a full justification for believing that it is a zebra, not a mere excuse.[17]

---

[16] The example is of course a variant of Carl Ginet's fake barns, described in Goldman (1976).

[17] For the conception of knowledge as justifying belief see Williamson (2000). On the conception developed there, what justifies belief is the subject's total evidence, which is simply the subject's total knowledge; one's degree of belief in a proposition is ideally its probability conditional on one's total evidence. Thus, if one knows that P, one's degree of belief that P should be 1. However, even if one does not know that P, the probability that P (or even that one knows that P) on one's total evidence may be close to 1, so that one's degree of belief should be close to 1. That is consistent with what is said in the text, for 'degree of belief' here does not mean degree of outright belief; one can have degree of belief 0.5 or 0.9 in a proposition and no outright belief in it whatsoever. To call belief in a proposition that has probability 0.5 on one's evidence 'half-justified' is like calling a glass 'half-full'; to call the belief 'justified' would still be straightforwardly false, just as calling the glass 'full' would be straightforwardly false.

Whether one believes that P naturally has many further implications for what one does with the proposition that P, in particular, for whether one uses it as a premise in practical reasoning. Indirectly, therefore, it has widespread ramifications for what one does.[18]

Imagine a typical scenario for contextualism about 'know'. On the basis of memory, Mary believes truly that she had her purse yesterday morning; background conditions are normal. In an ordinary context, Speaker(low) says 'Mary knows that she had her purse yesterday morning'. Simultaneously, in a seminar on scepticism, Speaker(high) says, of the same person, 'Mary does not know that she had her purse yesterday morning'. The contextualist insists that both speakers speak truly. Suppose that both speakers endorse and apply the argument of the preceding paragraphs, as uttered in their respective contexts. Thus Speaker(low) says 'It is not wrong for Mary to believe that she had her purse yesterday'. Speaker(high) says 'It is wrong for Mary to believe that she had her purse yesterday'. Both speak truly only on a context-ualist account of 'wrong'. The relevant sense of 'wrong' is doubtless not specifically moral. Nevertheless, this contextualist resolution of the apparent disagreement still seems glib and superficial. Since epistemic standards vary so wildly between the ordinary context and the epistemological context, they vary markedly between at least one of those contexts and the agent's context, Mary's context. Yet the primary question seems to be 'Is it wrong for me to believe that I had my purse yesterday?' as uttered by Mary. The epistemic standards relevant to answering that question are those operative in Mary's context. Hence at least one of Speaker(low) and Speaker(high) is judging Mary by inappropriate epistemic standards.

A contextualist about 'know' but not about 'wrong' might accept that diagnosis, and adjust the original line of thought according to those com-

Awkwardly, since a probability distribution can give probability 1 to a false proposition conditional on some true propositions, even a false proposition may have probability 1 on one's evidence, so that belief in it might count as justified to degree 1 without counting as justified. Any other theory of real-valued evidential probability is likely to encounter similar awkwardnesses, which arise mathematically from the slightly coarse-grained nature of real-valued measures on infinite probability spaces, independently of the theorist's epistemological outlook. Discussion with Alexander Bird helped me to clarify my thinking about the relation between knowledge and justification. Sutton (forthcoming) argues in detail that one's belief that P is justified only if one knows that P. Williamson (2000) also sketches an analogy between justified belief and warranted assertion, and argues that one's assertion that P is warranted only if one knows that P.

[18] The connection between being known and being apt for use as a premise in practical reasoning is explored in Hawthorne (2003).

mitments, as follows. If 'I know that P' is true in the context of agent S at time *t*, then it is not wrong for S at *t* to believe that P; if 'I know that P' is false in the context of S at *t*, then it is wrong for S at *t* to believe that P.[19] Thus epistemic standards in the agent's context, not the speaker's, determine what it is wrong for the agent to believe. Suppose, for example, that Mary, like Speaker(low), is in an ordinary context (she might even be Speaker(low)). Thus epistemic standards in Speaker(high)'s context are much higher than in Mary's. Speaker(high) should say 'Although Mary does not know that P, it is not wrong for her to believe that P, because she can truly say "I know that P"'.[20]

From Speaker(high)'s perspective, the context of the epistemology seminar, is Mary's outright belief that P justified or just excused? Her belief is true, but she is ignoring various sceptical possibilities of error. Since they do not obtain, she gets away with it. Pragmatically, her attitude may be the most sensible or only one to take. Taking account in real time of many heterogeneous distant possibilities is computationally infeasible for a human brain. But that sounds like a very good *excuse* for cutting corners. If Mary knew that P, she would not be cutting corners in believing outright that P; no pragmatic excuse would be needed, for she would be justified in a stronger sense. Since Mary does not know that P, it is strictly speaking wrong for her to believe outright that P, because some excuse is needed. But then the attempt to be contextualist about 'know' but not about 'wrong' collapses.

The argument so far has relied on a contested connection between 'know' and justification for belief. However, even without assuming such a connection, we can develop a variant of the anti-contextualist argument. For if contextualism about 'know' is well-motivated, so is contextualism about 'justified'. The contextual shifts in epistemic standards that appear to involve the reference of 'know' appear equally to involve the reference of 'justified'. For example, confronted with a sceptical scenario in which the universe was created an hour ago (with misleading apparent traces of millions of years of past history...), Mary is liable to think 'Oh dear, I was not really justified in taking for granted that the universe has existed for millions of years, so none

---

[19] For simplicity, 'P' is treated as context-invariant.

[20] DeRose (2002) argues for contextualism about 'know' *via* an account that connects the assertibility of 'P' with the truth of 'I know that P' in the context of assertion, although his arguments there do not obviously favour contextualist against the subject-sensitive invariantism suggested by Hawthorne and Stanley (see n. 4). DeRose argues elsewhere (2004) against subject-sensitive invariantism. The arguments of the present chapter could be rephrased in terms of assertibility rather than the justifiability of belief.

of my beliefs which rest on that assumption are justified', just as she is liable to think 'Oh dear, I do not really know that the universe has existed for millions of years'. To give a contextualist explanation of the latter reaction but not of the former would be suspiciously *ad hoc*. But contextualism about 'justified' is open to a more direct form of the objection that it grants inappropriate autonomy to the speaker's context in judging the agent, in setting the standard for when she needs an excuse.

Quite generally, it is plausible that, for some readings of some terms of epistemic evaluation, the appropriate standard will be set by the agent's context, the speaker's context will lack autonomy, and, on those very readings, the sorts of conversational phenomena that are supposed to motivate contextualism will nevertheless occur. In those cases, the real explanation of the phenomena will be non-contextualist. Indeed, just as with disagreements over the application of 'wrong', such an explanation is not far to seek. When standards are low, little is at stake and the sceptic is not bothering us, few possibilities of error are psychologically salient: no wonder that we do not doubt that cases which are or seem similar to socially accepted paradigms of knowledge (perception, memory, testimony, . . .) are indeed cases of knowledge (or whatever privileged status is at issue). When standards are high, much is at stake or the sceptic is bothering us, more possibilities of error are psychologically salient: no wonder that we give the newly salient cases more weight than before in assessing claims to knowledge (or whatever privileged status is at issue). In order to apply terms like 'know', 'justified', and 'wrong', we must often balance conflicting considerations, with no formula to tell us how to assign them comparative weights. It would be astonishing if considerations for or against did not weigh more heavily with us when they are salient than when they are not. Much of the rhetorical work in sceptical arguments goes into making the chosen scenarios of error as vivid and pressing as possible; of course that has an effect on our judgement. On the hypothesis that epistemological contextualism is false, the phenomena that are supposed to support it remain entirely predictable. Why invoke contextualism to explain them?[21]

[21] Discussions with John Hawthorne and Jason Stanley played an important role in developing the ideas in this chapter. Earlier versions of the material were presented in talks at a summer school on epistemology in Paris and at the following universities: Oxford, Queen's University (Ontario), Cornell (with Sydney Shoemaker as respondent), Nebraska (Lincoln), Minnesota, Manchester, East Anglia, Glasgow, York, Padua, and Michigan; I thank the audiences and an anonymous referee for helpful comments.

BIBLIOGRAPHY

Armstrong, D. (1973). *Belief, Truth and Knowledge* (Cambridge: Cambridge University Press).

Cohen, S. (1987). 'Knowledge, Context, and Social Standards', *Synthese*, 73: 3–26.

—— (1988). 'How to be a Fallibilist', *Philosophical Perspectives*, 2: 91–123.

—— (1999). 'Contextualism, Skepticism, and the Structure of Reasons', *Philosophical Perspectives*, 13: 57–89.

—— (2001). 'Contextualism Defended: Comments on Richard Feldman's "Skeptical Problems, Contextualist Solutions" '. *Philosophical Studies*, 103: 87–98.

Craig, E. (1990). *Knowledge and the State of Nature: An Essay in Conceptual Synthesis* (Oxford: Clarendon Press).

DeRose, K. (1992). 'Contextualism and Knowledge Attributions', *Philosophy and Phenomenological Research*, 52: 913–29.

—— (1995). 'Solving the Skeptical Puzzle', *Philosophical Review*, 104: 1–52.

—— (2002). 'Assertion, Knowledge, and Context', *Philosophical Review* 111: 167–203.

—— (2004). 'The Problem with Subject-Sensitive Invariantism', *Philosophy and Phenomenological Research* 68: 346–50.

Dretske, F. (1970). 'Epistemic Operators', *Journal of Philosophy*, 67: 1007–23.

—— (1981). *Knowledge and the Flow of Information* (Cambridge, Mass.: MIT Press).

Feldman, R. (2001). 'Skeptical Problems, Contextualist Solutions', *Philosophical Studies*, 103: 61–85.

Goldman, A. (1976). 'Discrimination and Perceptual Knowledge', *Journal of Philosophy*, 73: 771–91.

—— (1986). *Epistemology and Cognition* (Cambridge, Mass.: Harvard University Press).

Hawthorne, J. (2003). *Knowledge and Lotteries* (Oxford: Oxford University Press).

Hofweber, T. (1999). 'Contextualism and the Meaning-Intention Problem', in K. Korta, E. Sosa, and X. Arrazola (eds.), *Cognition, Agency and Rationality: Proceedings of the Fifth International Colloquium on Cognitive Science* (Dordrecht: Reidel).

Kamp, H. (1981). 'The Paradox of the Heap', in U. Mönnich (ed.), *Aspects of Philosophical Logic* (Dordrecht: Reidel).

Kaplan, D. (1989). 'Demonstratives: An Essay on the Semantics, Logic, Metaphysics, and Epistemology of Demonstratives and Other Indexicals', in J. Almog, J. Perry, and H. Wettstein (eds.), *Themes from Kaplan* (New York: Oxford University Press).

Lewis, D. (1979). 'Scorekeeping in a Language Game', *Journal of Philosophical Logic*, 8: 339–59.

—— (1996). 'Elusive Knowledge', *Australasian Journal of Philosophy*, 74: 549–67.

Nozick, R. (1981). *Philosophical Explanations* (Oxford: Oxford University Press).

Rysiew, P. (2001). 'The Context-Sensitivity of Knowledge Attributions', *Noûs*, 35: 477–514.

Schiffer, S. (1996). 'Contextualist Solutions to Scepticism', *Proceedings of the Aristotelian Society*, 96: 317–33.

Stanley, J. (2003). 'Context, Interest-Relativity and the Sorites', *Analysis*, 63: 269–80.

—— (forthcoming). *Knowledge and Interests* (Oxford: Oxford University Press).

Stine, G. (1976). 'Skepticism, Relevant Alternatives, and Deductive Closure', *Philosophical Studies*, 29: 249–61.

Sutton, J. (forthcoming). 'Stick to What you Know', *Noûs*.

Unger, P. (1986). 'The Cone Model of Knowledge', *Philosophical Topics*, 14: 125–78.

Williamson, T. (2000). *Knowledge and its Limits* (Oxford: Oxford University Press).

—— (2001). 'Comments on Michael Williams' "Contextualism, Externalism and Epistemic Standards" ', *Philosophical Studies*, 103: 25–33.

—— (2005). 'Contextualism, Subject-Sensitive Invariantism and Knowledge of Knowledge', *Philosophical Quarterly*, 55: 213-35.

5

What Shifts? Thresholds, Standards, or Alternatives?

Jonathan Schaffer

1. What Shifts?

Much of the extant discussion of epistemic contextualism focuses on the question of whether contextualism resolves skeptical paradoxes.[1] Understandably. Yet there has been less discussion as to the internal structure of contextualist theories. Regrettably. Here, for instance, are two questions that could stand further discussion: (i) what is the *linguistic basis* for contextualism, and (ii) what is the *parameter that shifts* with context?

The question of linguistic basis can be understood as a request for an explanation of how the truth conditions for knowledge ascriptions are supposed to shift with context. Is there some extra *variable* hidden in the syntax? Is 'knows' to be treated as a semantic *indexical*? Are there general *indices* of semantic evaluation that impact knowledge ascriptions? Or...? (Here the range of options will depend on one's overall view of the levels of linguistic structure—further discussion of this issue is under way in this volume.)

The question of what parameter shifts can be understood as a request for an explanation of which epistemic gear the wheels of context turn. Is there some shifting *threshold* for justification? Is there a shifting *standard* of epistemic

---

[1] Including such foundational presentations of contextualism as Stewart Cohen 1988 and 1999, Keith DeRose 1995, David Lewis 1996, and Mark Heller 1999.

position? Or is there a shifting set of epistemic *alternatives*? Or...? (Here it is not even *prima facie* clear how or whether these options differ, though I will clarify the differences below.)

In what follows, I will focus on the question of what parameter shifts with context. In section 2, I will display four desiderata for an answer to what shifts. In sections 3–5, I will consider thresholds, standards, and alternatives (respectively) in light of these desiderata, and uphold alternatives as the parameter of shift. In section 6, I will cast a parting glance at the linguistic basis for contextualism.

(While the discussion to follow will presuppose that some form of contextualism is true, it may still be of interest to invariantists who want to shunt contextual dependency into the pragmatics. For invariantists also face the question of what shifts with context, in developing their pragmatic account.)

2. Desiderata

What parameter shifts with context? Before considering candidate answers to this question, it will prove useful to display some desiderata for the candidates to meet. I offer four (interrelated) desiderata.

First, the parameter of shift must be *linguistically plausible*. That is, the alleged parameter associated with 'knows' should be a linguistically general parameter, associated with a natural class of expressions of which 'knows' is an instance. In other words, it will not do to invent a special parameter just for 'knows', or to import one from an unrelated class of expressions. Thus:

> D1. What shifts should be a linguistically general parameter, associated with a natural class of expressions of which 'knows' is an instance.

Second, the parameter of shift must be *predictively adequate*. That is, the alleged parameter associated with 'knows' should shift in ways that match intuitions about the acceptability of knowledge ascriptions. In other words, it will not do to associate a parameter whose shifts are triggered by considerations such as whether it is Wednesday, or any considerations different from those that trigger shifts in intuitions about knowledge ascriptions. Thus:

> D2. What shifts should sway with intuitions about the acceptability of knowledge ascriptions.

Third, an answer to what shifts must be *skeptically resolving*. That is, the alleged parameter associated with 'knows' should shift in ways that vindicate contextualist solutions to both moderate and radical skepticism. To do so, it should render most ordinary knowledge ascriptions true in ordinary contexts, some (those associated with the specific doubts in play) false in moderately skeptical contexts, and most (or perhaps all) false in radically skeptical contexts. For instance, in ordinary contexts the following sorts of claims should count as true (the reader should fill in the background details in the obvious ways): (i) 'I know that my car is parked on Elm', and (ii) 'I know that the movie starts at nine'. In a moderately skeptical context in which unresolved doubts have been raised as to whether my car has been stolen and relocated, (i) should count as false, though (ii) should still count as true (no doubts have yet been raised about *that*). Whereas in a radically skeptical context in which unresolved doubts have been raised as to whether one is dreaming, or a brain-in-a-vat, etc., (i) and (ii) should both count as false. Thus:

> D3. What shifts should vindicate contextualist treatments of both moderate and radical skepticism.

Fourth, an answer to what shifts must *illuminate inquiry*. That is, the alleged parameter associated with 'knows' should connect to the practical role that knowledge ascriptions play within the larger project of inquiry. The practical role of knowledge ascriptions is (at least in part) to certify that the subject can answer the question.[2] To connect to this role, the parameter must be capable of scoring the question. For instance, consider the following inquiries: (i) 'Is there a goldfinch in the garden, or a blue jay?', (ii) 'Is there a goldfinch in the garden, or a canary?', and (iii) 'Is there a goldfinch in the garden, or at the neighbor's?' The role of an ascription of 'I know that there is a goldfinch in the garden' differs in the context of (i)–(iii). With (i), such an ascription certifies that the speaker can tell a goldfinch from a blue jay; with (ii), it certifies that the speaker can tell a goldfinch from a canary (a harder task); while with (iii), it certifies

---

[2] Thus Christopher Hookway remarks: "The central focus of epistemic evaluation is ... the activity of inquiry ... When we conduct an inquiry ... we attempt to formulate questions and to answer them correctly." (1996, p. 7) And Hector-Neri Castañeda maintains: "[K]nowledge involves essentially the non-doxastic component of a power to answer a question." (1980, p. 194) Connections between knowledge ascriptions and the ability to answer questions emerge in our practice of testing students and fielding questions. Thus the professor may preface the test with: "Let's see what you know". One may field a question with "I know", or pass it with "Ask Pam, she knows". Such connections emerge most directly with knowledge-*wh* ascriptions. Thus James Higginbotham suggests that the sentence: "Mary knows who John saw" should be interpreted as: "Mary knows the (or an) answer to the question who John saw." (1993, p. 205) For further discussion, see Schaffer *manuscript*.

that the speaker can to tell the garden from the neighbor's (an entirely different task). The parameter of shift should explain how this can happen. Thus:

D4. What shifts should illuminate the role of knowledge ascriptions in our practices of inquiry, by keeping score of the question.

I think (D1)–(D3) should be relatively uncontroversial among contextualists. Perhaps (D4) will be somewhat controversial, if only because the role of knowledge ascriptions in inquiry is not so well explored. But never mind. For I will argue that thresholds and standards parameters fail all of (D1)–(D4), while an alternatives parameter satisfies them all.

3. Thresholds

So what parameter shifts with context? Let me begin by considering one possible answer (suggested by some remarks in Cohen, 1988), according to which what shifts is the *threshold* required for 'justified'. More precisely, for a subject s with a belief p, s is assigned an absolute degree d of justification for p. What shifts is whether d suffices for 'justified'. Thus:

T. What shifts is the threshold of justification sufficient for 'justified'.

Picturesquely, think of degrees of justification as measured on the interval $[0, 1]$, and think of context as selecting a threshold t for 'justified' on this interval. What shifts is whether $d<t$ or $d≥t$. See Figure 5.1. Here s's belief that p counts as 'justified' in context1, 'unjustified' in context2.

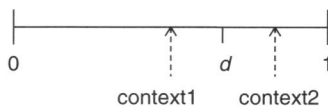

Figure 5.1

(T) derives its plausibility from the following observations: (i) justification is a necessary condition for knowledge, (ii) justification is a *vague* notion (or at least, 'justified' bears all the hallmarks of a vague predicate), and (iii) vague notions generally have contextually variable thresholds. Thus, a given subject s has an absolute degree h of height, an absolute degree w of income, etc. What shifts is whether s's degree of height h suffices for 'tall', whether s's degree of income w suffices for 'rich', etc.[3] So far, so good.

---

[3] This is an oversimplification. For a detailed account see Christopher Kennedy 1999.

But does (T) respect desiderata (D1)–(D4)? I am afraid that the answer is *no* in each case. Starting with (D1), while a linguistically general parameter has been identified, it is *not* a parameter associated with expressions of which 'knows' is an instance. It is rather a parameter associated with *gradable adjectives* like 'tall', 'rich', and 'justified'. And 'knows' is not an adjective, much less a gradable one (Stanley, *forthcoming*).

The fact that a threshold parameter is associated with 'justified' does not help, as that *predicate* does not occur in knowledge ascriptions. Thus the vagueness it bears should not be triggered. Knowledge may well entail justification, but that does not render 'knows' itself vague. After all, possessing precisely zero hairs entails baldness, but that hardly renders 'possesses precisely zero hairs' vague. The mere conceptual entailments of a term play no role here.

Turning to (D2), (T) predicts the wrong shifts. That is, (T) predicts that we would flit from 'knows' to 'does not know' and back, as the bar of justification rises and falls. Think of how we may flit from 'rich' to 'not rich' and back. Here we may invoke *comparison classes* ('he, like all professors, is not rich' and 'he, like all Americans, is rich'), or we may simply *draw the line* ('I mean: at least a millionaire'). But none of this comparing or line drawing seems to trigger any shifts with 'knows'. Instead, what seems to get us to shift from 'knows' to 'does not know' is the invocation of *specific doubts*. And what seems to get us to shift back to 'knows' is forgetting such doubts entirely.[4] The pattern of shift for 'knows' does not match the overall pattern of a shifting threshold.

Moving to (D3), (T) does not fit contextualist solutions to skepticism, for two reasons. First, it is it is unclear why raising skeptical doubts should generate *any shift at all* in the threshold. Why should raising doubts about whether one is a brain-in-a-vat have any impact on the threshold at all, much less drive it to the max? By analogy, it would be as if the mention of a humanly unreachable height (say, 1 mile) would drive the threshold for 'tall' through the roof. *That* would be surprising.

Second, and most crucially, raising doubts would shift the threshold in the wrong way for *moderate skepticism*. When thresholds shift, they do so in ways that *globally infect* other truth-values in that context. For instance, raising the bar of tallness for anyone raises it for everyone. If x does not satisfy 'tall' in

---

[4] As David Lewis 1979 points out, there is an asymmetry between (i) the *ease* by which the skeptic can shift to "does not know", and (ii) the *difficulty* for the dogmatist in shifting back to "knows". Skeptical doubts do not dissipate until the conversation is forgotten.

context c, and y has a height less than or equal to x's, then y cannot satisfy 'tall' in c either.[5]

Yet such global infection does not occur in moderately skeptical scenarios. Here our doubts are *localized*. For instance, if unresolved doubts are raised as to whether one's car has been stolen and relocated, car-location knowledge claims should now count as false, though movie-schedule knowledge claims should still count as true (§2). Conversely, if unresolved doubts are raised as to whether the movie schedule has been misprinted, then car-location knowledge claims should still count as true, though movie-schedule knowledge claims should now count as false. But with thresholds, this localization of doubt cannot happen. These claims will be assigned absolute degrees d_1 and d_2 of justification. If $d_1 = d_2$ (as is roughly plausible), then the threshold cannot be raised past d_1 without passing d_2 as well. Whereas if $d_1 \neq d_2$, then the threshold cannot be raised past whichever is greater without passing the other as well. In general, (T) renders local skeptical scenarios overly global. It means that raising the bar of justification anywhere raises it everywhere.[6]

Shifting finally to (D4), (T) does not keep score of the question, for two reasons. First, it is unclear that there is any relation at all between a line of inquiry and a threshold of justification. Why should the threshold of justification for 'I know that there is a goldfinch in the garden' respond at all to whether the inquiry is between (i) a goldfinch and a blue jay, (ii) a goldfinch and a canary, or (iii) the garden and the neighbor's? There seems to be no connection here.

Second and most crucially, the globality of thresholds would conflate distinct lines of inquiry. For instance, in inquiry (i) it is presupposed that the bird is not a canary, and that it is in the garden; in (ii) it is presupposed that the bird is not a blue jay, and (still) that it is in the garden; while in (iii) it is presupposed that the bird is a goldfinch (*a fortiori* neither a blue jay nor a canary), but no longer presupposed that it is in the garden. But thresholds make no such distinctions. 'Knows' will require some threshold t_1 in (i), t_2 in (ii), and t_3 in (iii). Whichever one or more of the thresholds is highest will simply subsume the others. The use of a thresholds parameter will conflate resolving the inquiry/inquiries associated with the highest threshold(s) with

---

[5] Infection is related to the phenomenon of *penumbral connection*, in which judgments about borderline cases are related. See Kit Fine 1975 for further discussion.

[6] Nor can the contextualist hope that we can shift contexts rapidly enough to get the effects of localized doubts. For it is crucial to the contextualist explanation of why dogmatic claims ring false in skeptical contexts (rather than forcing accommodation so they ring true), that skeptical doubts do not dissipate easily (see footnote 5).

resolving all the other inquiries associated with equal or lesser thresholds, regardless of any differences in presupposition. (T) thus submerges specific differences in what is posed and what is presupposed, under a general bar of justification.

There is an overall moral to be drawn. What shifts with 'knows' needs to be *locally responsive to specific doubts and questions*. Thresholds are too monolithic.

4. Standards

I now turn to a second possible answer (developed by DeRose, 1995, and endorsed by Heller, 1999), according to which what shifts is the *strength of epistemic position* required for knowledge. More precisely, for a subject s with a belief p, s is assigned an absolute strength of position r for p relative to similarity metric m, where r is the maximal radius in logical space as ordered by m through which s can *track* the truth or falsity of p.[7] What shifts is both which similarity metric is in play, and whether r extends far enough for 'knows' on that metric. Thus:

> S. What shifts is the metric of similarity, together with the standard of how far one must track for 'knows'.

Picturesquely, think of logical space as ordered into nested spheres via the similarity metric m, and think of context as both selecting m and selecting a standards radius l out to which one must track to satisfy 'knows'. What shifts is both the metric m, and whether $r < l$ or $r \geq l$ given m. Thus consider a toy model in which s can track the truth at α and $w1$, but not at $w2$. Suppose that context1 sets m to $<\alpha, w1, w2>$ and sets l to 1 (see Figure 5.2). Then s's belief that p counts as 'knowledge' in context1. But suppose that context2, while keeping m at $<\alpha, w1, w2>$, sets l to 2 (see Figure 5.3). Then s's belief that p does not count as 'knowledge' in context2. Or suppose that context3 sets m to $<\alpha, w2, w1>$, while keeping l at 1 (see Figure 5.4). Then s's belief that p does not count as 'knowledge' in context3.

Standards may seem thematically similar to thresholds, if one assumes that s's position r (how far s can track p) is s's degree of justification d. But one

---

[7] The notion of tracking is borrowed from Robert Nozick 1981. The idea is that s tracks p through a sphere of radius r iff, for all worlds within r, s is right about p (that is, if p is true, then s believes it; if p is false, then s disbelieves it).

need not assume this, and should not, at least if one has anything like an *internalist* conception of justification.[8] One should not assume that distance in logical space and degree of justification will generate anything like the same orderings.

In any case, (T) and (S) are formally distinct in the following two ways. First, the degree of justification has an *upper bound* of 1, perhaps enjoyed in cases like the mathematician's belief that $2+2=4$. Whereas the position r presumably has no upper bound. Second, (S) involves an *additional parameter* of contextual variation, namely the similarity metric m.

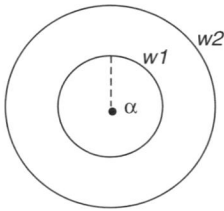

Context1 sets m to $<\alpha, w1, w2>$ and sets l to 1, so s needs to track one sphere out (to $w1$) to count as "knowing" that p.

Figure 5.2

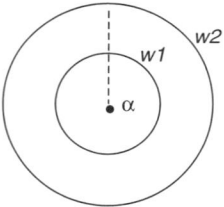

Context2 sets m to $<\alpha, w1, w2>$ and sets l to 2, so s needs to track two spheres out (to $w2$) to count as "knowing" that p.

Figure 5.3

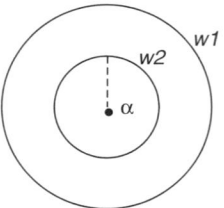

Context3 sets m to $<\alpha, w2, w1>$ and sets l to 1, so s needs to track one sphere out (which is now to $w2$) to count as "knowing" that p.

Figure 5.4

---

[8] By an internalist conception of justification, I mean one according to which a justification must be in principle accessible to s's conscious reflection. For further discussion see Richard Feldman and Earl Conee 1985, and Roderick Chisholm 1988, *inter alia*.

(S) derives its plausibility from the following observations: (i) knowledge entails an ability to track the truth,[9] (ii) how far out into logical space one tracks the truth may vary, such that (iii) there might be a parameter in the language corresponding to such variation. So far, so good. But does (S) respect desiderata (D1)–(D4)? I am afraid the answer is *no* in each case. Starting with (D1), no linguistically *general* parameter has been identified, much less one associated with expressions of which 'knows' is an instance. There seems to be no *precedent* for this form of parameter in the language. It seems a pure invention.

Turning to (D2), (S) predicts the wrong shifts. That is, (S) predicts that we would flit from 'knows' to 'does not know' and back, as the metric m contorts and as the standard l expands and contracts. But think of the sort of maneuvers that are commonly taken to contort the similarity metric, namely the emphasizing of certain *respects of similarity* as salient. That is, if one emphasizes the presence of the atom bomb, one will naturally take the closest world at which Caesar is a general in Korea as a world $w1$ in which Caesar uses the bomb. While if one emphasizes the beliefs of Romans, one will naturally take the closest world at which Caesar is a general in Korea as a world $w2$ in which Caesar uses catapults. But none of this weighing of respects seems to accomplish so much with 'knows'. Instead, what seems to get us to shift between 'knows' and 'does not know' is the invocation and revocation of specific doubts.[10]

Likewise think of the sorts of maneuvers that might expand and contract the standard of epistemic strength. Presumably, if anything can impact the standard, assertions of 'that is enough' and 'that is not enough' should do (though here the lack of a linguistic precedent makes it problematic to guess at which maneuvers would be appropriate). But once again such line drawing does not seem to accomplish much with 'knows'. Again, what does the work are specific doubts.

---

[9] Of course the tracking view of knowledge is highly contentious. Advocates of standards such as DeRose speak of tracking as being "at least roughly correct." (1995, p. 25) For present purposes I will not contest this. I should also add that (S) may help add to the plausibility of the tracking view, by reconciling it with closure principles (DeRose 1995).

[10] How would 'knows' behave, if it were sensitive to shifting respects of similarity? One would expect that, in contexts where one sufficiently emphasizes s's visual evidence, the nearest world in which s does not have hands would be one in which that evidence was held fixed but the reality behind the appearances shifted. That is, one would expect that emphasizing evidence should induce skepticism!

Moving to (D3), (S) does not fit contextualist solutions to skepticism, for two reasons. First, it is it is unclear why raising skeptical doubts should generate *any shift at all* in the standards. Why should raising doubts about whether one is a brain-in-a-vat have any impact on the standards at all, much less drive them so far into logical space?[11]

Second and most crucially, raising doubts would shift the standards in the wrong way for *moderate skepticism*. When standards shift, they do so in ways that *globally infect* other truth-values in that context. Thus suppose again that unresolved doubts are raised as to whether one knows where one is parked. By (S), what must have happened is that the standard l has been set to include a relatively wide sphere of worlds (given metric m), such that worlds at which s cannot track p (e.g., car theft worlds) are included. But now, assuming that movie schedule misprint worlds are at least as near as car theft worlds on m (an eminently reasonable assumption), it will follow that 'You know that the movie starts at nine' counts as false. And assuming that street sign prank worlds are at least as near as car theft worlds on m, it will follow that 'You know that you are now walking on Main' counts as false, etc. Yet that seems wrong—no *specific doubts* have been raised with respect to these claims. The movie schedule misprint and street sign prank scenarios should not count as relevant, where they have not been raised. Spheres encompass too much.

Shifting finally to (D4), (S) does not keep score of the question. The globality of standards would conflate distinct lines of inquiry. Thus compare again the inquiries into whether (i) there is a goldfinch in the garden or a blue jay, (ii) there is a goldfinch in the garden or a canary, and (iii) there is a goldfinch in the garden or at the neighbor's. Whichever scenario (blue jay, canary, neighbor's) is most distant will subsume the others. The use of a standards parameter will conflate resolving the inquiries associated with the most distant scenario(s) with resolving all the other inquiries associated with equal or nearer scenarios, regardless of any differences in presupposition. (S) thus submerges specific differences in what is posed and what is presupposed, under a general sphere.

Spheres simply are *too topologically limited* to keep score of questions. One might ask whether there is a goldfinch in the garden, or a fiendishly designed robot bird. Or one might ask whether one has hands, the claws of a great

---

[11] DeRose (1995, §12) says that one must track to the nearest $-p$ world, and farther to any contextually salient world (his *rule of sensitivity*). This does connect the raising of skeptical doubts with the expansion of the standards. But, as far as I can see, it is invented purely for such purposes, and has no independent support or precedent. It is just a stipulation.

horned owl, the tentacles of an octopus, or the pincers of a crab. Such questions do not describe a sphere. On any reasonable setting of the similarity metric m, such questions denote discrete cells in logical space, with the clumpy topology of cottage cheese (see Figure 5.5). In general, there is nothing in the nature of a question that forces (or even favors) spheres. Thus (S) imposes a topology far too restrictive for inquiry.

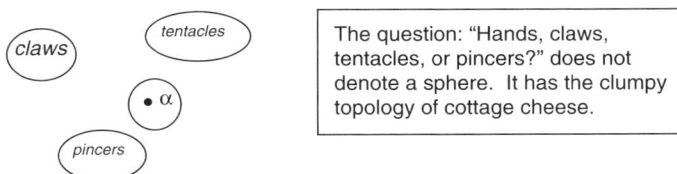

Figure 5.5

The same moral emerges with standards as with thresholds. What shifts with 'knows' needs to be *locally responsive to specific doubts and questions*. Standards are too monolithic.

5. Alternatives

I now turn to a third possible answer (rooted in relevant alternative views such as Austin (1946) and Dretske (1981), endorsed by Lewis (1996)), according to which what shifts is the set of *epistemic alternatives* in play. More precisely, for a subject s with a belief p, s is assigned an absolute eliminatory power e for p, where e is the set of possibilities that s can *eliminate*.[12] What shifts is whether e covers enough alternatives for 'knows'. The way this shifts is that there is a set of relevant alternatives Q, and 'knows' requires that all relevant possibilities be eliminated (e must cover Q). Thus:

A. What shifts is the range of alternatives s must eliminate.

Picturesquely, think of s's eliminatory power e for p as some region of arbitrary topology in logical space, and think of the relevant alternatives q as some other region also of arbitrary topology. What shifts is whether e covers Q. Thus picture the p-worlds as some box containing actuality, and picture the alternatives as the surrounding boxes, with s's eliminatory power e

---

[12] The notion of elimination is found in Dretske 1981 and Lewis 1996, *inter alia*. According to Lewis 1996, a possibility w is eliminated for s iff s's experience in w would differ from actuality. Though other definitions of elimination are, of course, possible.

for p as the shaded boxes (see Figure 5.6). Now suppose that context1 selects only shaded worlds as relevant alternatives. Then s's belief that p counts as 'knowledge' in context1. But suppose that context2 selects only unshaded worlds, and that context3 selects a mixture. Then s's belief that p does not count as 'knowledge' in context2 or context3. So far, so good.

But does (A) respect desiderata (D1)–(D4)? I believe that the answer is *yes* in each case. Or at least, I believe that the answer is *better than (T) or (S)* in each case.

Starting with (D1), there are precedents for semantic sensitivity to alternatives, such as with the *modal auxiliaries* (e.g. 'can' and 'must'). Claims like 'wood must burn' and 'I can run a four minute mile' have context-variable truth conditions, depending on which worlds count as *accessible*. 'Wood must burn' is true iff in every accessible possible world, wood burns. Whether this is true depends on whether worlds with different laws of nature are relevant. 'I can run a four minute mile' is true iff in some accessible world, I run a four minute mile. Whether this is true depends on whether worlds in which I am a (vastly) better athlete are relevant.[13]

The modal locutions are a decent precedent for the contextual variability of 'knows', given that 'knows' denotes *epistemic necessity*: K is box.[14] Hence it would be unsurprising if K can shift truth value depending on which alternatives are in play. Box always does. Thus (A) provides a linguistically general parameter, associated with a natural class of expressions of which 'knows' is an instance: the propositional attitude verbs, which model as modalities.

Perhaps an even better precedent is the verb 'regrets'. It is very plausible that the truth condition for regret ascriptions shift with the implicit alterna-

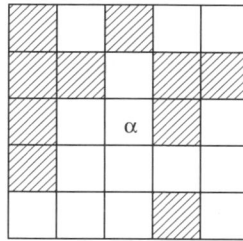

Figure 5.6

[13] See, for instance, Angelika Kratzer 1977 and 1991 for further discussion of modals.

[14] Or at least, in virtually every epistemic logic, K is treated as box. For some developments of this idea, see Jaakko Hintikka 1962 and G. E. Hughes and M. J. Cresswell 1996.

tives. For instance, 'I regret that Bush is president' is true when the relevant alternative is that Gore is president, but false when the relevant alternative is that Cheney is president. Whether 'I regret that Bush is president' is true seems to depend on who the alternative is.

The verb 'regrets' is an ideal precedent for 'knows', since both are members of the following lexical kind: *factive attitude verbs that permit either declarative (that-clause) or interrogative (wh-clause) complements.* (This kind also includes 'forgets', 'learns', and 'discovers', *inter alia*.) Indeed, given that 'regrets' is semantically alternatives-variable, the default hypothesis ought to be that 'knows' is too.

Turning to (D2), as mentioned above, what seems to get us to shift between 'knows' and 'does not know' is the invocation and revocation of specific doubts. If the invocation and revocation of specific doubts is understood in terms of the relevance and irrelevance of specific alternatives, then all works. Think of how we may shift from 'must' to 'might not' and back. Or from 'regrets' to 'does not regret' and back. Here we invoke and revoke specific scenarios. (That said, further investigation is called for as to how closely shifts with modal auxiliaries and shifts with knowledge ascriptions parallel. (A) predicts a perfect parallel, once other factors are controlled for.)

Moving to (D3), what is needed is an explanation for why radical skeptical scenarios generate global doubts, while moderate skeptical scenarios generate local doubts. To begin with, (A) explains why raising skeptical doubts should expand the alternatives. And (A) explains why radical doubts, such as whether one is a brain-in-a-vat, induce global skepticism. For the brain-in-a-vat hypothesis (or some suitable subcase of it) is an alternative to virtually every contingent proposition about the external world. And (A) explains why moderate doubts, such as whether one's car has been stolen and re-located, only induce local skepticism. For the car theft hypothesis (or some suitable subcase of it) is an alternative to the proposition that my car is parked on Elm. But it is not an alternative to the proposition that the movie starts at nine, or that I am now walking on Main, etc.

(T) and (S) had trouble with the local doubts of moderate skepticism, because thresholds *draw lines* and standards *draw spheres*, both of which are globally encompassing. (A) fares better because alternatives themselves are *pointlike* in logical space. That w is an alternative has no implications for whether other scenarios (be they associated with comparable degrees, or ringed around the same logical spheres, or whatnot) are relevant. Alternatives are not monolithic.

Shifting finally to (D4), what is needed is a parameter capable of illuminating inquiry by scoring the question. Alternatives work perfectly, because alternatives are exactly what questions denote. All well-formed questions are multiple-choice questions. As James Higginbotham writes, 'An *abstract question* [is] a nonempty *partition* Π of the possible states of nature into *cells*' (1993: 196) These cells are the semantic image of a (possibly infinite) *multiple-choice slate*.[15]

(T) and (S) had trouble with responding to specific questions, and distinguishing what is posed and what is presupposed. (A) fares better because alternatives can describe arbitrary topologies. Thus the question: 'Hands, claws, tentacles, or pincers?' denotes discrete cells in logical space with the topology of cottage cheese. It corresponds to the set of alternatives: {hands, claws, tentacles, pincers}. Thus the inquiries concerning the goldfinch in the garden pose different alternatives: {goldfinch in the garden, blue jay in the garden}, {goldfinch in the garden, canary in the garden}, {goldfinch in the garden, goldfinch at the neighbor's}. And they differ in presupposition, where what is presupposed is simply the union of what is posed.[16] What emerges is that only (A) has the flexibility to handle the full range of questions.

I conclude that what shifts with context are the epistemic alternatives. The epistemic gear that the wheels of context turn is the set of relevant alternatives. Or at least, as between thresholds, standards, and alternatives, with respect to the desiderata (D1)–(D4), alternatives are the runaway winner.

6. The Linguistic Basis

What constraints does a parameter of alternatives impose on the linguistic basis for contextualism? I have argued (§5) that an alternatives parameter is linguistically plausible, in so far as it fits the precedents of modal locutions, and of 'regrets'. Thus, the question of the linguistic basis for contextualism becomes the question of the linguistic basis for the accessibility relation for modals, and the alternatives-variability of 'regrets'.

---

[15] The association of questions with multiple-choice slates is known as *Hamblin's dictum* (C. I. Hamblin 1958), and is implemented in Nuel Belnap and Thomas Steel's (1976) erotetic logic, and maintained in the leading linguistic treatments of interrogatives, such as Jeroen Groenendijk and Martijn Stokhof 1997.

[16] Question Q presupposes proposition p iff p is entailed by all answers to Q (Belnap and Steel 1976). Picturesquely, what is entailed by all the cells is that the truth lies in those cells and not outside them.

Here I leave open whether the accessibility relation for modals, and the alternatives parameter for 'regrets', should be understood in terms of hidden syntactic variables, semantic indexicals, general indices of semantic evaluation, or whatnot. Though with precedents in hand, the way to approach the issue becomes clear: just figure out how things work in those cases.[17]

And with precedents in hand, the worry that there might be *no* linguistic basis for contextualism dissolves. Those who argue that contextualism is linguistically baseless must either (i) argue that 'regrets' is not semantically alternatives-variable, despite appearances; or (ii) maintain that 'regrets' is not fit precedent for 'knows', despite their kinship; or (iii) concede a precedent for a form of contextualism, in which what shifts are the alternatives.

REFERENCES

Austin, J. L. (1946). 'Other Minds', *Proceedings of the Aristotelian Society*, 20 (supp.): 149–87.

Bach, Kent (*forthcoming*). 'Context *ex Machina*', in Z. Szabo (ed.), *Semantics vs Pragmatics* (Oxford: Oxford University Press).

Belnap, Nuel, and Thomas Steel (1976). *The Logic of Questions and Answers* (New Haven: Yale University Press).

Castañeda, Hector-Neri (1980). 'The Theory of Questions, Epistemic Powers, and the Indexical Theory of Knowledge', in P. French, T. Uehling, Jr., and H. Wettstein (eds.), *Midwest Studies in Philosophy, v. Studies in Epistemology* (Minneapolis: University of Minnesota Press), 193–238.

Chisholm, Roderick (1988). 'The Indispensability of Internal Justification', *Synthese*, 74: 285–96.

Cohen, Stewart (1988). 'How to be a Fallibilist', *Philosophical Perspectives*, 2: 91–123.

—— (1999). 'Contextualism, Skepticism, and the Structure of Reasons', *Philosophical Perspectives*, 13: 57–89.

DeRose, Keith (1995). 'Solving the Skeptical Problem', *Philosophical Review*, 104: 1–52.

Dretske, Fred (1981). 'The Pragmatic Dimension of Knowledge', *Philosophical Studies*, 40: 363–78.

---

[17] See Schaffer 2004 and *forthcoming* for some further discussion. See Bach *forthcoming* for further options, including the option that what is said may be *incomplete*, in underdetermining which proposition the speaker is expressing. On this option, knowledge ascriptions may underdetermine the value of the alternatives variable Q. But knowledge propositions would invariably have the ternary, relational form: s knows that p relative to Q.

Feldman, Richard, and Earl Conee (1985). 'Evidentialism', *Philosophical Studies*, 48: 15–34.

Fine, Kit (1975). 'Vagueness, Truth, and Logic', *Synthese*, 30: 265–300.

Groenendijk, Jeroen, and Martijn Stokhof (1997). 'Questions', in Johan van Benthem and Alice ter Meulen (eds.), *Handbook of Logic and Language* (Amsterdam: Elsevier Science Publishers), 1055–1124.

Hamblin, C. L. (1958). 'Questions', *Australasian Journal of Philosophy*, 36: 159–68.

Heller, Mark (1999). 'Contextualism and Anti-Luck Epistemology', *Philosophical Perspectives*, 13: 115–29.

Higginbotham, James (1993). 'Interrogatives', in Kenneth Hale and Samuel Jay Keyser (eds.), *The View from Building 20: Essays in Honor of Sylvain Bromberger* (Cambridge, Mass.: MIT Press), 195–228.

Hintikka, Jaakko (1962). *Knowledge and Belief* (Ithaca, NY: Cornell University Press).

Hookway, Christopher (1996). 'Questions of Context', *Proceedings of the Aristotelian Society*, 96: 1–16.

Hughes, G. E., and M. J. Cresswell (1996). *A New Introduction to Modal Logic* (London: Routledge).

Kennedy, Christopher (1999). *Projecting the Adjective: The Syntax and Semantics of Gradability and Comparison* (New York: Garland).

Kratzer, Angelika (1977). 'What "Must" and "Can" Must and Can Mean', *Linguistics and Philosophy*, 1: 337–55.

—— (1991). 'Modality', in A. Von Stechow and D. Wunderlich (eds.) *Semantics: An International Handbook of Contemporary Research* (Berlin: de Gruyter), 639–50.

Lewis, David (1979). 'Scorekeeping in a Language Game', *Journal of Philosophical Logic*, 8: 339–59.

—— (1996). 'Elusive Knowledge', *Australasian Journal of Philosophy*, 74: 549–67.

Nozick, Robert (1981). *Philosophical Explanations* (Cambridge, Mass.: Harvard University Press).

Schaffer, Jonathan (2004). 'From Contextualism to Contrastivism', *Philosophical Studies*, 119: 73–103.

—— (*forthcoming*). 'Contrastive Knowledge', T. Grendler and J. Hawthorne (eds.), *Oxford Studies in Epistemology*, i.

Stanley, Jason (2004). 'On the Linguistic Basis for Contextualism', *Philosophical Studies*, 119: 119–46.

6

Epistemic Modals in Context

ANDY EGAN, JOHN HAWTHORNE, AND BRIAN
WEATHERSON

In the 1970s David Lewis argued for a contextualist treatment of modals
(Lewis, 1976, 1979*a*). Although Lewis was primarily interested in modals
connected with freedom and metaphysical possibility, his arguments for
contextualism could easily be taken to support contextualism about epistemic
modals. In the 1990s Keith DeRose argued for just that position (DeRose,
1991, 1998).

In all contextualist treatments, the method by which the contextual variables get their values is not completely specified. For contextualist treatments
of metaphysical modality, the important value is the class of salient worlds.
For contextualist treatments of epistemic modality, the important value is
which epistemic agents are salient. In this chapter, we start by investigating
how these values might be generated, and conclude that it is hard to come up
with a plausible story about how they are generated. There are too many
puzzle cases for a simple contextualist theory to be true, and a complicated
contextualist story is apt to be implausibly *ad hoc*.

We then look at what happens if we replace contextualism with relativism. On contextualist theories the truth of an utterance type is relative to
the context in which it is tokened. On relativist theories, the truth of
an utterance token is relative to the context in which it is evaluated. Many
of the puzzles for contextualism turn out to have natural, even elegant,
solutions given relativism. We conclude by comparing two versions of
relativism.

We begin with a puzzle about the role of epistemic modals in speech
reports.

A Puzzle

The celebrity reporter looked discomforted, perhaps because there were so few celebrities in Cleveland.

'Myles', asked the anchor, 'where are all the celebrities? Where is Professor Granger?'

'We don't know,' replied Myles. 'She might be in Prague. She was planning to travel there, and no one here knows whether she ended up there or whether she changed her plans at the last minute.'

This amused Professor Granger, who always enjoyed seeing how badly wrong CNN reporters could be about her location. She wasn't sure exactly where in the South Pacific she was, but she was certain it wasn't Prague. On the other hand, it wasn't clear what Myles had gotten wrong. His first and third sentences surely seemed true: after all, he and the others certainly *didn't* know where Professor Granger was, and she *had* been planning to travel to Prague before quietly changing her destination to Bora Bora.

The sentence causing all the trouble seemed to be the second: 'She might be in Prague.' As she wiggled her toes in the warm sand and listened to the gentle rustling of the palm fronds in the salty breeze, at least one thing seemed clear: she definitely wasn't in Prague—so how could it be true that she might be? But the more she thought about it, the less certain she became. She mused as follows: when I say something like *x might be F*, I normally regard myself to be speaking truly if neither I nor any of my mates know that x is not *F*. And it's hard to believe that what goes for me does not go for this CNN reporter. I might be special in many ways, but I'm not semantically special. So it looks like Myles can truly say that I might be in Prague just in case neither *he* nor any of *his* mates knows that I am not. And I'm sure none of them knows that, because I've taken great pains to make them think that I am, in fact, in Prague—and reporters always fall for such deceptions.

But something about this reasoning rather confused Professor Granger, for she was sure Myles had gotten something *wrong*. No matter how nice that theoretical reasoning looked, the fact was that she definitely wasn't in Prague, and he said that she might be. Trying to put her finger on just where the mistake was, she ran through the following little argument.

(1) When he says, 'She might be in Prague' Myles says that I might be in Prague.

(2) When he says, 'She might be in Prague' Myles speaks truly iff neither he nor any of his mates know that I'm not in Prague.

(3) Neither Myles nor any of his mates know that I'm not in Prague.

(4) If Myles speaks truly when he says that I might be in Prague, then I might be in Prague.

(5) I know I'm not in Prague.

(6) It's not the case that I know I'm not in Prague if I might be in Prague.

There must be a problem here somewhere, she thought, for (1)–(6) are jointly inconsistent. (Quick proof: (2) and (3) entail that Myles speaks truly when he says, 'She might be in Prague'. From that and (1) it follows he speaks truly when he says Professor Granger might be in Prague. From that and (4) it follows that Professor Granger might be in Prague. And that combined with (5) is obviously inconsistent with (6).) But wherein lies the fault? Unless some fairly radical kind of scepticism is true, Professor Granger can know by observing her South Pacific idyll that she's not in Prague—so (5) looks secure. And it seems pretty clear that neither Myles nor any of his mates know that she's not in Prague, since they all have very good reason to think that she is— so it looks like (3) is also OK. But the other four premises are all up for grabs.

Which exactly is the culprit is a difficult matter to settle. While the semantic theory underlying the reasoning in (1)–(6) is mistaken in its details, something like it is very plausible. The modal 'might' here is, most theorists agree, an *epistemic* modal. So its truth-value should depend on what someone knows. But who is this *someone*? If it is Myles, or the people around him, then the statement "she might be in Prague" is true, and it is unclear where to block the paradox. If it is Professor Granger, or the people around her, then the statement is false, but now it is unclear why a competent speaker would ever use this kind of epistemic modal. Assuming the *someone* is Professor Granger, and assuming Professor Granger knows where she is, then 'Granger might be in Prague' will be true iff 'Granger is in Prague' is true. But this seems to be a mistake. Saying 'Granger *might* be in Prague' is a way to weaken one's commitments, which it could not be if the two sentences have the same truth conditions under plausible assumptions. So neither option looks particularly promising.

To make the problem even more pressing, consider what happens if a friend of Professor Granger's who knows she is in the South Pacific overhears Myles's comment. Call this third party Charles. It is *prima facie* very implausible that when Myles says that Professor Granger might be in Prague he means to rule out that *Charles* knows that she is not. After all, Charles is not part of the conversation, and Myles need not even know that he exists. So if Myles knows what he is saying, what he is saying could be true even if Charles knows Professor Granger is not in Prague. But if Charles knows this, Charles cannot regard Myles's statement as true, else he will conclude that Professor Granger might be in Prague, and he knows she is not. So things are very complicated indeed.

In reasoning as we have been, we have been assuming that the following inferences are valid.

> (7) A competent English speaker says *It might be that S*

and

> (8) *S*, on that occasion of use, means that *p*

entail

> (9) That speaker says that it might be that *p*

Further, (9) plus

> (10) That speaker speaks truly

entail

> (11) It might be that *p*

If Charles accepts the validity of both of these inferences, then he is under considerable pressure to deny that Myles speaks truly. And it would be quite natural for him to do so—for instance, by interrupting Myles to say that 'That's wrong. Granger couldn't be in Prague, since she left on the midnight flight to Tahiti.' But it's very hard to find a plausible semantic theory that backs up this intervention, although such reactions are extremely common. (To solidify intuitions, here is another example: I overhear you say that a certain horse might have won a particular race. I happen to know that the horse is lame. I think: you are wrong to think that it might have won.)

Our solutions to this puzzle consist in proposed semantic theories for epistemic modals. We start with contextualist solutions, look briefly at invariantist solutions, and conclude with relativist solutions. Although we will look primarily at the costs and benefits of these theories with respect to intuitions about epistemic modals, it is worth remembering that they differ radically in their presuppositions about what kind of theory a semantic theory should be. Solving the puzzles to do with epistemic modals may require settling some of the deepest issues in philosophy of language.

Contextualist Solutions

Keith DeRose offers the following proposal (1991: 593–4):

S's assertion 'It is possible that P' is true if and only if (1) no member of the relevant community knows that P is false, and (2) there is no relevant way by which members of the relevant community can come to know that P is false.

DeRose intends 'possible' here to be an epistemic modal, and the proposal is meant to cover all epistemic modals, including those using 'might'. We will not discuss here the issues that arise under clause (2) of DeRose's account, since we'll have quite enough to consider just looking at whether clause (1) or anything like it is correct.

In our discussion below, we consider three promising versions of contextualist theory. What makes the theories contextualist is that they all say that Myles spoke truly when he said 'She might be in Prague', but hold that if Professor Granger had repeated his words she would have said something false. And the reason for the variation in truth-value is just that Myles and Professor Granger are in different contexts, which supply different relevant communities. Where the three theories differ is in which constraints they place on how context can supply the community in question.

The first is the kind of theory that DeRose originally proposed. On this theory, there is a side constraint that the relevant community always includes the speaker: whenever S truly utters *a might be F*, S does not know that *a* is not *F*. We'll call this *the speaker-inclusion constraint*, or sometimes just *speaker-inclusion*. There is some quite compelling evidence for speaker-inclusion. Consider, for example, the following sort of case. Whenever Jack eats pepperoni pizza, he forgets that he has ten fingers, and thinks 'I might only have eight fingers.' Jill (who knows full well that Jack has *ten* fingers) spots Jack sitting all alone finishing off a pepperoni pizza, and says, 'He might have eight fingers.' Jill has said something false. And what she's said is false because it's not compatible with what *she* knows that Jack has eight fingers. But if the relevant community could ever exclude the speaker, one would think it could do so here. After all, Jack is clearly contextually salient: he's the referent of 'he', the fingers in question are on his hand, and no one else is around. Now, a single case does not prove a universal—but the case does seem to provide good *prima-facie* evidence for DeRose's constraint.

One implication of DeRose's theory is that (1) is false, at least when Professor Granger says it. For when Professor Granger reports that Myles says 'She might be in Prague', she is reporting a claim he makes about his epistemic community—that her being in Prague is compatible with the things that they know. But when she says (in the second clause) that this means he is saying that she might be in Prague, she speaks falsely. For in her mouth the phrase 'that I might be in Prague' denotes the proposition that it's compatible with the knowledge of an epistemic community that includes Professor Granger (as the speaker) that Professor Granger is in Prague. And that is not a proposition that Myles assented to. So DeRose's theory implies that the very intuitive (1) is false when uttered by Granger.

> (1) When he says, 'She might be in Prague' Myles says that I might be in Prague.

It is worth emphasizing how counterintuitive this consequence of speaker-inclusion is. If the speaker-inclusion constraint holds universally then, in general, speech involving epistemic modals cannot be reported disquotation-ally. But notice how natural it is, when telling the story of Jack and Jill, to describe the situation (as we ourselves did in an earlier draft of this chapter) as being one where 'Whenever Jack eats pepperoni pizza, he forgets that he has ten fingers, and thinks he might only have eight.' Indeed, it is an important generalization about how we use language that speakers usually do not hesitate to disquote in reporting speeches using epistemic modals. So much so that exceptions to this general principle are striking—as when the tenses of the original speech and the report do not match up, and the tense difference matters to the plausibility of the attribution.

One might try to explain away the data just presented by maintaining a laxity for 'says that' reports. A chemist might say 'The bottle is empty' meaning it is empty of air, while a milkman might utter the same sentence, meaning in my context that it is empty of milk. Nevertheless, the milkman might be slightly ambivalent about denying:

> When the chemist says 'The bottle is empty', she says that the bottle is empty.

And this is no doubt because the overt 'says that' construction frequently deploys adjectives and verbs in a rather quotational way. After all, the chemist could get away with the following speech in ordinary discourse: 'I know the milkman said that the bottle is empty. But he didn't mean what I meant when I said that the bottle is empty. When he said that the bottle was empty he meant that it was empty of milk.' Thus the conventions of philosophers for using 'say that' involve regimenting ordinary use in a certain direction. But the disquotational facts that we are interested in cannot be explained away simply by invoking these peculiarities of 'says that' constructions, for the same disquotational ease surrounds the relevant belief reports. In the case just considered, while we might argue about whether it was acceptable for the chemist to say, in her conversational context, 'The milkman said that the bottle was empty', it is manifestly unacceptable for her to say 'The milkman believes that the bottle is empty'. This contrasts with the case of 'might'. If someone asked Professor Granger where Myles thought she was, she could quite properly have replied with (12).

(12) He thinks that/believes that I might be in Prague.

Indeed, we in general tend find the following inference pattern—a belief-theoretic version of (7) to (9) above—compelling: (i) A competent English speaker sincerely asserts *It might be that S*. (ii) S, in that context of use, means that *p*. Therefore, that speaker believes that it might be that *p*. Our puzzle cannot, then, be traced simply to a laxity in the 'says that' construction. Whatever the puzzle comes to, it certainly runs deeper than that.

Notice that (12) does not suggest that Myles thinks that for all Professor Granger knows, she is in Prague; it expresses the thought that Myles thinks that for all he knows, that is where she is. Moreover, this is hardly a case where Granger's utterance is of doubtful appropriateness: (12) is one of the ways canonically available for Granger to express that thought. But if we assume that what is reported in a belief report of this kind is belief in the proposition the reporter expresses by *I might be in Prague*, and we assume a broad-reaching speaker-inclusion constraint, we must concede that the proposition Granger expresses by uttering (12) is that Myles believes that, for all *Professor Granger* knows, Professor Granger is in Prague.

If the speaker-inclusion constraint holds universally, then anyone making such a report is wrong. There are two ways for this to happen—either they know what the sentences they're using to make the attributions mean, and they have radically false views about what other people believe, or they have non-crazy views about what people believe, but they're wrong about the meanings of the sentences they're using. The first option is incredibly im-plausible. So our first contextualist theory needs to postulate a widespread semantic blindness; in general speakers making reports are mistaken about the semantics of their own language. In particular, it requires that such speakers are often blind to semantic differences between sentence tokens involving epistemic modals. It is possible that some theories that require semantic blindness are true, but other things being equal we would prefer theories that do not assume this. In general the burden of proof is on those who think that the folk don't know the meaning of their own words. More carefully: the burden of proof is on those who think that the folk are severely handicapped in their ability to discriminate semantic sameness and difference in their home language.

So the plausibility of (1) counts as evidence against the first contextualist theory, and provides a suggestion for our second contextualist theory. The cases that provide the best intuitive support for the speaker-inclusion constraint and the case we used above involved unembedded epistemic modals. Perhaps this constraint is true for epistemic modals in simple sentences, but not for epistemic modals in 'that' clauses. Perhaps, that is, when S sincerely asserts *X Vs that a might be F,* she believes that X Vs that for all X (and her community) knows, *a* is *F.* (This is not meant as an account of the logical form of *X Vs that a might be F,* just an account of its truth conditions. We defer consideration of what hypothesis, if any, about the underlying syntax could generate those truth conditions.) To motivate this hypothesis, note how we introduced poor Jack, above. We said that he thinks he might have eight fingers. We certainly didn't mean by that that Jack thinks something about *our* epistemic state.

The other problem with the speaker-inclusion constraint is that it does not seem to hold when epistemic modals are bound by temporal modifiers, as in the following example. A military instructor is telling his troops about how to prepare for jungle warfare. He says, 'Before you walk into an area where there are lots of high trees, if there might be snipers hiding in the branches, clear away the foliage with flamethrowers.' Whatever the military and environmental merits of this tactic, the suggestion is clear. The military instructor is giving generic conditional advice: in any situation of type *S,* if *C* then do *A.* The situation *S* is easy to understand, it is when the troops are advancing into areas where there are high trees. And *A,* too, is clear: blaze 'em. But what about *C*? What does it mean to say that there might be snipers in the high branches? Surely not that it's compatible with the military instructor's knowledge that there are snipers in the high branches—he's sitting happily in West Point, watching boats sail lazily along the Hudson. What *he* thinks about where the snipers are is neither here nor there. Intuitively, what he meant was that the troops should use flamethrowers if *they* don't know whether there are snipers in the high branches. (Or if they know that there *are.*) So as well as leading to implausible claims about speech reports, the speaker-inclusion constraint seems clearly false when we consider temporal modifiers.

Here is a way to deal with both problems at once. There are constraints on the application of the speaker-inclusion constraint. It does not apply when the epistemic modal is in the scope of a temporal modifier (as the flame-thrower example shows) and it does not apply when the epistemic modal is in a 'that' clause. Our second contextualist theory then accepts the speaker-inclusion constraint, but puts constraints on its application.

This kind of theory, with a speaker-inclusion constraint only applying to relatively simple epistemic modals, allows us to accept (1). The problematic claim on this theory turns out to be (4):

(4) If Myles speaks truly when he says that I might be in Prague, then I might be in Prague.

When Myles said that Professor Granger might be in Prague, he was speaking truly. That utterance expressed a true proposition. So the antecedent of (4) is true. But the consequent is false: the 'might' that appears there is not in a that-clause or in the scope of a temporal modifier; so the speaker-inclusion constraint requires that Professor Granger be included in the relevant community; and since she knows that she is not in Prague, it's not true that she might be. We would similarly have to reject

(4'): If Myles has a true belief that I might be in Prague, then I might be in Prague.

But there are reasons to be worried about this version of contextualism, beyond the uneasiness that attaches to denying (4) (and, worse still, 4'). For one, this particular version of the speaker-inclusion constraint seems a bit *ad hoc*: why should there be just *these* restrictions on the relevant community? More importantly, the theory indicts certain inferential patterns that are intuitively valid. Suppose a bystander in our original example reasoned:

(13) [Myles] believes that it might be that [Professor Granger is in Prague].
(14) [Myles]'s belief is true

Therefore, (15) It might be that [Professor Granger is in Prague].

But this version of contextualism tells us that, while (13) and (14) are true, (15) is false. In general, there are going to be counter-intuitive results whenever we reason from cases where the speaker-inclusion constraint does not apply to cases where it does.

Finally, the theory is unable to deal with certain sorts of puzzle cases. The first kind of case directly challenges the speaker-inclusion constraint for simple sentences, although we are a little sceptical about how much such a case shows. Tom is stuck in a maze. Sally knows the way out, and knows she knows this, but doesn't want to tell Tom. Tom asks whether the exit is to the left. Sally says, 'It might be. It might not be.' Sally might be being unhelpful here, but it isn't clear that she is *lying*. Yet if the speaker-inclusion constraint applies to unembedded epistemic modals, then Sally is clearly saying something that she knows to be false, for she knows that she knows which way is out.

This case is not altogether convincing, for there is something slightly awkward about Sally's speech here. For example, if Sally knows the exit is not to the left, then even if she is prepared to utter, 'It might be [to the left]', she will not normally self-ascribe knowledge that it might be to the left. And normally speakers don't sincerely assert things they don't take themselves to know. So it is natural to suppose that a kind of pretense or projection is going on in Sally's speech that may well place it beyond the purview of the core semantic theory.

The following case makes more trouble for our second contextualist theory, though it too has complications. Ann is planning a surprise party for Bill. Unfortunately, Chris has discovered the surprise and told Bill all about it. Now Bill and Chris are having fun watching Ann try to set up the party without being discovered. Currently Ann is walking past Chris's apartment carrying a large supply of party hats. She sees a bus on which Bill frequently rides home, so she jumps into some nearby bushes to avoid being spotted. Bill, watching from Chris's window, is quite amused, but Chris is puzzled and asks Bill why Ann is hiding in the bushes. Bill says

(16) I might be on that bus.

It seems Bill has, somehow, conveyed the *correct* explanation for Ann's dive—he's said something that's both true and explanatory. But in his mouth, according to either contextualist theory we have considered, it is not true (and so it can't be explanatory) that he might have been on the bus. He knows that he is in Chris's apartment, which is not inside the bus.

Chris's question, like most questions asking for an explanation of an action, was ambiguous. Chris might have been asking what *motivated* Ann to hide in the bushes, or he might have been asking what *justified* her hiding in the bushes. This ambiguity is often harmless, because the same answer can be given for each. This looks to be just such a case. Bill seems to provide both a motivation and a justification for Ann's leap by uttering (16). That point somewhat undercuts a natural explanation of what's going on in (16). One might think that what he said was elliptical for *She believed that I might be on the bus*. And on our second contextualist theory that will be *true*. If Bill took himself to be answering a question about motivation, that might be a natural analysis. (Though there's the underlying problem that Ann presumably wasn't thinking about her mental state when she made the leap. She was thinking about the bus, and whether Bill would be on it.) But that analysis is less natural if we think that Bill was providing a justification of Ann's actions. And it seems plausible that he could utter (16) in the course of providing such a justification. This suggests that (16) simply means that for all *Ann* knew, Bill was on that bus. Alternatively, we could say that (16) is elliptical for *Because I might be on that bus*, and that the speaker-inclusion constraint does not apply to an epistemic modal connected to another sentence by 'because'. This may be right, but by this stage we imagine some will be thinking that the project of trying to find all the restrictions on the speaker-inclusion constraint is a degenerating research program, and a paradigm shift may be in order.

So our final contextualist theory is that DeRose's original semantic theory, before the addition of any sort of speaker-inclusion constraint, was correct and complete. So 'might' behaves like 'local' and 'nearby'. If Susie says 'There are snipers nearby', the truth condition for that might be that there are snipers near Susie, or that there are snipers near us, or that there are snipers near some other contextually salient individual or group. Similarly, if she utters "Professor Granger might be in Prague" the truth condition for that might be that for all she knows Professor Granger is in Prague, or that for all we know Professor Granger is in Prague, or that for all some other community knows, Professor Granger is in Prague. There are no universal rules requiring or preventing the speaker from being included in the class of salient epistemic agents.

According to the third version of contextualism, if Professor Granger does not equivocate when working through her paradox, then the problem lies with (6):

(6) It's not the case that I can know I'm not in Prague if I might be in Prague.

At the start of her reasoning process, Professor Granger's use of 'might' means (roughly) 'is compatible with what Myles and his friends know'. And if it keeps that meaning to the end, then the antecedent of (6) is true, because Professor Granger might (in that sense) be in Prague, even though she knows she is not. Any attempt to show that (1) through (6) form an inconsistent set will commit a fallacy of equivocation.

But (6) as uttered by Professor Granger sounds extremely plausible. And there are other, more general problems as well. It is difficult on such a theory to explain why it is so hard to get the relevant community to exclude the speaker in present tense cases. Why, for instance, can't Jill's statement about Jack, 'He might have eight fingers', be a statement about Jack's epistemic state rather than her own? The third theory offers us no guidance.

We'll close this section with a discussion of the interaction between syntax and semantics in these contextualist theories. As is well known, in the last decade many different contextualist theories have been proposed for various philosophically interesting terms. Jason Stanley (2000: 401) has argued that the following two constraints should put limits on when we posit contextualist semantic theories.

> VARIABLE. Any contextual effect on truth-conditions that is not traceable to an indexical, pronoun, or demonstrative in the narrow sense must be traceable to a structural position occupied by a variable. (Stanley, 2000: 401)

> SYNTACTIC EVIDENCE. The only good evidence for the existence of a variable in the semantic structure corresponding to a linguistic string is that the string, or another that we have reason to believe is syntactically like it, has interpretations that could only be accounted for by the presence of such a variable.

If any contextualist theory of epistemic modals is to be justifiably believed, then VARIABLE and SYNTACTIC EVIDENCE together entail the existence of sentences where the 'relevant community' is bound by some higher operator. So ideally we would have sentences like (17) with interpretations like (18).

(17) Everyone might be at the party tonight.

(18) For all x, it is consistent with all x knows that x will be at the party tonight.

Now (17) cannot have this interpretation, which might look like bad news for the contextualist theory. It's natural to think that if 'might' includes a variable whose value is the relevant community, that variable could be bound by a quantifier ranging over it. But if such a binding were possible, it's natural to think that it would be manifested in (17). So VARIABLE and SYNTACTIC EVIDENCE together entail that we ought not to endorse contextualism about epistemic modals.

This argument against contextualism fails in an interesting way, one that bears on the general question of what should count as evidence for or against a contextualist theory. The reason that any variable associated with 'might' in (17) cannot be bound by 'everyone' is that 'might' takes wider scope than 'everyone'. Note that (17) does not mean (19), but rather means (20).

(19) For all x, it is consistent with what we know that x will be at the party tonight.

(20) It is consistent with what we know that for all x, x will be at the party tonight.

As Kai von Fintel and Sabine Iatridou (2003) have shown, in any sentence of the form *Every F might be G*, the epistemic modal takes wide scope. For instance, (21) has no true reading if there is at most one winner of the election, even if there is no candidate that we know is going to lose.

(21) Every candidate might win.

More generally, epistemic modals take wide scope with respect to a wide class of quantifiers. This fact is called the Epistemic Containment Principle by von Fintel and Iatridou. Even if there is a variable position for the relevant community in the lexical entry for 'might', this might be unbindable because the epistemic modal always scopes over a quantifier that could bind it. If that's true then the requirement imposed by SYNTACTIC EVIDENCE is too strong. If the evidence from binding is genuinely neutral between the hypothesis that this variable place exists and the hypothesis that it does not, because there are no instances of epistemic modals that take narrow scope with respect to quantifiers, it seems reasonable to conclude that there are these variable places on the basis of other evidence.

Having said all that, there still may be direct evidence for the existence of a variable position for relevant communities. Consider again our example of the military instructor, reprinted here as (22).

(22) Before you walk into an area where there are lots of high trees, if there might be snipers hiding in the branches use your flamethrowers to clear away the foliage.

As von Fintel and Iatridou note, it is possible for epistemic modals to take narrow scope with respect to generic quantifiers. That's exactly what happens in (22). And it seems that the best interpretation of (22) requires a variable attached to 'might'. Intuitively, (22) means something like (23).

(23) Generally in situations where you are walking into an area where there are lots of high trees, if it's consistent with *your party's* knowledge that there are snipers hiding in the branches, use your flame-throwers to clear away the foliage.

The italicized *your party* seems to be the semantic contribution of the unenunciated variable. We are *not* saying that the existence of sentences like (23) shows that there are such variables in the logical form of sentences involving epistemic modals. We just want to make two points here. First, if you are a partisan of SYNTACTIC EVIDENCE, then (22) should convince you not to object to semantic accounts of epistemic modals that appeal to variables, as our contextualist theories do. Second, we note a general concern that principles like SYNTACTIC EVIDENCE presuppose that a certain kind of construction, where the contextually variable term is bound at a level like LF, is always possible. Since there are principles like the Epistemic Containment Principle, we note a mild concern that this presupposition will not always be satisfied.

Invariantist Solutions

The most plausible form of invariantism about epistemic modals is that DeRose's semantics is broadly correct, but the relevant community is not set by context—it is invariably the world. We will call this position *universalism*. Of course when we say *a might be F* we don't normally communicate the proposition that no one in the world knows whether *a* is *F*. The analogy here is to pragmatic theories of quantifier domain restriction, according to which when we say *Everyone is F*, we don't communicate the proposition that everyone in the world is *F*, even though that is the truth condition for our utterance.

The universalist position denies (2) in Professor Granger's argument. Myles did not speak truly when he said 'Professor Granger might be in Prague' because someone, namely Professor Granger, knew she was not in Prague. Although (2) is fairly plausible, it probably has weaker intuitive support than the other claims, so this is a virtue of the universalist theory.

The big advantage (besides its simplicity) of the universalist theory is that it explains some puzzle cases involving eavesdropping. Consider the following kind of case. Holmes and Watson are using a primitive bug to listen in on

Moriarty's discussions with his underlings as he struggles to avoid Holmes's plan to trap him. Moriarty says to his assistant

(24) Holmes might have gone to Paris to search for me.

Holmes and Watson are sitting in Baker Street listening to this. Watson, rather inexplicably, says 'That's right' on hearing Moriarty uttering (24). Holmes is quite perplexed. Surely Watson knows that he is sitting right here, in Baker Street, which is definitely not in Paris. But Watson's ignorance is semantic, not geographic. He was reasoning as follows. For all Moriarty (and his friends) know, Holmes is in Paris searching for him. If some kind of contextualism is true, then it seems that (24) is true in Moriarty's mouth. And, thought Watson, if someone says something true, it's OK to say 'That's right'.

Watson's conclusion is clearly wrong. It's not OK for him to say 'That's right', in response to Moriarty saying (24). So his reasoning must fail somewhere. The universalist says that where the reasoning fails is in saying the relevant community only contains Moriarty's gang members. If we include Holmes and Watson, as the universalist requires, then Moriarty speaks falsely when he says (24).

There are a number of serious (and fairly obvious) problems with the universalist account. According to universalism, the following three claims are inconsistent.

(25) x might be F.
(26) x might not be F.
(27) Someone knows whether x is F.

Since these don't *look* inconsistent, universalism looks to be false.

The universalist's move here has to be to appeal to the pragmatics. If (27) is true then one of (25) and (26) is false, although both might be appropriate to express in some contexts. But if we can appropriately utter sentences expressing false propositions in some contexts, then presumably we can inappropriately utter true sentences in other contexts. (Indeed, the latter possibility seems much more common.) So one could respond to the universalist's main argument, their analysis of eavesdropping cases like Watson's, by accepting that Watson can't *appropriately* say 'That's right' but he can *truly* say this. The universalist will have a hard time explaining why such a theory cannot work, assuming, of course, that she can explain how her own pragmatic theory can explain all the data.

The major problem here is one common to all appeals to radical pragmatics in order to defend semantic theories. If universalism is true then speakers regularly, and properly, express propositions they know to be false. (We assume here that radical scepticism is *not* true, so sometimes people know some things.) Myles knows full well that *someone* knows whether Professor Granger is in Prague, namely Professor Granger. But if he's a normal English speaker, this will *not* seem like a reason for him to not say, 'Professor Granger might be in Prague.' Some might not think this is a deep problem for the universalist theory, for speakers can be mistaken in their semantic views in ever so many ways. But many will regard it as a serious cost of the universalist claim.

This problem becomes more pressing when we look at what universalism says about beliefs involving epistemic modals. Myles does not just say that Professor Granger might be in Prague, he believes it. And he believes Professor Granger might not be in Prague. If he also believes that Professor Granger knows where she is, these beliefs are inconsistent given universalism. Perhaps the universalist can once again invoke pragmatics. It is not literally true in the story that Myles believes that Granger might be in Prague. But in describing the situation we use 'Myles believes that Granger might be in Prague', to pragmatically communicate truths by a literal falsehood. This appeal to a pragmatic escape route seems even more strained than the previous universalist claims.

In general, the universalism under discussion here seems to run up against a constraint on semantic theorizing imposed by Kripke's Weak Disquotation Principle. The principle says that if a speaker sincerely accepts a sentence, then she believes its semantic value. If we have some independent information about what a speaker believes, then we can draw certain conclusions about the content of the sentences she accepts, in particular that she only accepts sentences whose content she believes. The universalist now has two options. First, she can say that Myles here does accept inconsistent propositions. Second, she can deny the Weak Disquotation Principle, and say that, although Myles sincerely asserts, and accepts, 'Professor Granger might be in Prague', he doesn't really believe that Professor Granger might be in Prague. Generally, it's good to have options. But it's bad to have options as unappealing as these.

Reporting Epistemic Modals

Our third class of solutions will be relatively radical, so it's worth pausing to look at the evidence for it. Consider again the dialogue between Moriarty, Holmes, and Watson. Moriarty, recall, utters (24)

(24) Holmes might have gone to Paris to search for me.

Watson knows that Holmes is in Baker Street, as of course does Holmes. In the above case we imagined that both Watson and Holmes heard Moriarty say this. Change the story a little so Holmes does not hear Moriarty speak, instead when he comes back into the room he asks Watson what Moriarty thinks. Watson, quite properly, replies with (30).

(30) He thinks that you might have gone to Paris to search for him.

This is clearly not direct quotation because Watson changes the pronouns in Moriarty's statement. It is not as if Watson said 'He sincerely said, "Holmes might have gone to Paris to search for me." ' This might have been appropriate if Holmes suspected Moriarty was speaking in code so the proposition he expressed was very sensitive to the words he used.

Nor was Watson's quote a 'mixed' quote, in the sense of what happens in (31). The background is that Arnold always uses the phrase 'my little friend' to denote his Hummer H2, despite that vehicle being neither little nor friendly. No one else, however, approves of this terminology.

(31) Arnold: My little friend could drive up Mt Everest.
     Chaz: Arnold believes his little friend could drive up Mt Everest.

We've left off the punctuation here so as to not beg any questions, but there is a way this could be an acceptable report if Chaz's fourth and fifth word, and those two words only, are part of a quotation. This is clearly not ordinary direct quotation, for Arnold did not think, in English or Mentalese, 'His little friend could drive up Mt Everest.' Nevertheless, this is not ordinary indirect quotation. In ordinary spoken English Chaz's report will be unacceptable unless 'little friend' is stressed. The stress here seems to be just the same stress as is used in metalinguistic negation, as described in Horn (1989). Note the length of the pause between 'his' and 'little'. With an ordinary pause it sounds as if Chaz is using, not mentioning, 'little friend'. So it is possible *in principle* to have belief reports, like this one, that are neither strictly direct nor strictly indirect. Nevertheless, it does not seem like (30) needs such a case. In particular, there need be no distinctive metalinguistic stress on 'might' in Watson's utterance of (30), and such stress seems to be mandatory for this mixed report.

Assuming Moriarty was speaking ordinary English, Watson's report seems perfectly accurate. This is despite the fact that the relevant community one would naturally associate with Watson's use of 'might' is quite different to the community we would associate with Moriarty's use. When reporting speeches involving epistemic modals—and the beliefs express by sincere instances of such speeches—speakers can simply *disquote* the modal terms.

As is reasonably well known, there are many terms for which this kind of disquoting report is impermissible. In every case, Guildenstern's report of Ophelia's utterance is inappropriate.

(32) Ophelia: I love Hamlet.
      . . .
      Guildenstern: *Ophelia thinks that I love Hamlet.
(33) Guildenstern: What think you of Lord Hamlet?
      Ophelia: He is a jerk.
      . . .
      Rosencrantz: What does Ophelia think of the King?
      Guildenstern: *She thinks that he is a jerk.
(34) Guildenstern: Are you ready to teach the class on contextualism?
      Ophelia: I'm ready.
      . . .
      Rosencrantz: Does Ophelia think she is ready to defend her dissertation?
      Guildenstern: *She thinks she is ready.
(35) (*Guildenstern and Ophelia are on the telephone, Guildenstern in Miami, Ophelia in San Francisco*)
      Guildenstern: What do you like best about San Francisco?
      Ophelia: There are lots of wineries nearby.
      . . .
      Rosencrantz: Is it possible to grow wine in south Florida?
      Guildenstern: *Ophelia thinks that there are lots of wineries nearby.

Even when the contextualist claim is not *obviously* true, as with 'local' and 'enemy', disquotational reports are unacceptable after context shifts.

(36) (*Brian is calling from Providence, Hud and Andy are in Bellingham*)
      Brian: When I get all this work done, I'll head off to a local bar for some drinks.
      Andy: How much work is there?
      Brian: Not much. I should get to the bar in a couple of hours.
      Hud: Hey, is Brian in town? Where's he going tonight?
      Andy: *He thinks he'll be at a local bar in a couple of hours.

(37) The Enemy, speaking of us: The enemy have the advantage.
One of us: How are we doing?
Another of us: Someone just informed me that the enemy have the advantage.

(38) (*Terrell is an NFL player, and Dennis is his coach.*)
Terrell: Why are you cutting me coach?
Dennis: Because you are old and slow.
(*After this Terrell returns to academia. Kate and Leopold are students in his department.*)
Kate: Do you think Terrell would do well on our department ultimate frisbee team?
Leopold: ??I'm not sure. Someone thinks he's old and slow.

This data provides us with the penultimate argument against the contextualist theory of epistemic modals. We have already seen several such arguments.

First, as seen through the difficulties with each of the options discussed above, *any* version of contextualism faces serious problems, though by altering the version of contextualism we are using, we can alter what problems we have to face.

Second, there is nothing like the speaker-inclusion constraint for terms like 'local' and 'enemy' for which contextualism is quite plausible. This disanalogy tells against the contextualist theory of 'might'. With the right stage setting (and it doesn't usually take very much), we can get 'local' and 'enemy' to mean *local to x* and *enemy of x* for pretty much any x we happen to be interested in talking about. At least for 'bare' (unembedded) epistemic modals, the situation is markedly different. We can't, just by making Jack salient, make our own knowledge irrelevant to the truth of our utterance of, for example, 'Jack might have eight fingers'. The only way we can make our knowledge irrelevant is if we are using this sentence in an explanation or justification of Jack's actions.

Third, there is a difference in behaviour between embedded and unembedded occurrences of epistemic modals. When epistemic modals are embedded in belief contexts, conditionals, etc., they behave differently—the speaker-inclusion constraint seems to be lifted. (Think about belief reports and that military instructor case.) 'Local' and 'enemy' don't seem to show any analogous difference in their behaviour between their bare and embedded occurrences.

Fourth, 'local' and 'enemy' don't generate any of the peculiar phenomena about willingness to agree. If Myles (still in Cleveland), says

(39) Many local bars are full of Browns fans.

Professor Granger (still in the South Pacific) will not hesitate to say 'that's right' (as long as she knows that many bars in Cleveland really are, as usual, full of Browns fans). The fact that the relevant bars aren't local to *her* doesn't interfere with her willingness to agree with (39) in the way that the fact that *she* knew that she wasn't in Prague interfered with her willingness to agree with Myles's claim that she might be in Prague, or in the way that Watson's knowledge that Holmes was in London (should have) interfered with his willingness to assent to Moriarty's claim that Holmes might be in Paris.

Fifth, when there is a context shift, we are generally hesitant to produce belief reports by disquoting sincerely asserted sentences involving contextually variable terms. This is what the examples (32) through (36) show. For a wide range of contextually variable terms, speakers will quite naturally hesitate to make disquotational reports unless they are in the same context as the original speaker. Such hesitation is not shown by speakers reporting epistemic modals.

The sixth argument, that there is an alternative theory that does not have these flaws, will have to wait until the next section. For now, let's note that there are other words that seem at first to be contextually variable, but for which disquotational reports seem acceptable.

(40) Vinny the Vulture: Rotting flesh tastes great.
      John: Vinny thinks that rotting flesh tastes great.
(41) Ant Z: He's huge (*said of 5 foot 3, 141lb NBA player Muggsy Bogues*)
      Andy: Ant Z thinks that Muggsy's huge.
(42) Marvin the Martian: These are the same colour (*said of two colour swatches that look alike to Martians but not to humans*).
      Brian: Marvin thinks that these are the same colour.

In all three cases the report is accurate, or at least extremely natural. And in all three cases it would have been inappropriate for the reporter to continue 'and he's right'. But crucially, in none of the three cases is it *clear* that the original speaker made a mistake. In his context, it seems Vinny utters a truth by uttering, 'Rotting flesh tastes great', for rotting flesh does taste great to vultures. From Ant Z's perspective, Muggsy Bogues is huge. We assume here, a little controversially, that there is a use of comparative adjectives that is not relativized to a comparison class, but rather to a perspective. Ant Z does not say that Muggsy is huge for a human, or for an NBA player, but just relative to him. And he's right. Even Muggsy is huge relative to an ant.

Note the contrast with (36) here. There's something quite odd about Leopold's statement, which intuitively means that someone said Terrell is old and slow for a graduate student, when all that was said was that he is old and slow for an NFL player. And, relative to the Martian's classification of objects into colours, the two swatches are the same colour. So there's something very odd going on here.

The following *very* plausible principle looks like it is being violated.

TRUTH IN REPORTING. If *X* has a true belief, then *Y*'s report *X believes that S* accurately reports that belief only if in the context *Y* is in, *S* expresses a true proposition.

Not only do our three reports here seem to constitute counterexamples to TRUTH IN REPORTING, Watson's report in (30) is also such a counterexample, if Moriarty speaks truly (and sincerely). One response here would be to give up TRUTH IN REPORTING, but that seems like a desperate measure. And we would still have the puzzle of why we can't say 'and he's right' at the end of an accurate report.

Another response to these peculiar phenomena would be to follow the universalist and conclude that Moriarty, Vinny, Ant Z, and Marvin all believe something false. It should be clear how to formulate this kind of position: something tastes great iff every creature thinks it tastes great; something is huge iff it is huge relative to all observers; and two things are the same colour iff they look alike (in a colour kind of way) to every observer (in conditions that are normal for them). As we saw, there are problems for the universalist move for epistemic modals. And the attractiveness of universalism here seems to dissipate when we consider the cases from a different perspective.

(43) Brian: Cognac tastes great.
     Vinny: Brian believes that cognac tastes great.
(44) Andy: He's huge (*said of Buggsy Mogues, the shortest ever player in the Dinosaur Basketball Association*).
     Tyrone the T-Rex: Andy believes that Buggsy's huge.
(45) John: These are the same colour (*said of two colour swatches that look alike to humans but not to pigeons*).
     Pete the Pigeon: John believes that these are the same colour.

Again, every report seems acceptable, and in every case it would seem strange for the reporter to continue 'and he's right'. The universalist explanation in every case is that the original utterance is false. That certainly explains the data about reports, but look at the cost! All of our utterances about colours and tastes will turn out false, as will many of our utterances about sizes. It seems we have to find a way to avoid both contextualism and universalism. Our final suggestions for how to think about epistemic modals attempt to explain all this data.

Relativism and Centred Worlds

John MacFarlane (2003) has argued that believers in a metaphysically open future should accept that the truth of an utterance is *relative* to a context of evaluation. For example, if on Thursday Emily says, 'There will be a sea battle tomorrow', the believer in the open future wants to say that at the time her utterance is neither determinate true nor determinately false. One quick objection to this kind of theory is that if we look back at Emily's statement while the sea battle is raging on Friday, we are inclined to say that she got it right. From Friday's perspective, it looks like what Emily said is true. The orthodox way to reconcile these intuitions is that the only sense in which Emily's statement is *indeterminate* on Thursday is an *epistemic* sense—we simply don't know whether there will be a sea battle. MacFarlane argues instead that we should simply accept the intuitions as they stand. From Friday's perspective, Emily's statement is determinately true, from Thursday's it is not. Hence the truth of statements is relative to a context of evaluation.

There is a natural extension of this theory to the cases described above. Moriarty's statement is true relative to a context C iff it is compatible with what the people in C know that Holmes is in Paris. So in the context he uttered it, the statement is *true*, because it is consistent with what everyone in his context knows that Holmes is in Paris. But in the context of Watson's report, it is false, because Watson and Holmes know that Holmes is not in Paris.

We will call any such theory of epistemic modals a *relativist* theory, because it says that the truth of an utterance containing an epistemic modal is *relative* to a context of evaluation. As we will see, relativist theories do a much better job than contextualist theories of handling the data that troubled contextualist theories. Relativist theories are also plausible for the predicates we discussed at the end of the last section: 'huge', 'colour', and 'tastes'. On such a theory, any utterance that x *tastes F* is true iff x tastes F *to us*. Similarly, an utterance x *is huge* that doesn't have a comparison class, as in (41) or (44), is true iff x is huge relative *to us*. And *Those swatches are the same colour* is true iff they look the same colour *to us*. The reference to us in the truth conditions of these sentences isn't because there's a special reference to us in the lexical entry for any of these worlds. Rather, the truth of any utterance involving these terms is relative to a context of evaluation, and when that is *our* context of evaluation, *we* get to determine what is true and what is false. If the sentences were being evaluated in a different context, it would be the standards of that context that mattered to their truth.

So far we have not talked about the pragmatics of epistemic modals, assuming that their assertability conditions are given by their truth conditions plus some familiar Gricean norms. But it is not obvious how to apply some of those norms if utterance truth is contextually relative, because one of the norms is that one should say only what is true.

One option is to say that utterance appropriateness is, like utterance truth, relative to a context of evaluation. This is consistent, but it does not seem to respect the data. Watson might think that Moriarty's utterance is false, at least relative to his context of evaluation, but if he is aware of Moriarty's epistemic state he should think it is *appropriate*. So if something like truth is a norm of assertion, it must be truth relative to one or other context. But which one?

We could say that one should only say things that are true relative to all contexts. But that would mean John's statement about the two swatches being the same colour would be inappropriate, and that seems wrong.

We could say that one should only say things that are true relative to some contexts. But then Brian could have said, 'Rotting carcases taste great' and he would have said something appropriate, because that's true when evaluated by vultures.

The correct norm is that one should only say something that's true when evaluated in the context you are in. We assume here that contexts can include more than just the speaker. If Vinny the Vulture is speaking to a group of humans he arguably cannot say *'Rotting flesh tastes great'*. The reason is that rotting flesh does not taste great to the group of speakers in the conversation, most of whom are humans. This norm gives us the nice result that Myles's statement is appropriate, as is Moriarty's, even though in each case their most prominent audience member knows they speak falsely.

This helps explain, we think, the somewhat ambivalent attitude we have towards speakers who express epistemic modals that are false relative to our context, but true relative to their own. What the speaker said wasn't true, so we don't want to endorse what they said. Still, there is a distinction between such a speaker and someone who says that the sky is green or that grass is blue. That speaker would violate the properly relativized version of the *only say true things* rule, and Myles and Moriarty do not violate that rule.

As MacFarlane notes, relativist theories deny ABSOLUTENESS OF UTTERANCE TRUTH, the claim that if an utterance is true relative to one context of evaluation it is true relative to all of them. It is uncontroversial of course that the truth-value of an utterance *type* can be contextually variable. The interesting claim that relativists make is that the truth-value of utterance tokens can also be different relative to different contexts. So they must deny one or more premises in any argument for ABSOLUTENESS OF UTTERANCE TRUTH, such as this one.

> 1. ABSOLUTENESS OF PROPOSITIONAL CONTENT: If an utterance expresses the proposition p relative to some context of evaluation, then it expresses that proposition relative to all contexts of evaluation.
>
> 2. ABSOLUTENESS OF PROPOSITIONAL TRUTH-VALUE: If a proposition p is true relative to one context in a world it is true relative to all contexts in that world.
>
> C. ABSOLUTENESS OF UTTERANCE TRUTH

This argument provides a nice way of classifying relativist theories. One relativist approach is to say that Moriarty (or anyone else who utters an epistemic modal) says something different relative to each context of evaluation. Call this approach *content relativism*. Another approach is to say that there is a single proposition that he expresses with respect to every context, but the truth-value of that proposition is contextually variable. Call this approach *truth relativism*. (So that the meaning of 'proposition' is sufficiently understood here, let us stipulate that we understand propositions to be the things that are believed and asserted and thus, relatedly, the semantic values of 'that'-clauses.)

It might look like some of our behaviour is directly inconsistent with *any* sort of relativism. Consider the following dialogue.

> (46) Vinny: Rotting flesh tastes great
> Vinny's brother: That's true.
> John: That (i.e. what Vinny's brother said) is not true.

If what Vinny's brother is saying is that Vinny's utterance *Rotting flesh tastes great* is true in his context, then John is *wrong* in saying that what Vinny's brother said isn't true. For it is true, we claim, that *Rotting flesh tastes great* is true in Vinny's context. But this prediction seems unfortunate, because John's utterance seems perfectly appropriate in his context.

The solution here is to recognize a *disquotational* concept of truth, to go alongside the *binary* concept of truth that is at the heart of the relativist solution. The binary concept is a relation between an utterance and a context of evaluation. Call this $true_B$. So Vinny's utterance is $true_B$ relative to his context, and to his brother's context, and $false_B$ relative to John's context. One crucial feature of the binary concept is that it is not a relativist concept. If it is true relative to one context that an utterance is $true_B$ relative to context C, it is true relative to all contexts that the utterance is $true_B$ relative to context C. The disquotational concept is unary. Call this $true_T$. As far as is permitted by the semantic paradoxes, it claims that sentences of the form *S is true_T iff S* will be $true_B$ relative to any context (note here the primacy of $truth_B$ for semantic explanation). $True_T$ is a relative concept. An utterance can be $true_T$ relative to C and not $true_T$ relative to C'. When an utterance is given the honorific *true* in ordinary discourse, it is the unary relative concept $true_T$ that is being applied. That explains what is going on in (46). Vinny's brother says that Vinny's utterance is $true_T$. Relative to his context, that's right, since Vinny's utterance is true in his context. But relative to John's context, that's false, because an utterance is $true_T$ relative to John's context iff it is true relative to John's context. John spoke truly relative to his own context, so he spoke correctly. The important point is that assignments of $truth_T$ are relative rather than contextually rigid, so they might be judged true relative to some contexts and false relative to others.

Although both truth relativism and content relativism can explain (46) if they help themselves to the distinction between $truth_B$ and $truth_T$, there are four major problems for content relativism that seem to show it is not the correct theory.

The first problem concerns embeddings of 'might' clauses in belief contexts. Suppose Watson says,

(47) Moriarty believes that Holmes might be in Paris

On the content relativist view, (47) will say, relative to Watson, that Moriarty believes that, as far as Watson knows, Holmes is in Paris. That would be a crazy thing for Watson to assert. Suppose Watson is talking to Holmes. Then, relative to Holmes, Watson will have claimed that Moriarty believes that, as far as Holmes knows, Holmes is in Paris. That would *also* be a crazy thing for Watson to assert. But, given what he's just overheard, it would be perfectly natural—and pretty clearly *correct*, so long as nothing funny is going on behind the scenes—for Watson to assert (47). A view that tells us that Watson's saying something crazy relative to everybody who's likely to be a member of his audience is in pretty serious conflict with our pretheoretical judgements about the case. (Enlarging the context to include both Holmes and Watson obviously doesn't help, either.)

The second problem concerns the social function of assertion. In particular, content relativism causes difficulties for an attractive part of the Stalnakerian story about assertion that the central role of an assertion is to add the proposition asserted to the stock of conversational presuppositions (Stalnaker, 1978). On the content relativist view, it can't be that the essential effect of assertion is to add *the proposition asserted* to the stock of common presuppositions, because there's no such thing as *the* proposition asserted. There will be a different proposition asserted relative to each audience member. That's not part of an attractive theory. And it's not terribly clear what the replacement story about the essential effect of assertion—about the fundamental role of assertion in communication—is going to be. It may be that there's a story to be told about *assertability*—about when Moriarty is entitled to assert, for example, 'it might be that Holmes is in Paris'—but there's no obvious story about what he's *up to* when he's making that assertion, about what the assertion is supposed to accomplish. (And if you think that appropriateness of assertion's got to be tied up with what your assertion's supposed to accomplish, then you'll be sceptical about even the first part.)

The third problem concerns epistemic modals in the scope of temporal modifiers. The content relativist has difficulties explaining what's going on with sentences like (48).

(48) The Trojans were hesitant in attacking because Achilles might have been with the Greek army.

On the content relativist view, (48) will be false relative to pretty much everybody, certainly relative to everybody alive today. It's certainly false that the Trojans were hesitant because, as far as *we* know, Achilles was with the Greek army. (Or worse, because, as far as we knew *then*, Achilles was with the Greek army.) But, depending on how the Trojan war went, (48) could be *true* relative to everybody.

Finally, content relativism has a problem with commands. Keith's Mom says:

(49) For all days *d*, you should carry an umbrella on *d* if and only if it might rain on *d*.

Suppose on Monday Keith checks the forecast and it says there's a 50 per cent chance of rain. So he takes an umbrella. It doesn't rain, and on Tuesday he wonders whether what he did on Monday was what his Mom said he should. On the content relativist view, we get the following strange result: on Monday, it would have been true to say that he was doing what his Mom said he should, since at the time, the embedded clause expressed a proposition that was true relative to him. Looking back on Tuesday, though, it looks like he did what his Mom said he shouldn't, because now the embedded clause expresses a proposition that's false relative to him. But that's not right. He just plain did what his Mom told him to do.

The same thing happens with the soldiers trying to follow the imperative issued as (22). Assume one of them attempts to follow the command by burning down some trees that seem to contain snipers. Relative to the time she is doing the burning, she will be complying with the command. But later, when it turns out the trees were sniper-free, she will not have been following the command. If we assume there's an overarching command to not use flamethrowers unless explicitly instructed to do so, then it will turn out that, as of *now*, she violated her orders *then*. But that's not right. She just plain followed her orders.

There's a similar problem with the other terms about which relativism seems plausible. Consider the following commands:

(50) Don't pick fights with huge opponents.
(51) Stack all of the things that are the same colour together.
(52) If it tastes lousy, spit it out.

It's possible to sensibly issue these commands, even in relevantly mixed company. And if we're going to get the right compliance conditions, we don't want *content* relativism about great-tastingness, hugeness, and same-colouredness here. When we hear a command like (52), we take (*a*) the same command to have been issued to everybody, and (*b*) everybody to be following it if we all spit out the things that taste lousy to us. On the content relativist view, we've each gotten different commands, and the philosopher who spits out the chunk of week-old antelope hasn't complied with the command that Vinny was given. This seems wrong.

So the content relativist theory has several problems. The truth relativist theory does much better. Let us begin with the familiar notion of a function from worlds to truth values. Call any such function a Modal Profile. On the standard way of looking at things, propositions—the objects of belief and assertion, the semantic values of 'that'-clauses—are or at least determine a Modal Profile. The truth relativist denies this. According to the truth relativist, the relevant propositions are true or false not relative to *worlds*, but relative to *positions* within worlds—that is, they're true or false relative to *centred worlds*. (A centred world is a triple of a possible world, an individual, and a time.) There's a few ways to formally spell out this idea. One is to replace talk of Modal Profiles with Centring Profiles, that is, functions from *centred* worlds to truth-values. Another is to say that a centred world and proposition combine to determine a Modal Profile, so propositions determine functions from centred worlds to Modal Profiles. Each of these proposals has some costs and benefits, and we postpone discussion of their comparative virtues to an appendix. For now we are interested in the idea, common to these proposals, that propositions only determine truth-values relative to something much more fine-grained than a world. (We take no stand here on whether propositions should be *identified* with either Modal Profiles or Centring Profiles or functions from Centred Worlds to Modal Profiles.)

Truth relativism is not threatened by the four problems that undermine content relativism.

According to truth relativism, Watson and Moriarty express the very same proposition by the words *Holmes might be in Paris*, so it is no surprise that Watson can report Moriarty's assertive utterance by using the very same words. Similarly, it is no surprise that, if Moriarty has a belief that he would express by saying *Holmes might be in Paris*, Watson can report that by (53).

(53) Moriarty believes that Holmes might be in Paris.

Above we noted that it's unlikely that Watson could use this to express the proposition that, for all *Watson* knows, Holmes is in Paris. We used that fact to argue that DeRose's constraint did not apply when an epistemic modal is inside a propositional attitude report. The truth relativist theory predicts not only that DeRose's constraint should not apply, but that a different constraint should apply. When one says that *a believes that b might be F*, one says that *a* believes the proposition *b might be F*. And *a* believes that proposition iff *a* believes it is consistent with what they know that *b* is *F*. And that prediction seems to be entirely correct. It is impossible for Watson to use (53) to mean that Moriarty believes that for all Holmes knows he is in Paris, or that for all Watson knows Holmes is in Paris. This seems to be an interesting generalization, and while it falls out nicely from the truth relativist theory, it needs to be imposed as a special constraint on contextualist theories.

Since there is a proposition that is common to speakers and hearers when an epistemic modal is uttered, we can keep Stalnaker's nice idea that the role of assertion is to add propositions to the conversational context. Since propositions are no longer identified with sets of possible worlds we will have to modify other parts of Stalnaker's theory, but those parts are considerably more controversial.

The truth relativist can also explain how (48) can be true, though the explanation requires a small detour through the nature of psychological explanations involving relativist expressions.

> (48) The Trojans were hesitant in attacking because Achilles might have been with the Greek army.

All of the following could be true, and not because the things in question are rude, huge, or great tasting for us.

> (54) Marvin the Martian dropped his pants as the Queen passed by because it would have been rude not to.
>
> (55) Children are scared of adults because they are huge.
>
> (56) Vultures eat rotting flesh because it tastes great.

In general it seems that the truth of an explanatory claim of the form, *X φed because p* depends only on whether *p* is true in *X*'s context (plus whether the truth of *p* in *X*'s context bears the right relation to *X*'s φing). Whether or not *p* is true in *our* context is neither here nor there. Adults are not huge, rotting flesh does not taste great, and it is rude to drop one's pants as the Queen passes by, but (54)–(56) could still be true, and could all count as good explanations. Similarly, (48) can be true because *Achilles might have been with the Greek army* could be true relative to the Trojans.

Similarly, what it is to comply with a command is to act in a way that makes the command true in the context of action. This is not a particular feature of epistemic modals, but just a general property of how commands involving propositions with centred-worlds truth conditions behave. If Don picks a fight with Pedro after Don has shrunk so much that Pedro is now relatively huge, he violates (50), even if Pedro was not huge when the command was issued. And he still violates it from a later perspective when Pedro and Don are the same size. The general point is that whether the command is violated depends on the applicability of the salient terms from the perspective of the person to whom the command applies. Similarly, Keith does not violate his Mom's command if he takes an umbrella where *It might rain* is true in the context the action is performed. And this, of course, matches up perfectly with intuitions about the case.

It's a little tricky to say just which statement in Professor Granger's original hexalemma gets denied by the truth relativist. It all depends what we mean by *spoke truly*. If *Myles spoke truly* means that Myles said something true$_T$, then (2) is false (relative to Granger's context), for its right-hand side is true but its left-hand side is false. If, on the other hand, it means he said something true$_B$

relative to his own context, then (4) is false, for he did speak truly$_B$ relative to his context, but it's not the case that Professor Granger might be in Prague. This is awkward, but we might expect that any good solution to the paradox will be awkward.

Objections to Truth Relativism

It might be thought that the truth relativist has to deny TRUTH IN REPORT-ING, but in fact this can be retained in its entirety provided we understand it the right way. The following situation is possible on the truth relativist theory. *X* has a belief that is true in her context, and *Y* properly reports this by saying *X believes that S*, where *S* in *Y*'s mouth expresses a proposition that is false in *Y*'s mouth in her context. But this is no violation of TRUTH IN REPORTING. What would be a violation is if *X*'s belief was true in *Y*'s context, and still *Y* could report it as described here. But there's no case where, intuitively, we properly report an epistemic modal but violate that constraint. And the same holds for reports of uses of *huge*, *colour*, or *tastes*. Even if Vinny (truly) believes that rotting flesh tastes great, and the words 'Rotting flesh tastes great' in John's mouth express a false proposition, John's report, 'Vinny believes that rotting flesh tastes great' would only violate TRUTH IN REPORTING if Vinny's belief is still true in *John's* context. And it is not.

Given that the relativist has the concept of truth$_T$, or as we might put it truth *simpliciter*, what should be done with it? The answer seems to be not much. We certainly shouldn't restate the norms of assertion in terms of it, because that will lead to the appropriateness of assertion being oddly relativized. Whether it was appropriate for Vinny to *say* 'Rotting flesh tastes great', is independent of the context of evaluation, even if the truth of what he uttered is context relative. (It would not be at all appropriate for him to have said 'Rotting flesh tastes terrible' even though we should think he would have said something true by that remark, and something false by what he actually said.) And the same thing seems to hold for generalizations about truth as the end of belief. It is entirely appropriate for Myles to *believe* that Granger might be in Prague, because it's true$_B$ relative to his context. Relatedly, if knowledge is tied to truth$_T$ rather than truth$_B$, knowledge can't be the norm of assertion or end of belief. On the other hand, using truth$_T$ we can say that TRUTH IN REPORTING is true in the truth relativist theory without reinterpreting it in terms of relative truth concepts. Moreover, we can invoke truth$_T$ to explain why we got confused when thinking about the original puzzle. It is arguable that, even if we should distinguish truth$_T$ from truth$_B$ in our semantic theorizing, we aren't unreflectively as clear about that distinction as we might be. No wonder then that we get a little confused as we think about the Granger case. We want to say Myles doesn't make a mistake. And we also want to say 'That's wrong' speaking of the object of his assertion and belief, and what's more, when we say that, we don't seem to be making a binary claim about the relation between ourselves and what is believed. Once we clearly distinguish truth$_T$ from truth$_B$ things become clear. Using the disquotational notion, we can say 'That is false$_T$', which is a monadic claim, and not a binary one. The binary truth$_B$ explains why that claim is assertable (it is assertable because 'That is false$_T$' is true$_B$ at my context), but doesn't figure in the proposition believed. Meanwhile, the relevant notion of mistake—that of an agent believing a proposition that is not true$_B$ at her context—can only be properly articulated once the distinction between the more explanatory truth$_T$ is carefully distinguished from the (arguably) conceptually more basic truth$_B$.

One final expository point. In general, truth relativism makes for irresolvable disputes. Let us say that two conversational partners are in deadlock concerning a claim when the following situation arises. There is a pair of conversational participants, x and y, and a sentence S, under dispute, such that each express the same proposition (in the sense explained) by S but that S is true$_B$ at each of the contexts x is in during the conversation, and false$_B$ at each of the contexts y is in during the conversation. Neither speaks past one another in alternately asserting and denying the same sentence, since each expresses the same proposition by it. And each asserts what they should be asserting when each says: What I say is true$_T$ and what the other says is false$_T$, since each makes a speech that is true$_T$ at the respective contexts. In general, truth relativism about a term will lead one to predict deadlock for certain conversations, traceable to the truth relativity of the term. But in the case of 'might', it is arguable that conversation tends to force a situation where, even if at the outset, a 'might' sentence was true relative to x and not to y (on account of the truth relativity of the 'might' sentence), x and y will, in the course of engagement and dispute, be quickly put into a pair of contexts which do not differ with respect to truth$_B$ (unless the 'might' sentence contained other terms that themselves made for deadlock). This is not merely because the conversational participants will, through testimony, pool knowledge about the sentence embedded in the 'might' claim. It is in any case arguable that the relevant community whose body of knowledge determines whether a 'might' claim is true$_B$ at a context always includes not just that of the person at that context but also that of his conversational partners. In the special case of 'might', then, truth relativism may well generate far less by way of deadlock than in other cases.

There are two primary objections to the truth relativist theory: it doesn't quite handle all the cases and that it is too radical.

There are some cases that seem to tell directly against the truth relativist position. Consider the case again of Tom and Sally stuck in a maze. Sally knows the way out, but doesn't want to tell Tom. She says, *inter alia*, (57), and does not seem to violate any *semantic* norms in doing so, even though she knows the exit is some other way.

(57) The exit might be that way.

This seems to directly contradict the relativist claim that the norm for assertion is speaking truly in one's own context. We suspect that what's going on here is that Sally is projecting herself into Tom's context. She is, we think, merely trying to verbalize thoughts that are, or should be, going through *Tom's* head, rather than making a simple assertion. As some evidence for this, note (as was mentioned above) that it would be wrong to take (57) as evidence that Sally believes the exit might be that way, whereas when a speaker asserts that p that is usually strong evidence that she believes that p. It is unfortunate for the relativist to have to appeal to something like projection, but we think it is the simplest explanation of these cases that any theorist can provide.

The idea that utterances have their truth-value absolutely is well entrenched in contemporary semantics, so it should only be overturned with caution. And it might be worried that once we add another degree of relativization, it will be open to relativize in all sorts of directions. We are sensitive to these concerns, but we think the virtues of the relativist theory, and the vices of the contextualist and invariantist theories, provide a decent response to them. Invariantist theories are simply implausible, and any contextualist theory will have to include so many *ad hoc* conditions, conditions that seem to be natural consequences of relativism, that there are methodological considerations telling in favour of relativism. (Let us be clear: we are not recommending a general preference for relativism over contextualism in semantic theory. As we have been trying to make clear, for example, the case of 'might' is very different from, say, the case of 'ready'.) It is (as always) hard to tell which way the balance tips when all these methodological considerations are weighed together, but we think the relativist has a good case.

APPENDIX ON TYPES OF CONTENT

Robert Stalnaker has long promoted the idea that the content of an assertoric utterance is a set of possible worlds, or a function from worlds to truth-values. This idea has been enormously influential in formal semantics, although it has come in for detailed criticism by various philosophers. (See especially Soames, 1987; King, 1994, 1995, 1998.) But even philosophers who think that there is more to content than a set of possible worlds would agree that propositions determine a function from worlds to truth-values. Some would agree that such a function exhausts the 'discriminatory role' of a proposition, although this depends on the (highly contestable) assumption that the role of propositions is to discriminate amongst *metaphysical* possibilities. Still, even philosophers who disagree with what Stalnaker says about the nature of propositions could agree that if all we wanted from a proposition was to divide up some metaphysical possibilities, propositions could be functions from worlds to truth-values, but they think some propositions that divide up the metaphysical possibilities the same way should be distinguished.

We don't want to take sides in that debate, because our truth relativism means we are in conflict with even the idea that a proposition determines a function from worlds to truth-values. To see this, consider a sentence whose truth-value is relative to a context of evaluation, such as *Vegemite tastes great*. The truth relativist says that this sentence should be evaluated as true from a context where people like the taste of Vegemite (call this the Australian context) and should be evaluated as false from a context where people dislike this taste (call that the American context) and both evaluations are correct (from their own perspective) even though the Australians and Americans agree about what the content of *Vegemite tastes great* is, and they are in the same world. There's just no such thing as *the* truth-value of *Vegemite tastes great* in the actual world, so it does not determine a function from worlds to truth-values. What kind of function does it determine then?

One option, inspired by Lewis's work on *de se* belief, is to say that it determines a function from centred worlds to truth values. The idea is that we can identify a context of evaluation with a centred world, and then *Vegemite tastes great* will be true relative to a centred world iff it is properly evaluated as true within that context. Alternatively, the content of *Vegemite tastes great* will determine a set of centred worlds, the set of contexts from which that sentence would be evaluated as true. Just as propositions were traditionally thought to determine (or be) sets of possible worlds, properties were traditionally thought to determine (or be) functions from worlds to sets of individuals. Now if we identify centred worlds with <individual, world> pairs, a function from worlds to sets of individuals just is a set of centred worlds. So the content of *Vegemite tastes great* could just be a *property*, very roughly the property of being in a context where most people are disposed to find Vegemite great-tasting.

This proposal has three nice features. First, even though the content of *Vegemite tastes great* is not, and does not even determine, a proposition as Stalnaker conceived of propositions, it does determine a property. So the proposal is not as radical as it might at first look. Second, properties are the kind of things that divide up possibilities. The possibilities they divide are individuals, not worlds, but the basic idea that to represent is to represent yourself as being in one class of possible states rather than another is retained. The only change is that, instead of representing yourself as being in one class of worlds rather than another, you represent yourself as being in one class of <individual, world> pairs rather than another. Third, the proposal links up nicely with David Lewis's account of *de se* belief, and offers some prospects for connecting the contents of beliefs with the contents of assertions, even when both of these contents have ceased to be propositions in Stalnaker's sense.

But there's a problem for this account. Consider what we want to say about *Possibly Vegemite tastes great*, where context makes it clear that the 'possibly' is a metaphysical modal. There's a trivial problem and a potentially deep problem for this account. The trivial problem is that we know what the meaning of *possibly* is. It's a function that takes propositions as inputs and delivers as output a proposition that is true iff the input proposition is true at an accessible world. If the content of *Vegemite tastes great* is a property rather than a proposition, then we have a type mismatch. This is a trivial problem because it's a fairly routine exercise to convert the meanings of words like *possibly* so they are the right kind of things to operate on what we now take the meaning of *Vegemite tastes great* to be.

The deep problem is that when we go through that routine exercise, we get the wrong results. We don't want *Possibly Vegemite tastes great* to be true in virtue of there being an accessible world where the people *there* like the taste of Vegemite. We want it to be true in virtue of there being a world where Vegemite's taste is a taste that in this context we'd properly describe as great. And it's not clear how to get that on the current story. To see how big a problem this is, consider (58), where the modal is meant to be metaphysical and have wide scope.

(58) Possibly everyone hates Vegemite but it tastes great.

That's true, on its most natural reading. But the content of *Everyone hates Vegemite but it tastes great* will be the empty set of centred worlds, for there is no centred world on which this is true. Now it's not clear just what the meaning of *possibly* could be that delivers the correct result that (58) is true.

So we are tempted to consider an alternative proposal. Start with a very natural way of thinking about why the relativist has to modify the Stalnakerian story about content. The problem is that (even given a context of utterance) *tastes great* does not determine a property. Rather, relative to any context of evaluation, that is, centred world, it determines a property. That is, its content is (or at least determines) a function from centred worlds to properties. So given our actual context, it determines the property of having a taste that people around here think is great. Now properties combine with individuals to form Stalnakerian propositions. So *tastes great* is a function from centred worlds to functions from individuals to sets of worlds. Hence *Vegemite tastes great* is a function from centred worlds to sets of worlds, the previous function with the value for the 'individual' being fixed as Vegemite.

Our second option then is that in general sentences containing 'relative' terms like 'tastes' or 'huge' or 'might' determine a function from centred worlds to sets of worlds. This makes it quite easy to understand how (58) could work. *Possibly* type-shifts so that it is now a function from functions from centred worlds to sets of worlds to functions from centred worlds to sets of worlds. It's fairly easy to say what this function is. If the content of p is (or determines) f, a function from centred worlds to sets of worlds, then the content of $\Diamond p$ is (or determines) g, the function such that for any centred world c, $w \in g(c)$ iff for some w' accessible from w, $w' \in f(c)$. The core idea is just that we ignore the role of the centred worlds until the end of our semantic evaluation, and otherwise just treat $\Diamond$ as we'd treated it in traditional semantics. This is a rather nice position in many ways, but there are two issues to be addressed.

First, it is not clear that functions from centred worlds to sets of worlds are really kinds of content. They are not things that divide up intuitive possibilities, in the way that sets of individuals, and sets of <individual, world> pairs do. It's no good to say that relative to a centred world a content is determined. That would be fine if we were content relativists, and we said the content was meant to be determined relative to a centred world. But as argued in the text the content of *Vegemite tastes great* should be the same across various contexts of evaluation. A better response is to say functions from centred worlds to sets of worlds do determine a kind of content. For any such function f, we can determine the set of centred worlds $<i, w>$ such that $w \in f(<i, w>)$. These will be the centred worlds that the proposition is true at. It's not necessarily a problem that the proposition does *more* than determine this set. (It's not an objection to King's account of propositions that on his theory propositions do more than determine a set of possibilities.)

Second, it isn't exactly clear how to fill out these functions when we get back to our core case: epistemic modals. It's easy to say what it is for *Vegemite tastes great* to be true in a world relative to our context of evaluation; indeed we did so above. It's a lot harder to say what it is for *Granger might be in Prague* to be true in an arbitrary world w relative to an arbitrary context of evaluation c. As a first pass, we might say this is true in w iff for all the people in c know, it is true in w that Granger is in Prague. But the problem is that whenever c is not a centre in w, it's very hard to say just what the people in c know about w. Under different descriptions of w they will know different things about it. If w is described as a nearby world in which Granger is in Cleveland, they will know Granger is not in Prague in w. If it is described as a nearby world in which Myles knows where Granger is they may not know anything about whether Granger is in Prague is in w, even if those descriptions pick out the same worlds. Ideally we would cut through this by talking about their *de re* knowledge about w, but most folks have very little *de re* knowledge about other possible worlds. It's not clear this is a huge problem though. Remember that a sentence containing an epistemic modal is meant to determine a function from centred worlds to functions from worlds to truth-values. Provided we have a semantics that allows for semantic indeterminacy, we can just say that the functions from worlds to truth-values are partial functions, and they simply aren't determined when it's unclear what the people in c know about w. Or we can say there's a default semantic rule such that w is not in $f(c)$ (where f is the function determined by the sentence) whenever this is unclear. Since the sentences whose meanings are determined by these values of the function, like *Possibly Granger might be in Prague*, are similarly vague, it is no harm if the function is a little vague.

So we have two options on the table for what kind of functions sentences might determine if they don't determine functions from world to truth-values. One option is that they determine functions from centred worlds to truth-values, another that they determine functions from centred worlds to functions from worlds to truth-values. Neither is free from criticism, and the authors aren't in agreement about which is the best approach, so it isn't entirely clear what the best way to formally implement truth relativism is. But it does not look like there are no possible moves here. Moving to truth relativism does not mean that we will have to totally abandon the fruitful approaches to formal semantics that are built on ideas like Stalnaker's, although it does mean that those semantic theories will need to be modified in places.

REFERENCES

Cappelen, Herman, and Ernest Lepore (1997). 'On an Alleged Connection between Indirect Quotation and Semantic Theory', *Mind and Language*, 12: 278–96.

DeRose, Keith (1991). 'Epistemic Possibilities', *Philosophical Review*, 100: 581–605.

—— (1998). 'Simple Might's, Indicative Possibilities, and the Open Future', *Philosophical Quarterly*, 48: 67–82.

Egan, Andy (2004). 'Second-Order Predication and the Metaphysics of Properties', *Australasian Journal of Philosophy* (March).

Fintel, Kaivon, and Sabine Iatridou (2003). 'Epistemic Containment', *Linguistic Inquiry*, 34: 173–98.

Hawthorne, John (2004). *Knowledge and Lotteries* (Oxford: Oxford University Press).

Horn, Laurence (1989). *A Natural History of Negation* (Chicago: University of Chicago Press).

Jacobson, Pauline (1999). 'Towards a Variable Free Semantics', *Linguistics and Philosophy*, 22: 117–84.

King, Jeffrey (1994). 'Can Propositions be Naturalistically Acceptable?', *Midwest Studies in Philosophy*, 19.

—— (1995). 'Structured Propositions and Complex Predicates', *Noûs*, 29: 516–35.

—— (1998). 'What is a Philosophical Analysis?', *Philosophical Studies*, 90: 155–79.

Lewis, David (1976). 'The Paradoxes of Time Travel', *American Philosophical Quarterly*, 13: 145–52.

—— (1979a). 'Scorekeeping in a Language Game', *Journal of Philosophical Logic*, 8: 339–59.

—— (1979b). 'Attitudes *De Dicto* and *De Se*', *Philosophical Review*, 88: 513–43.

MacFarlane, John (2003). 'Future Contingents and Relative Truth', *Philosophical Quarterly*, 53: 321–36.

—— (n.d.) 'Epistemic Modalities and Relative Truth', unpublished MS.

Soames, Scott (1987). 'Direct Reference, Propositional Attitudes and Semantic Content', *Philosophical Topics*, 15: 47–87.

—— (2002). *Beyond Rigidity* (Oxford: Oxford University Press).

Stalnaker, Robert (1978). 'Assertion', *Syntax and Semantics*, 9: 315–32.

Stanley, Jason (2000). 'Context and Logical Form', *Linguistics and Philosophy*, 23: 391–434.

—— and Zoltan Gendler Szabó (2000). 'On Quantifier Domain Restriction', *Mind and Language*, 15: 219–61.

Part II

Compositionality, Meaning, and Context

7

Literalism and Contextualism: Some Varieties

François Recanati

According to the dominant position in the philosophy of language, we may legitimately ascribe truth-conditional content to sentences, independently of the speech act which the sentence is used to perform. This position, which I call 'literalism', contrasts with another view, reminiscent of that held by ordinary language philosophers half a century ago. That other view, which I call 'contextualism', holds that *speech acts* are the primary bearers of content. Only in the context of a speech act does a sentence express a determinate content.[1]

Both literalism and contextualism come in many varieties. There are radical, and less radical, versions of both literalism and contextualism. Some intermediate positions are mixtures of literalism and contextualism. In this chapter I will describe several literalist positions, several contextualist positions, and a couple of intermediate positions. My aim is to convince the reader that the literalism/contextualism controversy is far from being settled.

In the first section, I will look at the historical development of literalism. We will see that this development reveals a gradual weakening. The question that naturally arises is: How far can we go in this direction? Where will this tendency ultimately lead us? And the obvious answer is: to contextualism. In the second section I will describe the steps which, from a critique of the currently dominant literalist position (minimalism), can lead to contextualism. In the last three

---

[1] As James Conant (1998) pointed out, this is a Wittgensteinian extension of Frege's Context Principle.

sections I will describe various contextualist positions, and I will discuss possible literalist replies to the contextualist challenge.

I. The Development of Literalism

Indexicality raises a prima facie difficulty for literalism—a difficulty that was emphasized by its contextualist opponents. Indexical sentences possess a determinate (truth-evaluable) content only when uttered. Hence it is not obvious that such sentences, qua grammatical entities, possess content. As the ordinary language philosophers used to insist, we must draw a distinction between the sentence and the statement it is used to make. The content is the content of the statement, and only derivatively that of the sentence that is used to make that statement.

But indexicality is a feature of natural language sentences, and the philosophers in the literalist tradition were not originally concerned with natural language. They were primarily concerned with the formal languages of logic and, through them, with 'language' in general. Vernacular languages such as English or French were considered messy and defective. It was only in the middle of the twentieth century that things began to change, and that a descriptive attitude was adopted towards natural language within the literalist tradition.[2] Before that change occurred, context-sensitivity was taken to be a *defect* of natural language, like ambiguity. The fact that natural language sentences are indexical and therefore carry content only when uttered could therefore be deliberately ignored. Let us refer to this view (or rather, this attitude) as 'proto-literalism'.

Next in the development of the literalist tradition came 'eternalism'. In contrast to proto-literalism, eternalism was a substantial view regarding the phenomenon of indexicality in natural language. Indexicality was regarded as *not essential from a theoretical standpoint*. It was so considered because the following principle was widely accepted:

Eternalization Principle
For every statement that can be made in a natural language using a context-sensitive sentence in a given context, there is an eternal sentence, in that language (or in a suitable extension of that language), which can be used to make the same statement in any context.[3]

---

[2] See e.g. Reichenbach (1947), Bar-Hillel (1954).

[3] To obtain an eternal sentence from a context-sensitive one, one has only to replace the indexical constituents of the latter by non-indexical constituents with the same semantic value.

Thus indexicality turns out to be eliminable. Were it not for the necessities of practical life, we might utter only eternal sentences.

The eternalization principle has progressively been abandoned. It is now more or less accepted that natural language sentences are *irreducibly* context-sensitive. Some theorists even doubt the existence of eternal sentences in natural language. Eternalism, therefore, is out. But there still are fallback positions for literalism. Indeed literalism has been maintained, in progressively weaker forms, until today.

The strongest fallback position for literalism consists in acknowledging the extent (and ineliminability) of context-dependence, while insisting that it still is the *sentence* which, in virtue of the rules of the language, expresses a content in context. This semantic notion of the content of a sentence (with respect to context) is held to be distinct from the pragmatic notion of the content of a speech act. For it is the linguistic conventions, not the speaker's intentions (or the hearer's beliefs regarding the speaker's intentions), which fix the content of the sentence with respect to context. Hence the name 'conventionalism' for the view that *the truth-conditions of a sentence are fixed by the rules of the language independently of pragmatic considerations*. What determines the content of an indexical expression is not what is in the head of the language users, but a linguistic rule—the rule which constitutes the conventional meaning of that expression. As Barwise and Perry write, 'even if I am fully convinced that I am Napoleon, my use of "I" designates me, not him. Similarly, I may be fully convinced that it is 1789, but it does not make my use of "now" about a time in 1789' (Barwise and Perry, 1983: 148). It can therefore be maintained that natural language sentences possess a content (with respect to context) independently of the speech act which it is used to perform. The content of the speech act arguably depends upon the communicative intentions of the speaker which the utterance makes manifest to the hearer; but the content of the sentence is fixed directly by the rules of the language—with respect to context, admittedly, but independently of both the speaker's intentions and their recognition by the hearer.

Conventionalism replaced eternalism when the eternalization principle was abandoned; and it still has advocates today. But conventionalism is no longer the dominant position. It is widely acknowledged that the speaker's meaning has a role to play in fixing the truth-conditions of indexical sentences. To be sure, the reference of a pure indexical like 'I' is determined by a linguistic rule: the rule that 'I' refers to the speaker. But the reference of a demonstrative is not determined by a rule in this manner. It is generally assumed that there is such a rule, namely the rule that the demonstrative refers to the object which happens to be demonstrated or which happens to be the most salient, in the context at hand. But the notions of 'demonstration' and 'salience' are pragmatic notions in disguise. Ultimately, a demonstrative refers to *what the speaker who uses it refers to by using it*. Semantic reference turns out to be parasitic on speaker's reference here. Even expressions like 'here' and 'now' which Kaplan classifies as *pure* indexicals (as opposed to demonstratives) are highly sensitive to the speaker's intent. The alleged rule of reference which is said to govern them is the rule that they refer to the time or place of the context respectively; but what counts as the time and place of the context? How inclusive must the time or place in question be? It depends on what the speaker means, so that determining the content of words like 'here' and 'now' ultimately is a matter of pragmatics.

The alleged automaticity of content-determination and its independence from pragmatic considerations is an illusion due to an excessive concern with a sub-class of 'pure indexicals', namely words such as 'I', 'today', etc. In most cases, however, the reference of a context-sensitive expression is determined on a pragmatic basis.[4] That is true not only of standard indexical expressions, but also of many constructions involving something like a free variable. For example, a possessive phrase such as 'John's car' arguably means something like *the car that bears relation R to John*. The free variable 'R' must be contextually assigned a particular value; but that value is not determined by a rule. What a given occurrence of the phrase 'John's car' means ultimately depends upon what the speaker who utters it means. That dependence upon speaker's meaning is a characteristic feature of semantically underdeterminate expressions, which are pervasive in natural language. Their semantic value varies from occurrence to occurrence, yet it varies not as a function of some objective feature of the situation of utterance but as a function of *what the speaker means*.

So we cannot maintain that the content of the sentence is fixed in context by linguistic rules. We must acknowledge the role of pragmatic considerations in determining truth-conditional content. This means that we must depart from conventionalism; but there still is an ultimate fallback position for literalism. According to that position, which I call 'minimalism', the appeal to speaker's meaning in determining truth-conditional content is not free and unconstrained, but regulated by linguistic conventions. We appeal to speaker's meaning only when there is, in the meaning of the sentence type, a 'slot' to be filled pragmatically.

---

[4] Thus John Perry (1997: 595–6) distinguishes between 'automatic' indexicals and 'intentional' indexicals.

In the minimalist framework, the semantic content of the utterance departs only minimally from the linguistic meaning of the sentence type (hence the name 'minimalism'); it departs from it only when the meaning of the sentence itself requires that some contextual value be assigned to a context-sensitive word or morpheme, or to a free variable in logical form. The contextual assignment of values to indexicals and free variables is allowed to affect semantic content, because it is a bottom–up, linguistically controlled pragmatic process, that is, a pragmatic process triggered (and made obligatory) by a linguistic expression in the sentence itself. But no other contextual influence is allowed to affect semantic content. In particular, 'top–down' pragmatic processes are banned. Such processes are not triggered by a particular expression in virtue of a linguistic rule, but take place in order to make sense of the speaker's communicative act in context. For example, sometimes we interpret what the speaker says nonliterally, because a literal interpretation would clash with the presumption that the speaker respects Grice's Cooperative Principle. Because they are not linguistically controlled, such interpretive processes have no impact on truth-conditions, according to minimalism. They can only affect the overall content of the speech act performed by the speaker.

To sum up, four stages can be discerned in the historical development of the literalist tradition that started with Frege and is still dominant today. First came proto-literalism, according to which context-sensitivity is a defect of natural language, to be ignored in theorizing about language. Then came eternalism, which holds that indexicality is a practical convenience rather than an essential feature of natural language. Next came conventionalism, the view that the conventional meaning of the sentence-type fully determines the content of the sentence (in context) independently of the speaker's meaning. Finally, minimalism acknowledges the role of speaker's meaning in determining truth-conditions, but insists that the appeal to speaker's meaning is always subordinated to (controlled by) the conventional meaning of the sentence.

II. Towards Contextualism

As we have just seen, the strong forms of literalism have been replaced by progressively weaker forms, in the historical development of the tradition stemming from Frege's work. How far will that process go? The currently accepted position is minimalism. Will minimalism be superseded by still weaker positions, and if so, at what point will literalism have to be squarely given up in favour of contextualism? These are the questions I address in this section.

According to minimalism, no contextual influences are allowed to affect the truth-conditional content of an utterance unless the sentence itself demands it. Yet, sometimes, the truth-conditions of an utterance seem to be affected by context in a top–down manner. For example, if I say 'It is raining', I mean that it is raining where I am (or at another contextually salient place), but nothing in the sentence seems to correspond to the place, which is provided by context without being linguistically 'articulated' (Perry, 1986). Faced with such cases, a defender of minimalism has two options. He (or she) may bravely re-analyse the example so as to show that the pragmatic process at issue—here, the provision of a specific place—is a bottom–up process triggered by some expression in the sentence, appearances notwithstanding. Thus he may posit a free location variable in the logical form of the sentence (Stanley, 2000).[5] Alternatively, the minimalist may draw a distinction between the semantic content of the sentence (here, the location-less proposition that it's raining at some place or other) and the content actually conveyed (namely, the proposition that it's raining where the speaker is). In contrast to the former, the latter need not obey the minimalist constraint.

The second of the two positions I have just described as available to the minimalist *concedes* that there are pragmatic processes that affect the interpretation of an utterance in a top–down manner, and that affect it at the level of (intuitive) truth-conditions. Therefore, by choosing this option rather than the first one, we move one step further in the direction of contextualism. But we remain within the confines of literalism because we maintain that the content of the sentence is the 'minimal' proposition determined by the linguistic meaning of the sentence when indexicals, free variables and other context-sensitive elements have been assigned contextual values. This position—which I call 'the syncretic view' (Recanati, 2001, 2004)—is a compromise. On the one hand, the semantic content of the sentence is said to obey the minimalist constraint; on the other hand the intuitive content of the utterance can be freely enriched, as in this typical example from Scott Soames:

A man goes into a coffee shop and sits at the counter. The waitress asks him what he wants. He says, 'I would like coffee, please.' The sentence uttered is unspecific in several respects—its semantic content does not indicate whether the coffee is to be in

---

[5] This strategy defines the version of minimalism which, in Recanati (2004), I call 'indexicalism'.

form of beans, grounds, or liquid, nor does it indicate whether the amount in question is a drop, a cup, a gallon, a sack, or a barrel. Nevertheless, it is obvious from the situation what the man has in mind, and the waitress is in no doubt about what to do. She brings him a cup of freshly brewed coffee. If asked to describe the transaction, she might well say, 'He ordered a cup of coffee' or 'He said he wanted a cup of coffee', meaning, of course, the brewed, drinkable kind. In so doing, she would, quite correctly, be reporting the content of the man's order, or assertion, as going beyond the semantic content of the sentence he uttered. (Soames, 2002: 78)

Free enrichment—the process responsible for making the interpretation of an utterance more specific than its literal interpretation (as when 'coffee' is contextually understood as *coffee of the brewed, drinkable kind*)—is a top–down, pragmatically controlled pragmatic process. Another process of the same sort, 'predicate transfer' (Nunberg, 1995), takes us from a certain property, conventionally expressed by some predicative expression, to a distinct property bearing a systematic relation to it. For example, in 'I am parked out back', the property that is literally encoded by the verb phrase is a property of cars (the property of being parked out back), but the property which the expression actually contributes to the (intuitive) truth-conditions in this utterance is not a property of cars but another, systematically related property, namely the property a car-owner has when his or her car has the former property. In an utterance such as 'I am parked out back', transfer takes place because there is a linguistic mismatch between the predicate (which denotes a property of cars) and what it is applied to (a person). But such mismatch is not necessary for predicate transfer. Just as, through transfer, 'The ham sandwich left without paying' is understood as saying something about the customer who ordered the sandwich, 'The ham sandwich stinks' can be so understood, in a suitable context, even though the property of stinking potentially applies to sandwiches as well as to customers. Like free enrichment, the process of transfer is not a linguistically controlled but a pragmatically controlled pragmatic process: it is not triggered by something linguistic—some aspect of the linguistic signal being processed—but takes place in order to make sense of the communicative act performed by the speaker.

Predicate transfer and free enrichment are only two among a family of top–down pragmatic processes that affect the intuitive truth-conditions of utterances. This family of processes I call 'modulation', as opposed to the (bottom–up) process of assigning contextual values to indexicals, free variables etc. (Recanati, 2004). The syncretic view acknowledges modulation, but limits its effects to the intuitive content of the utterance, that is, to the content of the speech act performed by the speaker. The content of the *sentence* (the 'minimal proposition' it expresses) is said to be unaffected, in accordance with minimalism. But the syncretic view can be criticized, on the grounds that the 'minimal proposition' it posits has no useful work to do. It is supposed to give us the semantic content of the sentence (as opposed to the content of the speech act), but do we really need to posit such a level of semantic content for the global sentence? Maybe we don't. What must ultimately be accounted for is what speakers say in the pragmatic sense, the content of their assertions (or of whatever speech acts they perform by their utterances). The job of linguistic meanings, semantic contents, etc. is to contribute to the overall explanation. But, one may argue, it is sufficient to assign semantic contents (in context) to simple expressions. Modulation will operate on those contents, and the composition rules will compose the resulting senses, thereby yielding the content of the speaker's assertion. Of course it is possible to let the composition rules compose the plain semantic contents of the constituent expressions, thereby yielding the minimal proposition expressed by the sentence (an absurd proposition, in many cases). However, the content of the speaker's assertion will still be determined by composing the modulated senses resulting from the operation of pragmatic processes on the contents of the constituent expressions; so it is unclear what additional job the minimal proposition is supposed to be doing.[6]

Many people think that we need the minimal proposition because it is the input to the pragmatic processes which take us from what the speaker literally says to what she actually conveys. Those processes are said to operate globally on the output of the grammar. But that view has been rightly criticized. In 'There is a lion in the courtyard', 'lion' can be understood, through transfer, in the representational sense: the thing that is said to be in the courtyard is not a (real) lion but a *representation* (more specifically, a statue) *of* lion. Now consider 'There is a stone lion in the courtyard'. What is said to be made of stone here? Clearly, it is the statue, rather than the lion which the statue represents. This simple fact shows that the process of representational transfer must take place *before* the composition rule associated with the noun-noun construction applies to the semantic values of the nouns 'stone' and 'lion'.[7] If

---

[6] King and Stanley (2005) offer an analogous argument purporting to show that it is fruitless to ascribe functional 'characters' to sentences: it is sufficient to ascribe characters to the parts, and redundant to ascribe characters also to the whole.

[7] Note that this composition rule itself is context-sensitive (Partee, 1984: 294–5). The denotation of the compound results from intersecting the (literal, or pragmatically derived) denotation of the head noun with the set of objects that bear a certain relation R to

predicate transfer applied globally, after the grammatically triggered composition rules have applied, the interpretation we would get for the noun-phrase
'a stone lion' would be something like: *a representation of (a lion that is made of
stone)*. But the correct interpretation is: *(a representation of a lion) that is made
of stone*. We must therefore give up the Gricean idea that pragmatic processes
operate globally on the output of the grammar.[8] And this means that we don't
really need the 'minimal proposition'.

The position I have just described I call 'quasi-contextualism'. It is very
close to full-fledged contextualism, but to get to the latter we need to take one
more step.

So far we have granted that the pragmatic processes involved in modulation (free enrichment, transfer, etc.) are optional. For example, nothing
prevents the sentence 'There is a lion in the courtyard' from being understood
literally, as talking about a real lion. Or consider the following instance of free
enrichment:

She took out her key and opened the door.

The pragmatic process that enriches the meaning of this sentence so as to
convey both a sense of temporal order (giving to 'and' the sense of 'and then')
and a notion of the instrument used in opening the door (giving to 'opened
the door' the sense of 'opened the door with the key')—that process might
also not take place. As Grice emphasized, such pragmatic suggestions are
always cancellable, explicitly or contextually. Once the pragmatic suggestion
has been cancelled, what the words contribute to truth-conditional content is
their bare linguistic senses.

From the optional character of modulation, it follows that the minimal
proposition, even if it plays no causal-explanatory role, has at least the
following, counterfactual status: it is the proposition which the utterance
would express if no pragmatic process of modulation took place (Recanati,
1993: 318). To get full-fledged contextualism we must deprive the minimal
proposition even of this counterfactual status. While quasi-contextualism
considers the minimal proposition as a theoretically useless entity, and denies
that it plays any effective role in communication, contextualism goes much
further: it denies that the notion even makes sense. Contextualism ascribes to

the (literal, or pragmatically derived) denotation of the modifying noun. That relation can
only be contextually determined. In 'stone lion', 'R' is typically assigned the relation *being made
of*, but in less accessible contexts a different relation will be assigned to the variable.

[8] See Sag (1981), Recanati (1995), and Jackendoff (1997: 55 and 65–6).

modulation a form of necessity which makes it ineliminable. *Without contextual modulation, no proposition could be expressed*—that is the gist of contextualism. In this framework the notion of a 'minimal' proposition collapses: there *is* no proposition that is expressed in a purely 'bottom–up' manner.

III. Pragmatic Composition

To say that the pragmatic processes of modulation are optional is to say that in a suitable context, the senses expressed by the words would be, simply, the senses they possess in virtue of the rules of the language. The first of the three contextualist positions I am about to discuss—the pragmatic composition view (PC)—accepts that the literal, input sense undergoing modulation could, in a suitable context, be the expressed sense. So it construes the pragmatic processes of modulation as optional. But it construes them as optional only *with respect to the word whose sense is modulated*. If we consider not words in isolation, but the complex expressions in which they occur, we see that the pragmatic processes of modulation are not always contingent and dispensable, but often essential. Even though the linguistic meaning of a given word (or the semantic content we get after indexical resolution) could be the expressed sense, still the process of semantic composition, that is, the putting together of that sense with the senses of other expressions, cannot proceed unless appropriate adjustments take place so as to make the parts fit together within an appropriate whole. On this view words have meanings which could go directly into the interpretation, without modulation, but it is the composition process that forces modulation to take place, or at least invites it: often the meanings of individual words do not cohere by themselves, and can be fitted together only by undergoing a process of mutual adjustment.

Let us start with a simple example in which modulation is required to overcome a semantic mismatch:[9]

John hears the piano.

The verb 'hear' arguably denotes a relation between sentient organisms and sounds. Only sounds can be heard. Since a piano is not a sound, but a musical instrument, some adjustment is needed to make sense of 'hear the piano':

---

[9] This example is borrowed from Langacker (1991: 193–6).

either the noun-phrase 'the piano' must be given a metonymical interpretation, so that it stands for the sounds emitted by the piano; or (more plausibly) the verb 'hear' itself must be understood, not in its basic sense, but in a derived sense resulting from semantic transfer. An object is heard in the derived sense whenever the sound it emits is heard in the literal, basic sense.[10]

We need to adjust or modulate the meaning of words even in the absence of linguistic mismatch. Think of an example like

John hates the piano.

A piano is certainly an object that *can* be hated, however strictly one construes the predicate 'hate'. Still, some contextual enrichment is in order, because to hate the piano is to hate it *under some aspect or dimension*. One may hate the sounds emitted by the piano, or one can hate playing the piano, or one can hate the piano as a piece of furniture, etc. The relevant dimension is contextually provided through the process of enrichment. (Similarly, if I say that Jim likes John's sister, the sense of 'like' will be—defeasibly—modulated so as to mean something different from what it means in 'Jim likes pork'.)

The crucial question is whether the sentence expresses a proposition independently of this type of modulation. To address this issue, let us consider another example, due to John Searle. The word 'cut' is not ambiguous, Searle says, yet it makes quite different contributions to the truth-conditions of the utterance in 'Bill cut the grass' and 'Sally cut the cake'. That is because background assumptions play a role in fixing satisfaction-conditions for the verb-phrase, and different background assumptions underlie the use of 'cut' in connection with grass and cakes respectively. We (defeasibly) assume that grass is cut in a certain way, and cakes in another way. Through enrichment the assumed way of cutting finds its way into the utterance's truth-conditions:

Though the occurrence of the word 'cut' is literal in [both] utterances . . . , and though the word is not ambiguous, it determines different sets of truth conditions for the different sentences. The sort of thing that constitutes cutting the grass is quite different from, e.g., the sort of thing that constitutes cutting a cake. One way to see

---

[10] It is a bit excessive to talk of the 'literal' sense of 'hear', as if the other sense was not literal. It is better to speak of a family of (literal) senses, one of them being basic or primary. But even that is debatable, as a reader for Oxford University Press pointed out: maybe there is a family of (systematically related) senses for 'hear' and other perception verbs, none of which is more basic than the others. Nunberg discusses that sort of case in his early paper on semantic transfer (Nunberg, 1979).

this is to imagine what constitutes obeying the order to cut something. If someone tells me to cut the grass and I rush out and stab it with a knife, or if I am ordered to cut the cake and I run over it with a lawnmower, in each case I will have failed to obey the order. That is not what the speaker meant by his literal and serious utterance of the sentence. (Searle, 1980: 222–3)

Now an advocate of the syncretic view will insist that a sentence such as 'Cut the grass' expresses something that has literal conditions of satisfaction quite independent of any background assumption; something very abstract, involving the constant meaning of 'cut' and not the variable senses it takes on particular uses (or types of use). Stabbing the grass with a knife and running over it with a lawnmower are two ways of literally obeying the order 'Cut the grass', on this view. But the contextualist remains sceptical. To get something genuinely evaluable, he claims, that is, something which enables us to partition possible worlds into those in which the relevant condition is satisfied and those in which it is not, we need background assumptions (Searle, 1978). We cannot specify a determinate proposition which the sentence can be said literally to express, without building unarticulated assumptions into that proposition. The best we can do is to construct a disjunction of the propositions which could be determinately expressed by that sentence against alternative background assumptions.

In support of this controversial claim, Searle (1980) sets up an example for which no background assumption is readily available: 'Cut the sun'. What counts as obeying that order? We don't quite know. The abstract condition we can associate with that sentence (involving some form of linear separation affecting the integrity of the sun) is, precisely, too abstract to enable us to tell the worlds in which the condition is satisfied from the worlds in which it is not. It is not determinate enough to give us specific truth-conditions or obedience-conditions.

In previous writings I gave a real-life example of the phenomenon Searle is drawing our attention to.[11] Consider the following dialogue from *Desire*, a film by Frank Borsage (1936):

—Pedro!
—Yes sir.
—Take the plate to the kitchen and disarm the fricassee.

What does the complex phrase 'disarm the fricassee' literally mean? It is hard to tell, even though we know the meanings of all the constituents. To make

---

[11] See Recanati (1997: 120; 1999: 162–3).

sense of that phrase, we must know the context. In the film, the context is as follows: (i) Gary Cooper (the speaker) is handing a fricassee plate to the waiter (Pedro); (ii) the fricassee plate contains a gun; (iii) that gun has just fallen from the hands of someone during a brief fight around the dinner table. With respect to that situation, the phrase 'disarm the fricassee' makes perfect sense: it means that the waiter is to remove the gun from the plate. Without a proper background, however, we no more know the obedience-conditions of Cooper's utterance 'Disarm the fricassee' than we know the obedience-conditions of 'Cut the sun'.

In these examples, composing the senses of the parts so as to get a coherent sense for the whole involves imagining (or retrieving from memory) a possible scenario in which the senses of the parts fit together. That imaginative exercise involves elaborating what the meanings of the words give us—going beyond that linguistic meaning and, for example, interpreting 'disarm' in the specific sense of 'take the gun out of' or 'remove the gun from'.

As we shall see, a more radical version of contextualism denies that words like 'cut' possess a determinate sense: the constant meaning of 'cut' is more like an abstract schema which has to be fleshed out in context, and that is why elaboration is needed to get a determinate proposition. But the pragmatic composition view traces the need for modulation to the composition process, and some examples clearly support that view. Thus consider the adjective 'red'. Vagueness notwithstanding, it expresses a definite property: the property of being red or having the colour red. That property could, in principle, go into the interpretation of a sentence in which the adjective 'red' occurs. (For example: 'Imagine a red surface.') But in most cases the following question will arise: what is it for the thing talked about to count as having that colour? *Unless that question is answered, the utterance ascribing redness to the thing talked about (John's car, say) will not be truth-evaluable.* It is not enough to know the colour that is in question (red) and the thing to which that colour is ascribed (John's car). To fix the utterance's truth-conditions, we need to know something more—something which the meanings of the words do not and cannot give us: we need to know *what it is for that thing (or for that sort of thing) to count as being that colour.* What is it for a car, a bird, a house, a pen, or a pair of shoes to count as red? To answer such questions, we need to appeal to background assumptions and world knowledge.[12] Linguistic competence does not suffice: pragmatic fine-tuning is called for.

---

[12] 'For a bird to be red (in the normal case), it should have most of the surface of its body red, though not its beak, legs, eyes, and of course its inner organs. Furthermore, the red color

To sum up, on the view (PC) under discussion, even if the semantic content of a word is fixed by language (and context, if the expression is indexical), composing it with the contents of other words often requires help from above. It is semantic composition which has a fundamentally pragmatic character. So there is a sense in which modulation is necessary, but that is not quite the sense in which indexical resolution is. With indexical resolution there is a semantic gap and an instruction to fill the gap—both the gap and the instruction being part of the linguistic meaning of the expression. With modulation, there need be no gap and there is no instruction to search for some contextual filler. The expression means something, and that meaning could go into the interpretation—so modulation is optional—but to determine a suitable sense for complex expressions, we need to go beyond the meaning of individual words and creatively enrich or otherwise adjust what we are given in virtue purely of linguistic meaning. We must go beyond linguistic meaning, without being linguistically instructed to do so, if we are to make sense of the utterance.

IV. Literalist Responses to the Contextualist Challenge

According to Emma Borg (and other defenders of the syncretic view), the fact that we are unable to specify intuitive conditions of application for the predicate 'cut the sun' does not support the contextualist conclusion that sentences per se do not have truth-conditions. There is, she claims, a crucial difference between 'knowledge of truth-conditions and the knowledge that

should be the bird's natural color, since we normally regard a bird as being "really" red even if it is painted white all over. A kitchen table, on the other hand, is red even if it is only painted red, and even if its "natural" color underneath the paint is, say, white. Morever, for a table to be red only its upper surface needs to be red, but not necessarily its legs and its bottom surface. Similarly, a red apple, as Quine pointed out, needs to be red only on the outside, but a red hat needs to be red only in its external upper surface, a red crystal is red both inside and outside, and a red watermelon is red only inside. For a book to be red is for its cover but not necessarily for its inner pages to be mostly red, while for a newspaper to be red is for all of its pages to be red. For a house to be red is for its outside walls, but not necessarily its roof (and windows and door) to be mostly red, while a red car must be red in its external surface including its roof (but not its windows, wheels, bumper, etc.). A red star only needs to appear red from the earth, a red glaze needs to be red only after it is fired, and a red mist or a red powder are red not simply inside or ouside. A red pen need not even have any red part (the ink may turn red only when in contact with the paper). In short, what counts for one type of thing to be red is not what counts for another.' (Lahav, 1989: 264) truth-conditions are satisfied' (Borg, forthcoming). We may know the obedience-conditions of 'Cut the sun' in a purely 'disquotational' manner (i.e. we may know that 'Cut the sun' is obeyed iff the addressee cuts the sun), without knowing *what counts as* cutting the sun, in the context at hand. So there is no reason to deny sentences genuine truth-conditions. The sentence 'Oscar cuts the sun' does possess truth-conditions; such truth-conditions are determined by a recursive truth-theory for the language, which issues theorems such as '*Oscar cuts the sun* is true iff Oscar cuts the sun'. We know those truth-conditions provided we know the language. What we don't know, simply in virtue of knowing the language, is 'a method of verification for those truth-conditions' (Borg, forthcoming). This, then, is the syncretist's ultimate reply to the contextualist. According to the syncretist, the contextualist is guilty of endorsing a form of (so-called) 'verificationism'.[13]

This move strikes me as an unacceptable weakening of the notion of truth-condition. The central idea of truth-conditional semantics (as opposed to mere 'translational semantics') is the idea that, via truth, we connect words and the world.[14] If we know the truth-conditions of a sentence, we know *which state of affairs must hold for the sentence to be true*. T-sentences display knowledge of truth-conditions in that sense only if the right-hand-side of the biconditional is *used*, that is, only if the necessary and sufficient condition which it states is transparent to the utterer of the T-sentence. If I say '*Oscar cuts the sun* is true iff Oscar cuts the sun', without knowing what it is to 'cut the sun', then the T-sentence I utter no more counts as displaying knowledge of truth-conditions than if I utter it without knowing who Oscar is (i.e. if I use the name 'Oscar' deferentially, in such a way that the right-hand side is not really *used*, but involves some kind of mention).[15]

One may doubt the feasibility of referential or truth-conditional semantics and defend translational semantics as a viable alternative. I have heard

---

[13]   Ibid. The first occurrence of this line of reply to contextualism can be found in Marcelo Dascal's discussion of Searle's 'Literal Meaning' (Dascal, 1981: 173–4). The most recent occurrence I have seen is in Cappelen and Lepore (2005).

[14]   See Lewis (1970: 18–19), Evans and McDowell (1976: pp. vii–xi).

[15]   As Harman pointed out, if pure disquotational knowledge counts as knowledge of truth-conditions (in a suitably weak sense), then knowledge of truth-conditions (in that sense) does not count as knowledge of meaning. 'There is a sense in which we can know the truth conditions of an English sentence without knowing the first thing about the meaning of the English sentence. To borrow David Wiggins's (1972) example, we might know that the sentence "All mimsy were the borogroves" is true if and only if all mimsy were the borogroves. However, in knowing this we would not know the first thing about the meaning of the sentence, "All mimsy were the borogroves".' (Harman, 1999: 196)

(or read) arguments to that effect. My point however is that *if* we stick to the standard truth-conditional project (as Davidsonians like Cappelen and Lepore surely ought to do) then we should not accept the syncretist's claim that we somehow know the truth-conditions of 'Harry cut the sun'. (For we don't.)

The contextualist challenge is likely to elicit another unsatisfactory response, this time from the 'indexicalist'. To each dimension of contextual elaboration, the indexicalist may argue, there corresponds a slot in logical form, which must be filled for the utterance to say something definite. To illustrate that point, let us consider another contextualist example from Searle (1983: 145–7).

When we ask someone to open the door, the content of the request goes beyond what is linguistically encoded. Not only is it necessary for the addressee to identify the relevant door (i.e. to complete or otherwise enrich the incomplete definite description 'the door'). She must also determine in what sense the door must be 'opened'. Besides doors and windows, eyes and wounds can be opened. Now if the addressee 'opened' the door by making an incision in it with a scalpel, as when opening a wound, she would not have satisfied the request. Still, in a special context, it could be that the request to open the door must be satisfied precisely by incising it by means of a scalpel. The manner of opening is thus defeasibly indicated by context, it is not determinable on the basis of just the linguistic meaning of the sentence (including the direct object of the verb). To be sure, we can make it explicit in the sentence itself by introducing supplementary details, but each addition of this sort cannot fail to introduce other underdeterminacies. If, for example, we add that the door must be opened 'with a key', we don't specify whether the key must be inserted into the lock or rather used like an axe to break the door open (Searle, 1992: 182). However explicit the sentence, there will always be some aspect of truth-conditional content that is contextually determined without being explicitly articulated.

At this point, the imagined indexicalist response consists in saying that, like all verbs, 'open' (or 'disarm' or 'cut') is associated with a complex frame,[16] involving a certain number of argument roles: a location playing the role of INSIDE; another location operating as OUTSIDE; a BOUNDARY separating the two; a MOVING OBJECT liable to pass from inside to outside (or the other way round); an OBSTACLE, that is, an entity preventing the passage of

---

[16] The notion of frame which I am using is that elaborated by Fillmore in a series of papers. See Fillmore (1976, 1982, 1985), and Fillmore and Atkins (1992).

the moving object; an AGENT liable to free the passage by means of ACTION on the obstacle; an INSTRUMENT serving to accomplish the action; and so on and so forth. In context, each of the variables I have enumerated must be assigned a particular value: the INSIDE, the OUTSIDE, the OBSTACLE, the PATH, etc., all must be contextually identified. In the case of 'opening a wound', the INSIDE is the interior of the wound, the OUTSIDE is the exterior of the body, the MOVING OBJECT is the internal secretions of the wound, and so on. This contextual assignment of values to the variables is what determines the specific interpretation given to 'open' in a particular context, and it is no different from what is required for interpreting a context-sensitive expression. It is therefore unnecessary to modify semantic theory in order to give an account of Searle's examples; it is enough to extend the list of context-sensitive expressions, so as to include all verbs (in so far as they are all associated with frames which comprise a number of argument roles, the fillers of which must be contextually assigned).

This indexicalist response is no more convincing than the syncretist response was. Let's admit that the verb 'to open' is associated with the complex frame I have mentioned. Does that make it an indexical or context-sensitive expression, whose use triggers, indeed mandates, a contextual process of value assignment? No. There is an important difference between the argument roles of a frame and the indexical variables associated with context-sensitive expressions. Indexical variables *must* be contextually assigned values for the expression to acquire a definite semantic content. If the referent of 'he' in 'He boarded John's boat' is not contextually specified, or if the relation between John and the boat remains indefinite, the utterance does not have definite truth-conditions. In contrast, the argument roles of a frame may but need not be assigned contextual values. The contextual assignment process is optional; it may, or may not, take place, depending on what is contextually relevant. In other words, it is the context (not the sentence) which determines which, among the many argument roles of a given frame, are contextually assigned particular values, and which remain indefinite (existentially quantified). In many contexts, it is of no importance whether the door is opened with a key or in another way; what counts is simply that it is opened. To be sure, for any given verb (or verb plus syntactic context), there is a small number of argument roles in the frame for which the contextual assignment of value is linguistically mandated; but the indexicalist response presupposes something much stronger: that the verb 'open' is like an indexical expression, which acquires a definite content only when the argument roles of the associated frame (*all* the argument roles, in so far as they can all be contextually foregrounded) are contextually assigned values. That is evidently too strong. In a given context, many of the argument roles which feature in the frame are existentially quantified rather than contextually assigned values. This does not prevent the verb 'open' from expressing a definite content, in such a context.

To sum up, for indexicals it is the conventional meaning of the expression which triggers the process of indexical resolution and makes it mandatory. With ordinary expressions such as 'open', it is the context, not the conventional meaning of the expression, which is responsible for foregrounding certain aspects of the described situation and triggering a process of contextual specification which goes well beyond what is linguistically encoded. The process in question is top–down, not bottom–up. It is a pragmatically controlled pragmatic process, rather than a linguistically controlled pragmatic process, like indexical resolution.

V. Radical Contextualism

PC is not the only possible contextualist position. According to another one— the wrong format view (WF)—it is not just semantic composition which requires adjustment and modulation of word meaning. Individual word meanings themselves are such that they *could not* go directly into the interpretation. They do not have the proper format for that. They are either too abstract and schematic, in such a way that elaboration or fleshing out is needed to reach a determinate content; or they are too rich and must undergo 'feature-cancellation', or some other screening process through which some aspects will be backgrounded and others focused on. Note that there are versions of this view which take the meaning of a word to consist both in some abstract schema in need of elaboration *and* a large store of encyclopedic representations most of which must be screened off as irrelevant on any particular use.

WF is more radical than PC, but a third contextualist position, meaning eliminativism, is by far the most radical: it is a sort of WF pushed to the extremes. That position comes close to what I think Austin and Wittgenstein had in mind. Let me introduce it by contrasting it with WF.

According to WF, the sense expressed by an expression must always be contextually constructed on the basis of the (overly rich or overly abstract) meaning, or semantic potential, of the word type. Just as the reference of an indexical expression is not linguistically given but must be contextually determined, the sense of an ordinary expression is not linguistically given but must be constructed. In that framework there still is a role for the linguistic meaning of word types: it is the input (or part of the input) to the construction process.

The difference between meaning eliminativism (ME) and WF is that, according to ME, we don't need linguistic meanings even to serve as input to the construction process. The senses that are the words' contributions to contents are constructed, but the construction can proceed without the help of conventional, context-independent word meanings.

Note that, according to a trivial extension of WF, the linguistic meaning of a word is not merely the input to the process of semantic modulation: it is also the output of a process of induction through which the child, or anyone learning the language, abstracts the meaning of the word from the specific senses which it expresses, or seems to express, on the observed occasions of use. It is a truism that the child or language learner starts not with pre-formatted linguistic meanings, but with actual uses of words and the contextualized senses that words assume on such uses. So both contextualized senses and context-independent linguistic meanings are input, and both are output, in some construction process. The linguistic meaning of a word type is the output of an abstraction process; that process takes as input the contextualized senses used as evidence by the language learner. On the other hand, the linguistic meaning of a word type also serves as input to the modulation process which yields as output the contextualized sense of the word on a particular occasion of use (Figure 7.1).

ME purports to simplify WF by *suppressing the intermediary step* (linguistic meaning) and computing directly the contextual sense which an expression assumes on a particular occasion of use on the basis of the contextual senses which that expression had on previous occasions of use—without ever abstracting, or needing to abstract, 'the' linguistic meaning of the expression type.[17] This amounts to merging the two construction processes: the abstraction of meaning from use, and the modulation of meaning in use (Figure 7.2).

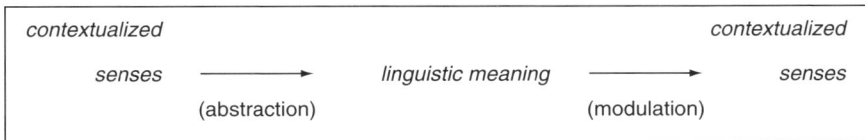

Figure 7.1

[17] For a psychological model supporting ME, see Hintzman (1986, 1988). Similar ideas can be found in Bartsch (1998).

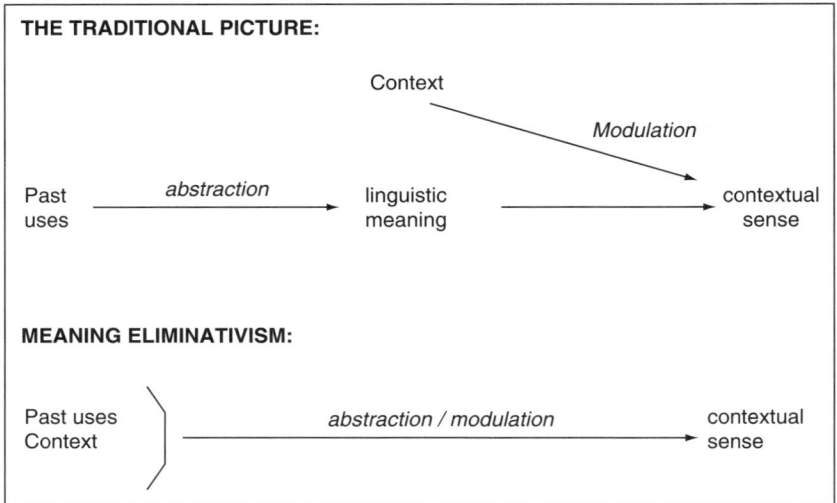

Figure 7.2

According to ME, there is a single process of abstraction-modulation which takes as input previous uses of the expression and yields as output the contextual sense assumed by the expression on the current use.

On the resulting picture, words are not primitively associated with abstract 'conditions of application', constituting their conventional meaning (as on the Fregean picture). The conditions of application for words must be contextually determined, like the reference of indexicals. What words, *qua* linguistic types, are associated with are not abstract conditions of application, but rather *particular applications*.

In the spirit of Wittgenstein, consider what it is for someone to learn a predicate P. The learner, whom I'll call Tom, observes the application of P in a particular situation S_1; he associates P and S_1. At this stage, the semantic potential of P for Tom is the fact that P is applicable to S_1. In a new situation S_2, Tom will judge that P applies only if he finds that S_2 sufficiently resembles S_1. To be sure, it is possible for S_2 to resemble S_1 in a way that is not pertinent for the application of P. The application of P to S_2 will then be judged faulty by the community, who will correct Tom. The learning phase for Tom consists in noting a sufficient number of situations which, like S_1, legitimate the application of P, as opposed to those, like S_2, which do not legitimate it. The semantic potential of P for Tom at the end of his learning phase can thus be thought of as *a collection of legitimate situations of application*; that is, a collection of situations such that the members of the community agree that P applies in or to those situations. The situations in question are the *source-situations*. The future applications of P will be underpinned, in Tom's usage, by the judgement that the situation of application (or *target-situation*) is similar to the source-situations.

In this theory the semantic potential of P is *a collection of source-situations*, and the conditions of application of P in a given use, involving a given target-situation S_3, are *a set of features which S_3 must possess to be similar to the source-situations*. The set of features in question, and so the conditions of application for P, will not be the same for all uses; it is going to depend, among other things, on the target-situation. One target-situation can be similar to the source-situations in certain respects and another target-situation can be similar to them in different respects. But the contextual variability of the conditions of application does not end there. Even when the target-situation is fixed, the relevant dimensions for evaluating the similarity between that situation and the source-situations remain underdetermined: those dimensions will vary as a function of the subject of conversation, the concerns of the speech participants, etc.

One particularly important factor in the contextual variation is the relevant 'contrast set'. As Tversky (1977) has pointed out, judgements of similarity are very much affected by variations along that dimension. If we ask which country, Sweden or Hungary, most resembles Austria (without specifying the relevant dimension of similarity), the answer will depend on the set of countries considered. If that set includes not just Sweden, Hungary, and Austria but also Poland, then Sweden will be judged more like Austria than Hungary; but if the last of the four countries considered is Norway and not Poland, then it is Hungary which will be judged more like Austria than Sweden. The explanation for that fact is simple. Poland and Hungary have certain salient geopolitical features in common which can serve as basis for the classification: Hungary and Poland are then put together and opposed to Austria and Sweden. If we replace Poland by Norway in the contrast set a new principle of classification emerges, based on the salient features shared by Norway and Sweden: in this new classification Hungary and Austria go together. Tversky concludes that judgements of similarity appeal to features having a high 'diagnostic value' (or classificatory significance), and that the diagnostic value of features itself depends on the available contrast set.

So the set of similarity features on which sense depends itself depends upon the relevant contrast set, and the relevant contrast set depends upon the current interests of the conversational participants. It follows that one can, by simply shifting the background interests ascribed to the conversational participants, change the truth-conditions of a given utterance, even though the facts (including the target-situation) don't change, and the semantic values of indexicals remain fixed. Charles Travis has produced dozens of examples of this phenomenon of truth-conditional shiftiness over the last thirty years, and his examples often involve manipulating the relevant contrast set.[18]

VI. Conclusion

In this chapter I have discussed a number of positions, going from the early literalists' blatant underestimation of context-sensitivity, to the most radical form of contextualism. The positions are:

- proto-literalism
- eternalism
- conventionalism
- indexicalism
- the syncretic view
- quasi-contextualism
- pragmatic composition
- the wrong format view
- meaning eliminativism

The first four positions stand squarely on the literalist side; the last three, squarely on the contextualist side. The syncretic view and quasi-contextualism fall in between.

Literalism, in general, minimizes context-sensitivity. It strives to preserve the view that the proposition expressed by a (complete) sentence *is* the linguistic meaning of that sentence—or one of its meanings, if the sentence is ambiguous. The only exception that is allowed for is indexicality, which is

---

[18] See Travis (1975, 1981, 1989, 2000). The following example, inspired from Austin, is taken almost at random from a list of Travis-examples compiled by Claudia Bianchi (then a graduate student of mine): 'Fred is walking with his young nephew beside a pond where a decoy duck is floating. Pointing to the decoy, he says, "That's a duck". Again we might ask whether what he said is true or false. But again, the above description is not enough for us to tell. If Fred has just finished laughing at a sportsman who blasted a decoy out of the pond, and if he has been trying to show his nephew how to avoid similar mistakes, then what he said is false. But suppose that Fred and his nephew are attending the annual national decoy exhibition, and the boy has been having trouble distinguishing ducks from geese. Then what Fred said may well be true. It would also be true had Fred said what he did in pointing out the fact that all the other ducks were poor copies (perhaps on the order of Donald Duck).' (Travis, 1975: 51)

not considered as a threat to the general picture because it is a form of context-sensitivity which remains under linguistic control. Indexicalism goes as far as to generalize indexicality in order to protect semantic content from 'top–down' or 'strong' pragmatic effects—a form of context-sensitivity that is *not* under linguistic control.

Such an exclusion of 'top–down' or 'strong' pragmatic effects on truth-conditions I find dogmatic. If we give up the stronger forms of literalism and admit that the content of an utterance is not entirely fixed by linguistic rules, but has to be contextually determined by making sense of the speaker's speech act, is it not obvious that some aspects of content may happen to be contributed entirely by context? Why insist that *all* aspects of content must be traceable to aspects of linguistic form, if not because one is still in the grip of the literalist prejudice?

Minimalism can be defended, by explicitly going stipulative. One may grant the existence, or at least the possibility, of strong pragmatic effects, while defining 'the proposition literally expressed by an utterance' in such a way that it can only satisfy the minimalist constraint. In other words, one may draw a distinction between what is said in the intuitive sense—the actual content of one's utterance—and the proposition which can be assigned to that utterance as its 'literal' content, that is, the minimal content that results from contextually assigning values to all indexical or free variables. That is the gist of the 'syncretic view'. In this framework the proposition literally expressed satisfies minimalism by definition: it does not incorporate the output of pragmatic processes unless they are mandatory and triggered by elements in the syntactic structure of the sentence.

What is the point of positing such a minimal proposition? As I have emphasized, it is unclear that it plays any role in the actual process of interpretation. This much must be conceded to the quasi-contextualist. It has been argued that we need the minimal proposition to account for 'the character of the information available to the hearer' (Bach, 1994: 158). The minimal proposition, Bach says, is 'included in the information available to the hearer in understanding an utterance' (1994: 159). What this means, presumably, is that the hearer knows the literal semantic values of the constituents, and knows the appropriate composition rules. He should therefore be credited with the ability to compose those values so as to determine the literal semantic value of the whole—the minimal proposition. In practice, that need not be done. Since modulation takes place locally, the interpreter does not actually compose the literal semantic values of the constituents to determine the minimal proposition; rather, he directly determines what is said (in the intuitive sense) by composing the pragmatic values resulting from whatever pragmatic processes locally operate on the literal semantic values of the constituents. Be that as it may, the minimal proposition is said to be 'available to the hearer, even if not actually accessed' (Bach, 1994: 158). The interpreter does not compute it, but he could.

Full-fledged contextualism questions the claim that, independent of modulation, it is possible to determine a minimal proposition by mechanically composing the meanings of the constituents. I have briefly indicated the sort of argument a contextualist may put forward in support of this denial, but the issue is far from being settled. My intention was not to argue for (or against) contextualism in this chapter, but only to convince you that the debate ought to take place. This means that we must get rid of the last literalist prejudice: we must stop *presupposing* that there is such a thing as the minimal proposition expressed by an utterance. It is important to realize that that literalist assumption, pervasive though it is among philosophers of language, rests on a substantial and highly controversial conception of both word meaning and sentence meaning. There is no reason to rule out, a priori, a contextualist account of word and sentence meaning, even if such an account entails the nonexistence of 'minimal propositions'.

REFERENCES

Bach, Kent (1994). 'Conversational Impliciture', *Mind and Language,* 9: 124–62.
Bar-Hillel, Yehoshua (1954). 'Indexical Expressions', *Mind,* 63: 359–79.
Bartsch, Renate (1998). *Dynamic Conceptual Semantics* (Stanford, Calif.: CSLI Publications/Folli).
Barwise, Jon, and Perry, John (1983). *Situations and Attitudes* (Cambridge, Mass.: MIT Press).
Borg, Emma (forthcoming). 'Saying What You Mean: Unarticulated Constituents and Communication'.
Cappelen, Herman, and Lepore, Ernie (2005). 'Radical and Moderate Pragmatics: Does Meaning Determine Truth-Conditions?', in Zoltan Szabó (ed.), *Semantics versus Pragmatics* (Oxford: Oxford University Press), 45–71.
Cohen, Jonathan (1971). 'Some Remarks on Grice's Views about the Logical Particles of Natural Language', in Yehoshua Bar-Hillel (ed.), *Pragmatics of Natural Languages* (Dordrecht: Reidel), 50–68.
—— (1993). 'The Semantics of Metaphor', in Andrew Ortony (ed.), *Metaphor and Thought* (2nd edn., Cambridge: Cambridge University Press), 58–70.

Conant, J. (1998). 'Wittgenstein on Meaning and Use', *Philosophical Investigations*, 21: 232–50.

Dascal, Marcelo (1981). 'Contextualism', in Herman Parret, Marina Sbisà, and Jeff Verschueren (eds.), *Possibilities and Limitations of Pragmatics* (Amsterdam: Benjamins), 153–77.

Evans, Gareth, and McDowell, John (1976). 'Introduction' to *Truth and Meaning: Essays in Semantics* (Oxford: Clarendon Press), pp. vii–xxiii.

Fillmore, Charles (1976). 'Frame Semantics and the Nature of Language', *Annals of the New York Academy of Sciences*, 280: 20–32.

—— (1982). 'Frame Semantics', in the Linguistic Society of Korea (ed.), *Linguistics in the Morning Calm* (Seoul: Hanshin), 111–38.

—— (1985). 'Frames and the Semantics of Understanding', *Quaderni di Semantica*, 6: 222–54.

—— and Atkins, Sue (1992). 'Toward a Frame-Based Lexicon: The Semantics of RISK and its Neighbors', in Adrienne Lehrer and Eva Kittay (eds.), *Frames, Fields and Contrasts: New Essays in Semantic and Lexical Organization* (Hillsdale, NJ: Lawrence Erlbaum Associates), 75–102.

Grice, Paul (1989). *Studies in the Way of Words* (Cambridge, Mass.: Harvard University Press).

Harman, Gilbert (1999). 'Meaning and Semantics', in his *Reasoning, Meaning, and Mind* (Oxford: Clarendon Press), 192–205.

Hintzman, Douglas (1986). ' "Schema Abstraction" in a Multiple-Trace Memory Model', *Psychological Review*, 93: 411–28.

—— (1988). 'Judgments of Frequency and Recognition Memory in a Multiple-Trace Memory Model', *Psychological Review*, 95: 528–51.

Jackendoff, Ray (1997). *The Architecture of the Language Faculty* (Cambridge, Mass.: MIT Press).

Kaplan, David (1989). 'Demonstratives', in Joseph Almog, Howard Wettstein, and John Perry (eds.), *Themes from Kaplan* (New York: Oxford University Press), 481–563.

King, Jeffrey, and Stanley, Jason (2005). 'Semantics, Pragmatics, and the Role of Semantic Content', in Zoltan Szabó (ed.), *Semantics versus Pragmatics* (Oxford: Oxford University Press), 111–164.

Lahav, Ron (1989). 'Against Compositionality: The Case of Adjectives', *Philosophical Studies*, 57: 261–79.

Langacker, Ronald (1991). *Concept, Image, and Symbol: The Cognitive Basis of Grammar* (Berlin: Mouton/De Gruyter).

Lewis, David (1970). 'General Semantics', *Synthese*, 22: 18–67.

Nunberg, Geoffrey (1979). 'The Non-Uniqueness of Semantic Solutions: Polysemy', *Linguistics and Philosophy*, 3: 143–84.

—— (1995). 'Transfers of Meaning', *Journal of Semantics*, 12: 109–32.

Partee, Barbara (1984). 'Compositionality', in Fred Landman and Frank Veltman (eds.), *Varieties of Formal Semantics* (Dordrecht: Foris), 281–312.

Perry, John (1986). 'Thought without Representation', *Proceedings of the Aristotelian Society, supplementary volume*, 60: 137–52.

—— (1997). 'Indexicals and Demonstratives', in Bob Hale and Crispin Wright (eds.), *A Companion to the Philosophy of Language* (Oxford: Blackwell), 586–612.

Recanati, François (1993). *Direct Reference: From Language to Thought* (Oxford: Blackwell).

—— (1995). 'The Alleged Priority of Literal Interpretation', *Cognitive Science,* 19: 207–32.

—— (1997). 'La Polysémie contre le fixisme', *Langue Française,* 113: 107–23.

—— (1999). 'Situations and the Structure of Content', in Kumiko Murasugi and Rob Stainton (eds.), *Philosophy and Linguistics* (Boulder, Colo.: Westview Press), 113–65.

—— (2001). 'What is Said', *Synthese,* 128: 75–91.

—— (2004). *Literal Meaning* (Cambridge: Cambridge University Press).

Reichenbach, Hans (1947). *Elements of Symbolic Logic* (London: Macmillan).

Sag, Ivan (1981). 'Formal Semantics and Extralinguistic Context', in Peter Cole (ed.), *Radical Pragmatics* (London: Academic Press), 273–94.

Searle, John (1978). 'Literal Meaning', *Erkenntnis,* 13: 207–24.

—— (1980). 'The Background of Meaning', in John Searle, Ferenc Kiefer, and Manfred Bierwisch (eds.), *Speech Act Theory and Pragmatics* (Dordrecht: Reidel), 221–32.

—— (1983). *Intentionality* (Cambridge: Cambridge University Press).

—— (1992). *The Rediscovery of the Mind* (Cambridge, Mass.: MIT Press).

Soames, Scott (2002). *Beyond Rigidity: The Unfinished Semantic Agenda of* Naming and Necessity (New York: Oxford University Press).

Stanley, Jason (2000). 'Context and Logical Form', *Linguistics and Philosophy,* 23: 391–434.

Travis, Charles (1975). *Saying and Understanding* (Oxford: Blackwell).

—— (1981). *The True and the False: The Domain of the Pragmatic* (Amsterdam: Benjamins).

—— (1989). *The Uses of Sense: Wittgenstein's Philosophy of Language* (Oxford: Clarendon Press).

—— (2000). *Unshadowed Thought* (Cambridge, Mass.: Harvard University Press).

Tversky, Amos (1977). 'Features of Similarity', *Psychological Review,* 84: 327–52.

8

A Tall Tale
In Defense of Semantic Minimalism and Speech Act Pluralism

HERMAN CAPPELEN AND ERNIE LEPORE

In *Insensitive Semantics* (2005), we argue for two theses—Semantic Minimalism and Speech Act Pluralism. In this chapter, we outline our defense against two objections often raised against Semantic Minimalism. We begin with five stage-setting sections. These lead to the first objection, namely, that it might follow from our view that comparative adjectives are context *in*sensitive. We defend our view against that objection (not, as you might expect, by denying that implication, but by endorsing it). Having done so, we address a second objection, namely, that Semantic Minimalism makes it difficult to see what role semantic content plays in communicative exchanges. We respond and end with a reversal, that is, we argue that even though the second objection fails against us, it works against those who raise the objection. In particular, we show that our critics, in particular, Carston (2002) and Recanati (2004), end up with a notion of communicated content that fails various tests for psychological reality.

Stage Setting 1: Semantic Minimalism

Three features of Semantic Minimalism are important in the context of this chapter (all elaborated on in *Insensitive Semantics*):

(*a*) The most salient feature of Semantic Minimalism is that it recognizes few context sensitive expressions, and hence, acknowledges a very limited effect of the context of utterance on the semantic content of an utterance. The only context sensitive expressions are the completely obvious ones ('I', 'here', 'now', 'that', etc., essentially those Kaplan lists in 'Demonstratives' (1989: 489)). These also pass certain tests for context sensitivity we spell out below.

(*b*) It follows that all semantic context sensitivity is grammatically (i.e. syntactically or morphemically) triggered.

(*c*) Beyond fixing the semantic value of these obviously context sensitive expressions, the context of utterance has no effect on the proposition semantically expressed or the semantic truth conditions. In this sense, the semantic content of a sentence S is that proposition that all utterances of S express (when we adjust for or keep stable the semantic values of the obvious context sensitive expressions in S).

Some illustrations: keeping tense fixed,[1] any utterance of (1)

(1) Rudolf is a reindeer.

is true just in case Rudolf is a reindeer, and expresses the proposition that Rudolf is a reindeer.[2] Any utterance of (2)

(2) Rudolf has a red nose.

is true just in case Rudolf has a red nose, and expresses the proposition that Rudolf has a red nose. Any utterance of (3)

(3) Rudolf is happy.

is true just in case Rudolf is happy, and expresses the proposition that Rudolf is happy. Any utterance of (4)

(4) Rudolf has had breakfast.

is true just in case Rudolf has had breakfast, and expresses the proposition that Rudolf has had breakfast. Any utterance of (5)

(5) Rudolf doesn't know that penguins eat fish.

is true just in case Rudolf doesn't know that penguins eat fish and expresses the proposition that Rudolf doesn't know that penguins eat fish.

---

[1] As we will throughout this chapter.

[2] Semantic Minimalism need not take a stand on whether semantic content is a proposition, or truth conditions or what have you. Throughout we try to remain neutral by couching the issues both in terms of truth conditions and in terms of propositions.

If you find it surprising that we are writing a chapter or (worse) a book defending conclusions so obvious, we have a great deal of sympathy. The problem is that a wide range of our contemporary colleagues rejects these views. (It's probably no exaggeration to say that our views about (1)–(5) are now held only by a small minority of philosophers, at least among those who have thought about the surrounding issues.[3]) In our book, we rebut these influential objections; here we want to elaborate on some implications of the view defended.

Stage Setting 2: Speech Act Pluralism

Here's one way to summarize Speech Act Pluralism:

> No one thing is said (or asserted, or claimed or . . .) by any utterance: rather, indefinitely many propositions are said, asserted, claimed, or stated. What is said (asserted, claimed, etc.) depends on a wide range of factors other than the proposition semantically expressed. It depends on a potential infinitude of features of the context of utterance and of the context of those who report on (or think about) what was said by the utterance.

It follows from this view that an utterance can assert propositions not even (logically) implied by the proposition semantically expressed. Nothing even prevents an utterance from asserting (saying, claiming, etc.) propositions incompatible with the proposition semantically expressed by that utterance.

From this it further follows that if you want to use intuitions about speech act content to fix semantic content, you must be extremely careful. It can be done, but it's a subtle and an easily corrupted process.[4]

These points are connected to our defense of Semantic Minimalism because one underlying assumption in many anti-minimalist arguments is the idea that semantic content has to be closely connected to speech act content. If Speech Act Pluralism is correct, then no such close connection exists, and so this requirement is revealed to be a philosophical prejudice. (Another way to see the connection is this: If there really were (or had to be) a close connection between speech act content and semantic content, then all the data we think support Speech Act Pluralism would also serve to undermine Semantic Minimalism.)

---

[3] See ch. 2 of *Insensitive Semantics* for extensive discussion of this point.
[4] For some instructions on how to proceed, see ch. 7 of *Insensitive Semantics*.

At this initial stage it's worth highlighting one more aspect of Speech Act Pluralism that has both wide-ranging implications and sets our view apart from (all?) other contemporary accounts of context sensitivity. We don't think everything speakers say by uttering a sentence in a context C is determined by features of C. The speaker's intentions, facts about the audience, the place and time of utterance, background knowledge salient in C, previous conversations salient in C, etc., are not even together sufficient to fix what the speaker said. According to Speech Act Pluralism, a theory of speech act content has to take into account the context of those who say or think about what the speaker said, that is, the context of those who report on what's said by the utterance can, in part, determine what was said by that utterance. (As far as we can tell, we are on our own defending this view; see Cappelen and Lepore, 1997.)

Stage Setting 3: Opponents

We have many opponents; indeed, it often feels as if we have only opponents. What our opponents have in common is a commitment to some form of semantic contextualism. Semantic contextualists, as we mark them, posit more semantic context sensitivity than is generally recognized. Sometimes their motives are opportunistic: for example, they claim they can solve Sorites, Liar, Skeptical, Moral and Fregean puzzles/paradoxes by positing that vague, semantic, knowledge, moral and psychological attributions are semantically context sensitive. Sometimes they posit context sensitivity because they believe themselves to have uncovered more of it than linguists/philosophers have so far recognized. Sometimes they conclude that entire semantic programs collapse under the weight of their discoveries; sometimes they are more modest, concluding only that their contributions are to the general project of semantics for natural language—namely, modest extensions to the already recognized indexicals and demonstratives. No matter how ambitious or modest their motivations, we have come to the same conclusion: they are all wrong; none of the contextualist candidates are semantically context sensitive.

We have argued against contextualism with a variety of dialectical strategies: One of our favorite argumentative strategies is to present direct and simple tests for context sensitivity; and to show that traditionally recognized context sensitive expressions pass these tests with flying colors, while contextualist candidates all fail them. In order to present the first objection to Semantic Minimalism, we'll briefly rehearse a couple of these tests (both discussed at greater length in chapter 7 of *Insensitive Semantics*).

Stage Setting 4: Test 1—Context Sensitive Expressions Block Inter-Contextual Disquotational Indirect Reports

Take an utterance u of S in C. Let C′ be a context relevantly different from C (i.e. different according to the standards significant according to contextualists about S). If there's a true disquotational indirect report of u in C′, then that's evidence S is context insensitive. So, take an obviously context sensitive expression, for example, the first person pronoun 'I' and its utterance in the sentence 'I went to Ottawa' made by Sarah-Jane. If Rich tries to report what Sarah-Jane said with 'Sarah-Jane said that I went to Ottawa', his report is false because the expression 'I' fails to pick out what it picked out in Sarah-Jane's mouth. The presence of 'I' in the disquotational report figures prominently in an explanation of why the report is false.

It's (almost) a matter of definition that context sensitive expressions tend to block inter-contextual disquotational indirect reports. The reason why is obvious: e is context sensitive only if e shifts semantic value between relevantly different contexts of utterance. It's obvious that all the traditionally recognized context sensitive expressions ('he', 'now' 'that', 'you', etc.) block inter-contextual disquotational indirect reports.

Stage Setting 5: Test 2—Context Sensitive Expressions Block Collective Descriptions

Here's another test applied to verbs first. If a verb phrase *v* is context sensitive (i.e. if it changes its semantic value from one context of use to another), then on the basis of merely knowing that there are two contexts of utterance in which 'A v-s' and 'B v-s' are true respectively, we *cannot* automatically infer that there is a context in which 'v' can be used to describe what A and B have both done.

In short, from there being contexts of utterance in which 'A v-s' and 'B v-s' are true it doesn't *follow* that there is a true utterance of 'A and B both v.' This is because the semantic value of 'v' in the previous collective sentence is determined in one context, and we have no guarantee that that semantic value, whatever it is, 'captures' (whatever that means) the semantic values of 'v' in those contexts of utterance where they were used alone.

On the other hand, *if* for a range of true utterances of the form 'A v-s' and 'B v-s' we obviously *can* describe what they all have in common by *using* 'v' (i.e. by using 'A and B v'), then that's evidence in favor of the view that 'v' in these different utterances has the same semantic content, and hence is not context sensitive. A parallel point extends to singular terms.

If an (unambiguous) singular term N is context *in*sensitive and there's a range of true utterances of the form 'N is F' and 'N is G', then we, for example, in *this* context, can truly utter 'N is F and G'. Similarly, if N is context sensitive, we shouldn't be able to do this. As an illustration consider the context sensitive 'yesterday': Suppose we know of two contexts in which 'Yesterday John left' and 'Yesterday Bill left' are true respectively (though we don't know the days of these contexts). It doesn't follow that there is a context in which 'Yesterday John and Bill left' is true.

Again, all traditionally recognized context sensitive expressions pass this test of collectivity.

There are other tests for context sensitivity; one of our favorites we call the Inter-Contextual Disquotational Test (different from Test 1 above). In discussing this test we distinguish between two kinds of context shifting arguments, Real and Impoverished, arguing that only the former identifies context sensitive expressions. (Context shifting arguments involve an appeal to speaker intuitions about distinct utterances of a single unambiguous sentence shifting in truth-value, or in proposition expressed, or in what's said.)

The Inter-Contextual Disquotation Test was our first and we feel a sentimental attachment to it. However, audiences tend to find it a bit confusing, so we'll leave it alone for now and direct those interested to our published work (Cappelen and Lepore, 2003). Instead, we'll take our two tests involving indirect reporting and collectivity and turn to what most contextualists take to be a fundamental flaw in our position.

First Objection: 'Tall' Is Self-Evidently Context Sensitive

We have argued that the contextualist candidates fail the various tests for context sensitivity. This applies to 'know', 'good', 'red', quantifier words, and so on. A standard reply is that there must be something wrong with our reasoning since words self-evidently context sensitive also seem to fail our tests: for example, comparative adjectives like 'tall'.

So, for example, look at our first test. Suppose A utters in a context C 'Rudolf is tall'. Suppose that in C the contextually salient comparison class consists of giraffes. According to contextualists, the proposition semantically expressed by A's utterance is *that Rudolf is tall for a giraffe*. This result is rendered possible because 'is tall' is alleged to be context sensitive. But look at our tests: we take it as obvious that anyone reporting A's utterance can accurately utter 'A said that Rudolf is tall' and this is so regardless of the context the reporter happens to find herself in, that is, even if the context of the report and the context of the reported utterance are relevantly different, that is, even if giraffes are not particularly salient in the context of the report. The reporter might not know that Rudolf is a giraffe; she might be unsure what kind of animal Rudolf is; or suspect he is a reindeer. The point is this: If the context of the first utterance and the context of the second utterance are relevantly dissimilar, then this report ought to be impossible—*if* 'tall' really is context sensitive.

Now turn to the second test. Take distinct utterances of 'Mount Everest is tall' and 'Kobe Bryant is tall' and 'The Empire State Building is tall'. Suppose in the first context, mountains are salient, in the second NBA players are, and in the third skyscrapers are. Suppose you are collecting these utterances into a context in which mountains and basketball players and skyscrapers are *not* (particularly) salient. Then any utterance of 'Mount Everest, Kobe Bryant, and the Empire State Building are all tall' (or 'Mount Everest is tall, and Kobe Bryant and the Empire State Building are too'—an appeal to a fourth test involving VP deletion; cf. *Insensitive Semantics*, ch 7) should be false, on the assumption that 'tall' is context sensitive. It's our intuition, however, that there *are* contexts in which such utterances can be true; it's hard to see how that could be so if 'tall' isn't taking as its semantic value something the original utterances have in common.

Contextualists of every flavor have mocked, ridiculed, snickered, flat out laughed, and even worse, completely ignored our views because of these results. The current attitude seems to be that any argument that leads to the view that 'tall' (or any other comparative adjective) is not semantically context sensitive must be seriously flawed.

There are at least three responses to our arguments:

(*a*) Our tests for semantic context sensitivity are no good.

(*b*) Comparative adjectives do pass our tests, but for one reason or another, we can't hear their uses as passing these tests.

(*c*) Or, one might say: That's right. These words fail the tests and they are context *in*sensitive—contrary to what we all once thought.

We have considered and replied to the first two options elsewhere (cf. Cappelen and Lepore, 2003). Here we would like to try something bolder: we'd like to run with option (*c*). This requires investigating what others have thought of as the absolute absurdity of Semantic Minimalism, that comparative adjectives are (semantically) context insensitive.

To this end, we'll tease out our critics' argument; and try to establish it has nothing to do with semantics but rather reflects a metaphysical concern—one we do not think semanticists have to address. We present the objection in three stages, only the third of which will require an extended answer (though it is important to see how that stage is different from the first two).

First Stage Objection to (*c*): Dismissive Incredulous Stare

The objection to the view that 'tall' is context insensitive typically starts out with the kind of stare Lewis characterized as incredulous. This stare is typically accompanied by a dismissive utterance of something along the lines of:

Are you crazy! Of course, there can be both true and false utterances of (6):

(6) Osama Bin Laden is tall.

If in one context the topic of discussion is the heights of NBA players, your utterance will be (taken to be) false; and if in another, the topic is the heights of Saudi Arabians, your utterance will be (taken to be) true.

Reply to First Stage

If you followed our brief introduction of Semantic Minimalism and Speech Act Pluralism above, you'll immediately understand that this reply can be pushed only by someone who does not understand our view. It is based on nothing but confusion. It should be obvious that our Speech Act Pluralism can accommodate the same data. In one context, the utterance *says* something true and in another an utterance of the same sentence *says* something false. But intuitions about the speech act content of these distinct utterances are *not* reliable guides to the semantic content of (6) or even its utterances, and so intuitions about the former need not be a good guide for conclusions about the latter.

Second Stage of Objection to (*c*): Honest Request for Further Elaboration

Opponents who bypass the deeply confused first stage typically move on to a second stage of confusion. They ask, Well, what is it to be tall *simpliciter*? That is, what is it to satisfy the semantic truth conditions of 'A is tall'? If it is not to be tall for an X, or according to some standard, what then is it?

Reply to Second Stage

Our quick, and we think completely satisfactory, reply is given by (6_{TC}) and (6_P):

> (6_{TC}) 'Osama Bin Laden is tall' is true iff Osama Bin Laden is tall.
> (6_P) 'Osama Bin Laden is tall' semantically expresses the proposition *that Osama Bin Laden is tall.*

Here is our problem: We think this is a conclusive reply, but our opponents insist on further elaboration. They move on to the third stage of the objection.

Third Stage of Objection to (*c*): Confused Demand for Further Elaboration

Faced with (6_{TC}) and (6_P) our opponents tend to react with something like this:

(6_{TC}) and (6_P) just aren't enough. I can't take this theory seriously unless you tell me more about what the right-hand side of those biconditionals mean (or require, or demand or . . .). You just don't have a semantic theory unless you say more. If you can't tell me what it is to be tall, then you don't have a semantic theory.

Reply to Third Stage

We've presented this third stage of the objection so that it both reflects innumerable conversations we have had about this topic, but (we hope) also reflects how unreasonable the demand is. We really don't think we, qua semanticists, are required to respond to this challenge. To demand that semanticists tell you what it is *to be tall* is to start down a most slippery slope. For example, why not also require that semanticists tell us what it takes, or is, to *be tall for a man*? Is that something semanticists are supposed to explore? Or take the word 'change'. Are semanticists required to reveal what the property *of change* is in order to do their job? Or what it is to be funny in order to deal with the semantics of the word 'funny'?

Though we take the answers to these various questions, qua semanticists, to be quite obvious, we also realize that sticking to our position is almost impossible (certainly unrewarding) since all the people that we like to talk to about these issues seem to lose interest if we don't elaborate. So, partly for selfish reasons (we don't want people to ignore us), partly out of the goodness of our hearts (we seek philosophical harmony), we'll engage in a little bit of metaphysics. We do this, however, filled with resentment and, ultimately, with the goal of getting our opponents to realize how absurd it is to require that we respond to their challenge.

Here goes. Think about dancing: Some people dance by stepping, some crawl around the floor (like Martha Graham), some have music, some don't have music, some jump in the air, some wave their arms, some hold on to other people, some are alone, some slide on ice, some fly in the air, etc. What do all these activities have in common in virtue of which they are all dancing? This is certainly not our area of expertise but suppose the dance metaphysicians will inform us that to dance is to move in some way W, where W is what all those different events of dancing have in common. There can be different accounts of W, and as far as we can tell both Semantic Minimalism and Semantic Contextualism are compatible with each and every one of them.

Or, think about eating. Some people eat sandwiches, some soup, some apples, some eat in Norway, some in the East Village of New York City, some eat with a spoon, some with their fingers. More generally, there are many things to eat, many places to do it, and many ways to eat. Any event of eating is of a specific thing, in some way, in some location. What is this property of eating? Well, isn't the simplest answer something along the lines of: to engage in the kind of activity that all these different events have in common, that is, what eating soup, apples, sandwiches, with finger, spoons, in Norway or New York, etc., have in common. Again, we're not specialists, but whatever they all have in common, that's what the activity of eating is. Notice, Semantic Minimalism and Semantic Contextualism are compatible with any answer to these questions. Neither the former nor the latter need take a stand on what eating is.

Now think about funny things: There are funny people, funny jokes, funny paintings, funny movements, etc. People who are funny can be so by moving around funny, by saying funny things, by writing funny, etc. The expression 'funny' presumably has as its semantic value whatever all these things have in common. Here are some conjectures about this property. It might be dispositional: for an object to be funny is for it to trigger a certain reaction in an audience. Whether an act is funny might depend on the context in which it is performed (e.g. the interests, expectations, etc., of the salient audience). Any such account of the semantic value of 'funny' is compatible with Semantic Minimalism and with Semantic Contextualism.[5]

Finally, turn to the property of being tall. We suppose that to figure out what tallness is, you proceed much as in these earlier cases. Engage in a little bit of tallness metaphysics. Consider, for example, the Empire State Building, Mount Everest, and Kobe Bryant. Ask, what, if anything, do they all have in common? Naturally, one answer is that they are all tall. If that's so, and it is, then it triggers the following metaphysical question. What is it in virtue of which these three objects are all tall? Or, what do they all have in common? Tallness? But what's that? What does it take for something to instantiate tallness? Because, as in all matters metaphysical, we are rank amateurs, we don't have much to say, but here are four preliminary options (there are obviously others):

1. For something to instantiate tallness there must be *some* comparison class or other with respect to which it's tall. If that's all it takes to instantiate tallness, it's very easy to do so. We take this to be an exceedingly unpromising account of tallness.

2. It might be that to instantiate tallness it's insufficient to be tall with respect to *some* comparison class. For each object there might be one such class that's privileged, say, for natural kinds, the natural kind they belong to, for artifacts the artifact they instantiate. Since objects belong to many kinds, work would have to be done to show one of these is privileged.

3. A third option is that the circumstances the object is in at a time t singles out a comparison class that's the one the object has to be tall with

---

[5] In all these cases you could attempt to respond that it is a philosophical prejudice that there is something that all these things have in common. That it is a pun to say they are all dancing, eating, funny. We do not address that response here, but see ch. 11 of *Insensitive Semantics* for further discussion.

respect to in order to be tall at t. Again, work would have to be done to figure out how this comparison class is picked out.

4. The property of being tall corresponds to being taller than the average height for all objects that have height. Since we have no idea how many objects have heights we have no idea exactly what has this property.[6]

If you agree that there's a property of tallness—how could you not?—but have a better account of what it is to instantiate it, that's fine with us. Try it out on us. Which one is correct? We are not sure even how to determine an answer to this question. However, the only serious objection we can contemplate is to deny that there's any such thing as the property of being tall. Such cynicism would be to endorse Metaphysical Nihilism about tallness: that is, it would be to endorse the view that there's nothing A and B have in common if A is tall for a G and B is tall for an F. That view is, as far as we can tell, a rather bizarre view to hold because no one, as far as we know, denies there is any such a thing as *being tall with respect to some comparison class*. No one can deny there's such a thing as *being tall with respect to a privileged comparison class* or *a contextually salient comparison class*; or having the property of *being taller than the average height of all objects that have heights*. If this is so, then everyone agrees with us that at least for these four accounts of what the property of tallness is, each picks out something that exists. Whether it's the 'right' account is another topic.

In sum, our response to the first objection is this. If you think there is such a thing as tallness, then let that be the semantic value of 'tall' in 'Osama bin Laden is tall' and in answer to the question as to what it takes for that sentence to be true we say that it is whatever it takes for Osama bin Laden to have that property. To keep this answer in perspective remember:

(a) We don't accept that it is a necessary condition on an acceptable semantic theory for English that it tells us what tallness is (even though we have given you some modest pointers for how to proceed).

(b) According to Speech Act Pluralism, the semantic content of 'Osama bin Laden is tall' is not all of what the speaker who utters that sentence says; more generally, it does not fully determine the content of speech acts performed by people who utter that sentence.

---

[6] A more elaborate discussion of these options would, in some ways, mirror contemporary debates about knowledge attributions. Both Stanley and Hawthorne propose theories according to which knowledge is some kind of interest relative property, but where this does not necessarily make 'know' a context sensitive expression (see Stanley, n.d.; Hawthorne, 2003). We imagine analogous arguments being made in connection with comparative adjectives. For some suggestions along these lines, see Graff (2002), and a reply by Stanley (2003).

First (and Only) Digression: Being Tall for an F is No Better than Being Tall

Suppose you're baffled by the idea that there's such a thing as tallness. We'll now try to show that if you are, you should be equally baffled by the idea that there is such a thing as, for example, being tall for a giraffe, or more generally, by the sort of property expressed by *being tall for an F*. This claim is dialectically significant because Semantic Contextualists tend to hold that this alleged problem occurs only for those who are Semantic Minimalists (as applied to comparative adjectives in particular). The fix, according to Semantic Contextualists, is supposed to reside with relativizing comparative adjectives to comparison classes, that is, with a commitment to contextualism for 'tall' and other comparative adjectives.

Adjectives like 'tall' are to be treated as relational with, for example, an unpronounced place for a comparison class that gets indexed in a context of use. So, for example, in effect, the sentence 'A is tall' is equivalent, on this contextualist suggestion, at some level of linguistic analysis, say, at the level of LF, with the representation 'A is tall for an F', where 'F' is an indexical that somehow receives its semantic value in context. For a sentence like (6), in one context of utterance the indexed comparison class (or property, or whatever) might be NBA players; and in another it might be Saudi Arabians.

Recall that the alleged problem for *tallness* is that it's mysterious what it is to be tall *simpliciter*: 'There can be no such thing as tallness *simpliciter*. To claim Kobe Bryant, Mount Everest, and the Empire State Building all have something in common—namely, *tallness*—is a mistake, and any semantics that presupposes there could be such a thing must be mistaken. Since Semantic Minimalism, as characterized, is committed to this possibility, it should be rejected.'

If this objection issues from anyone content with properties like *being tall for an F*, then it is terribly misplaced. Take the property of *being tall for a giraffe* as an example, that is, we're imagining an opponent who thinks that many things can instantiate the property of *being tall for giraffes*. Before proceeding with our inquiry, consider the following basic giraffe facts. Giraffes have hairy ears. The fleshy part of the ear stops before the hairs on the ears stop. Not every giraffe can stretch his neck all the way up; some are old and arthritic. (With assistance they might be able to stretch their necks further than without help.) Giraffes can stand on their back legs and lift their front legs into the air, and thereby, push themselves further up into the air. That makes them longer. They have hoofs, and these hoofs wear down with usage.

Holding these simple giraffe facts in mind, consider two giraffes, say, A and B. What would it be for A and B to both instantiate the property of being tall for giraffes? The problem is this: there are many ways to be tall for a giraffe. For starters, there are indefinitely many ways to measure the tallness of giraffes. Consider these few illustrations. A giraffe's height can be measured:

- from bottom of his hoof to the fleshy tip of his ear with a self-stretched neck;
- from the bottom of a hoof to the tip of his snout with a self-stretched neck;
- from the bottom of a hoof to the hairy tip of an ear with a self-stretched neck;
- from the bottom of a hoof to the tip of a snout when standing on his back legs with his front legs lifted into the air;
- all of the above, with an artificially stretched neck, that is, by a machine or something else that can stretch the neck out further than the giraffe can by herself. (Remember, some giraffes are arthritic, and have very stiff necks.)

Then, of course, there's the question of which comparison class or property or whatever we are to compare any given giraffe to. Here are but a few options:

- all living giraffes;
- a stereotypical giraffe;
- french giraffes;
- all giraffes that have ever lived, are alive, and will ever live;
- all possible giraffes;
- all giraffes in the vicinity of a certain giraffe.

Then, of course, there's the question of the (optimum) conditions under which to measure a particular giraffe (holding the method of measurement and the comparison class fixed). Here are but a few of indefinitely many options:

- right after a bath (giraffes shrink a bit after having taken a bath);
- right after a long walk (their hoofs wear down);
- when dead (again, death shrinks us all);
- when hungry (they tend to stretch their necks further);
- when pregnant (their necks are rendered less flexible).

Let's stop here even though there is much else that has to be settled. But now ask yourself: what is it to *be tall for a giraffe*? what is *giraffe-tallness*? It all depends on *which giraffes* you compare any given giraffe to, *how* you measure it, the conditions of the giraffe when being measured, and so on. The 'and so on' here is vital. There are no obvious or a priori limits on the different variations on giraffe-tallness.

Just to remind you why this matters. We're imagining a Semantic Contextualist opponent who's completely baffled by the idea that there's such a thing as tallness and that it can be the semantic value of 'tall'. We've just tried to make that seem a little less peculiar by showing that the kind of worry that triggers befuddlement with respect to being tall should also, if legitimate, trigger the same sort of befuddlement with respect to being *tall for a giraffe*. Now, since we expect at least some opponents to be completely non-befuddled about being *tall for a giraffe,* at least before seeing our examples, this discussion might remove or alleviate some of their resistance to tallness.

Of course, we expect many opponents to say: 'Of course, there's no such thing as being tall for a giraffe *simpliciter.* You have to fill it out: you have to add something about the class of giraffes, the condition of the giraffes, the measuring methods, and so on.' To these critics we say: OK, just do it. Let's see how that gets incorporated into semantics and then we'll continue the debate.

Second Objection: Role of Semantic Content in Communication

Remember, according to Speech Act Pluralism, speakers use sentences to make claims, assertions, suggestions, requests, claims, statements, raise hypotheses, inquiries, etc., the contents of which can be (and typically are) radically different from the semantic contents of (the propositions semantically expressed by) these utterances. The speech act content (i.e. what was said, asserted, claimed, asked, etc.) depends on a potentially indefinite range of facts about the speaker, his audience, their shared context, the reporter (i.e. the person recounting what was said), the reporter's audience, and their shared context. These facts have no bearing on the semantic content of the utterance.

Here's a potential worry for this position. What communicators actually *care* about in a discourse exchange *is* the speech act content and *only* the speech act content. What they care about is what the speaker said, asserted, claimed, stated, suggested, asked, etc. If this *isn't* the semantic content, if the semantic content is, so to speak, always hidden, if it never surfaces, then what purpose does it serve? Isn't it just an idle wheel? What would be lost if our theory just let it go? So, even if there is tallness, and even if the semantic value of 'is tall' somehow involves it, what role can this peculiar property play in communication? Does it have any kind of psychological reality? Let's call this the Psychological Challenge to Semantic Minimalism.

Reply to Second Objection: Semantic Content Does Have a Role to Play in Communication

We think the answer is simple and obvious but we can't overemphasize its importance. We begin by reminding you of some basic facts about communication. Then we respond directly to this psychological challenge. What we are about to say presupposes there being a clear notion of *a shared context*. We doubt there is one, but we'll place our reservations to the side for now. If there are shared contexts, then that will make life even harder for the Semantic Contextualist.

Basic Facts About Speakers and Audiences who Share a Context

Speakers are sometimes wrong (or have incomplete information) about their audience, for example, about:

- what the audience believes and knows;
- what the audience remembers about prior conversations;
- how the audience has interpreted previous conversations;
- how the audience perceives their shared environment; and
- what the audience believes about the speaker.

Audiences are sometimes wrong (or have incomplete information) about speakers, for example, about:

- what the speaker believes and knows;
- what the speaker remembers about previous conversations;
- how the speaker has interpreted previous conversations;
- how the speaker perceives their shared environment; and
- what the speaker believes about the audience.

Audiences and speakers are both often wrong (or have incomplete information) about the context that they find themselves in, for example, about:

- what their perceptual environment is; and
- what the contents of preceding conversations were.

Speakers and audiences know that they can be wrong and have incomplete information about each other in the ways just specified.

Basic Facts about Speakers and Audiences who do Not Share a Context

Sometimes the audience of an utterance doesn't share a context with the speaker. This can happen in any of several ways, the most salient of which being the reproduction of a speech act, as in published articles. Writers often have no idea who their reader is; they know next to nothing about her beliefs; or about her perceptual environment; all they know is that it is not shared. Yet, nonetheless, writers have audiences (no matter how small they might be).

Another typical device through which a speech act can reach an audience in another context is indirect quotation. This is when S says in C to A what another speaker S′ said in another context C′ to another audience A′. In these cases the sources of confusion are multiplied. The added complications should be obvious; there is not even the illusion of a shared context.

Basic Facts about Inter-Contextual Content Sharing

First, people can and often do say the same thing in different contexts. People in different contexts can say that Napoleon was short.

Second, according to Semantic Contextualists, no two contexts (are likely to) share exactly the same content fixing parameters, for example, the intentions are not the same; the background knowledge is not the same; previous conversations are not the same; what's normal is not the same; and so on (cf. e.g. Sperber and Wilson, 1986: 118, 192–3; Carston, 2001: 26–7; Recanati, 2004: 149; Bezuidenhout, 1997: 212–13).

Third, it is possible to say in a context C that people in a range of contexts $C_1–C_n$ said the same thing, for example, there are true reports, say, in C, of the form 'They all said that Napoleon was short' about different speakers' utterances in contexts C_1–C_n. (Similarly, distinct utterances can be collected; true utterances of the form 'A is tall', 'B is tall', and 'C is tall' said in contexts C_1, C_2 and C_3 can be collected in a single context C_4 with an utterance of 'A, B, and C are tall'.)

Note that if someone denies these three points we don't want to talk to her or about her (because she doesn't think she can say what we say, so she can't deny what we say, and (according to her) we can't say what she said, and so we can't say that we disagree with what she said).

The Cognitive Role of Minimal Semantic Content

What, then, is the cognitive role of minimal semantic content? The answer should be (almost) self-evident by now:

1. Speakers know that their audience can be (and often are) mistaken (or have incomplete information) about the communication-relevant facts about the context of utterance. The proposition semantically expressed is that content the speaker can expect the audience to grasp (and expect the audience to expect the speaker to expect them to grasp) even if they have mistaken or incomplete communication-relevant information.

2. Audiences know that the speaker can be (and often is) mistaken (or has incomplete information) about the communication-relevant facts about the context of utterance. The proposition semantically expressed is that content the audience can expect the speaker to grasp (and expect the audience to grasp) even if she has such mistaken or incomplete information.

3. The proposition semantically expressed is that content which can be grasped and expressed by someone who isn't even a participant in the context of utterance.

4. The proposition semantically expressed is that content which speakers and audiences know can be transmitted through indirect quotation or reproduction (in the form of tapes, video recordings, etc.) to, or collected by, those who find themselves in contexts radically different from the original context of utterance.

In short: the proposition semantically expressed is our minimal defense against confusion/misunderstanding/indifference, and it is that which guarantees communication across contexts of utterance. It's what allows us to collect, report, and reproduce others' utterances.

Possible Counter-Reply

We expect this sort of reply: 'Hold it: You're saying that the minimal semantic content is a "shared fallback content" and that this content serves to guard against confusion and misunderstandings. But given what you've told us about minimal propositions, how could they serve that purpose? Consider, for example, an utterance of (6). Suppose a speaker utters it to communicate that Osama Bin Laden is tall for a Saudi Arabian (or something like that). That's what the speaker is trying to say. How would it help an audience to know that the minimal proposition, that is, *that Osama bin Laden is tall*, was expressed? It might not be what the speaker wanted to assert. What help could it be to know that this proposition was expressed?'

Our response is simple: it is a starting point. The audience knows that the speaker is talking about Osama Bin Laden and attributes tallness to him, and not, for example, to Sprite cans, Sweden, Britney Spears, or pig ears. There's lots to talk about in the universe. The proposition semantically expressed pares it down considerably. Knowledge that this proposition was semantically expressed provides the audience with the *best possible* access to the speaker's mind, given the restricted knowledge she has of that speaker. In general, audiences know what to look for in such situations; they know what kind of information would help narrow down more closely what the speaker wanted to communicate.[7]

To sum up our reply, consider the following charge from Recanati against Semantic Minimalism and our reply. Recanati writes of minimal propositions:

Let the semanticist use it if he or she wants to, provided he or she agrees that ... the minimal proposition has no psychological reality. It does not correspond to any stage in the process of understanding the utterance, and need not be entertained or represented at any point in that process. (Recanati, 2004: 89)

If there's a difference between having a cognitive function and corresponding to a stage in processing/having psychological reality, we don't know what that difference consists in. If (1)–(4) above are insufficient to 'correspond to a stage in the process of understanding the utterance and need not be entertained or represented at any point in that process', then we don't know what is.

---

[7] There are many theories about how speakers go from semantic content to speech act content and we do not mean to, nor do we need to, endorse any one of those here.

In some sense, we're taking a stab in the dark here since we're not at all sure what Semantic Contextualists have in mind by the psychological requirement. What we have said is sufficient to render the propositions semantically expressed psychologically real, but we're genuinely confused since we have no idea how Semantic Contextualists satisfy their own requirement.

Concluding Point: The Second Objection Reversed (or Why Recanati's Account of What-Is-Said Doesn't Satisfy his own Availability Principle)

Suppose we focus, as Semantic Contextualists tend to, on the context of the speaker and her audience. The factors that figure into fixing the what-was-said/explicature include, *inter alia*, (i)–(iv):

   (i) information triggered in the speaker and the audience by prior discourse contents;
  (ii) information conversational partners share about each other;
 (iii) information the conversational partners have acquired through observation of their mutual perceptual environment;
  (iv) information conversational partners have about each other's purposes and abilities (e.g. whether the person is being deceitful or sincere, whether the person tends to verbosity, or is a person of few words).

These in no way exhaust the facts that, according to Semantic Contextualists, are content determinants, but what we have to say about (i)–(iv) generalizes. The problem is this. Suppose (i)–(iv) are factors that fix the explicature (i.e. the proposition expressed) of an utterance u of some sentence S. Now (i)–(iv) involve the mental states of several people (i.e. the speaker and her audience). None of the participants knows all the relevant facts about all the other participants: Herman doesn't know all the information triggered in Ernie by their many previous discussions; Ernie doesn't know what information Herman has about him. (He undoubtedly knows things about him that he doesn't even know he knows.) He doesn't always know what he will pay attention to in their sometimes shared perceptual environment; and so on.

The point here is obvious: if the explicature is fixed by these sorts of facts (what else?), then no one of the participants has direct access to the explicature. It is fixed intra-personally, and so there's no reason to think the resulting content is 'represented' at any stage of that person's processing of the relevant utterance. There is no reason to think that the resulting proposition is psychologically real.

Recanati discusses a version of this objection and the utter failure of his reply illustrates just how hard it is for Semantic Contextualists to satisfy their own psychological reality requirement. In particular, it illustrates why Recanati can't satisfy his Availability Principle (his version of the Psychological Requirement).

Hence my 'Availability Principle' (Recanati 1993: 248), according to which 'what is said' must be analysed in conformity to the intuitions shared by those who fully understand the utterance—typically the speaker and the hearer, in a normal conversational setting. I take the conversational participants' intuitions concerning what is said to be revealed by their views concerning the utterance's truth-conditions. I assume that whoever fully understands a declarative utterance knows which state of affairs would possibly constitute a truth-maker for that utterance, i.e., knows in what sort of circumstance it would be true. (Recanati, 2004: 20–1).

Recanati's theory, based on his Availability Principle, is supposed to be an alternative to theories according to which the explicature/content/what-is-said is not psychologically accessible. Recanati's idea is that, since his what-is-said corresponds to the speaker's intuitions about what is said, it will figure in the process of understanding (an utterance of) the sentence. He raises this worry:

Have we not equated what is said with their [i.e. the speaker and audience] understanding of what is said?. . . . We have not. We have equated what is said with what a normal interpreter would understand as being said, in the context at hand. A normal interpreter knows which sentence was uttered, knows the meaning of that sentence, knows the relevant contextual facts (who is being pointed to, etc.) Ordinary users of the language are normal interpreters, in most situations. They know the relevant facts and have the relevant abilities. But there are situations . . . where the actual users make mistakes and are not normal interpreters. In such situations their interpretations do not fix what is said. To determine what is said, we need to look at the interpretation that a normal interpreter would give. This is objective enough, yet remains within the confines of the pragmatic construal. (Recanati, 2004: 27)

But what's *normal* is not something speakers have psychological access to. What's normal need not 'be in the speaker's mind when the sentence is understood'; it certainly needn't figure into any psychological processes that the speaker goes through when understanding (an utterance of) a sentence. This is so for several obvious reasons; here are perhaps the most obvious ones:

- A speaker can be abnormal, but think that she is normal.
- A speaker might know that she is not normal, but not know what normal is.
- A speaker might think that she is not normal, but not be.
- More generally: even for speakers who are normal and know that they are normal, they might not know what counts as a normal understanding of some specific feature of a context that they happen to find themselves in.

A lot of situations have no 'normal' set of expectations associated with them. Suppose you meet someone in a cafe on a hot New York City summer day. What 'normality' are we looking for? Normal for you when talking to strangers in a cafe in New York City on a hot summer day? There's no such thing!

In other words, if what's normal, in part, determines what-is-said, and if what is normal is not represented at any stage in the processing of the utterance, then the resulting what-is-said cannot be so represented. Then, we suppose (though, as we have admitted, we're not sure we entirely understand the Semantic Contextualists here), Recanati's what-is-said is not psychologically real.

In sum: the Semantic Minimalist has a response to the Psychological Objection; it is the Semantic Contextualist who surprisingly does not.[8]

---

[8] Reply to Stanley on Binding

This is not the place to rehearse our arguments for Semantic Minimalism (for a summary see our 2005), but we would like to indulge in one retrospective digression. In his contribution to this volume, Stanley responds to our criticism against his Binding Argument and we thought it appropriate to comment on his response. Stanley writes:

> If the intuitive reading of (5) is (5*), then it would seem that the advocate of the binding argument is committed to postulating a place variable in the logical form of '2 + 2 = 4'.
>
> [(5) Everywhere I go, 2 + 2 = 4
> (5*) For all places x, if Sally goes to x, then 2 + 2 = 4 at x.]
>
> (Where we imagine (5) uttered by a confused mathematical anthropologist who travels the world to find out if mathematical statements are universal.)

I do not see that (5*) is the intuitive reading of (5), and I do not see that Cappelen and Lepore even believe that (5*) is a reading of (5). As Cappelen and Lepore (*ibid.*) point out, '. . . it is close to indisputable that arithmetical statements lack hidden indexicals referring to places.' Presumably, the reason they are so convinced of this is that it is unclear what it even means to speak of an arithmetical statement being true at a place.

What we agree with Stanley about is (1) and (2):

1. If (5*) is the intuitive reading of (5), then Stanley is committed to postulating a place variable in '2 + 2 = 4'.

REFERENCES

Bezuidenhout, A. (1997). 'The Communication of De Re Thoughts', *Noûs*, 31/2: 197–225.

Cappelen, H., and E. Lepore (1997). 'On an Alleged Connection between Indirect Quotation and Semantic Theory', *Mind and Language*, 12: 278–96.

—— (2003). 'Context Shifting Arguments', *Philosophical Perspectives*, 17: 25–50.

—— (2005). *Insensitive Semantics* (Oxford: Basil Blackwell).

Carston, R. (2001). 'Explicature and Semantics', in S. Davis and B. Gillon (eds.), *Semantics: A Reader* (Oxford: Oxford University Press).

—— (2002). *Thoughts and Utterances: The Pragmatics of Explicit Communication* (Oxford: Basil Blackwell).

Graff, Delia (2002). 'Shifting Sands: An Interest Relative Theory of Vagueness', *Philosophical Topics*, 28/1: 45–81.

Hawthorne, J. (2003). *Knowledge and Lotteries* (Oxford: Oxford University Press).

Kaplan, David (1989). 'Demonstratives', in J. Almog, J. Perry, and H. Wettstein (eds.), *Themes from Kaplan* (Oxford: Oxford University Press), 481–563.

Recanati F. (1993). *Direct Reference: From Language to Thought* (Cambridge: Blackwell).

—— (2002). 'Unarticulated Constituents', *Linguistics and Philosophy*, 24: 299–345.

—— (2004). *Literal Meaning* (Cambridge: Cambridge University Press).

Sperber, D., and D. Wilson (1986). *Relevance* (Oxford: Basil Blackwell).

Stanley, J. (2003). 'Context, Interest-Relativity, and the Sorites' *Analysis*, 63/4: 269–80.

—— (n.d.). 'Context, Interest-Relativity, and Knowledge', unpublished MS.

2. There is no hidden argument place for location in arithmetical statements. (Note that Stanley himself uses the factive 'point out'.)

Where disagree with him is over (3) and (4):

3. That (5⁺) is the intuitive reading of the described utterance of (5).
4. That it is unclear (and we think it is unclear) what it means to speak of an arithmetical statement being true at a place.

About (4): We have no difficulty whatsoever making sense of the idea of an arithmetical statement being true at a place. We can all make sense of the claim that $2 + 2 = 4$ is a necessary truth, i.e. that it is true *in every possible world*. If you make sense of that, surely you can make sense of it being true *at a place* or a time (for a time traveler). Test: ask yourself if you agree that our imagined mathematical anthropologist is wrong in assuming that there are places where $2 + 2 = 4$ is false, *because* $2 + 2 = 4$ everywhere.

About (3): The reason we think (5⁺) is a natural reading of (5) is that every one (read unrestrictedly) we have asked whether (5⁺) is a natural reading of (5) have agreed that it is. Also: the speaker of (5) might use (5⁺) to say what she said, if asked to elaborate (or if asked: 'what do you mean?') Exercise: If you think (5) isn't the best way to say what she's wants to say, try finding a more natural way to say it.

If (5⁺) is the correct reading of (5) and if it is not generated by quantifying over an argument place in all arithmetical statements, we owe an account of how this reading is generated. This note is not the place to present that account.

9

Semantics in Context

JASON STANLEY

Consider an utterance of the sentence 'Some philosophers are from New York'. If no philosopher in the world comes from New York, competent speakers of English know that it is false. They also know that this utterance is true if six philosophers in the world come from New York. In other words, competent English speakers have clear intuitions about the conditions under which what is said by an utterance of this sentence is true or false.

The apparent *source* of such intuitions is not difficult to locate. Competent English speakers know the meanings of the words in the sentence 'Some philosophers are from New York.' They also know how to combine the meanings of each of the words in this sentence to arrive at what is said by the utterance of the sentence, 'Some philosophers are from New York.' It is that linguistic competence that seems to be the source of their ability to report correctly about the truth of what is said by that sentence relative to different possible circumstances, for example, the circumstance in which there are no philosophers from New York, or the circumstance in which six philosophers come from New York.

So, the explanation for our ability to report about the truth and falsity of what is said by an utterance of 'Some philosophers are from New York' in various possible situations is as follows. Competent English speakers know the meanings of the words used, and understand how they are combined. Their grasp of the truth-conditions of the utterance of that sentence is due to their ability to combine the meanings of the words, relative to the context of utterance.

With this explanation in mind, consider an utterance of the sentence 'Every philosopher is from New York', made at a small philosophy conference.

It is natural to take this utterance to say something that is true if and only if every philosopher *at the conference* is from New York. If we cleave to the model of understanding just described, we will seek to explain our understanding of the truth-conditions of this utterance by appeal to a process of combining the elements of the sentence 'Every philosopher is from New York', using our understanding of the words used in the sentence. But of course, there appears to be no expression in the sentence 'Every philosopher is from New York' that corresponds to the understood constituent expressed by 'at this conference'.

Similarly, suppose, pointing at a 5 foot tall 7-year-old child, I utter the sentence 'He is tall.' I am most naturally understood as saying something that is true if and only if the child in question is tall *for a 7-year-old child*. Preserving the model of understanding we began with, according to which our intuitions about the truth-conditions of an utterance are due to a process of combining meanings of the parts of the sentence uttered, would require us to find some constituent in the sentence that could be taken to supply the understood property of *being a 7-year-old child*. But again, it appears that the sentence 'He is tall' contains no such constituent.

So, we have a predicament. If we look at certain sentences, there seems to be a clear and elegant explanation of why we have the intuitions we do about the truth-conditions of utterances of those sentences. But if we consider utterances of other sentences, the explanation appears to break down. The first response to this predicament is to attempt to preserve the clear and elegant explanation in the face of the apparently recalcitrant data. The second is to abandon the clear and elegant explanation of the source of our truth-conditional intuitions in favor of a different one.

My concern with the second response to the predicament is that the suggestions I am aware of for dealing with the additional complexity essentially end up abandoning the project of giving a systematic explanation of the source of our intuitions. They invariably involve appeal to unconstrained and non-explanatory notions or processes (cf. Stanley, 2002*a*). I have therefore been inclined to pursue the first of these options (cf. Stanley, 2000).

My purpose in this chapter is to continue the project of defending the clear and elegant explanation of the source of our intuitions about the truth-conditions of utterances. I will do so by considering some replies to previous arguments in favor of it. I will argue that proponents of abandoning the clear and elegant explanation have not yet made their case.

I. The Challenge from Context-Sensitivity

On the simple explanation of the source of our intuitions about the truth-conditions of utterances of sentences we understand, it is due primarily to a compositional process of interpretation. Our knowledge of meaning, together with our knowledge of relevant contextual facts, allows us to assign meanings to the parts of a sentence, and the intuitive truth-conditions of an utterance of that sentence are what result from combining these values. Somewhat tendentiously, I will call proponents of the simple explanation *semanticists*.

Innumerable researchers from pragmatics have challenged the semanticist's model. Here is the form of the standard challenge. First, a linguistic construction C is produced that appears intuitively to have a certain reading R. Secondly, the researcher claims that the readings cannot be due to the semantics of that construction. That is, the claim is that R cannot be due to the compositional semantic interpretation of C, relative to the envisaged context of use. The conclusion the researcher draws is that the assumption that the intuitive truth-conditions of a sentence relative to a context are due to semantics is incorrect.

A large number of researchers opposed to the semanticist employ arguments of this sort (a brief list of the most prominent exponents includes Kent Bach, Herman Cappelen, Robyn Carston, Ernie Lepore, Stephen Levinson, François Recanati, Dan Sperber, Charles Travis, and Deirdre Wilson; there are many more). Typically, such researchers do not just supply a single example, but a list of disparate examples. For example, the following is a representative list that could occur in any one of a hundred papers written in the past decade by researchers in this tradition:

(1) John is tall (for a fifth grader)
(2) John is finished (with grading)
(3) Every boy (in the class) is seated.
(4) John and Mary went to Paris (together/separately)
(5) If Lincoln hadn't gone to the theater, he wouldn't have been assassinated (fixing certain background assumptions)
(6) John ate breakfast (this morning)
(7) John had breakfast this morning (in the normal way, through his mouth)
(8) John ate (mushrooms)

(9) The ham sandwich (person who ordered the ham sandwich) is getting annoyed.

(10) The apple is green (on the inside)

The bracketed material is intended to indicate the material that cannot be provided by semantics, but only by pragmatics.

As one may imagine, any such list will include cases that virtually all proponents of the simple model of interpretation believe are uncontroversially generated by the compositional interpretation of the sentence uttered. For example, there is much recent investigation into the syntax and semantics of gradable adjectives that generates the supposedly pragmatic material as the semantic value of some element in the syntax (either a comparison class variable, or a degree variable). Semantic treatments of plurals treat collective-distributive ambiguities in a variety of ways. For example, some treat collective-distributive ambiguities as structural ambiguities due to the relative scope of an event quantifier. On such a treatment, the two readings of (4) are due to scope facts in the syntax, rather than pragmatics. Since Partee (1973), most linguists have defended the view that verbs are associated with temporal variables that have their references filled via deixis. On this view, generating the relevant reading of (6) simply involves speaker intentions determining the value of a temporal variable in the syntactic structure of the sentence uttered. Finally, few semanticists would balk at associating the provision of an accessibility relation for counterfactuals to some element in the syntax, either the conditionals words themselves, or some covert element.

On the other side of the spectrum, some of the examples that are provided in such lists seem to require pragmatic treatment, on the grounds that the alleged intuitive truth-conditions are richer than those delivered by tutored intuitions about truth-conditions. For example, as I will argue in the final section, with the help of recent work by Luisa Marti, it is clearly accessible to a native speaker of English that it is no part of the truth-conditions of an utterance of (7) that John ingested his breakfast through his mouth. Of course, when someone tells us that John ate this morning, we assume he did so in the normal way. But no one would deem an utterance of (7) *false* if, contrary to default assumptions, they discovered that John ingested breakfast in some non-standard way, such as being spoon fed. So the manner of eating is no part of the intuitive truth-conditions of (7), but is rather pragmatically conveyed information. We also assume other things when we hear an utterance of (7), for example, that John's breakfast wasn't prepared by a Martian. But none of this is information that is carried semantically, and *pace* Carston

(2002: 203) and Wilson and Sperber (2002), it is odd to suppose that anyone has ever advanced a theoretical position that would commit them otherwise.

Nevertheless, between the two extremes I have just discussed, there are some examples that are genuinely worrying for the semanticist. For instance, it certainly appears that the intuitive truth-conditions of an utterance of (9) involve a person, rather than a ham sandwich. Yet it's not clear that a process that maps ham sandwiches onto persons counts as genuinely semantic. To take another example, the intuitive truth-conditions of (3) certainly involve reference to a domain of quantification. But if domain restriction is a matter of information being freely provided by context, that too does not seem to be a process that can be considered genuinely semantic.

Some have tried to respond to this predicament by arguing that the semantic content of a sentence, relative to a context, is only a minimal part of the intuitive truth-conditions of that utterance, a version of what King and Stanley (2005) call *semantic modesty*. As King and Stanley emphasize, the worry with this response is that it is unclear what role the minimal semantic core ends up playing in an account of the intuitive truth-conditions, if one accepts that processes such as free enrichment account for much of our intuitions in examples such as (1)–(10). If free pragmatic enrichment is a process hearers regularly use to interpret utterances, and speakers are aware of this, then why can't speakers utter sentences whose semantic content is minimal or vacuous, and rely on such pragmatic processes to do the bulk of the expressive work? So I am not sanguine about semantic modesty as an intermediate position for the semanticist.

So much the worse for the semanticist, one might think. However, if our intuitions about truth and falsity are responsive to processes that are not linguistically controlled, we need an *explanatory* account of information freely provided by context. And it's not clear that such an account is in the offing. The most serious problem facing the advocate of free pragmatic enrichment to intuitive truth-conditions is that of *over-generation* (cf. Stanley, 2002*a*). If our intuitions about the truth-conditions of utterances of quantified sentences are due to a process of free pragmatic enrichment, then it would be a mystery why utterances of certain sentences lack certain readings. For example, why is it the case that an utterance of (11) can express the same proposition as an utterance of (12), but never the same proposition as an utterance of (13)?

(11) Every Frenchman is seated.
(12) Every Frenchman in the classroom is seated.
(13) Every Frenchman or Dutchman is seated.

In short, since these 'enrichment' processes are not linguistically constrained, they should be constrained only by general pragmatic reasoning. But why do general pragmatic facts allow (11) to express (12) but not (13)?

In the light of these worries with free pragmatic enrichment accounts of intuitive truth-conditions, it is important to investigate the possibility that the intuitive truth-conditions of utterances of sentences such as those in (1)–(10) are due to linguistically determined content. Linguistically determined content is content that is constrained not just by pragmatic means. Particularized conversational implicatures, for example, are constrained only by pragmatic means, and hence are not part of linguistically determined content. In contrast, the value of a term such as 'she', relative to a context, is linguistically determined, because the speaker intentions that determine its value must be referential intentions consistent with the literal meaning of 'she'. So the question posed by such examples is how to establish that the intuitive readings of the problematic sentences in (1)–(10) are due to linguistically determined content.

II. Responding to the Challenge

I adopt the conception of semantics at work in Stanley (2000) and spelled out in detail in King and Stanley (2005). The semantic content of a sentence relative to a context is derived by taking the semantic contents of the parts of that sentence, relative to that context, and composing them in accord with the composition rules governing the syntactic structure of that sentence. The semantic value of a basic constituent of a sentence is what is determined by speaker intentions together with features of the context, in accord with the standing meaning of that lexical item. Given this conception of semantics, the position of the semanticist is then that the source of our intuitions about the truth and falsity of utterances relative to various possible circumstances is due to semantics.

When faced with the claim that a certain construction C has a reading R that prima facie does not seem traceable to the semantics, the semanticist has three options. The first option is to establish that the alleged reading is not part of the intuitive truth-conditions of an utterance of that sentence, but is instead due to the pragmatics (as in the discussion of (7), above). The second option is to argue that the claim that reading R is not due to the semantics is due to an overly simplistic conception of the semantic content of some elements of C. When the correct semantics for the relevant expression is given, the reading does emerge from the semantics (cf. King and Stanley (2005: s. 5) on 'implicature intrusion'). The third option is to argue that the claim that reading R is not to the semantics is due to an overly simplistic conception of the syntactic structure of C. In fact, C contains covert structure, and once this is recognized, reading R does emerge from the semantics (cf. Stanley and Szabo (2000) on domain restriction, and Stanley (2000) for discussion of other constructions).

So, when faced with a list such as that given in the previous section, the semanticist has, in each case, three alternatives. The first is to reject the semantic significance of the data, the second is to give an alternative semantic assignment to some overt element, and the third is to argue for covert syntactic structure. As I have indicated, it is a construction specific matter which of these options is preferable. The difficulty facing the semanticist's opponent is that she must establish, for each case, that none of the three very different alternatives is available as an account of the data.[1]

Of all the constructions on the list, I think the central worry for the semanticist is (9), the case of deferred reference. Not only is there a strong intuition that the deferred meaning is part of the intuitive truth-conditions, but the deferred meaning enters into certain linguistic processes, such as anaphora and ellipsis. For example, the natural reading of (14) is one in which the anaphoric element 'his' receives its value not from the 'literal' content of 'the ham sandwich', but from its deferred meaning:

(14) The ham sandwich wants his bill now.

Similarly, when we consider someone uttering (15) in the kitchen of a restaurant, describing the predicaments of two waiters, it is the deferred meaning of 'an annoying ham sandwich' that is carried over to the ellided constituent:

(15) Bill served a ham sandwich, and John did too.

In particular, (15) cannot be interpreted as conveying that Bill served a person who ordered a ham sandwich, whereas John served a ham sandwich. Finally, one could argue that the literal meaning of an expression provides a guide for its deferred meaning, and so the deferred meaning is semantic after all.

I think neither of these points show that deferred reference is semantic. In a nominative metaphor such as (16a), we see the same phenomenon as in (14),

---

[1] The only pragmaticist I know of who seems to recognize the daunting challenge this poses to the opponent of the semanticist is Stephen Levinson (cf. Levinson, 2000: 214).

and in (16*b*), we see the same phenomenon as in (15), where the metaphorical reading is what is carried over in ellipsis:

(16) *a*. The pig in the next room wants his check immediately.
   b. John is a pig, and Bill is too.

We cannot interpret (16*b*) to mean that John is a person who is a sloppy eater, and Bill is (e.g.) a pig, perhaps John's pet. But on a standard view of metaphor, metaphor is not semantic. If the metaphorical meaning of an expression does not affect the semantic content of sentences containing it, relative to a context, then the fact that deferred reference behaves in a similar manner should not lead us to believe that deferred reference is semantic.

Joseph Stern (2000: 69–70) has recently used facts such as (16*b*) to argue that metaphor affects semantic content, that (as he would put it), there is such a thing as semantically significant metaphorical *meaning*. But, as Elizabeth Camp (n.d.) has pointed out, we also see the same phenomenon with *irony*. Consider:

(17) John: Bill is a fine friend.
   Sally: Sue is too.

If John's utterance is intended ironically, then the ellided constituent 'fine friend' in Sally's utterance must be understood ironically as well. But this does not show that irony is semantic, or that there is such a thing as semantically significant ironical *meaning*. As Stern (2000: 232) writes, 'Now, whatever controversy surrounds the status of metaphorical meaning, the ironic "meaning" of an utterance is surely not a semantic meaning.' So, such ellipsis facts do not demonstrate that a phenomenon is semantic.

The second argument that deferred reference is semantic is that the literal meaning of an expression in context provides a guide to its deferred meaning. For example, the literal meaning of 'the ham sandwich' provides a guide to the deferred meaning of 'the ham sandwich' in (14), which is *the person who ordered the ham sandwich*. So if the mark of the semantic is guidance (in some sense) by literal meaning, then there is evidence that deferred reference is semantic.

But it is also the case that the literal meaning of 'has nice handwriting', in the context of an utterance of 'John has nice handwriting' in a reference letter, provides a guide for the implicated property, *is a bad philosopher*. So the fact that the literal meaning is used in deriving the deferred meaning does not show that the deferred meaning is linguistically controlled in the relevant sense (i.e. semantic).[2]

---

[2] Thanks to Hanna Kim for discussion here.

I think a more general argument can be given that deferred reference should not be treated as semantic. The mark of the semantic is that semantic content is *constrained* by linguistic meaning. At the very least, the semantic content of an expression, relative to a context, must be something of which that expression is true. If it is not, it is hard to see how the semantic content of that expression has been constrained by the conventional meaning of that expression. But in the case of deferred reference, that is not true. If deferred reference were semantic, the denotation of 'the ham sandwich' would be something of which the predicate 'ham sandwich' were not true. So it is hard to see how the deferred reference of 'the ham sandwich', in (9), is semantic, since it is not constrained by the conventional meaning of the words used. So, one theoretical consideration that should lead us to deny that deferred reference (as in example (9)) is not semantic is that the deferred reference of an expression is not something of which the conventional meaning need be true.[3]

A second consideration involves the *scope* of the phenomenon. One reason against taking metaphor to be semantic is that virtually any term can be used metaphorically. This suggests that metaphor has to do with the *use* of a term, rather than the semantics of a particular expression. Similarly, virtually any term can be used with a deferred reference.[4] This suggests that the phenomenon of deferred reference does not have to do with the semantics of any particular construction. Rather, it involves how we can *use* constructions that have a certain semantics to communicate something different than such constructions semantically express.

A final theoretical consideration that can be brought to bear in arguing that deferred reference is not semantic has to do with the unconstrained nature of any semantic theory adequate to the task. This emerges when one considers the details of the semantic resources one would need to adopt in order to incorporate deferred reference into the semantics. Sag (1981) gives a semantic theory appropriate to the task of incorporating deferred reference into semantic content. Sag introduces 'sense-transfer functions' into contexts, and then uses them to interpret expressions in a sentence interpreted relative

---

[3] As Jeff King has pointed out to me, this distinguishes deferred reference from deferred *ostension*. Suppose, pointing at a parked car festooned with tickets, I utter 'That driver is going to be upset.' The reference of 'that driver' is the driver of the indicated car, even though what I demonstrated is the car. But the driver is still who is denoted by my use of 'that driver', because he satisfies the predicative material 'driver'. This distinguishes deferred reference from deferred ostension; the former is not semantic, whereas the latter is.

[4] For example, we can have 'Two ham sandwiches are getting irritated', 'Every ham sandwich is clamoring for her check', 'John ham-sandwiched again' (where this latter may mean the same as 'John ordered a ham sandwich again').

to a context. On his account, an expression is interpreted relative to a sense-transfer function, which can map the meaning of that expression onto any other meaning. The class of sense-transfer functions is restricted only by pragmatics.

Something like Sag's semantic proposal is required to account for deferred reference. But notice what the resulting 'semantic' theory has the power to do. In no sense can it be said that semantic content is 'constrained' by conventional meaning. Since, as we just discussed, virtually any word can have a deferred meaning, it follows that any word could in principle acquire any meaning, via a sense-transfer function. The available sense-transfer functions are constrained only by pragmatics. So, the resulting semantic theory is one according to which semantic content is unconstrained by conventional meaning. The semantic content of the word 'house' could be the property of being a dog—the only thing that would prevent it from acquiring this semantic content is pragmatic facts about a context.

The moral of this final consideration is that, to capture deferred reference semantically, one would need to adopt a semantic theory where semantic content is not constrained by conventional meaning; in short, an unconstrained semantic theory (that is, constrained only by pragmatics). When capturing a phenomenon within the semantics would result in an unconstrained semantic theory, that suggests that the phenomenon is not semantic. For example, if in order to capture a phenomenon within the semantics, one needs to exploit resources that could allow the semantic content of 'Grass is green', relative to a context, to be the proposition that snow is white, then the phenomenon is not semantic. This is the principal theoretical reason for denying that deferred reference is semantic.

So, I have given three theoretical reasons for denying that deferred reference is semantic. These considerations are not arguments based on intuitions. As I have already indicated, there is a sense of 'intuitive truth-conditions' in which deferred reference enters into intuitive truth-conditions. So one might think that to draw the distinction between semantic content and what is only pragmatic in such a way that the deferred reference of a use of an expression is not part of the semantic content is to abandon the semanticist's view that semantics is the source of our intuitions about the truth-conditions of an utterance.

I don't think that any reasonable way of delineating the border between the semantic and the non-semantic will deliver results that will satisfy all. The responsibility of the semanticist is rather to provide some way of drawing the distinction that preserves the core semanticist claim that the source of our intuitions about truth-conditions is the semantics. Cases like deferred reference are cases in which tutored intuitions *diverge*. It is certainly the case that the non-deferred meaning of (9) is available to all competent users of the language, as in the discourse:

(18) A: The ham sandwich is getting annoyed.
     B: That's absurd; sandwiches do not get annoyed.

In such a case, where the putatively literal semantic content is clearly available to all competent users of the language, it is perfectly permissible to let theoretical considerations decide between the putatively literal semantic content and the enriched content (that is, the content enriched with the deferred meaning). This is consistent with the semanticist's position, since this is a case in which speakers have several intuitions easily available to them.

The case of deferred reference contrasts, then, with the case of comparative adjectives. Suppose that a theorist maintained (cf. Cappelen and Lepore in this volume) that the semantic contribution of 'tall' was something like the semantic content 'tall for some comparison class', so that everything in the universe except the smallest thing is tall. Suppose then that I showed a speaker a picture of a tiny dwarfish man, surrounded by normal-sized men. Pointing at the dwarfish man, I uttered 'That man is tall'. On the envisaged theory, the semantic content of my sentence, relative to this context, is a true proposition. The person in question is tall, relative to some comparison class (e.g. the class of mice). But this semantic content is utterly inaccessible to the speaker. Unlike the case of deferred reference, there is no possibility of a sensible discourse along the following lines:

(19) A (*pointing at the dwarfish man*): That person is not tall.
     B: That's absurd; everyone and everything is tall, except for the smallest thing.

What this indicates is that the putative semantic content—that the indicated person is tall for some comparison class—is not available to the competent user of the language. Therefore, it is not consistent with the view I am suggesting to take it as the actual semantic content of the sentence, in context.[5]

---

[5] There are other powerful objections against the view in question. For example, 'tall', like other comparative adjectives, is *gradable*. On a degree theoretic view, the function of an intensifier such as 'very' is to raise the contextually salient degree of height that something must meet in order to be tall. But, on the Cappelen and Lepore view, it is mysterious what the semantic function of 'very' would be in a sentence such as 'Bill is tall, but John is very tall.'

I have said that, when the putative semantic content is clearly accessible and tutored intuitions about semantic content diverge, theoretical considerations may enter in to decide where to draw the line between semantic content proper and the rest of what is conveyed in a speech act. As we have seen, deferred reference is one such case. In this case, I gave two theoretical reasons to take the semantic content of a sentence not to be sensitive to deferred meanings. It is instructive to look at another such case in which tutored intuitions may diverge, but theoretical considerations impel us to draw a different sort of line between the semantic and the non-semantic: the case of domain restriction.

When a sentence such as (3) or (20) is uttered, we naturally interpret it with respect to a salient domain of quantification:

(20) Every bottle is in the fridge.

For example, (20) could be used to communicate the proposition that every bottle in the house is in the fridge. However, like the case of deferred reference (and unlike the case of comparative adjectives), the unrestricted interpretation is also available to competent language users, as the coherence of the following sort of discourse illustrates:

(21) A: Every bottle is in the fridge.
       B: Well, your fridge couldn't possibly be that large! There are bottles somewhere in the world that aren't in your fridge.

So, like the case of deferred reference, though intuitions are sensitive to the domain of quantification, it is nevertheless possible for competent speakers to detect the unrestricted reading of quantified sentences. If, as in the case of deferred reference, there were overwhelming theoretical considerations that mitigated against building the restricted reading of quantified sentences into the semantics, then it would then be acceptable to do so, consistently with the thesis that semantic content delivers intuitive truth-conditions.

However, there are no good theoretical reasons against incorporating domain restriction in the semantics. As we saw, incorporating deferred meaning into semantic content has at least two disturbing results. First, the semantic content of an expression may be something that does not satisfy the conventional meaning of that expression. Secondly, in order to treat the phenomenon, one needs to employ resources that trivialize the semantics. In contrast, incorporating domain restriction into the semantics brings no such costs.

On the theory of domain restriction in Stanley and Szabo (2000) and Stanley (2002*b*), the effect of domain restriction is to restrict the extension of the head noun in a quantified noun phrase. That is, in a sentence such as (19), the effect of domain restriction is just to restrict the interpretation of the property expressed by 'bottle', by intersecting its extension with the extension of the property that is the domain restriction. The semantic content of the result will be a subset of the set of bottles. So, the semantic content of the restriction of 'bottle' will be something that satisfies the conventional meaning of 'bottle'. Secondly, in incorporating domain restriction into the semantics, there is no risk of giving the semantics the resources to make 'Grass is green' express the proposition that snow is white. The only effect context can have is to restrict the interpretation delivered by the conventional meaning of the head noun in a quantified noun phrase. So, incorporating domain restriction into the semantics is perfectly consistent with the nature of semantic content as intrinsically constrained by conventional meaning.

Since incorporating domain restriction into the semantics does not have theoretical costs, given that domain restriction does affect some level of intuitive truth-conditions, it ought to be incorporated into the semantics. Of course, it is only possible to incorporate domain restriction into the semantics if it is due to semantics, that is, due to the compositional assignment of content to a sentence in context. In previous work, I have argued that there is covert structure in quantified noun phrases to which provision of a domain to the semantic content of the sentence containing that noun phrase is due. One argument I have used for this conclusion (in the case of domain restriction as well as other constructions) is what has since been called *the binding argument*. Note that the sentences in (22) are most naturally interpreted as in (23):

(22) *a.* In every room, every bottle is in the corner.
       b. Every student answered every question.
(23) *a.* In every room r, every bottle in r is in the corner.
       b. Every student x answered every question y on x's exam.

One way to generate the readings in (23) is to suppose that there are bound variables in the structure of quantified noun phrases, whose values, relative to a context, generate a domain of quantification.

More specifically, the theory of domain restriction I favor (Stanley and Szabo 2000; Stanley, 2002*b*) captures these readings in the following way. Syntactically associated with each nominal are domain restriction indices, of the form 'f(i)'. Relative to a context, 'f' is assigned a function from objects to properties, and 'i' is assigned an object.[6] So, the syntactic structure of the sentences in (23) is similar to the sentences in (24):

(24) *a.* Every fireman is tired.
      b. Every student answered every question.
(25) *a.* Every <fireman, f(i)> is tired.
      b. [Every <student, f(j)>]-i answered every <question, f(i)>.

Given an utterance of, for example, (23*b*), the speaker intends the value of 'f' to be a function from students to their exams, and 'i' is bound by the higher quantifier 'every student', yielding the desired reading (23*b*).[7]

If these are the right representations, then domain restriction is due to the semantics, since it is due to the assignment of values to constituents of a sentence, relative to a context. Evidence that these are the right representations comes from the fact that one detects operator-variable interactions involving quantifier domains, and operator-variable interactions are syntactic in nature.

Of course, binding considerations are certainly not the only way to argue that an allegedly non-semantic phenomenon is due to semantics. For example, the view that the phenomenon in question is non-semantic could be due to an overly simplistic conception of the semantics of some overt expression, and so one way of establishing that the phenomenon is semantic is by giving a more complex semantic clause for some overt expression (cf. again King and Stanley (2005) on implicature intrusion). Furthermore, binding considerations are not the only way to establish covert structure, since nothing bars the language system from employing syntactic structures containing covert non-bindable indexicals, akin to the overt non-bindable indexicals 'I' and 'here' of English. But binding considerations are still one way to argue for covert structure, and one that generalizes to a wide range of constructions (cf. Stanley, 2000). Because such considerations do provide an argument for the semantic treatment of a wide range of data that pragmaticists have long claimed to be non-semantic in nature, they

---

[6] To my knowledge, the need for such a function variable in an account of domain restriction was first pointed out in Von Fintel (1994: 31). Von Fintel's theory differs from Stanley and Szabo (2000) in that his representations associate the domain indices with determiners, rather than nominals.

[7] The values for the domain indices for the first nominal 'student' could be, for example, the classroom (for 'j') and a function from the classroom to its inhabitants (for 'f'). For more discussion of the values of unbound domain indices, cf. Stanley (2002*b*: 371).

have recently been widely criticized. In the rest of this chapter, I will look at some of the criticisms of the argument from binding, to see whether they undermine the status of these considerations as arguments for syntactic structure.

III. The Binding Argument

According to the binding argument, if there is a genuine bound reading of a certain construction, that supports the hypothesis that the quantifier in question binds a variable in the syntactic structure of the sentence. For the binding argument to have force, the bound reading must be generated by an expression that is an uncontroversial example of a quantificational expression. The binding argument, *considered as an argument for syntactic structure*, has been interpreted in several different ways. In this section, I discuss the three different ways it has been interpreted.[8]

On the first interpretation of the binding argument, which occurs in unpublished work by Michael Nelson, and in Cappelen and Lepore (2002), the binding argument establishes the existence of covert structure, on pain of ungrammaticality due to vacuous binding. For instance, in the case of (18*a*), the quantifier 'every room' must bind a variable in the syntactic structure of the sentence 'every bottle is in the corner', on pain of ungrammaticality. On the second interpretation of the binding argument, a bound reading of a sentence is evidence for syntactic structure, since bound readings are the semantic effect of a syntactic process (see Stanley, 2000: 412–14 for details). On this version of the binding argument, it is not potential ungrammaticality that is at issue. Rather, certain kinds of semantic phenomena (e.g. bound readings, scope ambiguities) have ultimately a syntactic explanation. On the third (and weakest) interpretation of the binding argument, it is an inference to the best explanation. By postulating a covert variable, one can account for

---

[8] Many authors have used bound readings of various constructions to draw disparate morals. Partee (1989) uses bound readings of relational expressions such as 'local' and 'enemy' to argue that binding is *not* always represented linguistically (thereby drawing the *opposite* conclusion from such data to Stanley, 2000). Cooper (1993) provides bound readings to argue for the semantic reality of situation variables. Von Fintel uses bound readings of quantifier phrases to argue that resource domain variables are indexical in nature, but stops just short of arguing that they are syntactically present (1994: 33). Nevertheless, it's natural to read von Fintel as endorsing that thesis.

the bound reading, and there is no other satisfactory way to account for it. In Stanley (2002*a*: 152), for argument's sake, I employed this third interpretation in arguing against 'free enrichment' accounts of binding.

There are two basic kinds of challenges to the binding argument. First, there are attempts to argue that, whatever the right account of the data, the methodology behind the binding argument is unsound. However, the point of the third version of the binding argument is that merely objecting to the postulation of variables without providing an alternative account is insufficient. It is one thing to raise faults with the methodology, but quite another to provide an account that is equally adequate to the explanatory task. The second kind of response to the binding argument is to attempt to fulfill this obligation by explaining bound readings without postulating covert structure.

Since the most important task for the person who objects to the binding argument is to explain bound readings without postulating covert structure, I will focus first on accounts that attempt to accomplish this. But before I begin my discussion of such accounts, I want to discuss briefly two approaches to the data that I will *not* discuss at length: variable free semantics and free pragmatic enrichment.

A variable free semantic framework can provide an account of bound readings of sentences without postulating covert structure. There are many different versions of variable-free semantics, but I'll briefly focus on the elegant version given in Jacobson (1999). On Jacobson's account, work that might ordinarily be done by postulating syntactic movement or covert structure is done instead by type-shifting in the semantics; a pronoun in the complement of a verb induces a *type-shift* in that verb. A transitive verb has potentially different semantic types, depending upon the number of pronouns that occur within its complement. Complexity in the syntax, on a variable-free account, is replaced by complexity in semantic type assignments to lexical items.

I will not discuss variable-free semantics, because I think the question of whether to implement binding syntactically or semantically is orthogonal to the question at hand, which is whether certain examples demonstrate that intuitive truth-conditions are not generated within the semantics. Both the proponent of variable-free semantics and the more traditional syntactician and semanticist should agree that bound readings of a sentence are of semantic significance. The more traditional syntactician and semanticist should think they are of semantic significance because they indicate hidden syntactic structure, whereas the variable-free semanticist should think they are of semantic significance because they demonstrate that a lexical item is associated with potentially distinct semantic types. Variable-free semantics does not make it easier to argue that certain readings cannot be generated in the semantics; it is irrelevant to this issue.[9]

The second topic I will not discuss is free enrichment accounts of the data. There are two styles of such accounts. According to the first, when one utters a sentence, via a pragmatic process, the sentence itself is 'enriched' into a longer sentence with the addition of lexical material. We may call this *free syntactic enrichment*. According to the second, when one utters a sentence, the semantic content of that sentence (a proposition or a property or propositional function) is enriched by the addition of additional semantic constituents. We may call this *free semantic enrichment*.[10]

I shall not discuss either enrichment account of the intuitive data, not because it is not topical (it clearly is), but because I have discussed such accounts in detail already (Stanley, 2002*a*). As I have previously indicated, my objection to such accounts is that they over-generate. If free pragmatic enrichment of either kind were a regular mechanism we could appeal to in communication, it would be a mystery why many sentences cannot serve greater communicative functions than they do.

In the next sections, I shall rather discuss two challenges to the binding argument that seek to account for the intuitive data without free pragmatic enrichment, either syntactic or semantic. If there were viable alternative accounts of some of the binding data, then that would raise worries about

[9] An interesting issue arises with what would be captured as free readings of variables in a more traditional framework (Jacobson, 1999: 134–5). On a variable-free framework, there really are no free variables. Explicit pronouns are semantically empty (express the identity function). The effect of a free variable (or a free reading of a relational expression such as 'enemy') is to induce type-shifts so that the resulting sentence expresses a propositional function (e.g. in the case of 'enemy', a function from persons to singular propositions). On this view, a sentence containing a free variable does not express a proposition, but rather a function from a certain kind of entity (determined by the type of the free-variable) to a proposition (or truth-value, depending on one's framework). Satisfying this function is not a matter of free enrichment, but rather closer to what Kent Bach (1994) calls 'completion'.

[10] Some philosophers of language hold that a sentence expresses a structured semantic content, with specific holes that are saturated by context. I do not consider this to be free semantic enrichment. In the envisaged process, the role of context is constrained to supply elements of a particular semantic type. Thus, it is conventionally constrained. In contrast, free semantic enrichment is, by its nature, not so constrained. Elements of any semantic type, consistently with the conversational context, could be added.

the soundness of the underlying methodology, and thereby threaten to rob the defender of the binding argument of a useful tool by which to establish covert structure in a wide variety of problem cases.

IV. Binding and Comparative Adjectives

In Stanley (2000), the binding argument was used to argue for the syntactic representation of comparison classes for comparative adjectives, such as 'tall' and 'old'. The target of the arguments there was the following kind of unarticulated constituent clause:

> (R) Relative to any context c, 'old' expresses the property of being old for a thing of the kind that is salient in context c.

In Stanley (2000: 418), I pointed out that (R) cannot capture the most natural reading of a sentence such as:

> (26) Most species have members that are old.

The problem with (R) is that it predicts that the occurrence of 'old' in (26) must be fixed to a particular species salient in the context of use of (26). But, in the natural reading of (26), the values introduced by the initial quantifier 'most species' vary the comparison class to which 'old' is applied. (R) cannot account for this reading.

In conversation, I have encountered philosophers challenging this line of argument, by contending that 'old' in (26) simply means *old for a thing of its kind*. If so, then (R) produces the desired reading, because the variation is part of the lexical meaning of the adjective 'old'. However, this suggestion does not rescue (R), as a similar example shows:

> (27) Every sports team has a member who is old.

Intuitively, (27) may express the proposition that every sports team has a member that is old for that sport. But on the view we are considering, 'old' expresses the property of being old for x's kind; that is λx(old for x's kind). But each member of a sports team belongs to many different kinds. So it is unclear how to use this suggestion to obtain this reading of (27).

Perhaps we can use this suggestion to emend (R):

> (R*) Relative to any context c, 'old' expresses the property λx(x is old for x's N), where N is the contextually salient property.

Unlike (R), (R*) has no trouble with (26). For relative to a context of utterance for (26), the salient property is *species*. So, relative to a context of utterance of (26), 'old' expresses λx(old for x's species), which delivers the correct reading. But (R*) also promises to help with (27). Relative to a context of utterance of (27), the contextually salient property is *sport*. So, relative to a context of utterance of (27), 'old' expresses the property λx(old for x's sport). According to this clause, then, in a context of utterance of the appropriate sort, (27) expresses the proposition that every sports team has a member who is old for his sport. And this seems to be the desired reading.

However, (R*) does not work. It faces what we may call *the Bo Jackson problem*. Someone may play more than one sport. In such a case, (R*) will not deliver a result, since (R*) requires that there is one unique sport played by each person. Nevertheless, relative to such a situation, (27) may still express a coherent and indeed true proposition, namely the proposition that every sports team S has a member who is old for the sport played by S.

Here is a possible repair to (R*) in light of the Bo Jackson problem:

(R**)   Relative to any context c, 'old' expresses the property λx(x is old for some N in which x participates), where N is the contextually salient property.

(R**) evades the Bo Jackson problem, since it does not require, of each thing, that it participates in only one kind of the contextually salient property (in the case of (26), only one kind of sport). However, (R**) also fails.

According to (R**), in a context of the appropriate sort, (26) expresses the proposition that every sports team has a member that is old for some sport he plays. Suppose that there are three sports teams, a gymnastics team, a chess club, and a baseball team. One person, Bob, plays for all three teams. Bob is old for a gymnast, but not old for a chess player or a baseball player. No other members of the teams are old for their sports. Intuitively, what an utterance of (27) expresses, relative to this situation, is false. However, according to (R**), the proposition expressed by (27) should be true in this situation. For each sports team does have a member who is old for some sport he plays. Each sports team contains Bob, who is old for a gymnast.

So there does not seem to be any easy repair of a rule such as (R). If one wishes to capture semantically all of the intuitive judgements about truth and falsity we have discussed, examples such as (26) and (27) seem to require a syntactically represented comparison class (or some other mechanism that imitates binding).

V. Quantifying over Contexts

One classic example of an unarticulated constituent analysis of a construction involves example (28), from Perry (1986):

(28) It's raining.
(U) 'It is raining(t)' is true in a context c if and only if the denotation of 'rain' takes $<t,l>$ to the true, where l is the contextually salient location in c.

In Stanley (2000: 415–23), I used binding considerations against an unarticulated constituent analysis like this. In particular, I used examples such as:

(29) Every time John lights a cigarette, it rains.

The unarticulated constituent analysis suggested in (U) cannot derive the natural reading of (29), where the location of the raining varies with the values of the initial quantifier, 'every time John lights a cigarette'.

My purpose in giving this argument was not so much to advance my own account of such examples as to reject an unarticulated constituent analysis. But I did propose two positive 'articulated' accounts of the data (2000: 416–17). According to the first, 'rain' is associated with an event or situation variable, which is bound by the initial quantifier 'every time'. According to the second, 'rain' is associated with a pair of variable positions, one of which determines a time, and the other a location, both bound into by the initial quantifier.

Peter Pagin (this volume) seeks to evade the need for either kind of analysis, by treating quantifications such as 'every time John lights a cigarette' as quantifiers over contexts. On Pagin's analysis, (29) ends up having the truth-conditions in (30):

(30) For every context c' differing from c at most in its time and location indices, 'if John lights a cigarette, then it rains' is true in c'.

On Pagin's treatment, there is no need for a variable for events or locations, because the initial quantifier is over contexts.

My concern with Pagin's analysis is a familiar one with operators that shift contextual features, noted originally by Lewis (1981: 86):

. . . we need to know what happens to the truth values of constituent sentences when one feature of context is shifted and the rest are held fixed. But features of context do not vary independently. No two contexts differ by only one feature. Shift one feature only, and the result of the shift is not a context at all.

Suppose I utter (29) in a context c. I am the speaker of c. But to obtain the right truth-conditions, we need to quantify over all n-tuples that differ from c only in their location and time indices. But some n-tuples of indices will not be possible contexts of use.

To make Lewis's point vivid, consider the sentences in (31)

(31) *a.* Whenever I'm politely listening to someone speaking, it starts to rain.
      b. Whenever wind blows through a mountain pass, it starts to rain.

Pagin's truth-conditions for the sentences in (31), considered as uttered in a context c, are:

(32) *a.* For every context c′ differing from c in at most its location and time indices, 'If I'm politely listening to someone speaking, it rains' is true in c′.
      b. For every context c′ differing from c in at most its location and time indices, 'If the wind blows through a mountain pass, it starts to rain' is true in c′.

Now consider the contexts c′ involved in obtaining the correct truth-conditions. To obtain the right truth-conditions, many of these must be packages of indices that are not possible contexts of use. For example, to obtain the right truth-conditions for (31*a*) via (32*a*), we need contexts in which the speaker in c is the addressee in c′, rather than the speaker. But these will not be contexts that differ from c only in their location and time indices. A different problem surfaces for (31*b*). A context is one in which the agent of the context is at the time and location of the context. So Pagin predicts that (31*b*) is true just in case, whenever the speaker in c is at the time and location of the relevant mountain pass, it starts to rain when the wind blows through. But clearly, these truth-conditions are too weak. (31*b*) would be falsified if there are situations with no one around (and hence no agents) in which the wind blows through a mountain pass and it doesn't start to rain at that location.[11]

So, I'm skeptical that appealing to quantifiers over contexts will help in accounting for bound readings of alleged unarticulated constituents. The problem is that quantifying over contexts results in truth-conditions that are too weak, given the paucity of contexts of use.

---

[11] Pagin discusses a similar problem (see the discussion surrounding principle (I)). But his discussion cannot accommodate (31*b*), since his approach involves quantifying only over contexts, and to obtain the right truth-conditions for (31*b*), one needs to quantify over indices that are not possible contexts of use.

VI. The Challenge from Over-Generation

In the past two sections, I have discussed attempts to capture the binding data without postulating unpronounced structure. I now turn to challenges to the binding argument. The most common sort of objection involves *over-generation*.[12] According to this kind of challenge, if one postulates variables when bound readings are available, what results is an over-generation of variables in the syntax.

In what follows, I will respond to the over-generation concern for the binding argument. But first, I want to note an oddity about the strategy of advancing over-generation objection against the binding arguments. Those who advance such objections typically do so in support of *pragmatic* accounts of the bound readings. But pragmatic accounts of the data, as I have

---

[12] One different type of objection to the binding argument, discussed in Cappelen and Lepore (2002: 276–7) is that the variables the binding argument would have us postulate behave differently than overt pronouns, in particular in anaphora. For example, as they point out, it is odd to follow up an utterance of 'Tigers are mammals', by 'and it is a big domain' (with the 'it' referring to the domain associated with 'tigers'). This objection deserves more attention than I can give it here (unpublished work by Adam Sennett and Brett Sherman is important in this regard). But one reason to be suspicious of the argument is that it would apply to an alarmingly large range of constructions. Of course Cappelen and Lepore revel in this fact; as they note (2002: 279), these considerations would also tell against postulating variables for comparison classes for comparative adjectives (cf. also Cappelen and Lepore, this volume). Their argument would also tell against postulating variables for degrees for adjectival constructions, as witnessed by the oddity of 'John is tall, and it is a high degree'. More problematically, the considerations also entail that the implicit anaphoric elements associated with relational expressions such as 'local' and 'enemy' are not syntactically realized. For example, suppose Bill utters 'John talked to an enemy in 2004', thereby expressing the proposition that John talked to an enemy of Bill in 2004. It is not possible for someone to follow this utterance up by saying 'He has many enemies', where the 'he' is genuinely *discourse anaphoric* on the covert variable that refers to Bill. Similarly, suppose Bill utters 'John talked to an enemy', meaning an enemy of the USA. It is not possible to follow this up with, 'And it is a big country', where 'it' is discourse anaphoric on the covert variable. So, if this argument were correct, *implicit anaphora* would not be syntactically realized. Similarly, it is plausible to take epistemic modals to involve implicit anaphora; the occurrence of 'might' in a token of 'It might be raining in Paris on 19 July 2004' is to be taken relative to the knowledge state of the person making the utterance. But one cannot follow up someone's utterance of 'It might be raining in Paris' with 'He is strange', where 'he' is an anaphoric pronoun (contrast this with the acceptability of following 'According to John, it might be raining in Paris' with 'He is strange', where 'he' is uttered with anaphoric intent). The argument therefore proves too much, unless Cappelen and Lepore are also willing to use it to reject the syntactic representation of implicit anaphora.

emphasized, over-generate more than any other account possibly could. For pragmatic accounts are, by their nature, *unconstrained* by linguistic meaning. Were some pragmatic account to be correct, there would be numerous sentences that would allow readings that they actually do not allow (Stanley, 2002*a*).[13]

The first over-generation objection I will discuss is due to Cappelen and Lepore (2002: 273). A confused mathematical anthropologist (call her 'Sally') trying to find out if mathematical truths are universal utters (5) as a summary of her findings:

(5) Everywhere I go, $2 + 2 = 4$

Here's the binding argument applied to (5). Intuitively, (5) says that for every place Sally goes, $2 + 2 = 4$ at that place. So we should present the logical form of (5) along the following lines:

(5*) For all places x, if Sally goes to x, then $2 + 2 = 4$ at x.

The quantifier phrase 'Everywhere Sally goes' is binding a place variable in the logical form of '$2 + 2 = 4$'—otherwise, there would be nothing for the quantifier phrase to bind. This establishes that the logical form of the sentence '$2 + 2 = 4$' has a freely occurring place variable.

Since there is obviously *no* variable ranging over locations in '$2 + 2 = 4$', this is a *reductio* of the binding argument.

Before responding to this argument, we should be clear about what version of the binding argument Cappelen and Lepore have in mind. As I discussed above, there are three versions of the binding argument. According to the first, it has to do with grammaticality; one must postulate a place variable in the logical form of a sentence, or else one cannot explain the grammaticality of the larger construction. According to the second, it does not have to do with grammaticality; bound readings are taken to be a reflection of syntactic binding. According to the third reading, it is an inference to the best explanation of the bound reading.

---

[13] Indeed, in the thousands of pages that have been written over the last decade arguing for pragmatic (non-semantic) accounts of a wide range of apparently semantic phenomena, I am not aware of a single attempt to provide a response to the threat of over-generation to pragmatic theories. Indeed, I am not even aware, aside from passing footnote references, to a discussion of the over-generation threat facing such theories. Given this silence, there is some irony involved in such theorists' extreme sensitivity to over-generation worries with alternative positions. I hope that the sensitivity such theorists evince to over-generation objections will soon be reflected in greater attention to these worries with their favored accounts.

Cappelen and Lepore address the first of these versions of the binding argument. Since I am not aware of that version being promoted in published work, I'm not sure it should be the focus of critical attention.[14] That is, the obvious *grammaticality* of example (5) poses no worries for the advocate of the binding argument. So I take it that the feature of the example that is supposed to concern the advocate of the binding argument is the claim that the intuitive reading of the example is (5*). If the intuitive reading of (5) is (5*), then it would seem that the advocate of the binding argument is committed to postulating a place variable in the logical form of '2 + 2 = 4'.

However, I do not see that (5*) is the intuitive reading of (5), and I do not see that Cappelen and Lepore even believe that (5*) is a reading of (5). As Cappelen and Lepore (2002) point out, 'it is close to indisputable that arithmetical statements lack hidden indexicals referring to places'. Presumably, the reason they are so convinced of this is that it is unclear what it even means to speak of an arithmetical statement being true *at a place*. If that is the intuition, then it is equally hard to see how (5*) is a legitimate reading of (5). Sally may intend (5*) as a reading of (5), because, as Cappelen and Lepore put it, she is a 'confused mathematical anthropologist.' But the fact that someone confusedly believes a sentence has a certain reading does not give that sentence that reading.

Of course, it is uncontroversial that (5) is grammatical. But nothing follows from this, other than a rejection of the first version of the binding argument. But since the first version of binding argument is not one that has ever been advanced in print, it is not germane to the issue.

Breheny (2004) has leveled another sort of over-generation objection against the binding argument, this involving what he calls the problem of multiple dependencies. Since Breheny's arguments are interesting and illustrate important points, it is worth going over them in detail.

Recall that on my favored account of domain restriction, motivated by binding considerations, each noun is syntactically associated with two indices, a function index and an argument index. Relative to a context, the function index is assigned a function from objects to properties, and the argument index an object. So, if I have New Jersey in mind when I say 'Every

---

[14] Cappelen and Lepore cite Nelson (2001), who seems to have the first interpretation of the Binding Argument in mind. But the relevant passages in Nelson (2001) involve a summary and subsequent critique of Stanley (2000), and in that paper, I certainly did not have the first interpretation of the Binding Argument in mind.

politician is saintly', then New Jersey is the value of the object index, and perhaps the function index is assigned a function from states to the property of being an inhabitant of that state. It is this view that is Breheny's target.[15]

The first sort of example Breheny discusses is:

(33) Every student was feeling particularly lucky and thought no examiner would notice every mistake.

Breheny argues that (33) has the reading in:

(34) [Every student]$_x$ thought [no examiner]$_y$ would notice [every mistake made on a paper x turned in and y examines]$_z$.

Breheny argues that this sort of example is problematic, because the approach I advocate cannot generate reading (34) of (33), without postulating more syntactic variables. That is, Breheny worries that the methodology of the binding argument commits its proponent to postulating implausibly many variables, certainly more than just the domain variables discussed above.

But I don't see the worry with this particular example. The noun 'examiner' is a relational noun. It is associated (cf. Stanley, 2000) with a syntactically represented index. This fact straightforwardly generates the desired reading. That is, an independently motivated claim about relational expressions, together with an independently motivated theory of domain restriction, straightforwardly predicts that (33) has the reading:

(35) [Every student]$_x$ thought [no examiner, x]$_y$ would notice [every mistake f(x)]$_z$.

We may assume 'f'' is assigned a function from students to their exam questions. So, we can straightforwardly predict a reading of (33) according to which every student thought no examiner of that student would notice every mistake on that student's exam. So recognizing the relational nature of

---

[15] In previous work (Stanley and Szabó, 2000; Stanley, 2002*b*) I took the function index and the object index to 'co-habit' a node with the head noun. I no longer think this is correct. Talk of 'cohabiting a node' with a lexical item suggests that domain indices are part of lexical structure. But the position that domain indices are merely part of lexical structure is not consistent with the general view (advocated in Stanley, 2000) that considerations such as binding, weak-crossover, and ellipsis are evidence for genuine syntactic structure, rather than mere lexical structure. Secondly, both Breheny (2004) and Williamson (2003) provide evidence that the domain index must sometimes be outside the scope of adjectives modifying the head noun. Since the domain indices must sometimes be inside the scope of modifying adjectives (cf. Stanley, 2002*b*: 372–3), this suggests that the domain indices occupy their own terminal nodes that can have different adjunction sites.

'examiner' enables us to derive the natural reading with only independently motivated resources.

Breheny also has examples that do not involve relational nouns. However, they do not raise problems for any view I have defended. Consider Breheny's 'multiple dependence' example (36a), which he claims to have reading (36b):

(36) *a*. Every paranoid artist thinks no dealer will stop at selling every forged painting.

    b. [Every paranoid artist]$_x$ thinks [no dealer]$_y$ will stop at selling every [[forged [painting by x]] coming into y's possession.

On my account, every noun (or N′) in every QNP is associated with a domain index. So (36a) is predicted to have a reading as in (37):

(37) [Every paranoid artist]$_x$ thinks [no dealer f(x)]$_y$ will stop at selling [every forged painting f′(y)].

Relative to the envisaged context, 'f' is assigned a function from artists to people in possession of forged paintings of that artist, and 'f′' is assigned a function from dealers to their collections. So, the theory predicts that (36a) has the reading:

(38) Every paranoid artist thinks that no dealer in possession of forged paintings of that artist will stop at selling every forged painting in their collection.

Intuitions are subtle here. But both of my informants think that (36a) clearly has reading (38), and none of my informants think that (36a) has reading (36b). In other words, there is a strong difference among my informants between (36a) and (39):

(36) *a*. Every paranoid artist thinks no dealer will stop at selling every forged painting.

(39)   [Every paranoid artist]$_x$ thinks no dealer will stop at selling every forged painting of his$_x$.

My informants do not obtain reading (39) of (36a). They only obtain reading (38) of (36a). And that is precisely what an account that only postulates a single pair of domain variables (one argument and one function variable) would suggest.

A final example of Breheny is:

(40) Every company knows that none of the pension fund can be diverted away from any former employee.

Breheny claims this example has the following reading:

(41) [Every company]$_x$ knows that [none of the pension fund]$_y$ can be diverted away from any [[former employee of x] who is due some of y].

But again, no additional variables are needed to capture the appropriate reading semantically. Since 'employee' is a relational noun, (40) is predicted to have the reading in (42):

(42) [Every company]$_x$ knows that [none of the pension fund f(x)]$_y$ can be diverted away from any former [employee, x].

Relative to the envisaged context, 'f' is assigned a function from (e.g.) companies to their benefit programs. So, (41) expresses the proposition that every company knows that none of the pension funds of that company can be diverted away from any former employee of that company. And this is precisely the desired reading.

Breheny writes that 'if we wanted to pursue a variable-rich approach, given these multiple dependencies, we seem to need to assume that QNP structures contain a plethora of hidden variables at different levels which are vacuously assigned (to what?) when not used.' But, as I have argued, this worry is unfounded. The assumption that relational nouns are associated with syntactically realized implicit arguments, together with the assumption that QNPs are each associated with a single domain index, is sufficient to explain all the data. Indeed, the framework even explains why certain sentences *lack* readings, as in reading (36*b*) of (36*a*).

There is a final sort of over-generation objection against the binding argument that I wish to discuss. Because I think this sort of objection hinges on a confusion about the methodology of semantics, responding to it involves less focus on empirical detail, and more on foundational matters.

According to François Recanati, the binding argument involves what he calls the 'Binding Criterion'. The Binding Criterion is that intuitively bound readings must be reflected by bound variables in the syntax. Given his assumption, here is his objection (Recanati, 2004: 106–7). We can say:

(15) John is anorexic, but whenever his father cooks mushrooms, he eats.

On a natural interpretation, we understand that John eats the mushrooms his father has cooked. Intuitively, a form of binding is operative here; for the food eaten by John co-varies with the food cooked by his father. Such examples show that intuitive binding, per se, does not entail the existence of a free variable in logical form. The Binding Criterion, on which Stanley's argument rests, must be rejected.

Recanati's argument against the Binding Criterion has two premises. The first premise is that the intuitive reading of his sentence (15) is that, whenever John's father cooks mushrooms, John eats the mushrooms his father cooks. Recanati's second premise is that is that there is no covert variable for *what John eats* in the logical form of 'he eats'. Assuming these two premises, Recanati concludes that the Binding Criterion, which requires such a covert variable, must be rejected.

Recanati's example is deliberately modeled upon examples discussed in Stanley (2000), such as:

(43) Whenever John lights a cigarette, it rains.

There, I concluded that 'it rains' does contain a variable that can be bound by the initial quantifier, 'whenever John lights a cigarette.' The evidence that it can be is due to the fact that the intuitive reading of (43) is:

(44) Whenever John lights a cigarette, it rains at the location of that lighting.

I also suggested various ways of accounting for the bound reading in question (2000: 416). Recanati's suggestion is that his example (15) is analogous to (43), so that whatever methodology leads one to postulate an unpronounced variable in 'it rains' to account for the bound reading in (43) should lead one, incorrectly, to postulate an unpronounced variable for what is eaten in 'John eats'.

However, Recanati's (15) is simply not analogous to (43). In particular, the first premise of Recanati's argument is false (whereas the corresponding premise for (43) is true). As Luisa Marti (n.d.) has shown, it is not the case that the intuitive truth-conditions of (15) are what Recanati says they are. The following two discourses, due essentially to Marti, reveal the clear difference between (15) and (43):

(45) A. Whenever John's father cooks mushrooms, John eats.
      B. #No he doesn't—he eats broccoli when his father cooks mushrooms.
(46) A. Whenever John lights a cigarette, it rains.
      B. No it doesn't—though it rains somewhere else.

As the oddity of Marti's discourse in (45) clearly demonstrates, it is not permissible to deny the content of A's assertion on the grounds that one thinks that John eats broccoli, rather than mushrooms, when his father cooks mushrooms. This demonstrates that the intuitive truth-conditions of an utterance of Recanati's (15) is not that whenever John's father cooks mushrooms, John eats the mushrooms his father cooks. It is rather that whenever John's father cooks mushrooms, John eats *something*. In contrast, the acceptability of the discourse in (46) demonstrates that the intuitive content of (43) is (44).

According to the binding argument, when a bound reading is part of the intuitive truth-conditions of an utterance, it is the result of a quantifier–variable interaction. The problem with Recanati's example is that (as Marti's argument demonstrates), it is no part of the intuitive truth-conditions of an utterance of (15) that John ate the mushrooms his father cooked. Our intuitions about truth and falsity clearly reveal this to be a reflection of our background assumptions, combined with the semantic content of (15), which is just that in whatever situation John's father cooked mushrooms, John ate something in that situation. In contrast, our intuitions about the truth-conditions of utterances of sentences such as (43) clearly reveal that relativity to a location parameter is part of their intuitive truth-conditions.

The distinction between a verb like 'rains' and a verb like 'eats' can be seen even in non-embedded sentences. Suppose Bill has cooked a mushroom dinner. Pointing at a dirty plate on the table, and intending to communicate that John has eaten the mushrooms Bill cooked, I utter:

(47) John ate.

Suppose one knew that John had just eaten, but he did not eat the mushrooms Bill cooked. It is still clearly not permissible to follow my assertion with:

(48) No he didn't; he ate broccoli instead.

In contrast, suppose that it is raining in New York City, where I am located. Speaking on the phone with Delia, who is in Ithaca, I utter:

(49) It's raining.

Delia, seeing on television that the sky is clear in New York, utters:

(50) No it isn't. But it's raining here.

Delia's reply is perfectly acceptable, in contrast to the unacceptable (48). This demonstrates that the location is part of the intuitive truth-conditions of an utterance of (49), whereas what is eaten, even when it is salient, is clearly not part of the intuitive truth-conditions of an utterance of (47).

Of course, when we hear an utterance of Recanati's (15), we are liable to assume that John ate the mushrooms his father cooked. The reason we assume this has nothing whatever to do with semantics. Rather, we assume that when your father is cooking a meal, and you're eating together with him, it is expected behavior to eat what your father has cooked. We also assume, when we hear an utterance of Recanati's (15), that John's father is not a Martian. But it would be absurd to suppose that it is the semantics that 'tells' us that John's father is not a Martian. It is similarly absurd to suppose that information we acquire via the background assumption that people generally eat the meals that are cooked for them must be supplied semantically, if the semanticist is right.[16]

Similar mistakes to these have been made by other pragmaticists, in their discussions of the view of Stanley (2000) that the source of the intuitive truth-conditions of an utterance are covert structure. For example, Wilson and Sperber (2002) exploit the example:

(51) I must wash my hands: I've eaten [using my hands, rather than, say, being spoon-fed].

According to Wilson and Sperber, the bracketed material is part of the intuitive truth-conditions of an utterance of 'I must wash my hands: I've eaten.' So, they conclude that anyone who defends the clear and elegant explanation of the source of intuitive truth-conditions is committed to the view that 'eat' has an argument place for *the manner of eating* (see also Carston, 2002: 203–4). But it is false that the manner of eating, even in the example they envisage, enters into the intuitive truth-conditions, as the oddity of Bill's utterance in the Marti-style discourse in (52) demonstrates:

(52) John: I must wash my hands: I've eaten.
      Bill: No you didn't; you got spoon-fed.

---

[16] Iliria Frana (n.d.) provides an argument against the binding argument that is also undermined by these considerations. Frana considers the sentence 'Paolo is a real curious guy; every time he finds something, he opens it.' According to Frana, an utterance of this sentence has the intuitive truth-conditions that Paolo always opens the thing he finds in a manner appropriate to that thing. But intuitively, what is said would not be *false* if Paolo always opened what he found in a manner that was not appropriate to that thing. Therefore, this is no part of the intuitive truth-conditions of Frana's sentence. A similar point dispenses with the reply to the binding argument in Stalnaker (2004: 110–11).

Of course, we would naturally assume, given John's discourse, that he ate with his hands. We would also assume that he was not from Mars, and that he was not the product of in-vitro fertilization. It is just as absurd to take it as an objection to the semanticist that such information is not provided by the semantics of the verb 'eat' as it is to take it as an objection to the semanticist that the semantics does not provide for a manner of eating. Such information has nothing to do with intuitive truth-conditions of an utterance.

The responsibility of the semanticist is rather to show that speaker intuitions about the truth-conditions of an utterance are due to semantics. Unfortunately, too many objections to the semanticist assume that the responsibility of the semanticist is to generate within the semantics all information that a competent speaker and member of a culture may derive from a communicative act. Such objections seem to presume, absurdly, that the semanticist's position is incompatible with Grice. As Marti's tests show, being more subtle about judgements of truth and falsity can clearly reveal the distinction between what is part of intuitive truth-conditions proper and what is conveyed by the communicative act to a hearer who combines these truth-conditions with her background knowledge about the world.

Conclusion

My purpose in this chapter has been to defend the claim that the intuitive truth-conditions of an utterance are due to semantic interpretation. Many of those who have objected to it have done so by saddling the position with absurd theoretical commitments, such as the position that all information conveyed in any discourse is due to the semantics. Part of my goal has been to explain what costs the semanticist's position incurs, and what costs it doesn't, by elucidating the target concept of semantics. As I have argued, in certain cases (e.g. that of deferred reference), the semanticist must make decisions about the defiendum that are informed by theoretical considerations. But this is the ordinary practice even in the human sciences.

REFERENCES

Bach, Kent (1994). 'Conversational Impliciture', *Mind and Language*, 9: 124–62.
Breheny, Richard (2004). 'A Lexical Account of Implicit (Bound) Contextual Dependence', in *Semantics and Linguistic Theory* (SALT) 13.

Camp, Elizabeth (n.d.) 'Lodging in the Words', MS.

Cappelen, Herman, and Ernie Lepore (2002). 'Indexicality, Binding, Anaphora, and a Priori Truth', *Analysis*, 62/4: 271–81.

Carston, Robyn (2002). *Thoughts and Utterances: The Pragmatics of Explicit Communication*. (Oxford: Blackwell).

Cooper, Robin (1993). 'Generalized Quantifiers and Resource Situations', in Aczel, Israel, Katagiri, and Peters (eds.), *Situation Theory and its Applications*. (Stanford, Calif.: Stanford University Press).

Fintel, Kai von (1994). '*Restrictions on Quantifier Domains*', University of Massachusetts dissertation.

Frana, Ilaria (n.d.) 'The Constituents of Meaning', MS.

Jacobson, Pauline (1999). 'Towards a Variable-Free Semantics', *Linguistics and Philosophy*, 22: 117–84.

King, Jeffrey C., and Jason Stanley, (2005). 'Semantics, Pragmatics and the Role of Semantic Content', in Z. G. Szabo (ed.), *Semantics versus Pragmatics* (Oxford: Oxford University Press), 111–64.

Levinson, Stephen (2000). *Presumptive Meanings: The Theory of Generalized Conversational Implicature* (Cambridge, Mass.: MIT Press).

Lewis, David (1981). 'Index, Context, and Content', in Stig Kanger and Sven Ohman (eds.), *Philosophy and Grammar: Papers on the Occasion of the Quincentennial of Uppsala University*. (Dordrecht: D. Reidel), 79–100.

Marti, Luisa (n.d.). 'Unarticulated Constituents Revisited', MS.

Nelson, Michael (2001). 'When is an Expression Context-Sensitive?', unpublished MS.

Partee, Barbara (1973). 'Some Structural Analogies between Pronouns and Tense', *Journal of Philosophy*.

—— (1989). 'Binding Implicit Variables in Quantified Contexts', *Proceedings of the Chicago Linguistics Society*, 25 (Chicago: University of Chicago Press), 342–65.

Perry, John (1986). 'Thought without Representation', *Supplementary Proceedings of the Aristotelean Society*, 60: 137–52.

Recanati, François (2004). *Literal Meaning* (Cambridge: Cambridge University Press).

Sag, Ivan (1981). 'Formal Semantics and Extra-Linguistic Context', in Peter Cole (ed.), *Syntax and Semantics*, 13. *Radical Pragmatics* (New York: Academic Press), 273–94.

Stalnaker, Robert (2004). 'Comments on "From Contextualism to Contrastivism"', *Philosophical Studies*, 119/1–2: 105–17.

Stanley, Jason (2000). 'Context and Logical Form', *Linguistics and Philosophy*, 23/4: 391–434.

—— (2002a). 'Making it Articulated', *Mind and Language*, 17/1–2: 149–68.

—— (2002b). 'Nominal Restriction', in Gerhard Preyer and Geory Peter (eds.), *Logical Form and Language* (Oxford: Oxford University Press).

—— and Zoltan Szabó (2000). 'On Quantifier Domain Restriction', *Mind and Language*, 15/2: 219–61.

Stern, Josef (2000). *Metaphor in Context*. (Cambridge, Mass.: MIT Press).

Williamson, Timothy (2003). 'Everything', *Philosophical Perspectives*, 17/1: 415–65.

10

Meaning before Truth

PAUL M. PIETROSKI

According to Chomsky (1996: 52),

> we cannot assume that statements (let alone sentences) have truth conditions. At most, they have something more complex: 'truth indications', in some sense. The issue is not 'open texture' or 'family resemblance' in the Wittgensteinian sense. Nor does the conclusion lend any weight to the belief that semantics is 'holistic' in the Quinean sense that semantic properties are assigned to the whole array of words, not to each individually. Each of these familiar pictures of the nature of meaning seems partially correct, but only partially. There is good evidence that words have intrinsic properties of sound, form, and meaning; but also open texture, which allows their meanings to be extended and sharpened in certain ways; and also holistic properties that allow some mutual adjustment. The intrinsic properties suffice to establish certain formal relations among expressions, interpreted as rhyme, entailment, and in other ways by the performance systems ...

If this is right, and I think it is, we must re-evaluate many widely accepted assumptions about meaning, truth, and context-sensitivity.

1 Overview

Chomsky offers a plausible though often ignored conception of linguistic meaning and its relation to truth: the meaning of a natural language sentence S is an internalistic property of S, determined by the human language faculty and the relevant lexical items; the semantic properties of sentences, which reflect how human beings understand natural language, are theoretically tractable; but if an utterance of S is true or false, its truth or falsity is typically a massive interaction effect due to the meaning of S and many factors not indicated by elements of S.[1] In my view, this conception is preferable to more standard alternatives, which either (i) burden theories of meaning with implausible predictions, or (ii) abandon good explanations.

Davidson (1967a, 1984) conjectured that there are Tarski-style theories of truth for natural languages, and that such theories can serve as theories of meaning. This proposal was very useful, but too bold. Sentences like (1–3) illustrate difficulties, discussed in later sections.

(1) France is hexagonal, and it is a republic
(2) This government does little for the sake of the average American, whose children will inherit the massive deficit that is accumulating
(3) Hamlet lived with his parents in Denmark

For example, I don't think 'France' has the semantic correlate it would need to have, given a compositional theory of truth. But we shouldn't conclude that there are no theories of meaning for natural languages. We should conclude that such theories are not theories of truth. Correlatively, the meanings of declarative sentences do not specify truth-conditions, not even relative to contexts. In epistemic mode: knowing what sentence S means—that is, understanding S—is not a matter of somehow associating S with a function from contexts to truth-conditions.

Rather, the meaning of S is a compositionally determined intrinsic property of S that *constrains and guides without determining* how S can be *used to make* true or false assertions in various conversational situations. A related theme, often stressed by Chomsky, is that we should combine the idea that sentences have intrinsic semantic properties with a cluster of claims associated with Wittgenstein, Austin, and Strawson: making truth-evaluable assertions is *one* of the things we can do with sentences, in contexts, though uses of this kind are highly variable; while people refer to things, words don't; and sentence *use* may not be a theoretically tractable phenomenon. So if we adopt the good idea that theories of meaning are theories of *understanding*, we should not expect a tight connection between meaning and truth.

---

[1] See Pietroski (2003a) for discussion focusing mainly on Chomsky (1977, 2000). Let me note that what I say there, and here, is partly a result of many conversations with Jim McGilvray. For similar views with different emphases, see Moravcsik (1977, 1998), Hornstein (1984), McGilvray (1996, 1999), Hinzen (2002); see Stainton (forthcoming) for useful review and discussion. Many linguists may adopt some such view in practice, and regard their claims to the contrary as dispensible idealizations; but cf. Higginbotham (1989a, 1989b).

This conflicts with some Quinean/Davidsonian claims about the nature and source of semantic phenomena. But we should reject these claims in any case. We may eventually earn the right to say that semantic theories associate sentences with 'truth indications' in some interesting sense. Until then, it may be best to just say that theories of meaning/ understanding for natural languages are *like* theories of truth for formal languages in certain specifiable respects. For this may be all we need, in order to explain what semantic theories actually explain—for example, facts about entailment relations, ambiguity, and how natural language *cannot* be understood.

In the next section, I lay out some spare assumptions about the enterprise of semantics. This precludes certain conceptions of meaning, given some observations due to Chomsky and others following him. These observations bolster the arguments, discussed below, for a Chomsky-style conception. Along the way, I briefly consider some alternatives. While my aim is not to establish that these alternatives are wrong, I do think they should be evaluated on their own merits, without assuming tendentious views about how meaning is related to truth.

2 Assumptions

Let's say that a *natural* language is one that human children can acquire, in the normal course of development, given a course of experience that is not atypical for members of the relevant linguistic community. For these purposes, I take as given that a theory of meaning for a natural language is a theory of understanding, and thus a theory of certain human capacities; see Chomsky (1965, 1986), Dummett (1975), Higginbotham (1985). Such a theory can take the form of an algorithm that associates signals of the relevant language (sounds, in the case of a spoken language) with interpretations, leaving it open for now what interpretations are. But a theory of meaning for a natural language L is not merely an algorithm of this sort. It also purports to explain, at least in part, *how* a speaker of L associates signals of L with interpretations.[2]

---

[2] Dummett (1975, 1976) makes the important observation that a theory of understanding might have the *formal character* of a Tarski-style truth-theory without *being* a theory of truth. One can offer such a theory without construing the labels for "truth values" in terms of classical truth and falsity. But my point will not be that we should replace 'is true' with 'is assertable'.

So if certain phenomena—ambiguity, entailment, indexicality, or what-ever—reflect the way that speakers associate linguistic signals with interpret-ations, then these phenomena bear on theories of meaning. I do not deny that the right level of abstraction, whatever that turns out to be, will let us ignore many details about how particular speakers make such associations. One can understand my idiolect of English without biochemically associating signals with interpretations in the *exactly* the way I do. But one cannot stipulate, in advance of inquiry, which facts are (not) relevant for theories about how speakers of a language understand that language. Our job as theorists is to describe and explain the relevant facts, whatever those turn out to be.

2.1 Negative Facts are Relevant

Chomsky (1957, 1965, 1970, 1977, 1981, 1986) drew our attention to the fact that for any signal σ of a natural language, there are endlessly many inter-pretations that σ cannot have, and that *non*ambiguity often calls for explan-ation. Consider the contrast between (4) and (5),

(4) John is easy to please
(5) John is eager to please

which can be paraphrased with (4*a*) and (5*a*), but *not* with (4*b*) and (5*b*).

(4*a*) It is easy for us to please John
(4*b*) #It is easy for John to please us
(5*a*) John is eager that he please us
(5*b*) #John is eager for us to please him

Every adult speaker of English knows what (4) and (5) mean, *and* what they don't mean. So evidently, if any normal human child undergoes any ordinary course of experience in any English-speaking community, that child will acquire an idiolect according to which the sounds of (4) and (5) are associated with the interpretations indicated with (4*a*) and (5*a*) *but not* the interpret-ations indicated with (4*b*) and (5*b*). This is an interesting fact. For there is no general prohibition against ambiguity in natural language.

Lexical ambiguity is ubiquitous. The sound of 'bear' can be associated with more than one interpretation (and spelling). So if expressions are signal–interpretation pairs, there are homophonous but distinct lexical expressions. Different expressions composed from the same (overt) lexical items can also be homophonous, as illustrated with (6) and (7).

(6) The goose is ready to eat

(7) The millionaire called the senator from Texas

The words in (6) can be combined to form a sentence meaning that the goose is prepared to dine, or a sentence meaning that the goose is *pret-a-manger*; compare 'The goose is eager/easy to eat'. Similarly, (7) can be associated with the interpretations indicated with (7*a*) and (7*b*).

(7*a*) The millionaire called the senator, and the senator is from Texas

(7*b*) The millionaire called the senator, and the call was from Texas

But again, there is a negative fact, since (7) cannot have the interpretation indicated with (7*c*).

(7*c*) #The millionaire called the senator, and the millionaire is from Texas

So it seems that any "Englished" child—that is, any normal human child who undergoes an ordinary course of experience in an English-speaking community—will acquire an idiolect according to which: (7) has a reading on which it implies (7*a*), and a reading on which it implies (7*b*), but no reading on which it implies (7*c*). More generally, if σ is a signal of a natural language L in which σ is associated with certain interpretations $<\mu_1 \ldots \mu_n>$ but not others, then (other things equal) an L-ed child will come to associate signals with interpretations in a way that associates σ with $<\mu_1 \ldots \mu_n>$ but not other interpretations; and this is so even for the endlessly many signals that the child will never encounter, at least not prior to meeting a linguist.

This bears on theories of meaning, since facts about how humans *don't* associate signals with interpretations may well reveal important aspects of *how* humans understand language—especially if such facts raise theoretically interesting questions about how children manage to converge (in so far as they do converge) on agreement about signal–intepretation associations, despite disparate and often relatively impoverished experience. And once it is granted that the explananda for semantics need not be limited to facts about what signals *do* mean, it quickly becomes clear that these "positive" facts reflect the tip of an iceberg; see Higginbotham (1985). Consider, as another illustration, the much discussed facts concerning the (im)possibilities for antecedence of pronouns in (8)–(10); see Chomsky (1981, 1986).

(8) Pat thinks that Chris likes him/himself

(9) Pat wants to meet Chris and like him/himself

(10) Pat wants Chris to meet and like him/himself

In such cases, the unavailable interpretations do not correspond to incoherent or contradictory thoughts. And there are endlessly many word-strings for which an unavailable interpretation would be a *more* reasonable guess about what the speaker might have meant, compared with the mandatory interpretation (which may be initially hard to discern). Consider 'Pat wants Chris to meet and like himself' or 'Was the hiker who lost kept walking'. Such examples also constitute data for "poverty of stimulus" arguments, according to which humans impose arational constraints on the space of possible interpretations for linguistic signals.[3]

Nonambiguity is intimately connected with entailment. If one sentence follows from another, that is an interesting fact, because distinct sentences are not typically related in this way. For example, we learn something about how humans understand natural languages by trying—as Davidson (1967*b*, 1985) did—to explain the facts illustrated with (11)–(13).

(11) Brutus stabbed Caesar
(12) Brutus stabbed Caesar with a knife
(13) Brutus stabbed Caesar, and he did it with a knife.

The relevant explananda include the fact that (11) follows from (12) *and not conversely*, just as (11) follows from (13) *and not conversely*. Correspondingly, (12) can be paraphrased with (13) but not with (14), which follows from (11).

(14) Brutus stabbed Caesar, or something was done with a knife

Similar points apply to (4)–(10). In most dialects, the sound of 'Pat wants to meet Chris and like himself' does not have a natural interpretation on which it follows that Pat wants to like Chris. We want to know why not. For whatever keeps speakers from hearing 'himself' as linked to 'Chris' in this example is potentially relevant for theories of meaning/understanding.

2.2 Disquotation is Inadequate

Horwich (1997, 1998) outlines a conception of meaning heavily biased towards positive facts. And while few other theorists adopt Horwich's "deflationary" view in its entirety, I suspect that many are inclined to adopt something like it with regard to certain aspects of linguistic meaning. So

---

[3] For reviews of some relevant literature, including psycholinguistic studies of young children, see Crain and Pietroski (2001, 2002); see also Hornstein and Lightfoot (1981), Laurence and Margolis (2001).

it is worth being clear about the kinds of explanation that get lost on such a view.

Horwich begins with a plausible idea: the meaning of a complex expression E is a property of E that can be viewed as the result of combining the meanings of E's constituents in ways corresponding to ways (exhibited by E) of combining expressions. And he rightly notes that given this conception of meaning, accounting for the mere compositionality of semantic properties is not hard. In particular, one need not adopt a substantive theory of truth to say that the meaning of E is determined by (i) the meanings of E's basic constituents, and (ii) the relevant ways of combining those lexical meanings. But Horwich also says that "Understanding one of one's own complex expressions (nonidiomatically) is, by definition, nothing over and above understanding its parts and knowing how they are combined" (1997: 504). On this view, if "one has worked out how a certain sentence is constructed from primitive syntactic elements", then "provided one knows the meanings of those elements" one understands the sentence "automatically and without further ado . . . no further process needs to be involved, leading from these initial conditions to the state of understanding the sentence".

Horwich concludes that, given the grammatical structure of a complex expression, all a "theory" of meaning/understanding must provide is a specification of what the lexical items mean; where such a specification can be given disquotationally, using "axioms" like 'barked means BARKED' to report that a certain word means what it does. But this seems wrong, for reasons discussed by Higginbotham (1985) and others. To understand a complex expression E, one must also know how the form of E contributes to the meaning of E; and this imposes substantive constraints, not captured by disquotation, on what lexical items can(not) mean.

Recall (7), which has no reading on which it implies (7c).

(7)   The millionaire called the senator from Texas
(7c) #The millionaire called the senator, and the millionaire is from Texas

As a matter of natural language *grammatical* structure, 'from Texas' cannot modify 'millionaire' in (7). But let's assume, if only for illustration, that it can modify 'senator' or 'called the senator' as shown in the homophonous (7α) and (7β).

(7α) [[The millionaire][called [the [senator [from Texas]]]]]
(7β) [[The millionaire][[called [the senator]][from Texas]]]

262 COMPOSITIONALITY, MEANING, AND CONTEXT

This accounts for the ambiguity of (7). But it does not explain why (7) has no reading on which it implies (7c). We need some further theoretical claims according to which the structure indicated in (7β) does *not* support the following interpretation: the millionaire is *both* someone who called the senator *and* someone who is from Texas. Of course, the structure doesn't support this interpretation. Speakers know, and so children somehow figure out, that (7β) is not associated with the interpretation indicated with (7c). But this *isn't* just a matter of "working out" how (7) can be constructed from the relevant words, and knowing what the words mean. One must also associate each way of structuring the words in (7) with the right interpretation, while *not* associating (7β)—or whatever the relevant grammatical structure is—with the interpretation indicated in (7c). And this is not trivial.

Davidson's (1967*b*) event analysis suggests a hypothesis. On any reading, (7) is understood partly in terms of an event variable associated with the verb 'call'; the grammatical subject and object are understood as indicating a call*er* and a call*ee*; and in (7β), 'from Texas' is understood as a predicate linked to this variable, *but not* to potential callers. One can spell this out in several ways. Perhaps 'called' and 'called the senator' are understood as predicates associated with an event variable, *and not* with a variable corresponding to potential callers, while combining 'called the senator' with 'from Texas' signifies predicate-conjunction. On this view, the meaning of (7β) might be represented as follows: $\exists e[\text{Agent}(e, \text{the millionaire}) \ \& \ \text{Past-Calling}(e) \ \& \ \text{Theme}(e, \text{the senator}) \ \& \ \text{From}(e, \text{Texas})]$; where 'Past-Calling(e)' means that e was an event of calling. Alternatively, perhaps 'called' and 'called the senator' *are* associated with a variable for callers, but for some reason, 'from Texas' cannot be linked to this variable in (7β). On this view, the meaning of (7β) might be represented as follows: $\exists e[\text{Called}(e, \text{the millionaire}, \text{the senator}) \ \& \ \text{From}(e, \text{Texas})]$'; where 'Called(e, x, y)' means that e was a calling by x of y.[4]

For present purposes, the details do not matter. The important point is that the relevant negative fact, concerning the interpretation of 'from Texas' in (7β), is not even adequately described—much less explained—with a semantic "theory" that simply provides a disquotational algorithm for associating signals (relative to grammatical structures) with interpretations.

---

[4] For defense of the view that verbs like 'called' are understood as monadic predicates, whose grammatical arguments are associated with thematic roles, see Parsons (1990), Schein (1993, 2002, forthcoming), Pietroski (1998, 2002, 2003*c*, 2005), Herburger (2000); see Kratzer (1996) for a slightly different view that would have the same consequences for (7). For defense of the second view, see Higginbotham (1985); see also Taylor (1985).

One can say that just as 'called' and 'Texas' mean what they mean, so the grammatical relation corresponding to adverbial modification makes whatever semantic contribution it makes. But this does not explain why [[called [the senator]][from Texas]] cannot be understood as a predicate satisfied by x iff x called the senator and x is from Texas, or why (7) has a reading on which it implies that the *call* was from Texas. Explaining this requires substantive hypotheses about 'called', and the *specific* significance of combining expressions in certain ways.[5] Likewise, we want a theory that explains relevant negative facts concerning 'John is easy/eager to please'. And this will presumably require substantive hypotheses about what 'easy' and 'eager' mean.

One way or another, we need to capture the following idea: the meaning of 'easy' is lexicalized so that when this word combines with 'to please' and 'John', constraints on grammatical structure and compositional semantics conspire to ensure that John is said to be an individual who is easily *pleased*; while the meaning of 'eager' is lexicalized so that when this word combines with 'to please' and 'John', John is said to be an individual who is eager to be a *pleaser*. We want to know more about these facts, which seem to be symptoms of how lexicalization interacts with (syntactic and semantic) composition in natural language. But just saying that 'easy' has the semantic properties that it has, or that 'eager' applies to what it applies to, tells us nothing about how 'easy' and 'eager' differ in a way that 'easy' and 'hard' do not. And recall that 'The goose is ready to eat' *is* ambiguous; see Chomsky (1965, 1977, 1986). Thus, disquotational description blurs interesting distinctions, and it obscures relevant explananda.

In what follows, I assume that this is the normal case: interesting phenomena—relevant to theories of meaning, since they bear on linguistic understanding—are often due to subtle interactions between lexical items and natural composition; and explaining such phenomena typically requires substantive (nondisquotational) hypotheses about lexical meanings and

<hr>

[5] We could, after all, invent a language in which (7β) has the meaning indicated with (7c). And a Horwich-style theory would apply just as well to such a language. It is also worth noting that small grammatical differences can have significant semantic effects. In 'I heard Pat sang', 'Pat' occupies a referentially opaque position, but not so in 'I heard Pat sing'; see Higginbotham (1983), Vlach (1983). So one wants a theory that explains *why* the differences are significant in the ways that they are. And it's not clear that one can give deflationary descriptions of how the meaning of a sentence with *covert* constituents (that are somehow linked to overt constituents) is compositionally determined; see Pietroski (2000), Collins (2003).

composition principles. So a theory with axioms like '*easy* means EASY' or 'x satisfies *easy* iff x is easy', or theorems like 'x satisfies *called the senator* iff x called the senator', may be a poor theory of meaning. Even if such axioms/ theorems are true, it is a tendentious hypothesis that they are formulated in the right way for purposes of explaining how humans understand language.

2.3 Radical Interpreters would Misinterpret

One might claim that negative facts are irrelevant to theories of meaning, because: (i) there *could* be creatures who correctly associate English signals with interpretations, while having no views about whether additional inter-pretations of the signals are possible; and (ii) such creatures would under-stand English, despite being different from human speakers. But it is hardly obvious that (i) is true in any theoretically interesting sense of 'could'. And (ii) is blatantly question-begging. Why suppose that the right degree of abstrac-tion for the study of (how humans understand) natural language is one that abstracts away from differences between us and the imagined creatures? Or put another way, why assume that for purposes of theorizing about meaning, it is *irrelevant* that human children do not grow up to be such creatures? Nonetheless, a well-known line of thought starts with this assump-tion, and then invites the conclusion that theories of meaning are theories of truth. Unsurprisingly, the reasons for rejecting this line of thought are closely related to some reasons for adopting a Chomsky-style conception of meaning.

The semantic properties of sentences are often said to be somehow con-structable from, or at least determined by, facts concerning how utterances of those sentences *could be assigned interpretations* by a rational being in the position of someone learning the language. One imagines an alien trying to figure out, on the basis of limited evidence, what speakers are saying. By stipulation, the alien imposes only very general constraints (of rationality) on possible interpretations, and he appeals only to certain kinds of publicly available evidence; where this evidence is, at least "in principle", available to those who natually acquire the language. Given a suitably generous concep-tion of availability—according to which children *could* consider native speaker reports, across various languages, about the (im)possibility of certain interpretations for certain signals—the resulting thesis would be a version of verificationism about linguistic meaning. But if the alien is supposed to be an idealized version of a child (as "field linguist"), appealing only to evidence of a sort that typical children respond to in the course of language acquisition, the result is much less plausible than verificationism.[6]

The alien represents an arbitrary and unstable mix of two perspectives on linguistic meaning: that of a *scientist*, who will assume as little as possible about the space of possible interpretations, whatever they turn out to be; and that of a *child* who needs to figure out, on the basis of limited evidence, how signals are associated with interpretations in a given community. But actual scientists do not refuse to consider data unavailable to children. And poverty of stimulus arguments, based on negative facts like those discussed in section 2.1 strongly suggest that actual children impose substantive constraints on the space of possible interpretations for signals. Indeed, one way of summarizing the conclusion of such arguments is that human children are *not* alien interpreters of the imagined sort; see Chomsky (1969, 1993, 1995*a*, 2000*a*).

So the alien is not a reasonable idealization of *any* reasonable creature trying to figure out what expressions mean: not children, who impose arational constraints on interpretations; and not linguists, who do not impose alien limits on evidence (but rather try to figure out, by doing ordinary science, what constraints humans impose on interpretations). Nor does the alien try to determine *what portion* of the publicly available evidence actual children exploit. Instead, he considers *all* the evidence of some preferred kind. The alien thus embodies the theoretical assumption that any heuristics used by children are in principle dispensible, in favor of a more intensive search of the preferred evidence. But this assumption is quite implausible. If *all* normal children in each linguistic community converge (despite varied experience) on agreement about what signals cannot mean, this suggests that such agreement is due to properties of children, not properties of their environment. Correlatively, the challenge presented by negative facts is not "merely" to explain how *some learner could* acquire English on the basis of evidence available to a hyperattentive child. The deeper challenge is to explain how *all Englished children do* acquire English, despite variability in experience and attentiveness—and likewise for every other human language.

If semantic properties of expressions are what the alien takes them to be, this raises the question of how actual humans manage to understand human

---

[6] Thinking of the child as a "little linguist" can thus be misleading. Quine (1960) restricts attention to a speaker's disposition to endorse or reject sentential utterances. Davidson (1984) is less behavioristic, allowing for talk of speakers "holding sentences true" in a given situation (and wanting other sentences to be true). And there are alternatives to Davidson's "principle of charity"; see e.g. Grandy (1973). But these differences of detail do not matter if the underlying idea of "meaning as (radical/alien) interpretability" is fundamentally misguided.

languages. Some philosophers have been led to the extraordinary conclusion that we don't, at least not fully; see Dummett (1986). One can hypothesize that English is a "Communal-Language" that each speaker of English imperfectly grasps. But then one needs to argue that theories of understanding are primarily concerned with Communal-Languages, and not idiolects that speakers do understand, despite Chomsky's (1986, 1996, 2000a) reasons for not appealing to Communal-Languages (or what he calls "E-languages") in explaining how speakers understand natural language; cf. Burge (1989).

Moreover, whatever speakers understand, there is no independent reason for deferring to an alien conception of understanding. Prima facie, the alien would not conclude that (7) has no reading on which it implies that the millionaire is from Texas,

(7) The millionaire called the senator from Texas

(I assume that the alien, like the child, does not ask which strings of words are unambiguous in which ways.) But we theorists should not conclude that (7) may have a millionaire-from-Texas reading after all—or that there is no negative fact about (7) that a semantic theory should explain, unless the alien *would* conclude that (7) has no such reading.

The alien, recall, is an epistemic monster (half-child, half-scientist) charged with a bizarre task: given a restricted body of evidence, and minimal constraints on interpretation, find the class of viable interpretations for certain noises. This imagined exercise may have some interest, since it may help reveal the size of the *gap* between typical human experience and actual linguistic competence. But for just this reason, we should not say that the semantic facts about natural languages are determined by what the imagined alien would conclude. This hypothesis about the nature of semantic properties is evidently false, given that humans cannot understand complex expressions as having certain perfectly coherent readings. One might be led to the opposite conclusion by a chain of reasoning like the following: theories of meaning are theories of truth; so we need a conception of meaning/understanding according to which theories of truth can be theories of understanding; and the best such conception treats meaning as alien interpretability. But if the last premise is correct, we have an argument against the first.[7]

---

[7] One can say that a *philosophical* thesis about meaning is immune from such criticism. I don't see how any such (alleged) thesis could be evaluated in any nonstipulative way; see Chomsky (2000a) on methodological dualism. But in any case, one would have to *argue* that the thesis is relevant to the study of how human beings understand natural language. Likewise, for any "remark" about meaning offered to unconfuse a confused philosopher.

2.4 An Environment is No Substitute for a Mind

There are, of course, reasonable premises in the neighborhood. Facts about the meanings of expressions in a natural language are such that children can figure them out given evidence typically available to them. But this does not imply, or even suggest, that *any possible* learner can figure out what human sentences mean given *only* the evidence that is available to *actual* learners. In describing semantic facts, theorists will abstract away from many individual differences; and presumably, the semantic properties of an expression are not (in principle) detectable by only one person. (Even if each speaker has her own idiolect, this does not preclude understanding; two speakers can "share" a language, in the sense of associating signals with interpretations in the same way, modulo differences that are irrelevant for certain purposes.) But this does not imply, or even suggest, that the theoretically best level of abstraction will be public in the sense of ignoring any individual similarities not discernible by the alien.

If humans share a biology/psychology that imposes substantive constraints on how linguistic signals can be associated with interpretations, an inquirer will not discover this simply by attending to evidence available to any child without precocious investigation. Correlatively, the alien will be forced to look *in the wrong place* for semantic regularities that are due to constraints imposed by human biology/psychology. In his search for sources of inter-subjective linguistic stability, especially with regard to how speakers use expressions to make true claims, the alien will be forced to exaggerate the relevance of the fact that speakers inhabit a shared environment. Put another way, the alien will be led to blame the environment for (i) certain aspects of intersubjective linguistic stability that are indeed due to the environment, *and* (ii) certain aspects of intersubjective linguistic stability that are due to aspects of human nature rendered invisible by alien restrictions on what is potentially relevant to theories of meaning.

This will lead the alien, who knows model theory, to favor interpretations of human speech that associate names with hunks of the environment that can satisfy predicates. Facts of the sort discussed in sections 3 and 4, which tell against such interpretations, will be ignored entirely or discounted as "noise"; for the alien has no conceptual room for the possibility that such facts reflect relevant but invisible aspects of human nature. So he may well conclude, given the constraints imposed by *his* task, that the best interpretations are those that take the form of Tarski-style truth-theories. But none of this shows that semantic theories for natural languages should associate words like 'water' and 'France' with things in the environment. Expressions may have objective interpretations that are not—and do not involve relations to— Fregean *Bedeutungen*. I return to this point.

This is not to deny that talk of "triangulation" has its place; see Davidson (1989, 2001). The environment is surely responsible for some aspects of intersubjective stability with regard to how we *use* linguistic expressions to talk about things; although this kind of stability may well presuppose meaning. Perhaps serious investigation will eventually reveal that our shared understanding of the word 'water' has more to do with H_2O than with internalistic properties of the word. I doubt it. But in any case, the *alien's* tendency to look for associations between words and "stuff referred to" is not itself a reason for thinking that a theory of meaning/understanding should make such associations. We have independent reason for thinking that the best semantic theory will be one that the alien could not endorse. And in the end, I think the facts warrant a stronger conclusion: for purposes of theorizing about meaning/understanding, the best degree of abstraction will be one that (*a*) de-emphasizes facts about what speakers actually refer to when using language and (*b*) highlights internalistic properties of expressions that can be used in different environments to make semantically identical but truth-evaluably distinct claims. If this is correct, we must re-evaluate the influential idea that linguistic meanings should be specified in terms of context-sensitive rules for determining truth/reference/satisfaction conditions.

3 Systematicity with Flexibility

As Davidson (1967*a*, 1967*b*, 1984) noted, there seem to be counterexamples to his hypothesis that there are Tarski-style theories of truth for natural languages. My own view is that the constructions that Davidson himself addressed—action sentences with adverbial modification, and discourse reports—present no special difficulties, given subsequent developments of his seminal proposals.[8] But the deeper worry has less to do with specific constructions, and more to do with some ubiquitous features of natural language, illustrated with sentences like (1).

(1) France is hexagonal, and it is a republic

---

[8] Focusing on adverbial constructions turned out to be extremely productive. And the basic framework has many virues. See Larson and Segal (1995) for a wide-ranging and theoretically interesting illustration of a Davidsonian semantic program.

These examples, which also reveal subtle and interesting interactions between lexicalization and compositional effects, invite a Chomsky-style view. For as we shall see, this lets us retain many virtues of Davidson's conjecture without losing descriptive adequacy; cf. Austin (1962).

3.1 Lexical Flexibility: Implication and Typology

Utterances of (1) can be true. Imagine that the speaker is objecting to a crazy view according to which the shape of a country explains the local form of government. If there is a theory of truth for English, one might expect it to have a theorem according to which an utterance of (1) is true iff something in the relevant domain satisfies the following conditions, at least relative to the context of utterance: it is France, it is hexagonal, and it is a republic. But one might also suspect that nothing is both hexagonal and a republic. For even if one grants that the terrain of France is hexagonal, one might deny that the French terrain is the French republic; and one might think that republics, whatever they are, cannot be hexagonal. Moreover, even if there are such things, one might be suspicious of a *semantic* theory according to which it *follows* from (1) that there are hexagonal republics. Such a theory apparently *mis*characterizes the meaning of (1). For a competent speaker who asserts (1) might deny that at least one thing is both hexagonal and a republic. And a competent interpreter can deny that there is any such thing, while still taking the speaker's assertion to be true.

Chomsky (1977, 2000a) offers many examples of this sort. There are, of course, possible responses. Speakers may explicitly deny what they tacitly assume; and true theories of truth may not have the implications that critics expect. But the form of Chomsky's argument is familiar. One observes that if a certain kind of semantic theory is correct, sentences would have elementary implications that competent speakers evidently do not recognize. And at least prima facie, this tells against theories of that kind. Consider an analogy.

Acccording to many philosophers and some linguists, a theory of meaning for English should not imply that an utterance of 'Some bottles are red' is true only if: *there is a set* whose elements are all and only the bottles; or *there is a property* of redness instantiated by all and only the red things. Any such theory seems to mischaracterize the semantic properties of the mundane sentences. This may be harmless for many purposes, and useful for others. But intuitively, the *meaning* of 'Some bottles are red' does not ensure that an utterance of this sentence is true only if the world contains something—a set, property, or whatever—that is intimately related to but distinct from each bottle. One can illustrate this point vividly with examples like 'Some sets are nonselfelemental'; though a theory according to which this true sentence has provably false implications (e.g. that there is the *set* of nonselfelemental things) is just a special case of a theory that mischaracterizes meanings. There are potential responses. But these must be evaluated on their merits, not as resolutions of a paradox that any semantic theory will face. For we need not take it as given that a theory of meaning will associate 'bottle' with an abstract entity distinct from each bottle (and likewise for every other predicate, including 'set'); see Boolos (1998).

Returning to (1), speakers do recognize that it implies (1*a*) and (1*b*).

(1*a*) France is hexagonal
(1*b*) France is a republic

So we want to know why the inference from (1) to (1*c*) is not trivial in the same way.

(1*c*) France is a hexagonal republic

The point is not that (1*c*) is analytically false or meaningless. Natural languages are not like formal languages with formation rules any violation of which results in gibberish; see Higginbotham (1985). Indeed, an utterance of (1*c*) in the right context might be true. Still, (1*c*) is weird in a way that calls for explanation, and likewise for 'Something is a republic that is hexagonal'. An obvious thought is that by virtue of their meanings, 'hexagonal' and 'republic' cannot be comfortably combined to form a complex (presumably conjunctive) predicate; compare 'green idea' and 'sleep furiously' in Chomsky's well-known example. This isn't yet an explanation. But we can at least encode the explanandum by saying that the two monadic predicates, which are alike in some semantically relevant respects, are associated with variables of different types indicating different kinds of linguistic features. Then we can try to provide theories of how such features can be combined to create complex expressions that can be used (in ways natural for humans) to make various kinds of claims.

By contrast, it's not clear how to even start describing the relevant facts given a theory according to which 'France' is semantically associated with a language-independent entity that can satisfy both 'hexagonal' and 'republic'. On such a theory, 'hexagonal republic' is on a par with 'brown dog'. For certain elementary purposes, we can say that all of these expressions are predicates of type $<x, t>$, thus signifying a certain relation to names (for things in some domain) and truth-evaluable expressions. But it hardly follows that this exhausts the semantic typology of monadic predicates. And as noted in section 2, associating 'France' with something referred to by using 'France' may be the wrong kind of theoretical abstraction. If we assume that some hunk of the environment is the source of (stable intersubjective) semantic properties of 'France', we may obscure significant distinctions that a semantic theory should highlight. So perhaps we should focus less on the things we use 'France' to talk about, and more on whatever properties of 'France' make it possible for us to use a name of this sort in the ways we do use such names.

3.2 Flexible Meanings and Complex Concepts

The right conception of linguistic meaning may still be undreamt of. But even if one agrees that *'France' denotes France* is not a theory, it is at least a gesture in the direction of a theory that associates expressions with things referred to. So if only to loosen the hold of this idea, it may be useful to wave hands in an alternative direction: perhaps the meaning of an expression is an instruction for creating a concept from available mental resources.

To be sure, mentalistic conceptions of meaning are often combined with objectionable claims: that meanings are ideas, in a way that precludes successful communication; or that most words can be defined in terms of a relatively small stock of basic concepts, with the result that there is much more analyticity than there seems to be; or that there are no distinctively linguistic constraints on how humans associate signals with meanings.[9] But these claims need not be part of a Chomsky-style view. A related point is that many theorists, including some in the "generative semantics" tradition, have explored the idea meanings *are* mental representations (or "conceptual structures") somehow associated with expressions of natural language; see, for

---

[9] See Baker (1988, 1997) for a paradigm illustration of how insights from generative grammar can be incorporated into a view according to which syntax imposes severe constraints on interpretations, thereby explaining many negative facts of the sort discussed in section. 2. See Pietroski (2003*b*) for a discussion of analyticity in these terms. While I sympathize with Jackendoff (1990) in some respects, he stresses negative facts less than I do; and I think he underestimates the role of autonomous linguistic constraints on how expressions can(not) be associated with "conceptual structures". As he notes (p. 32), it has long been clear that features of expressions are "inadequate to the full task of conceptual description". But theories of meaning need not be theories of concepts any more than they need be theories of truth (or referents). And since Jackendoff (1997) regards 'Fritz is a cat, so Fritz is an animal' as a paradigmatic case of valid inference, I assume that he is interested in (alleged) conceptual relations that go well beyond formal validity and relations established by expressions themselves.

example, Katz and Fodor (1963), Lakoff (1970, 1987), Jackendoff (1990, 1997, 2002). But my suggestion is not that linguistic expressions have *Bedeutungen* that are mental as opposed to environmental.

Recall that Strawson (1950) urged us to characterize the meaning of a referential device R in terms of "general directions" for using R on particular occasions "to refer to or mention particular objects or persons," *and not* in terms of some entity allegedly denoted by R. This leaves room for talk of concepts as well. For we can try to characterize the meaning of R in terms of general directions for using R (on particular occasions) to express particular concepts and refer to, or mention, or think about specific things. Correlatively, one can avoid familiar pitfalls while adopting a view like the following: the word 'France' has certain features that get correlated in human minds with certain conceptual capacities, like the capacities to think about spatio-temporal coordinates, and about intentional properties of people who create institutions; these may not be capacities to think about (properties of) the *same* mind-independent things; and these capacities may themselves be complex and varied, in ways that tell against the claim that 'France' either denotes something or ambiguously denotes some things.[10]

Speakers can use 'France' to refer to various things—certain terrain, a particular nation, or whatever. Correlatively, predicates like 'hexagonal' and 'republic' seem to differ in kind. This does not yet show that *semantic* theories should mark such distinctions. Perhaps we should diagnose such facts as

---

[10] As Lewis (1972) noted, theories that "merely" associate expressions with (instructions for creating) mental representations do not associate sentences with *truth* or *truth-in-a-model*, in the way familiar from Frege–Tarski–Montague treatments of formal languages. This was taken to be a defect of such theories. But in retrospect, one might take it to be a virtue; and as Lepore (1983) argued, appeals to truth-in-a-model provided less than advertised; see also Higginbotham (1990). The trend towards externalism, invited by alien-interpretability conceptions of linguistic meaning, seemed to support rejection of mentalistic/internalistic conceptions. But as discussed in section four, a Chomsky-style view is not threatened by Twin-Earth thought-experiments, and it is fully compatible with Kripke's (1980) insights. Prior to "quantifier-raising" conceptions of grammatical structure, and appeals to "LF" as a level of natural language *syntax*—see May (1985), Higginbotham and May (1981), Chomsky (1981, 1995*b*)—it was also assumed that (as Frege–Russell–Wittgenstein had argued) grammatical form diverges significantly from logical form, even for relatively simple quantificational constructions like 'The dog saw every cat'. And this suggested, wrongly, that meaning was importantly independent of natural language syntax; see Pietroski (2003*c*) for review and discussion (see also Neale, 1990, 1993; Hornstein, 1984). So if the evidence now suggests that theories of meaning/understanding are *not* plausibly viewed as theories of truth, perhaps we should conclude that a reasonable conception of meaning was abandoned for a cluster of (what turned out to be) bad reasons.

reflections of what speakers know about France, and not what they know about 'France'; see Fodor and Lepore (1992, 2002). But we should also consider the following possibility: lexicalization is a process in which diverse mental representations can be linked via the language system. Perhaps without lexicalization, representations that are different in kind cannot be combined to form a complex concept that is usable in human thought, but (luckily for us) the language system provides resources for creating certain "common denominators", which make it possible to create endlessly many complex mental representations with constituents that are typologically disparate. This leaves ample room for grammatical expressions that *don't* provide ways of forming complex mental representations that are usable in fully natural ways by human minds; though such expressions may still trigger "degraded" mental representations that can be used in limited ways. The familiar idea would be that words often "fit together" in ways that the corresponding concepts by themselves do not; and in endlessly many though not all cases, linguistic expressions can be given natural interpretations.[11]

As a first approximation, one might think about a complex monadic predicate like 'brown dog' as (*inter alia*) an instruction for creating a monadic concept from disparate mental resources. We may naturally think about colors as properties *of* surfaces, and think about dogs as things that *have* surfaces, with the result that brute concatenation of the relevant concepts would be unnatural for us. And there is independent reason for thinking that natural language provides a constrained system of grammatical features that can be used as rough indicators of various possession relations; see, for example, Uriagereka (2002). Perhaps such features serve as "adaptors" that make it possible for us to connect concepts of different types, thereby forming the kinds of complex concepts that we regularly deploy in ordinary human thought.[12]

[11] And so not a "category mistake" (cf. Ryle, 1949) if this implies that the resulting expression is nonsense or contradictory; see also Evans's (1982) talk of "generality constraint" on distinctively human thought. Carruthers (2002) argues—drawing on lots of evidence from psychology, especially Hermer-Vasquez *et al.* (1999), Spelke (forthcoming)—that the language system plays something like this role in cognition. Variations on this theme underly a great deal of work in linguistics, both in lexical semantics (see e.g. Jackendoff, 1990; Pustejovsky, 1995; Levin and Rappaport-Hovav, 1995; Bloom, 2000) and appeals to "type adjustments" in compositional semantics (see e.g. Montague, 1974; Partee and Rooth, 1983). One need not agree with the details of such work to think that it is getting at *something* important about how the human language system relates to other human cognitive systems.

[12] Independently, it seems that some grammatical features of expressions (markers for case, person, number, etc.) do not reflect the basic architecture of the recursive system that allows for

If the idea of predicates as instructions for creating concepts seems foreign, it is worth noting—as Chomsky (1996, 2000*a*) does—that one can also think of 'brown dog' as an instruction (to the human articulatory system) for creating a complex sound. Indeed, an expression of a spoken language may just *be* a pair of instructions for creating a sound of a certain sort and a concept of a certain sort. Sentences can be viewed as instructions for pairing sentential sounds with sentential concepts.[13] And just as phonologists can try to explain relations of rhyme in terms of relations between certain instructions for creating sounds, semanticists can try to explain relations of entailment (say, between 'Fido is a brown dog' and 'Fido is a dog') in terms of relations between instructions for creating sentential concepts. One can use the apparatus of model-theory to characterize such relations. But the utility of this apparatus is not an argument for the *hypothesis* that entailment is best explained in terms of truth (or truth-in-a-model). We may pretheoretically characterize many semantic relations in terms of truth. But often, good explanation requires redescription of explananda in overtly theoretical terms. And notions like 'truth' may not make the right theoretical cuts for purposes of explaining the facts that semantic theories explain; see Hornstein (1984) for related discussion.

---

composition of expressions. So an obvious thought, developed by Chomsky (1995*b*, 2000*b*) and others, is that such features reflect modifications of a simpler (and perhaps nontransformational) system that became more usable as a device that "interfaces" with other cognitive systems. If this is plausible, it invites a more general conjecture: apparent quirks of the human language system—aspects of the system not required in order to recursively associate signals with interpretations—reflect a natural history in which a "minimal" system has been supplemented with devices that allow for the creation of expressions with cognitively useful properties; where such expressions are interpretable as instructions for creating complex concepts that are otherwise unavailable for natural use. See Hauser *et al.* (2002), Uriagereka and Piatelli-Palmarini (forthcoming).

[13] The details depend on the logical forms associated with sentences of natural language. But at least many sentences (like 'Brutus stabbed Caesar with a knife') can be viewed as instances of the logical form '$\exists x \Phi x$': existential closure of a monadic predicate. Any such sentence can be treated as an instruction for creating a complex monadic concept C, and then the corresponding thought of the form '$\exists x \Phi x$' with C as its main constituent. Elsewhere, I have argued that this paradigm covers far more than one might have thought, including quantificational examples like 'No theory covers every case'; see Pietroski (2002, 2003*c*, 2005). Indeed, my suspicion is that natural language is fundamentally a system that allows for combination of monadic predicates (and a small number of relational notions associated with "thematic roles" that are in turn associated with certain grammatical relations); see also Castañeda (1967), Parsons (1990), Schein (1993, 2002, forthcoming), and Baker (1997).

From this perspective, 'dog' provides instructions for accessing one or more concepts already available for natural use. This leaves open various issues about the concepts: are they structured or atomic; how many 'dog'-concepts do we have; is the species-concept dependent on the individual-concept (or vice versa, or neither); etc. Similarly, one can say that a name like 'France' provides instructions for accessing one or more singular concepts, which can be used to think about the various things that can count as France. This remains a vast oversimplification. But the idea, offered here as a quick illustration of *an* alternative to the idea that 'France' denotes a hexagonal republic, would be as follows: a speaker using (1*a*) can use 'France' to indicate a concept with which a human can think about something that has geometric properties; a speaker using (1*b*) can use the same lexical item to indicate a concept with which a human can think about something that has political (and hence, intentionally characterized) properties; and 'France' itself is an expression that makes a certain range of singular concepts available for use in the construction of various sentential concepts that can be used to make various truth-evaluable claims. But 'France' is not *ambiguous* in the way that 'bear' is. And in so far as there are French things that speakers cannot naturally refer to by using 'France', there are negative facts to explain. So the point is not merely that the relation of word-sounds to concepts is one-to-many. The facts are more subtle, interesting, and potentially revelatory of human thought.

In thinking about examples like (1), it is worth remembering that Plato's poverty of stimulus argument in the *Meno* involved geometry, and that humans understand words like 'triangle' in a very interesting way. We know that perceptible figures can count as triangles; and we can perceptibly distinguish triangles from circles and squares, which can be drawn in the sand (say, for purposes of illustrating a generalization). Yet we also know that "real" triangles, described by theorems of geometry, are imperceptible. Hypotheses about natural language must cohere with such facts, and the fact that utterances of 'Triangles are perceptibly different from circles' and 'Triangles are imperceptible' can be true, while utterances of 'Imperceptible triangles differ perceptibly from imperceptible circles' are not.

This invites the thought that linguistic meanings are involved in making it possible for humans to connect percepts with a *capacity* for abstract thought that would lie "untriggered" if not for the language faculty. Perhaps we could not think about (the various things that can count as) triangles, as opposed to merely being able to classify certain things as triangular, without two integrated and integrating capacities: an ability to lexically connect concepts corresponding to perceptual prototypes, an abstract notion of space, and the idea of proof or necessity; and an ability to create sentential concepts unavailable without mediation by linguistic expressions that have the right features. Hermer and Spelke (1994, 1996), Hermer-Vasquez *et al.* (1999), Spelke (2002), and Carruthers (2002) provide arguments that this is not mere rationalist speculation. For example, there is evidence that prelinguistic children—and animals without a language faculty—lack the ability to create some relatively simple structured concepts whose constituents are readily available. In any case, we should be wary of semantic theories according to which (i) linguistic meaning cannot play this kind of role in human *thought* because (ii) the relation between meaning and *truth* is relatively simple. This makes the study of thought and ontology even harder than it already is.

To repeat, the view is that speakers can use 'France' to make a variety of true claims, and that this kind of usage is possible in part because the meaning of 'France' does *not* associate the name with an environmental entity; though typically, a speaker uses 'France' to refer to something, like a government or a sports team. This view is often associated with Wittgenstein (1953). But as Chomsky (1966, 2000*a*) notes, it is also what traditional rationalists should expect, absent a benificent deity or wildly optimistic assumptions about the history of natural selection. Nativists should be unsurprised if commonsense thought and talk does not reflect the structure of the world, except perhaps by sheer luck; see McGilvray (1999). Even when speakers/thinkers use language in consciously regimented ways, with the express aim of trying to describe the world (as opposed to engaging in ordinary talk about the passing show), success is not guaranteed. On the contrary, success seems to be possible only in certain domains; see also McGinn (1993). Indeed, given poverty of stimulus arguments, why should *anyone*—apart from alien interpreters and naive empiricists—expect the structure of reality to "fit" the structure of our natural ways of talking/thinking about it? Chomsky offers a more realistic conception of language, without describing the intricately structured and highly constrained phenomena of understanding with unhelpful slogans like "meaning is use".

3.3 Typology and Ontology

We can speak quasi-commonsensically of France being a "truth-maker" for (1), (1*a*), (1*b*), and (1*c*). But it does not follow that France is an entity that satisfies the predicates in these sentences, at least not if 'satisfies' is used in its standard technical sense, derived from Frege (1879, 1892) and Tarski (1933).

This does not challenge the commonsense claim that France is a perfectly real country that one can visit. But ordinary vocabulary is often ill-suited to the task of describing the world in theoretically perspicuous ways. Correlatively, given some technical terminology that was introduced to talk about languages *invented* for purposes of describing the world in theoretically perspicuous ways, there is no guarantee that this technical terminology will also provide theoretically perspicuous ways of describing languages with ordinary vocabulary.

One can hypothesize that France is an "all-purpose thing", which somehow incorporates all the potential truth-makers for claims of the form 'France is Φ', as part of a proposal about the *semantic* properties of 'France'; cf. Meinong (1904) on squarable circles. But there are limits on what one can plausibly posit given the available evidence. And one can achieve implausibility without positing subsistent but nonexistent squarable circles. Put another way, if one sees nothing wrong with theories of meaning that posit Fregean *Bedeutungen* with both perimeters and politicians, one needs to say what (if anything) is wrong with more overtly Meinongian semantics. With this background in mind, I think comments like the following seem quite plausible, and in no way a denial of commonsense realism.

As far as is known, it is no more reasonable to seek some thing-in-the-world picked out by the word 'river' or 'tree' or 'water' or 'Boston' than to seek some collection of motions of molecules that is picked out by the first syllable or final consonant of the word 'Boston'. With sufficient heroism, one could defend such theses, but they seem to make no sense at all. Each such usage of the words may well pick out, in some sense, specific motions of molecules and things-in-the-world (the world as it is, or is conceived to be); but that is a different and entirely irrelevant matter. (Chomsky, 1996: 48.)

One *could* provide a "model" of English that associates syllables with *Bedeutungen*, treating words compositionally. So if one agrees that such a model would not teach us much about linguistic meaning, the question is how much more we learn from standard models.

Similar remarks apply to pronouns. If 'it' has 'France' as its antecedent in (1),

(1) France is hexagonal, and it is a republic

and 'France' does not have a *Bedeutung*, neither does 'it'. But there are independent reasons for thinking that antecedence is a *grammatical* relation; associating a pronoun with the same entity as another expression is neither necessary nor sufficient for antecedence. (Consider 'My square circle has a perimeter equal to its diameter' and 'He must be Bob, since he is driving Bob's car'; see Higginbotham, 1983, 1985.) So with regard to (1), an obvious thought is that while a pronoun makes the full range of its antecedent's features available for predication—modulo restrictions, like gender or number, imposed by the pronoun—only *some* of these features will be semantically "activated" by any given predicate. In (1), 'republic' may indirectly (i.e. at the occurrence of 'it') activate features of 'France' that cannot be naturally combined with 'hexagonal'. Examples like (15) provide further illustrations.

(15) The red book is too heavy, although it was favorably reviewed, and the blue one is boring, although everyone is reading it

A speaker can utter (15), talking about which book to bring on a trip, and say something true. But it does not follow that one satisfier of 'book' satisfies 'red', 'too heavy', and 'favorably reviewed', while another one satisfies 'blue', 'boring', and 'everyone is reading it'; see Chomsky (2000*a*), Pietroski (2003*a*). There are books; some are red, and some are heavy. But this does not imply that 'book', a predicate of *natural* language, has *satisfiers* at all— much less that books can satisfy other predicates that show signs of being typologically disparate. Prima facie, this theoretical claim mischaracterizes how speakers understand ordinary discourse. To be sure, there are important differences between predicates and their arguments. But this claim is detachable from more tendentious claims about how meaning is related to truth. Likewise, we can say that predicates are apt for use as devices for classifying, while names are apt for use as devices for referring, without saying that names denote satisfiers of predicates.

3.4 Ontology and Meaning

Given examples like (2) and (3), it seems that desperate measures will be needed to maintain the ontology required by theories of truth that can serve as theories of meaning for natural languages.

(2) The government does little for the sake of the average American, whose children will inherit the massive deficit that is accumulating.
(3) Hamlet lived with his parents in Denmark.

Other things being equal, one expects a (nontrivial) theory of truth for English to imply that an utterance of (2) is true only if the world includes: something that is a massive deficit, accumulating, and inheritable; something that has a sake, is the average American, and has children; and a government that does little for the sake in question. So one might suspect that no such theory will be true. And one can suspect this, while conceding that some paraphrases of (2), like (2*a*), don't raise all the same concerns.

(2*a*) The members of the current administration do little for average Americans, whose children will inherit a massive deficit due to current policies.

A theory of truth/meaning for English must associate (2), which is itself a perfectly good sentence of English, with a truth-specification. And one does not provide such a theory simply by saying that, for purposes of assigning a truth-specification, (2) is somehow associated with a more ontologically respectable paraphrase. One has to say *how* a speaker who understands (2) associates this sentence with the preferred paraphrase (and not others).[14]

It is often said that an utterance of (3)—sincerely produced by someone who knows that Hamlet is a fictional character in Shakespeare's play—is true iff *in* the relevant story, Hamlet lived with his parents in Denmark. Such biconditionals may well be true, at least as idealizations, and they may explain *something*. Certainly, utterances of (3*a*) can be true.

(3*a*) In Shakespeare's famous play, Hamlet lived with his parents in Denmark.

But prima facie, for any sentence S, the meaning of 'In the relevant story, S' depends on the meaning of S. So I don't think appeals to 'In the story' operators will help provide a theory of truth/meaning that accommodates (3), unless one adopts Lewis's (1986) view according to which both meanings and stories are characterized in terms of Lewisian possible worlds: totalities of things as real as you and me, just not things that exist in *this* world/spacetime. On this view, there really *are* worlds with a fleshy Hamlet and mortal Polonius, and there really *are* worlds at which Hesperus is not Phosphorus, *pace* Kripke (1980). But if one rejects Lewis's conception of reality and reference, while still holding out for a theory of truth that accommodates (3), trouble awaits. For 'Hamlet' is either satisfied by nothing or satisfied by something.

Like many others, I think that Lewis adopts ontologically desperate measures. While his picture is coherent and interesting, in ways that Meinong's

---

[14] Cf. Montague's (1974) treatment of quantificational constructions. Higginbotham (1985) notes the similarlity of 'The average American has 2.4 children' to 'On the average, an American has 2.4 children'. But it is not clear how to extend this analogy to examples like (2).

(1904) was not, it is still incredible. That said, Lewis may have been right about what theories of truth for natural language ultimately require, across the wide range of cases he discusses. And *if* we assume that such theories are needed, no matter how implausible their ontological implications, it becomes very hard to offer principled reasons for resisting Lewisian conclusions. One is free to speculate that a correct theory of truth for English will require hexagonal republics though not Lewisian possible worlds. But then one has to say why the considerations Lewis presses (simplicity, scope, etc.) don't tell in favor of his theory, which really ends up being a theory of a *regimented variant* of English—that is, a language for which a theory of truth can be given, assuming enough ontology.

I suspect that some philosophers want it both ways: a theory of meaning/truth according to which meanings themselves relate expressions to the things that speakers use expressions to talk about, so that *understanding* an expression is already a way of being "in contact with" the world that makes our claims true; and a theory of meaning/truth without substantive ontological commitments, so that understanding an expression does not require a *theory* of that which makes our claims true. I won't try to argue here that this is a shell game. But I do want to register respect for Lewis's honesty, which led him to work out in detail what a theory of truth might actually require.[15]

If we set aside Lewis's view, it is *very* hard to see how a theory of truth/meaning for English could avoid mischaracterizing the meaning of 'Hamlet' or 'Denmark' or both. This is, I think, one thing established by the vast literature on "fictional names"—names introduced for purposes of creating fiction. Such names exhibit the hexagonal republic phenomenon with a vengeance. We can say, truly, that Hamlet is a fictional character, and that Hamlet is a prince who at one point hallucinates and merely seems to see a dagger, but at another point (unintentionally) kills Polonius with a real sword; although the status of ghosts and witches in Shakespeare's plays is less clear, as illustrated by debates concerning Macbeth's interactions with the weird sisters. Theories of natural language must allow for the previous sentence.

Kripke (n.d.) provides an insightful starting point for a lexical semantics of fictional names. And of course, if 'France' can be used to refer to different

---

[15] Jackendoff (1990) is laudably clear about the difference between his psychological conception of meaning and Lewis-style formal semantics. Linguists who claim to be pursuing the latter, but without regard for metaphysics as philosophers understand it, are often less clear about what their theories are supposed to be theories of.

things, we should expect the same to be true of 'Hamlet'. Lots of other work may also find a place in an eventual account of how names without a preexisting bearer can be used to make true assertions. My point is (not to disparage the literature, but rather) to note that names like 'Hamlet' invite treatment in terms of the hypothesis that the meaning of a name should be specified (not by associating the name with some entity, but rather) in terms of some array of features that the name makes available for a variety of uses; where using all the features at once would be ungrammatical and incoherent. Similar remarks apply to (16), utterances of which can be true.

(16) Teddy bears are in the next aisle, and the unicorns are right here.

But utterances of 'There are no unicorns' can also be true.[16]

Once we consider the possibility that (1)–(16) illustrate related phenomena that are ubiquitous in natural language, as opposed to thinking about (1)–(16) as a hodgepodge of marginal cases to be set aside, I think it becomes clear just how bold Davidson's conjecture was. Linguistic meanings don't seem to be functions from contexts to truth/reference/satisfaction conditions (even setting aside the technical difficulties presented by 'Yesterday, I said that Hesperus is Phosphorus'). In section 4.3, I return to this point. But first, I want to enter some disclaimers, and briefly compare a Chomsky-style view with some alternatives that specialists will know about.

4 Caveats and More Doubts

My claim is not that we should abandon current semantic theories, or that standard textbooks are complete bunk. It is rather that "axioms" like *'France' denotes France* are best read, despite appearances to the contrary, as preliminary claims about intrinsic features of linguistic expressions—and that we should bear this in mind, as we revise our current theories. But the suggestion is not that each word has a unique array of grammatical features. And I am not denying that causal-historical facts, of the sort Kripke (1971, 1980) and others have discussed, bear on what speakers refer to with names.

---

[16] Generic plurals like 'Teddy bears' present their own complications, as Chomsky (1977) discusses—especially in examples like 'Unicycles have wheels', 'Beavers build dams', and 'Poems are written by fools like me'; cf. Carlson and Pelletier (1995).

4.1 Internalistic Meanings, Externalistic Truths

In many idiolects, 'Latvia' and 'Estonia' may be type-identical, modulo pronunciation. Perhaps the same is true for 'elm' and 'beech', or 'arthritis' and 'rheumatism'; see Putnam (1975), Burge (1979). But in the absence of evidence to the contrary, children seem to assume that different expressions in the same language have different meanings. So I assume that except for a few special cases, marked as such, distinct expressions are understood as semantically distinct. It doesn't follow, though, that understanding 'Latvia' is a matter of knowing that it denotes Latvia. Understanding the name may be a matter of tacitly knowing that (i) the name is distinct from other expressions of the same kind, and (ii) the name has certain features in virtue of which it can be used as a device for referring to a place, perhaps characterized in terms of intentional properties.

One might say that 'Latvia' is relevantly like 'water', and that understanding 'water' is relevantly like having seen water: one cannot be in such a state without bearing the right causal-historical relation to some H_2O. There is, however, little if any evidence in favor of this prima-facie implausible thesis. I am happy to say that understanding is importantly like perception. But one might have thought that understanding 'water' is more like seeing (or hearing) the expression 'water' than seeing water; where expressions are individuated so that creatures in H_2O-less environments could perceive and use 'water'. Since it has become common to think otherwise, let me stress: Putnam and Burge never showed that *theories of linguistic meaning* must employ a notion of expression such that my Twin-Earth duplicate and I use typologically distinct expressions. (Presumably, my twin is like me with respect to intuitions that linguists care about.) The thought-experiments suggest that some facts about *how humans use language* cannot be explained in internalistic terms; and this bears on certain philosophical projects and claims. But one needs a premise to get substantive claims about meaning from these claims about use.

Referring to water is relevantly like seeing water. It can't be done without *some* kind of contact with at least some H_2O. And for purposes of figuring out what a speaker is trying to say, Davidsonian triangulation is presumably important, even if alien interpreters exaggerate its importance. I am also inclined to agree with externalists like Burge (1979, 1989), who hold that the truth or falsity of an utterance can depend on the norms of a relevant community—and notions of rational commitment—in ways not captured by the ways in which the meanings of indexical/demonstrative expressions track certain aspects of conversational situations; cf. Fodor (1987), Stanley (2000). Externalism about truth may well be correct in this nontrivial sense. But one can deny that meaning and understanding are tightly connected to truth and reference and rationality; we need not say that *understanding* 'water' is relevantly like having seen water, or that 'water' is, by virtue of its linguistic *meaning*, an indexical or demonstrative expression like 'nearby' or 'that stuff'. Perhaps 'water' is, as it appears to be, a mass-noun with no part that somehow indexes H_2O on earth but not Twin-Earth; and perhaps the thought-experiments just reveal that the relation between meaning and truth is not as simple as some philosophers thought (or hoped).

If intuitions about Twin-Earth thought-experiments reflect our tacit views about truth and reference—and what speakers *commit themselves to* when they use language in certain ways—then such intuitions do not tell against a Chomsky-style internalism about linguistic meaning. For the internalist view on offer is one according to which linguistic meanings *guide and constrain without determining* truth, reference, and other (norm governed) expression–speaker–world relations. This leaves room for the claim that such relations are interestingly externalistic. So one can hardly use the thought-experiments to argue for this claim, and then use them again to argue that meaning is like truth and reference in this respect.[17]

We can *invent* a language in which: a predicate Φ is associated with a function from possible worlds to substances like H_2O; and some name α is associated with a function from possible worlds to either (i) all-purpose entities like the alleged hexagonal republic of France, or (ii) functions from contexts and n-tuples of Fregean *Bedeutungen* to purpose-specific entities. This may establish the coherence of corresponding hypotheses about natural

---

[17] One can try to provide independent arguments that the connnection between meaning and truth is tighter. But the premises must be more plausible than the claim that theorists should defer to the alien with respect to human understanding. Burge (1979) and others offer arguments that rationalizing explanations of human action unavoidably traffic in externalist notions of *intentional content*; cf. Fodor (1987). I happen to find this conception of human action plausible; see Pietroski (2000). But why think that linguistic meaning is like intentional content in this respect, especially since the study of the former has delivered better theoretical results than the study of the latter? For all we know, human intentional content may itself be an interaction effect one of whose determinants is (internalistic) linguistic meaning. Of course, one would like an account of how it all hangs together—thought, communication, meaning, reference, truth, confirmation, atoms, constellations, praise, condemnation, and everything else. And one can define 'Language' so that a Language would have the properties needed to make it all hang together in some envisioned way. But it doesn't follow that there are Languages, much less that they include natural spoken languages.

language; see Kaplan (1989). But plausibility is another matter. Stanley (2000, 2002) outlines an intriguing view according to which the truth of sentential utterances depends on the environment only in ways tracked by (the meanings of) overt or covert constituents of sentences. I don't think this generalization is warranted. But I won't try to argue against Stanley's view here; though see Blair (forthcoming) for an argument that the requisite covert constituents are not there, even in cases where positing them seems most plausible—for example, quantifier domain restriction (cf. Stanley and Szabó, 2000).

For present purposes, let me just say that Chomsky offers a less radical response to examples which suggest that truth depends on the environment in ways not tracked by theories of meaning for natural languages. One need not say that linguistic expressions have, in addition to all their other features, many covert indices not detectable with current tests. So Stanley's criticism of *other* responses does not yet undercut the force of all the apparent counterexamples to his very general thesis. That said, Stanley—and those he criticizes, like Bach (1994)—may be importantly right about *something*. The mental representations *indicated by* linguistic expressions may well have elements (not corresponding to elements of the sentences speakers utter) that track many ways in which the truth of utterances can depend on the environment.

There may also be symbol–world regularities not explained by theories of linguistic meaning. If there is a language of thought with its own "psychosemantics", this is presumably relevant to questions about truth. And *perhaps*, as Fodor (1987, 1998) argues, a correct theory of meaning for Mentalese will associate primitive expressions of Mentalese with Fregean *Bedeutungen*; perhaps sentences of Mentalese even have (context-sensitive) truth-conditions, not merely truth-indications. For present purposes, I take no stand on these issues. Though for all we know, the relation between Mentalese and truth is also less than fully systematic, while Mentalese and a spoken language and communal norms *together* impose enough constraints to make truth stable and interesting (*pace* deconstructionists). Even if we don't know how, it seems clear that at least on occasions of use where we are trying to be careful, we can think and talk about the world in ways that are objectively right or wrong. But this hardly shows that any language we ordinarily use to think or talk is a language that has a truth-theory. And in any case, a theory of denotation for Mentalese would not obviate the need for theories of meaning for spoken languages, if only because of the relevant negative facts.

Fodor (1998) sometimes speaks as if one can account for all the semantic facts regarding spoken languages by saying that each sentential utterance gets associated with a token of some mental sentence; see also Schiffer (1992, 1994*a*, 1994*b*, 2000). But this doesn't begin to explain why sentences of English are *not* associated with sentences of Mentalese in certain ways. One wants to know why (7)

(7) The millionaire called the senator from Texas

cannot indicate a Mentalese sentence that is true iff the millionaire from Texas placed a call to the senator. One wants to know why 'Brutus stabbed Caesar' cannot indicate a Mentalese sentence that is true iff there was a stabbing of Brutus by Caesar, and likewise for all the other facts regarding nonambiguity in natural language. These facts call for substantive assumptions about *how* grammatical structures of spoken languages can(not) be related to interpretations; see Higginbotham (1994), Matthews (2003). Since Fodor knows about negative facts, perhaps when he says that spoken languages do not have a compositional semantics, he just means that there are no systematic theories of truth for such languages.

One can define 'semantics' so that language L has a semantics only if there is a theory of truth for L. But one cannot stipulate that all the relevant explananda are explained by syntactic structures for spoken languages, a denotational semantics for Mentalese, and a mechanism that associates each sentential utterance *u* with a token of some mental sentence that expresses the thought expressed with *u*. Moreover, even if we identify the interpretations of certain "labels" in Mentalese with certain things that speakers can refer to by using certain names of a spoken language, it does not follow that the things referred to are the interpretations of spoken names.

Kripke (1980) noted that a speaker of English might see no significant difference between (i) the distinction between 'Feynman' and 'Gell-Mann', and (ii) the distinction between 'Cicero' and 'Tully'. For a speaker might have no way of distinguishing Feynman from Gell-Mann, except by recourse to metalinguistic predicates like *was called 'Feynman'*; and such a speaker might think, mistakenly, that Cicero and Tully were distinct Romans. Kripke made this observation in the context of arguing against theories according to which 'Feynman' and 'Gell-Mann' would be synonymous for such a speaker. But it also suggests that the semantic difference between these names has nothing to do with the difference between the physicists, since the semantic difference between 'Cicero' and 'Tully' cannot be even partly due to a way that Cicero differs from Tully. And Kripke does not say that 'Cicero' and 'Tully' are synonymous.[18]

One can hypothesize that understanding 'Cicero' is relevantly like being causally related to Cicero, that names for the same thing are synonymous, and that the relation between meaning and truth is relatively simple— arguments to the contrary notwithstanding. Given such a view, many contrasts that might have been explained as semantic contrasts will have to be explained in some other way; see Braun and Saul (2002) for a proposal that engages with the difficulties, instead of just labelling them as 'pragmatics'. But one wants to know if there is any *evidence* that motivates this conception of synonymy, given a Chomsky-style alternative, which leaves room for various projects concerned with the use of meaningful expressions (and notions of rational commitment); cf. Soames (1987, 1995). Perhaps alien interpreters would end up identifying the meanings of names with things named. But if anything, this should make us more skeptical of "direct reference" conceptions of linguistic meaning—even if we follow Frege in thinking that for certain norm-governed enterprises like scientific inquiry, we should use each expression as though its meaning is its *Bedeutung*.

Let me conclude this subsection with a brief remark about rigid designation. One need not say that 'Aristotle' denotes a certain long dead philosopher in order to accommodate Kripke's insights. As a matter of causal-historical fact, speakers use this "famous-person name" to talk about a certain long dead philosopher. Speakers also tacitly know that names have both causal-historical associations and descriptive associations; that these aspects of use can conflict, with regard to "who we are talking about" when we use the name; and that in such cases, the causal-historical associations trump the descriptive associations. But the plausible hypothesis that names are devices for referring "rigidly" (and not by description) does not require the implausible hypothesis that names denote things. On the contrary, one might ask which thing 'France' rigidly denotes. For we can coherently describe a possible situation in which the terrain of France is not inhabited by people who have a republican form of government, and a possible situation in which the republic of France has different borders.

This perfectly familiar point again suggests that there is no all-purpose *Bedeutung* for 'France'. Any such thing would be denoted rigidly by 'France';

---

[18] On a Chomsky-style view, names may be more like predicates than "logical constants" of the predicate calculus. But this is independently plausible; see Burge (1973), Longobardi (1994).

and so, given the truth of various counterfactual claims, it would need to have *both* its geometric *and* political properties *in*essentially. But what is this alleged thing, which conveniently has all the properties something needs to have to be a truth-maker for all claims of the form 'France is, or at least might have been, Φ'? Was the republic of France formerly a hexagonal monarchy? Could the republic have been a communist state, or a loose confederation of anarchist associations? If not, perhaps we should detach the idea that speakers use names to perform acts of rigid reference from the idea that names have referents rigidly.

4.2 Extensionality

I do not, however, want to argue about words like 'meaning', 'understanding', and 'semantics'. If someone insists that such words describe relations between expressions and potential objects of reference, my claim can be conditionalized: *if* such insistence is correct, there may be no theories of meaning for natural languages, since 'understanding' has been defined as a label for (what turns out to be) a massive interaction effect; and we do not need theories of the interaction effect to account for the facts, positive and negative, concerning how humans associated signals of a spoken language with interpretations. But whatever the terminology, we can try to provide theories of (speakers' tacit knowledge concerning) intrinsic properties of linguistic expressions, supplemented with claims (which may not rise to the level of theories) about the use of meaningful expressions. Likewise, I don't insist that semanticists eschew the term 'denotes'. Theorists can and do create special contexts in which a name can be used to talk about its semantic properties. The one that has become standard—writing axioms like *'France' denotes France*—makes it easy to ignore lexical flexibility. Such idealization is appropriate for certain purposes. And it is harmless, so long as we don't think that invoking the term 'denotes' magically dispels lexical flexibility, or shows how to accommodate it in a theory of truth.

Correspondingly, I am *not* objecting to the idea that theories of meaning can be formulated in a metalanguage governed by an *extensional* logic. One way to see this point is by thinking about other ways of using names to talk about their semantic properties. We could invent a technical term 'meanotes' and write axioms like *'France' meanotes France*, taking this to be shorthand for a cluster of claims like the following.

'France' is an expression (of a certain type) that makes certain linguistic features available for use. Speakers can use these features to perform referential acts of various kinds (and thereby refer to things of different kinds). Given the contingent history of how 'France' has been used, speakers of English can use it to refer to the various things that can count as France in various contexts, as opposed to other things (like those that can count as Germany). But these contingencies may be extraneous to theories of meaning/understanding, which may turn out to be theories of (speakers' tacit knowledge regarding) certain essential and internalistic properties of expressions. Although the contingences are relevant to questions of truth or falsity.

But then for purposes of writing down a real theory—with theorems concerning the semantic properties of complex expressions and axioms concerning the semantic properties of words—we would need a logic for claims of the form *expression Σ meanotes α*; where the logic can be combined with plausible hypotheses about how meaning/understanding is related to meanoting. And providing such a logic will be hard, given the stipulations governing what *meanotes α* means in the metalanguage.[19]

In general, it is bad methodology to adopt a theoretical vocabulary that forces one to come up with a complete correct theory before offering any theory from which theorems can be derived. Better to let oneself write down and later revise partial theories that are false, as part of a process that might eventually lead to reasonably good idealizations that partly explain a certain range of phenomena. So we want an alternative to 'meanotes' that does not require a special logic. We want to offer comprehensible theories, and see where the difficulties lie, without having to worry about what follows from what. In this spirit, Davidson (1967a, 1984) proposed that, instead of trying to provide theories with axioms like *'France' means France* and theorems like

---

[19] Should the logic licence the inference from *'Hesperus' meanotes Hesperus* and *Hesperus = Phosphorus* to *'Hesperus' meanotes Phosphorus*? If so, are we saying that 'Hesperus' and 'Phosphorus' are synonymous if Hesperus is Phosphorus? Suppose one speaker uses 'France' to refer to certain terrain (knowing full well that France is also a republic), while another speaker introduces 'Gaul' as a device for referring to the same *terrain* but stipulating that Gaul is the wrong sort of thing to be a republic. Is *'France' meanotes Gaul* true, false, or neither? Such questions need to be settled in order to know what a theory with axioms like *'France' meanotes France* implies. Putting the point in a way friendly to Quine (1951): one can try to accommodate the facts in various ways; but opting for a theory governed by a nonstandard logic will not be one's first choice. That said, I think there are good reasons for adopting a second-order metalanguage, which is *not* to say that the second-order variables range over sets of things that first-order variables range over; see Boolos (1998), Schein (1993, 2002), Higginbotham (1998), Pietroski (2005).

'France is a republic' means that France is a republic, we should try to do two things: provide theories with axioms like *'France' is true of France* and theorems like *'France is a republic' is true iff France is a republic*; and show how such theories can do the theoretical work that theories of meaning need to do.

This turned out to be a terrific methodological proposal. I fully endorse the strategy of supposing that the core semantic notions are extensional, and treating apparent counterexamples (propositional attitude reports, verbs like 'hunt' and 'worship', etc.) as special cases to be dealt with as such; see Larson *et al.* (forthcoming), cf. Montague (1974). But Davidson's replacement of 'means that' with 'is true iff' also reflected his implausible views about the nature and source of semantic phenomena; see 2.2 above. One can abandon these views and retain the practice of writing axioms like *'France' denotes France*. For engaging in the practice does not commit one to the hypothesis that a correct theory of meaning for English will associate 'France' with an entity that satisfies any predicate Φ, such that utterances of a sentence formed by combining 'France' with Φ are true. Instead, one can view the use of axioms like *'France' denotes France* as indications that certain idealizations like the following are operative:

> For purposes of explaining the limited range of facts this theory purports to explain, we're ignoring a lot of what makes 'France' the expression it is— an expression that can (given contingent facts) be used to refer to the various things that can count as France. Likewise, many typological differences between predicates (including those that distinguish 'hexagonal' from 'republic') will be ignored. Indeed, all that really matters for these purposes is that 'France' is (i) a potential grammatical argument of a predicate, (ii) a word that can be used to refer to something, and (iii) semantically distinct from other words of this type, unless some other axiom says otherwise.

This leaves room for the claim that 'France' has a hexagonal republic as its *Bedeutung*. But we should be clear that this is the analog of what we would need to say, in terms of rules governing the derivation of theorems, given axioms like *'France' meanotes France*. In my view, blaming the language-independent world for the apparent gap between meaning and truth is no more plausible than blaming logic. And if axioms like *'France' denotes France* reflect idealizations that abstract away from all the reasons for thinking that there are no theories of truth for natural languages, then the use of such axioms does not even suggest that there are such theories. So one can endorse much of the work done by theorists who use such axioms, typically as part of a scheme for encoding other more interesting claims about natural language, while remembering that the operative idealizations make it hard to use the virtues of current theories as arguments for the claim that theories of meaning are theories of truth. *If* subsequent theorizing leads to less idealized theories that are plausibly theories of truth, that will be another matter. But like Chomsky, I think the trend is in the other direction.

4.3 Lexical Flexibility and Standard-Shifting

Consider one last example of linguistic flexibility discussed by Austin (1962) and many others (see Travis, 1985, 1996). Some utterances of (1a) can be true, while others are false.

(1a) France is hexagonal

But a theory of truth for English will presumably have some theorem like the following, ignoring tense for simplicity: an utterance of (1a) is true iff the thing denoted by '*France*' is Φ; where Φ is a predicate of the metalanguage. So even setting aside worries about the alleged denontatum of 'France', there is a problem. The predicate Φ will be satisfied by whatever things it is satisfied by; and one will mischaracterize the meaning of 'hexagonal' by saying that it is a predicate satisfied by all and only those things—call them the Xs. The Xs may be the things that satisfy 'hexagonal' given *some* standards for what counts as hexagonal. But whatever the Xs are, competent speakers will know that 'hexagonal' can be used as a predicate *not* satisfied by all and only the Xs.

There are many potential replies to this kind of argument, and I cannot adequately address them here. But again, my point is more to raise the question of whether such replies are motivated, and less to argue that they are wrong. One might use 'hexagonal' itself in a theory of meaning—and not just as a temporary device to be replaced (eventually) with something else— even though 'hexagonal' is a poor candidate for a *theoretical* term, especially if France can satisfy it. But then metalanguage predicates like *satisfies 'hexagonal'* will have flexible meanings. So even if we allow for the use of such predicates in theories, despite Frege–Tarski admonitions against doing so, it seems that a "theoretical" sentence formed by combining *satisfies 'hexagonal'* with a suitable label for an entity is not a sentence that itself expresses a clear hypothesis. (This suggests that 'satisfies' is being used quasi-commonsensically, and so misleadingly.) Perhaps as used in a suitable theoretical context, *France satisfies 'hexagonal'* is a truth-evaluable claim that can be empirically assessed as a clear hypothesis about natural language. But once a context is fixed, *satisfies 'hexagonal'* will be satisfied by whatever things it is satisfied by relative to that context; and prima facie, one will mischaracterize the meaning of 'hexagonal' by saying that it is satisfied by all and only those things.

Cappelen and Lepore (2003*a*, 2003*b*, 2005)—henceforth, C&L—claim that this difficulty can be avoided. On their view, theorems of the form *S is true iff p* do indeed have meanings as flexible as the meanings of the object language expressions in question; and likewise for the corresponding axioms. C&L maintain that such axioms nonetheless comprise an honest theory, which need not and should not be relativized to a context so that certain things are all and only the satisfiers of *satisfies 'hexagonal'*. I sympathize with the spirit of this proposal, which is to relieve semantic theories of the burdens imposed by the idea that theories of meaning should reflect all the ways that truth can depend on the environment. As C&L argue, one can and evidently should theorize about meaning/understanding in abstraction from many factors relevant to truth. They say, and I agree, that one should abstract away from aspects of context-sensitivity not indexed by *expressions* of the language in question. But once one accepts this point, I don't see any theoretical motivation for retaining the idea that theories of meaning are theories of truth.

My suspicion, which I won't try to argue for here, is that appeal to flexible truth-theoretic axioms amounts to vascillation between two perspectives: a Chomsky-style view, combined with a preference for encoding semantic theories in terms of *constraints on truth* imposed by expressions, as opposed to *features of expressions* that impose constraints on truth; and a much less plausible "deflationary" view, combined with the idea that a "philosophical" theory of meaning need not account for explananda that go unexplained by adopting axioms like *x satisfies 'easy' iff x is easy*. For present purposes, let me just note that appeal to *theories* whose axioms have flexible meanings is itself a nonstandard response to Wittgenstein–Austin–Chomsky examples. And if C&L offer the best alternative to a Chomsky-style view, then the initial motivations for adopting the latter are relatively clear, at least if one assumes that we do not know a priori what theories of meaning should (not) explain.

One can, of course, hypothesize that all context-sensitivity is relevantly like indexicality. Perhaps 'hexagonal' indexes standards, much as 'I' indexes speakers. But one wants to see the evidence, independent of the dogma that theories of meaning are theories of truth. Prima facie, the flexibility of 'hexagonal' is importantly different than the indexicality of 'I'.[20] With regard to the former, context matters because, for some things, there is no *clear-cut* answer as to whether or not they are hexagonal. But with regard to 'I', it is not just that there is no *clear-cut* answer to the question of whether or not some individual satisfies 'I' independent of how (i.e. by whom) the pronoun is being used. The question isn't even coherent until the speaker is identified, at which point there is no question left. By contrast, as many authors have noted, standard-shifting seems more like—and may well be intimately related to—vagueness; see Graff (2000) for discussion. Though for just this reason, assimilating phenomena of standard-shifting to indexicality seems to mis-characterize both.

This is not to deny that the interesting questions about vagueness remain. One still wants to know what is wrong with the reasoning in Sorites para-doxes. But we should not assume that understanding is so tightly connected to truth that the following conditional holds: if the dependence of truth on the environment is vague and situation-sensitive, then *expressions of natural language* track even this dependence in the way that indexicals track other kinds of dependence. This assumption does not help resolve the paradoxes; and it may make them worse.

Correspondingly, even given a conversational situation, it can be vague as to whether or not a given entity is hexagonal. One can say that there there are many contexts for each conversational situation, perhaps with no fact of the matter as to which is *the* context relevant to the truth of an utterance in the conversational situation. I think this gets the (one-to-many) relation between contexts and conversational situations backwards, thereby making it mysteri-ous how contexts could be related to linguistic understanding. But in any case, with regard to borderline cases of hexagonalness, there is no independ-ent reason for thinking there was a clearer standard "there" that the speaker somehow failed to indicate; prima facie, there is nothing that would settle the question.

---

[20] Given any particular context, 'hexagaonal' would have to index (not an entity of the usual sort, but rather) something that associates 'hexagaonal' with some thing*s*; and one might wonder how this works, even setting aside concerns about whether it requires the paradoxical assumption that every predicate has an extension. And if the claim ends up being that contexts are (not just Kaplan-style n-tuples of potential satisifers for indexed expressions, but also) entire possible worlds, the resulting "theory" is trivial: the meanings of sentences determine truth-conditions relative to contexts, because truth is determined by meaning and everything else relevant to truth; see Pietroski (2003*a*) for related discussion. But put these concerns aside.

Again, it's important not to be misled by the fact that we can invent formal languages governed by a supervaluationist logic. Such languages may illuminate certain aspects of vagueness. But it hardly follows that natural languages *are* languages of this sort, or that the phenomenon of natural language vagueness *is* the phenomenon of "supervaluationism"; see Williamson (1994) for trenchant criticism. So if one rejects Williamson's own conclusion—according to which 'hexagonal' and 'bald' have precise extensions, unbeknownst to competent speakers—one might conclude that Williamson (like Lewis) offers a nice *reductio* of the idea that predicates of natural language have meanings that can be correctly characterized with Tarski-style theories of truth. But this leaves room for possibility that Williamson is right about how we *ought to use* language for purposes of theorizing. It may well be that we have a "regulative ideal" according to which truth is tightly connected to the meanings of expressions in a *Begriffsschrift*. And it may well be that some surprising claims about natural language *would* be descriptively correct *if* natural language meaning/understanding was related to truth this way.

One can still maintain that the meaning of 'hexagonal' somehow determines a function from contexts to satisfaction conditions. But I don't think this is any better motivated than the idea that speakers *understand* vague monadic predicates like 'red' and 'bald' by associating such predicates with *functions from numbers to* functions from entities to truth-values; where the numbers correspond to "precisifications" of the predicate (cf. Lewis, 1972). Supervaluationist *models* of understanding may be useful for certain purposes. But as Sainsbury (1990) and others have noted, we shouldn't conclude that a word like 'bald' or 'red' is a predicate semantically associated with a function from precisifications to functions. For such a predicate is no more vague than any other predicate associated with a function. And prima facie, natural language predicates have flexible meanings that make it impossible to characterize their meanings in terms of functions, without ignoring their vagueness (and thus *mis*characterizing their meanings). One can often idealize away from vagueness, but not when it comes to accounting for vagueness.[21]

---

[21] See also McGee and McLaughlin (1994), Fodor and Lepore (1996), Pietroski (2003*a*). The general point is clear from Benacerraf (1965): if a theoretical picture forces us to say that Xs (numbers, meanings, or whatever) are things of a certain sort, Ys, but identifying any particular X with any particular Y seems to mischaracterize Xs—say, by *over*describing them, with consequent indeterminacy as to which Y a given X is—perhaps we should look for another theoretical picture.

That said, the caveats of this section apply. I am not saying that causal-historical facts are irrelevant with regard to what a given predicate is intuitively true of. Nor am I saying "axioms" like *x satisfies 'hexagonal' iff x is hexagonal* are bunk. This is one way of encoding a perfectly fine idea: 'hexagonal' is a monadic predicate; and given some things to talk about, such a predicate is apt for use (on a given occasion) as a device for sorting the things in a certain way, just as 'France' is apt for use as a device for referring (on a given occasion) to one of the things. But given some things, there are many overlapping ways of sorting them such that for each of those ways, a speaker of English can use the word 'hexagonal' to sort the things in that way. The question is whether we theorists should describe this fact about language use by characterizing the *meaning* of 'hexagonal' in terms of a mapping from things to ways of sorting them—and not in terms of *intrinsic features of the word that make it possible* to use 'hexagonal' as a device for sorting things in certain ways across various conversational situations. The theoretical task, as always in this domain, is to figure out *how* meaning is related to use. It is not enough to just say that each aspect of use reflects meaning; but encoding each aspect of use in claims about meaning is just a special case of ensuring descriptive adequacy at the cost of explaining nothing.

5 Concluding Remarks

Many examples tell against the idea that theories of meaning/understanding will be theories of truth. Perhaps these are all special cases requiring special treatment; one theorist's *reductio* is another's research program. But at some point, one has to wonder what *truth*-conditional semantics explains, over and above what can be explained without supposing that theories of meaning are theories of *truth*.[22] Are there any nonspecial cases, apart from rarefied sentences like 'Two plus three equals five'? Natural language may not fit the model of a language in which names are semantically associated with entities that are satisfiers of predicates. This was a fruitful model that allowed theorists to start accounting for a certain range of elementary facts. And it simplifies discussion, in harmless ways, when the flexibility of lexical items is

---

[22] Higginbotham (1989*a*, 1989*b*) offers suggestions about what knowledge of reference might explain. But given apparent counterexamples to theories of truth, one needs to argue that such knowledge (in so far as speakers have it) is knowledge of *meaning*, as opposed to an interaction of linguistic understanding and other aspects of human cognition; see Pietroski (2003*a*).

not at issue. But the explanatory value of the model may be limited, in ways that now require attention, if we want *better* models that start to account for ways in which lexicalization and composition *interact*—and other ways in which natural languages are importantly unlike a *Begriffsschrift*.

We may have reached the stage at which the simplications frustrate theorizing more than they promote it. One can say this while agreeing that, at an earlier stage of theorizing, it was more important to stress that the Frege–Tarski toolkit was applicable in (theoretically illuminating ways) to the study of natural language—and that natural languages are importantly like a Fregean *Begriffsschrift*. It may be convenient to express this last point, in reply to those who still deny it, by saying that there are theories of truth for natural language. But one shouldn't confuse a slogan for a plausible hypothesis. Likewise, since it is part of a theorist's job to invent hypotheses that intially seem like wild overgeneralizations, it may be convenient to remind theorists of certain facts (that really do tell against *certain* generalizations) by saying 'meaning is use'. But in fact, meaning *constrains* both use and truth, in subtle and interesting ways. An account that does justice to natural language will have to accommodate facts which suggest both that (i) use and truth are *very* complicated, perhaps in many intractable ways, and (ii) meaning is systematic and in many ways theoretically tractable, even for creatures with our limited cognitive powers.

I began this chapter with a quote from Chomsky. Let me end with one from Kripke.

> I find myself torn between two conflicting feelings—a 'Chomskyan' feeling that deep regularities in natural language must be discoverable by an appropriate combination of formal, empirical, and intuitive techniques, and a contrary (late) 'Wittgensteinian' feeling that many of the 'deep structures', 'logical forms', 'underlying semantics' and 'ontological commitments', etc., which philosophers have claimed to discover by such techniques are *Luftgebaüde*. (1976: 412 n. 56).

Both sensibilities can also be found in Chomsky, who offers an attractive suggestion about how to resolve the apparent tension: meaning is less tightly connected to truth (and ontology and alien interpretability) than a lot of work suggests; expressions have semantic properties; but these are intrinsic properties of expressions that *constrain without determining* the truth-conditions of utterances. One can say that semantics is a species of syntax on this view. But that is not an objection. Given how form constrains meaning in natural languages, perhaps we should indeed replace the idea that semantic properties are *not* syntactic properties with a suitably expansive view of syntax. In any case, we should take Chomsky's view seriously—instead of insisting on a conception of meaning according to which his insights can bear essentially on syntax, but only tangentially on larger questions about understanding. That is, we should make conceptual room for the possibility that natural language is unlike a *Begriffsschrift*, in that the relation between meaning and truth is looser, while the relation between meaning and form is tighter.

We should evaluate claims about linguistic meaning, truth, and context-sensitivity in light of our best theories of natural language, instead of insisting that these theories conform to externalist dogma. Truth may well depend on communicative situations in ways that should *not* be indexed by theories of meaning/understanding for natural languages. In which case, we must revise many current claims about how meaning, truth, and context are inter-related.[23]

REFERENCES

Austin, J. (1961). *Philosophical Papers* (Oxford: Oxford University Press).

—— (1962). *How to Do Things with Words* (Oxford: Oxford University Press).

Bach, K. (1994). 'Conversational Impliciture', *Mind and Language*, 9: 124–62.

Baker, M. (1988). *Incorporation* (Chicago: University of Chicago Press).

—— (1997). 'Thematic Roles and Grammatical Categories', in L. Haegeman (ed.), *Elements of Grammar* (Dordrecht: Kluwer), 73–137.

Barber, A., ed. (2003). *Epistemology of Language* (Oxford: Oxford University Press).

Bäuerle, R., C., Schwarze, and A., von Stechow, eds. (1983). *Meaning, Use, and Interpretation of Language* (Berlin: de Gruyter).

Benacerraf, P. (1965). 'What Numbers Could Not Be', *Philosophical Review*, 74: 47–73.

Blair, D. (forthcoming). 'The Grammar of Context Dependence'.

Bloom, P. (2000). *How Children Learn the Meanings of Words* (Cambridge, Mass.: MIT Press).

Boolos, G. (1975). 'On Second-Order Logic', *Journal of Philosophy*, 72: 509–27.

—— (1998). *Logic, Logic, and Logic* (Cambridge, Mass.: Harvard University Press).

Burge, T. (1973). 'Reference and Proper Names', *Journal of Philosophy*, 70: 425–39.

---

[23] For helpful comments and discussion, my thanks to: Noam Chomsky, Susan Dwyer, Norbert Hornstein, Ernie Lepore, Jim McGilvray, and Georges Rey.

—— (1979). 'Individualism and the Mental', *Midwest Studies*, 4: 73–121.

—— (1989). 'Wherein is Language Social', in A. George (1989).

Braun, D., and J. Saul (2002). 'Simple Sentences, Substitutions, and Mistaken Evaluations', *Philosophical Studies*, 111: 1–41.

Cappelen, H., and E. Lepore (2003*a*). 'Radical and Moderate Pragmatics', in Z. Szabo (ed.), *Semantics and Pragmatics* (Oxford: Oxford University Press).

—— and —— (2003*b*). 'Unarticulated Constituents and Hidden Indexicals', in M. O'Rourke and C. Washington (eds.), *Essays in Honor of John Perry* (Cambridge, Mass.: MIT Press).

—— and —— (2005). *Insensitive Semantics* (Cambridge, Mass.: Blackwell).

Carlson, F., and F. Pelletier., eds. (1995). *The Generic Book* (Chicago: University of Chicago Press).

Carruthers, P. (2002). 'The Cognitive Functions of Language', *Behavioral and Brain Sciences*, 25: 261–316.

Castañeda, H. (1967). 'Comments', in N. Rescher (1967).

Chomsky, N. (1957). *Syntactic Structures* (The Hague: Mouton).

—— (1965). *Aspects of the Theory of Syntax* (Cambridge, Mass.: MIT Press).

—— (1966). *Cartesian Linguistics* (Lanham, Md.: University Press of America).

—— (1969). 'Quine's Empirical Assumptions', in D. Davidson and J. Hintikka (eds.), *Words and Objections: Essays on the Work of W. V. Quine* (Dordrecht: Reidel.)

—— (1970). 'Remarks on Nominalization', in R. Jacobs and R. Rosenbaum (eds.), *Readings in English Transformational Grammar* (Waltham: Ginn).

—— (1977). *Essays on Form and Interpretation* (New York: North Holland).

—— (1981). *Lectures on Government and Binding* (Dordrecht: Foris).

—— (1986). *Knowledge of Language* (New York: Praeger).

—— (1993). 'Explaining Language Use', *Philosophical Topics*, 20: 205–31.

—— (1995*a*). 'Language and Nature', *Mind*, 104: 1–61.

—— (1995*b*). *The Minimalist Program* (Cambridge, Mass.: MIT Press).

—— (1996). *Powers and Prospects* (Boston: South End Press).

—— (2000*a*). *New Horizons in the Study of Language and Mind* (Cambridge: Cambridge University Press).

—— (2000*b*). 'Minimalist Inquiries', in R. Martin, D. Michaels, and J. Uriagereka (eds.), *Step by Step: Essays on Minimalist Syntax in Honor of Howard Lasnik* (Cambridge, Mass.: MIT Press).

Collins, J. (2003). 'Horwich's Schemata Meet *Syntactic Structures*', *Mind*, 112: 399–432.

Crain, S., and P. Pietroski (2001). 'Nature, Nurture, and Universal Grammar', *Linguistics and Philosophy*, 24: 139–86.

—— (2002). 'Why Language Acquisition is a Snap', *Linguistic Review*, 19: 163–83.

Davidson, D. (1967*a*). 'Truth and Meaning', *Synthese*, 17: 304–23.

—— (1967*b*). 'The Logical Form of Action Sentences', in N. Rescher (1967).

Davidson, D. (1984). *Inquiries into Truth and Interpretation* (Oxford: Oxford University Press).

—— (1985). 'Adverbs of Action', in B. Vermazen and M. Hintikka (eds.), *Essays on Davidson: Actions and Events* (Oxford: Clarendon Press).

—— (1989). 'What is Present to the Mind?', in J. Brandl and W. Gombocz (eds.), *The Mind of Donald Davidson* (Amsterdam: Rodopi).

—— (2001). *Subjective, Intersubjective, Objective* (New York: Clarendon Press).

Dummett, M. (1975). 'What is a Theory of Meaning?', in S. Guttenplan (ed.), *Mind and Language* (Oxford: Oxford University Press).

—— (1976). 'What is a Theory of Meaning (II)?', in G. Evans and J. McDowell (1976).

—— (1986). 'A Nice Derangement of Epitaphs: Some Comments on Davidson and Hacking', in E. Lepore (1986).

Evans, G. (1982). *Varieties of Reference* (Oxford: Oxford University Press).

—— and McDowell, J., eds. (1986). *Truth and Meaning* (Oxford: Oxford University Press).

Fodor, J. (1987). *Psychosemantics* (Cambridge, Mass.: MIT).

—— (1998). *Concepts: Where Cognitive Science went Wrong* (New York: Oxford University Press).

—— and E. Lepore (1992). *Holism: A Shopper's Guide* (Oxford: Blackwell).

—— and —— (1996). 'What Cannot be Evaluated Cannot be Evaluated, and it Cannot be Supervalued Either', *Journal of Philosophy*, 93: 516–35.

—— and —— (2002). *The Compositionality Papers* (Oxford: Oxford University Press).

Frege, G. (1879). *Begriffsschrift* (Halle: Louis Nebert). English translation in J. van Heijenoort (ed.), *From Frege to Gödel: A Source Book in Mathematical Logic, 1879–1931* (Cambridge, Mass.: Harvard University Press, 1967).

—— (1892). 'Function and Concept', in P. Geach and M. Black (tr.), *Translations from the Philosophical Writings of Gottlob Frege* (Oxford: Blackwell, 1980).

George, A., ed. (1989). *Reflections on Chomsky* (Oxford: Blackwell).

Graff, D. (2000). 'Shifting Sands', *Philosophical Topics*, 28: 45–81.

Grandy, R. (1973). 'Reference, Meaning, and Belief', *Journal of Philosophy*, 70: 439–52.

Hauser, M., N. Chomsky, and W. Fitch (2002). 'The Faculty of Language', *Science*, 298: 1569–79.

Herburger, E. (2001). *What Counts* (Cambridge, Mass.: MIT Press).

Hermer, L., and E. Spelke (1994). 'A Geometric Process for Spatial Reorientation in Young Children', *Nature*, 370: 57–9.

—— and —— (1996). 'Modularity and Development: The Case of Spatial Reorientation', *Cognition*, 61: 195–232.

Hermer-Vazquez, L., E. Spelke, and A. Katsnelson (1999). 'Sources of Flexibility in Human Cognition', *Cognitive Psychology*, 39: 3–36.

Higginbotham, J. (1983*a*). 'Logical Form, Binding and Nominals', *Linguistic Inquiry*, 14: 395–420.

—— (1983*b*). 'The Logical Form of Perceptual Reports', *Journal of Philosophy*, 80: 100–27.

—— (1985). 'On Semantics', *Linguistic Inquiry*, 16: 547–93.

—— (1986). 'Lingustic Theory and Davidson's Program', in E. Lepore (1986).

—— (1989*a*). 'Knowledge of Reference', in A. George (ed.), *Reflections on Chomsky* (Oxford: Blackwell).

—— (1989*b*). 'Elucidations of Meaning', *Linguistics and Philosophy*, 12: 465–517.

—— (1990). 'Contexts, Models, and Meanings', in R. Kempson (ed.), *Mental Representations: The Interface between Language and Reality* (Cambridge: Cambridge University Press).

—— (1993). 'Grammatical Form and Logical Form', *Philosophical Perspectives*, 7: 173–96.

—— (1994). 'Priorities in the Philosophy of Thought', *Proc. Aristotelian Society* (supp. vol.) 20: 85–106.

—— (1998). 'On Higher-Order Logic and Natural Language', *Proc. of the British Academy*, 95: 1–27.

—— and R. May (1981). 'Questions, Quantifiers, and Crossing', *Linguistic Review*, 1: 47–79.

Hinzen, W. (2002). 'Meaning without Belief', in W. Hinzen and H. Rott (eds.), *Belief in Meaning: Essays at the Interface* (Frankfurt: Hansel-Hohenhausen).

Hornstein, N. (1984). *Logic as Grammar* (Cambridge, Mass.: MIT Press).

—— and D. Lightfoot (1981). *Explanation in Linguistics* (London: Longman).

Horwich, P. (1997). 'The Composition of Meanings', *Philosophical Review*, 106: 503–32.

—— (1998). *Meaning* (Oxford: Oxford University Press).

Jackendoff, R. (1990). *Semantic Structures* (Cambridge, Mass.: MIT Press).

—— (1997). *The Architecture of the Language Faculty* (Cambridge, Mass.: MIT Press).

—— (2002). *Foundations of Language* (Oxford: Oxford University Press).

Kaplan, D. (1989). 'Demonstratives', in J. Almog, J. Perry, and H. Wettstein (eds.), *Themes from Kaplan* (New York: Oxford University Press).

Katz, J., and J. Fodor (1963). 'The Structure of a Semantic Theory', *Language*, 39: 170–210.

Kratzer, A. (1996). 'Severing the External Argument from its Verb', in J. Rooryck and L. Zaring (eds.), *Phrase Structure and the Lexicon* (Dordrecht: Kluwer Academic Publishers).

Kripke, S. (1971). 'Identity and Necessity', in M. Kunitz (ed.), *Identity and Individuation* (New York: NYU Press).

—— (1976). 'Is there a Problem about Substitutional Quantification?', in E. Evans and J. McDowell (1976).

Kripke, S. (1980). *Naming and Necessity* (Cambridge, Mass.: Harvard University Press).

—— (n.d.). 'Reference and Existence: The John Locke Lectures for 1973', unpublished.

Lakoff, G. (1970). *Irregularity in Syntax* (New York: Holt, Rinehart, & Winston).

—— (1987). *Women, Fire, and Dangerous Things* (Chicago: University of Chicago Press).

Larson, R., P. Ludlow, and M. den Dikken (forthcoming). 'Intentional Transitives'.

Larson, R. and Segal, (1995), *Knowledge of Meaning* (Cambridge, Mass.: MIT Press).

Laurence, S., and E. Margolis (2001). 'The Poverty of Stimulus Argument', *British Journal for the Philosophy of Science*, 52: 217–76.

Lepore, E. (1983). 'What Model-Theoretic Semantics Cannot Do', *Synthese*, 54: 167–87.

—— ed. (1986). *Truth and Interpretation* (Oxford: Blackwell).

Levin, B., and M. Rappaport (1995). *Unaccusativity: at the Syntax–Semantics Interface* (Cambridge, Mass.: MIT Press).

Lewis, D. (1972). 'General Semantics', in D. Davidson and G. Harman (eds.), *Semantics of Natural Language* (Dordrecht: Reidel).

—— (1986). *On the Plurality of Worlds* (Oxford: Blackwell).

Longobardi, G. (1994). 'Reference and Proper Names', *Linguistic Inquiry*, 25: 609–65.

McGee, V., and B. McLaughlin (1994). 'Distinctions without a Difference', *Southern Journal of Philosophy*, 33: 203–53.

McGilvray, J. (1998). 'Meanings are Syntactically Individuated and Found in the Head', *Mind and Language*, 13: 225–80.

—— (1999). *Chomsky: Language, Mind and Politics* (Cambridge: Polity Press).

McGinn, C. (1993). *Problems in Philosophy* (Oxford: Blackwell).

Matthews, R. (2003). 'Does Linguistic Competence Require Knowledge of Language?', in Barber (2003).

May, R. (1985). *Logical Form: Its Structure and Derivation* (Cambridge, Mass.: MIT Press).

Meinong, A. (1904). 'Über Gegenstandstheorie', in A. Meinong (ed.), *Untersuchungen zur Gegenstandstheorie und Psychologie* (Leipzig: Barth).

Montague, R. (1970). 'English as a Formal Language', reprinted in Montague (1974).

—— (1974). *Formal Philosophy* (New Haven: Yale University Press).

Moravcsik, J. (1975). *Understanding Language* (The Hague: Mouton).

—— (1998). *Meaning, Creativity, and the Partial Inscrutability of the Human Mind* (Stanford, Calif.: CSLI).

Neale, S. (1990). *Descriptions* (Cambridge, Mass.: MIT Press).

—— (1993). 'Grammatical Form, Logical Form, and Incomplete Symbols', in A. Irvine and G. Wedeking (eds.), *Russell and Analytic Philosophy* (Toronto: University of Toronto).

Parsons, T. (1990). *Events in the Semantics of English* (Cambridge, Mass.: MIT Press).

Partee, B., and M. Rooth (1983). 'Generalized Conjunction and Type Ambiguity', in Bäuerle *et al.* (1993).

Pietroski, P. (1998). 'Actions, Adjuncts, and Agency', *Mind*, 107: 73–111.

—— (2000*a*). *Causing Actions* (Oxford: Oxford University Press).

—— (2000*b*). 'The Undeflated Domain of Semantics', *Sats, Nordic Journal of Philosophy*, 1: 161–76.

—— (2002). 'Function and Concatenation', in G. Preyer and G. Peter (2002).

—— (2003*a*). 'The Character of Natural Language Semantics', in A. Barber (2003).

—— (2003*b*). 'Small Verbs, Complex Events: Analyticity without Synonymy', in L. Antony and N. Hornstein (eds.), *Chomsky and his Critics* (Cambridge, Blackwell).

—— (2003*c*). 'Quantification and Second-Order Monadictity', *Philosophical Perspectives*, 17: 259–98.

—— (2005). *Events and Semantic Architecture* (Oxford: Oxford University Press).

Pustejovsky, J. (1995). *The Generative Lexicon* (Cambridge, MA: MIT Press).

Putnam, H. (1975). 'The Meaning of "Meaning" ', in K. Gunderson (ed.), *Language, Mind and Knowledge* (Minneapolis: University of Minnesota Press).

Preyer, G., and G. Peter eds. (2002) *Logical Form and Language* (Oxford: Oxford University Press).

Quine, W. V. O. (1951). 'Two Dogmas of Empiricism', *Philosophical Review*, 60: 20–43.

—— (1960). *Word and Object* (Cambridge, Mass.: MIT Press).

Rescher, N., ed. (1967). *The Logic of Decision and Action* (Pittsburgh: University of Pittsburgh Press).

Ryle, G. (1949). *The Concept of Mind* (Chicago: University of Chicago Press).

Sainsbury, M. (1990). 'Concepts without Boundaries', in R. Keefe and P. Smith (eds.), *Vagueness: A Reader* (Cambridge, Mass.: MIT Press).

Schein, B. (1993). *Events and Plurals* (Cambridge, Mass.: MIT Press).

—— (2002). 'Events and the Semantic Content of Thematic Relations', in G. Preyer and G. Peter (2002).

—— (forthcoming). *Conjunction Reduction Redux* (Cambridge, Mass.: MIT Press).

Schiffer, S. (1992). 'Belief Ascription', *Journal of Philosophy*, 89: 499–521.

—— (1994*a*). 'The Language-of-Thought Relation and its Implications', *Philosophical Studies*, 76: 263–85.

—— (1994*b*). 'A Paradox of Meaning', *Noûs*, 28: 279–324.

—— (2000). 'Critical Study: Horwich on Meaning', *Phiolsophical Studies*, 50: 527–36.

Soames, S. (1987). 'Direct Reference, Propositional Attitudes, and Semantic Content', *Philosophical Topics*, 15: 47–87.

—— (1995). 'Beyond Singular Propositions', *Canadian Journal of Philosophy*, 25: 515–50.

Spelke, E. (2002). 'Developing Knowledge of Space: Core Systems and New combinations', in S. Kosslyn and A. Galaburda (eds.), *Languages of the Brain* (Cambridge, Mass.: Harvard University Press).

—— (2003). 'What Makes Humans Smart?', in D. Gentner and S. Goldin-Meadow (eds.), *Advances in the Investigation of Language and Thought* (Cambridge, Mass.: MIT Press).

Stainton, R. (forthcoming). 'Meaning and Reference Some Chomskyan Themes', in E. Lepore and B. Smith (eds.), *Handbook of Philosophy of Language* (Oxford: Oxford University Press).

Stanley, J. (2000). 'Context and Logical Form', *Linguistics and Philosophy*, 23: 391–424.

—— (2002). 'Making it Articulated', *Mind and Language*, 17: 149–68.

—— and Z. Szabó (2000). 'Quantifer Domain Restriction', *Mind and Language*, 15: 219–62.

Strawson, P. (1950). 'On Referring', *Mind*, 59: 320–44.

Tarski, A. (1933). 'The Concept of Truth in Formalized Languages', reprinted in Tarski (1983).

—— (1983). *Logic, Semantics, Metamathematics*, tr. J. H. Woodger, 2nd edn., ed. J. Corcoran (Indianapolis: Hackett).

Taylor, B. (1985). *Modes of Occurrence* (Oxford: Blackwell).

Travis, C. (1985). 'On what is Strictly Speaking True', *Canadian Journal of Philosophy*, 15: 187–229.

—— (1996). 'Meaning's Role in Truth', *Mind*, 105: 451–66.

Uriagereka, J. (2002). *Derivations: Exploring the Dynamics of Syntax* (London: Routledge).

—— and M. Piatelli-Palmarini (forthcoming). 'The Immune Syntax', in L. Jenkins (ed.), *Variation and Universals in Biolinguistics* (Oxford: Elsevier).

Vlach, F. (1983). 'On Situation Semantics for Perception', *Synthese*, 54: 129–52.

Williamson, T. (1994). *Vagueness* (London: Routledge).

Wittgenstein, G. (1921). *Tractatus Logico-Philosophicus*, tr. D. Pears and B. McGuinness (London: Routledge & Kegan Paul).

—— (1953). *Philosophical Investigations* (New York: Macmillan).

11

Compositionality and Context

PETER PAGIN

1 Fodor on Linguistic Compositionality

In his contribution to a series of millennial articles in *Mind and Language*, Jerry Fodor (2001) confronts the question of the priority between thought and language. As Fodor adequately frames it, the question comes down to whether one of thought content and linguistic meaning is derived from the other. His chosen method is an appeal to *compositionality* (Fodor, 2001: 6): that which is primary must be compositional. For reasons of productivity and systematicity,[1] Fodor thinks, there must be compositionality of content (2001: 6–7). Hence, he says, 'if, as between language and thought, only one of the two has compositional content, then that must be the one whose content is underived'. Fodor then goes on to argue that linguistic meaning in fact is *not* compositional. He concludes that thought is prior to language.

At present I shall leave the question of the compositionality of mental content, as well as that of the priority between thought and language, to a footnote.[2] What will interest me in this context is Fodor's reason for the claim that natural language isn't compositional. Fodor's argument for this

---

[1] See e.g. Fodor, 1987: 147–53.

[2] I do in fact think that the arguments from productivity and systematicity give very poor support for the priority of the mental. To the extent that these arguments do provide good reasons for compositionality it is by appeal, sometimes tacit and sometimes not, to facts about linguistic communication: we frequently succeed when communicating with new sentences. That a speaker can *produce* arbitrarily many meaningful sentences does not by itself give a reason to think that there is some systematic connection between syntax and semantics. Only when we add the fact that novel sentences produced are understood *as meant* by other speakers

conclusion appeals to the heavy *context dependence* in natural language. Terminologically, I shall use 'context dependence' precisely for the *depending on context*. To make this more precise, let μ be a meaning function that takes linguistic expressions from a language L and contexts of utterance (i.e. actual or possible utterances) in a domain C of contexts to semantic values in a domain K. That is $\mu: L \times C \rightarrow K$. Then we say that μ, or K, is *context dependent* iff there is an expression e of L, and contexts c_1 and c_2 in C such that

$$\mu(e, c_1) \neq \mu(e, c_2)$$

We say that the K-value of e, or of expressions in L in general, depends on context.

If it holds for all $e \in L$ and all $c_1, c_2 \in C$ that

$$\mu(e, c_1) = \mu(e, c_2)$$

then μ, or K, is *context independent*.

If the sentence (or other expression) has a standing, context *invariant* meaning, such that what is expressed by way of this meaning in a context depends on the context, then that sentence has a meaning that is context *sensitive*, not context dependent. Again, let μ' be a context invariant function from L to a domain M of semantic values, $\mu': L \rightarrow M$. I shall say that μ' is *context sensitive* if the M-value in a context c determines a K-value where K is context dependent. We can then regard elements $\mu'(e) \in M$ of standing meanings as *functions* from contexts to K-values. We will then have, for all $e \in L$ and $c \in C$

---

do we get a reason for believing that this can be explained by appeal to such a systematic connection. The appeal to communicative success is explicit in some formulations by Chomsky of the productivity argument (Chomsky, 1966: 74, 1980: 76–8). It is emphasized in Frege, 1923: 1. The argument from systematicity suffers from the same problem: either there is an appeal to linguistic communication, or the argument is very weak (because needing an additional premise which in itself is not very plausible). Only in this case the situation is more complicated. Since there is no good argument for the compositionality of the mental that is independent of arguments for the compositionality of linguistic meaning, no support for the priority of the mental is forthcoming. This does not, however, mean that the order of priority is the reverse. For one thing, considerations about communicative success do provide reasons for the compositionality of mental representations, reasons not so far mentioned by Fodor (see Pagin, 2003: 315). Further, the proper definition of communicative success does appeal to an independent notion of thought content. In this sense it is a mentalistic definition (Pagin, n.d.). However, no assumption about semantic structure is needed in this definition. If any general conclusion is to be drawn, it is that Fodor's strategy of settling the priority issue by appeal to compositionality results in a draw. The issue of justifying compositionality is discussed in Pagin 1999 and 2002 and will be given a fuller treatment eventually.

(c-app) $(\mu'(e))(c)=\mu(e, c)$

That is, the standing meaning of e applies to a context argument and delivers a context dependent semantic value, the same value as the original context dependent function μ delivers for that expression in that context. To exemplify, David Kaplan's notion of *content* (Kaplan, 1989) is context dependent, for the content of

(1) I am walking

will vary with context, the content being the singular proposition

(2) $\langle walking,\langle S, t\rangle\rangle$

where the elements are the property of walking, the speaker S and the time t of utterance. With a different speaker or a different time, the content of the utterance of (1) will be different accordingly. By contrast, Kaplan's notion of *character*, that is, the standing meaning of an indexical like 'I' and a sentence like (1), does not vary between contexts. Kaplan considers it as a *function* from contexts to contents, that is, to context dependent values. In the present terminology, character is context sensitive while content is context dependent. Instead of Kaplan's terminology, and without any specific semantic theory in mind, I shall borrow terminology from Quine and speak of standing meaning (M-values), and *occasion* meaning (K-values).

There is a second, related phenomenon of context dependence, namely that contextual semantic variation can occur even though there is no surface part of the expression to which the variation can be traced. Both these phenomena are illustrated by a standard example. The sentence

(3) It rains

is used to say different things on different occasions of utterance. A speaker S who utters (3) says that it is raining where S is (or at some other contextually salient location) at the time of utterance (or at some other contextually salient time). So there is a variation in communicated content, which exemplifies the first phenomenon. But (3) also exemplifies the second, for there is a double context dependence, only one of which is explicit. First, the speaker says something about the time of utterance (that it is a rainy time), and the relation between the utterance and the time is articulated in the sentence by the present tense of the verb. Second, the speaker also says something about the contextually salient *location* (that it is a rainy place), but the relation between the utterance and the location is not articulated by anything overtly in the sentence. It can be made explicit as in

(4) It rains here

where the place of utterance is the referent of the indexical 'here', but that element is missing in (3), even though what is said or communicated is the same.

Other standard examples concern incomplete definite descriptions and domain restrictions of quantifiers. By uttering

(5) The book is on the table

the normal speaker is communicating something about a contextually salient book on a contextually salient table. He is not claiming nor presupposing that there is exactly one book and one table in the universe. However, the extra conditions (the book such that ... ; the table such that ...) that are needed to identify the objects are not overtly expressed in the sentence. And by uttering

(6) Everyone left at midnight

the normal speaker says that everyone in a contextually salient group of people (not everyone in the universe) left at midnight, and again the restriction of the quantifier 'everyone' to this group is not overtly expressed.

Fodor appeals to examples like these for showing that what we utter often is inexplicit about the thought expressed, and goes on to argue as follows. First, the content of a sentence is ('plus or minus a bit') the thought it is used to express (2001: 11). Second, language is 'strikingly elliptical and inexplicit about the thoughts it expresses' (2001: 11). Third, language cannot be elliptical and inexplicit about the thoughts it expresses if it is compositional ('in anything like strict detail') (2001: 11). The third point is expounded on as follows:

For, if it were (and assuming that the content of a sentence is, or is the same as, the content of the corresponding thought) the structure of a sentence would indeed have to be explicit about the structure of the thought it expresses; in particular, the constituents of the sentence would have to correspond in a straightforward way to the thought's constituents. For, if there are constituents of your thought that don't correspond to constituents of the sentence you utter, then since compositionality requires that the content of a thought contains all of the content of its constituents, it must be that there was something in the thought that the sentence left out. (Fodor, 2001: 11–12)

The conclusion is that language isn't compositional.

2 How to Refute Compositionality

A difficulty with this argument, as presented, is that Fodor hasn't said what compositionality is. On the contrary, he says explicitly that he is not going to tell us, and further that nobody knows exactly what it demands (2001: 6). This casts some doubt on Fodor's third premise. The doubt grows when we consider the standard conception of compositionality. The principle of compositionality is usually rendered something like

> (PoC) The meaning of a complex expression is a function of the meanings of its parts and its mode of composition.

This in turn is usually understood in a strong sense, as stating that the meaning of a complex expression is determined by the meanings of its *immediate* parts and its mode of composition. To make this formally more precise, let μ be a function from expressions of a language L to meanings in some domain M. Let 'σ' be a parameter for syntactic operations, and 'e_1' etc. terms for expressions of L. Then we can restate (PoC) as the requirement that μ be a compositional meaning function. μ is compositional just if there is a function g such that for any n, any σ of arity n and expressions $e_1, \ldots e_n$ (such that μ is defined for $\sigma(e_1, \ldots e_n)$)

> (comp) $\mu(\sigma(e_1, \ldots e_n))=g(\sigma,\mu(e_1), \ldots,\mu(e_n))$

A function g satisfying (comp) will be called a *composition function*, or, more precisely, a *composition function for* μ.[3]

Understood in this way, if the compositionality of a language consists in the fact that PoC is true of it, then Fodor's third premise certainly seems false. It is not a violation of compositionality, in this standard sense, that a complex expression has a meaning that is much richer than what you intuitively get out of the meanings of the parts. For instance, suppose we have expressions e_1 and e_2, a syntactic operation σ and a meaning function μ such that $\mu(e_1) =$ George W Bush, $\mu(e_2)=$Silvio Berlusconi and $\mu(\sigma(e_1, e_2))=$*the proposition that George W Bush and Silvio Berlusconi will never have visited Bhutan*

---

[3] (comp) amounts to the algebraic requirement that μ be a *homomorphism* from L to M. The requirement that natural language semantics be compositional in this sense was put forward by Richard Montague (cf. Montague, 1970*a*: 227), and elaborated on by Montague himself and others in the Montague tradition, including Partee (1984), Jansen (1984, 1997) and Hendriks (2001). A simplified algebraic treatement was later proposed by Hodges (1998, 2001). Hodges's framework is used in Westerståhl (2002, 2004) and Pagin (2003).

together. However odd, this wouldn't be a violation of PoC. Whether the sentence $\sigma(e_1, e_2)$ also is inexplicit about the thought it expresses, in Fodor's sense, is a further question, but since it, for example, does express a thought with reference to Bhutan, without there being any constituent in the sentence that carries that reference, it seems inexplicit enough.[4]

The claim that natural language is not compositional, given that compositionality is understood in terms of PoC and (comp), amounts to a claim that there is *no* function which, given such and such syntactic and semantic data, maps the meaning of constituent expressions and syntactic structure of a complex expression on the meaning of that expression. That is, the claim is that for a natural language (or any natural language) L, and any admissible meaning function μ for L, there is *no composition function* for μ.

There is one clear and definitive way of demonstrating that no composition function exists: by giving a *counterexample to functionality.* That is, we show that the language contains four expressions e_1, e_2, A, and $A[e_2/e_1]$, such that A contains e_1 as a constituent, $A[e_2/e_1]$ is the result of substituting e_2 for e_1 in A, and the meaning function μ for this language is such that $\mu(e_1)=\mu(e_2)$ and $\mu(A)\neq\mu(A[e_2/e_1])$. μ does not give the meanings of A, and $A[e_2/e_1]$ as a function of the meanings of the parts, for if it did A and $A[e_2/e_1]$ would mean the same. Moreover, no other meaning function that respects these semantic data, that is, agrees with μ on these four expressions, does either. This is a clear and definitive way of showing that a language fails to be compositional. It has been claimed, for example, by Jeff Pelletier (1994*b*), that because of the hyperintensionality of belief contexts, truth conditions as the meanings of sentences aren't functionally determined by the meanings of sentence parts. I shall refer to

(SF) $\mu(e_1)=\mu(e_2)$ and $\mu(A)\neq\mu(A[e_2/e_1])$,

understood as above, as the *substitution failure* schema.[5]

---

[4] Maybe in this context Fodor by 'compositionality' means what he also calls 'biconditional compositionality' (2001: 9). He says 'compositionality requires that host concepts receive their semantic properties solely from their constituents, *and also that constituent concepts transmit all of their semantic properties to their hosts*' (Fodor, 2001: 9; italics in the original). As stated, this principle concerns contents and the constituent relation between contents. It does not concern the expression–content *relation*, and so it is irrelevant to natural language semantics.

[5] It is assumed here that μ is defined for both A and $A[e_2/e_1]$. Substitutivity can fail in a weaker sense if μ fails to be defined for exactly one of them (A or $A[e_2/e_1]$ is meaningless), even though there is a composition function for μ (giving the value of μ for any argument for which it is defined). A semantics is called *Husserlian* by Hodges (2001: 11) if synonymous expressions

Are there other ways of establishing the failure of compositionality? In principle yes, but other ways do not easily take you all the way to the goal. For instance, you might want to claim that natural language fails to be compositional because some complex expressions have other meanings than they compositionally *ought* to. That is, we assume that we have identified the meanings of the parts of a complex expression, the syntactic operations by which it is formed and also the semantic significance of these operations, and then it turns out that the complex expression itself has a different meaning (in addition to or instead of) from what was to be expected. That is, we may assume that in general we have

$$\mu(\sigma(e_i, e_j)) = g(\mu(e_i), \mu(e_j))$$

for some composition function g, and now it turns out that

$$\mu(\sigma(e_1, e_2)) \neq g(\mu(e_1), \mu(e_2))$$

(or perhaps that in addition to $g(\mu(e_1), \mu(e_2))$, $\sigma(e_1, e_2)$ has another meaning). For instance, it has been claimed that because of the existence of idioms, like 'kick the bucket' (as meaning *die*), English isn't compositional. However, just because a certain familiar composition function g on the meanings of the parts does not give the right meaning of the whole, this does not mean that no *other* function does either. We might be able to define a modification or extension g^* of g, agreeing with g on all other arguments, such that

$$\mu(\sigma(e_i, e_j)) = g^*(\mu(e_i), \mu(e_j))$$

for all relevant e_i, e_j, including e_1 and e_2. Then the functionality condition is met after all.[6]

---

can always be intersubstituted without loss of meaningfulness. Conversely, if a constituent of a meaningful complex expression is itself meaningless, then the meaning of the complex expression is not a function of the meanings of its parts and the mode of composition. The substitutivity principle may still hold, in that any *meaningful* constituent may be exchanged for a synonymous one without change of meaning of the containing complex. The principle that meaningful compounds have only meaningful parts is called the *Domain principle*. If the Domain principle holds for a *Husserlian* semantics μ, then there is composition function for μ just in case μ has no substitution failure (cf. Hodges, 2001: 12–13). I shall in general assume that the conditions for this equivalence are met.

[6] For a comprehensive formal treatment of idioms in a compositional framework, see Westerståhl, 2002. Note that *learning* what this g^* is will involve learning the idiom separately. That much is right in calling idioms 'non-compositional'; the idiomatic meaning is not predictable from what you know in advance.

Secondly, you might want to claim that compositionality fails because some parts just don't *have* any meaning. You might have defined rules that give the meaning of every sentence on the basis of its syntax, but such that they do not invariantly make use of meanings of constituents. For instance, Jaakko Hintikka's game-theoretic semantics is of this kind, and Hintikka and Gabriel Sandu (1997) have claimed that, although there is a proper game-theoretic semantics for their *independence-friendly logic*, IF, no compositional semantics exists. This claim has been refuted by Wilfrid Hodges, who provided a compositional semantics for IF, and also proved that any partial semantics that satisfies certain conditions (including that of being *Husserlian*) can be extended into a total compositional semantics.[7] Hodges's theorem has since been generalized by Dag Westerståhl (dropping the *Husserlian* condition).[8]

Third, you might want to claim that compositionality fails because an expression contributes different meanings to different containing expressions, or contributes another meaning than what it has in isolation. That is, compositionality would fail because there is no single meaning that can be assigned to a certain expression so that the meaning of the containing expressions would follow compositionally. This is an argument from *linguistic* context dependence. Thus James Higginbotham (1986) has claimed that 'unless' means *and not* in

(7) No person will eat steak unless he eats lobster

but *or* in

(8) Every person will eat steak unless he eats lobster.

However, if this is a straight claim about difference in the meaning of 'unless' in different contexts, then it seems natural to conclude that we here have a case of lexical ambiguity, to be treated for example, as a case of homonymy, which then does not provide any difficulty for compositionality. This is one of the options suggested by Pelletier (1994a).

Therefore, the claim should rather be that on the one hand we have a single unambiguous word 'unless' such that no meaning can be assigned to it which gets the right truth conditions for both (7) and (8) in a compositional way. The range of solutions must be restricted so that intuitive or theoretically established facts about the meanings of the other words and the syntax are respected. But this still leaves the possibility of a composition function *g* such

---

[7] Hodges, 1997, 1998, 2001.   [8] Westerståhl, 2004.

that $g(\mu(\text{'no person'}), \mu(\text{'will eat steak unless he eats lobster'}))$ and $g(\mu(\text{'every person'}), \mu(\text{'will eat steak unless he eats lobster'}))$ are the truth conditions of (7) and (8) respectively, and which agrees with the data on meanings of unproblematic verb phrases. Non-compositionality has not been demonstrated.[9]

Fourth, you might claim that compositionality fails because of general speaker creativity. The claim is that speakers are creative in a more radical sense than having the ability to compose and interpret new sentences. We can also create new sentences with practically unpredictable intentions, and still be understood by equally creative interpretaters, as for example emphasized by Davidson (1986). However, this does not imply that compositionality fails for the set of sentences that *do* have well-defined meanings. Few if any have claimed that compositional semantics by itself is sufficient for explaining all of successful linguistic communication, and I certainly don't. Neither do I claim that there is a finite list of pragmatic principles that together with some compositional semantics for (some variety of) English can explain all episodes of successful communication in (that variety of) English. There is genuine novelty, and compositionality cannot be blamed for not assigning a meaning to an expression that does not yet have it.

It may also be claimed that natural language meanings are too fuzzy for serving as arguments and values to compositional functions. However, if we can talk about meanings at all, then they are not too fuzzy to be referred to by means of linguistic expressions, and if this is possible in general, then it is hard to see why this would be impossible precisely with expressions for compositional functions.

There are yet further options for rejecting compositionality, but this is enough to show that without a clear counterexample to functionality, it is difficult to find a conclusive refutation. Given this, the question is how context dependence can provide one.

---

[9] Pelletier (1994*a*: 606–8) suggests solving the semantic problem by giving a kind of higher order meaning to 'unless', taking linguistic contexts as arguments, but this move is not necessary. Moreover, Higginbotham's ambiguity claim is spurious. The incongruence in truth conditions between (7) and (8) does not depend on properties of 'unless'. To see this, note that if we generate (7′) and (8′) by substituting 'if he does not eat' for 'unless he eats' in (7) and (8), respectively, we preserve truth conditions ('No person eats steak if he does not eat lobster' has the same truth conditions as (7), in similarly for (8′) and (8)). However, it is plainly not the case that 'if not' means *and not* in (7′) and *or* in (8′). Rather, the phenomenon seems to depend on a difference between how the quantifiers 'no person' and 'every person' interact with the conditional. Notice that we preserve the truth conditions of (7) by replacing the *antecedent* with its logical equivalent 'everyone does not eat steak'.

3 Context Dependence against Compositionality

Assuming the need to counter functionality, how can context dependence conflict with compositionality? The key, I believe, lies in Fodor's first premise above:

>   (Rad) The *meaning* of a sentence is the thought (proposition) it is used to express.

Since Fodor actually says 'plus or minus a bit' (and 'content' instead of 'meaning') it is not clear how much one can hold him to, but let's put that question aside and consider the radical thesis itself. (Rad) amounts to one extreme view on the semantics/pragmatics distinction, according to which everything is semantics. That is, although conscious psychological processes are deeply involved in most linguistic communication, still there is no ingredient in what is expressed or communicated that is not held to be part of the meaning of the sentence used. Because of context dependence, what is communicated with a context dependent sentence varies from one utterance of it to the next. According to (Rad), the meaning changes as well. Thus, (almost) no standing meaning.

That the meaning of a sentence changes between contexts is not itself in conflict with compositionality. But we can get an intuitive conflict by combining *invariance* of occasion meaning of the sentence parts, with *variation* in occasion meaning of the sentence itself. Thus, suppose that in (3), the impersonal pronoun 'it' has context independent occasion meaning, and that the same holds for the feature placing verb 'rains'. With two occasions of utterance, c_1 and c_2, we get two different occasion meanings of (3), μ ('it rains', c_1), i.e. the meaning of 'it rains' in c_1, and μ('it rains', c_2). Since by assumption μ('it',c_1)=μ('it',c_2), μ('rains',c_1)=μ('rains',c_2), and μ('it rains', c_1)$\neq \mu$('it rains',c_2) (and there are no other parts, nor any change in syntax), we seem to have a counterexample to functionality.

However, when we extend the notion of compositionality from standing meaning to occasion meaning, the extra argument place for context creates a complication. We can extend it in two different ways, a weaker and a stronger. According to the weaker version, *e*-compositionality ('*e*' for expression) a meaning function μ counts as compositional iff there is an *e*-composition function *g* such that

>   (*e*-comp) $\mu(\sigma(e_1, \ldots e_n),c)=g(\sigma,\mu(e_1, c), \ldots,\mu(e_n, c),c)$.

Notice that the arguments for g are the syntactic operator σ, the meanings of the parts in the context, *and* the context itself. It may be that the context dependence is influenced by the syntax, and it may be that the context parameter contributes in a uniform way.[10] Either way, the extra context parameter is supposed to be non-vacuous. Having the context itself as an extra argument cannot be objected to as violating compositionality, since the meaning function μ itself takes a context argument to begin with.

If e-compositionality holds, then the substitutivity requirement is fulfilled. That is, for any context c, if $\mu(e_1, c){=}\mu(e_2, c)$, then $\mu(A, c){=}\mu(A[e_2/e_1],c)$. Moreover, the converse holds as well: if the substitutivity condition is met, then μ satisfies (e-comp).[11]   Hence, in one natural way of extending compositionality from standing meaning to occasion meaning, compositionality holds if e-compositionality holds. However, in another it doesn't, simply because the meaning of the whole in the context isn't a function of just the mode of composition and meanings of the parts in the context. There is therefore room for a stronger notion, ec-compositionality ('c' for context), requiring the existence of an ec-composition function g such that

(ec-comp) $\mu(\sigma(e_1, \ldots e_n),c){=}g(\sigma,\mu(e_1, c), \ldots ,\mu(e_n, c))$

where the extra context argument place is dropped. Since there is nothing but syntax and part meanings in context that is the arguments of the ec-composition function g, ec-compositionality is in one sense closer to compositionality for standing meaning.[12] Other things equal, ec-compositionality embodies a simpler method of determination of the occasion meaning of a compound than e-compositionality, and is therefore in general preferable. However, it is an open question whether an ec-compositional semantics can be given

---

[10] In the former case we could have two operations σ_1 and σ_2 such that
$g(\sigma_1, c){\neq}g(\sigma_2, c)$
(where $g(\sigma_1, c)g(\sigma_2, c)$ are functions from n occasion meanings of the parts to an occasion meaning for the compound), and a function h such that
$g(\sigma_1,\ c){=}g(\sigma_2, h(c))$
where the value of h depends only on c, such as mapping the time of c to a time k hours later.

[11] The argument is simple. If substitutivity holds, then it holds for each context c that there is a function g_c such that
$\mu(\sigma(e_1, \ldots e_n),c){=}g_c(\sigma,\mu(e_1, c), \ldots ,\mu(e_1, c))$.
But then there is a function g such that for any c, $g(c){=}g_c$. Such a function g is clearly an e-composition function for μ.

[12] I guess it is ec-compositionality that Recanati (1993: 268) and Crimmins and Perry (1989: 710–11) have in mind when they claim that natural language isn't fully compositional, and that they would agree that it is violated by instances of (CSF) below.

whenever an e-compositional semantics is available. Maybe in some cases that possibility is blocked.[13]

The example above, with variation in occasion meaning of the sentence 'it rains' without any corresponding variation in occasion meaning of the parts, is not a violation of e-compositionality, since it is allowed that the context influences occasion meaning over and above its influence on part meanings. However, it *is* a violation of ec-compositionality. It instantiates what we can call *the schema of context shift failure*: where $e_1, \ldots, e_n$ are the immediate constituents of A, we have

(CSF)　$\mu(e_i, c_1) = \mu(e_i, c_2)$, for $1 \leq i \leq n$, and $\mu(A, c_1) \neq \mu(A, c_2)$.

(CSF) provides an independent method of failing ec-compositionality.[14] Thus, the suggested semantics for 'it rains' violates ec-compositionality in a way clearly different from that of substitution failure.

Not many would accept the above view of the semantics of 'it rains', and for good reasons. The present tense in 'rains' is an explicitly context sensitive device, similar to referring indexicals. And we can characterize the meaning of the present tense form of the verb 'to sleep' by saying

[13] What is the relation between the compositionality for standing meaning and for occasion meaning? Given a meaning function μ for occasion meaning we can form a function μ' from expressions to functions h, where each function h applied to a context delivers an occasion meaning. This is done simply by functional abstraction on the context variables c and e, in that order. Thus the function $\lambda e(\lambda c(\mu(e, c)))$ is such that

$\lambda e(\lambda c(\mu(e, c)))(e_1) = \lambda c(\mu(e_1, c))$

It is natural to conclude that $\lambda e(\lambda c(\mu(e, c)))$ maps expressions on standing meanings, for standing meanings are precisely such functions. However, a radical contextualist denies that there are standing meanings. According to the radical thesis, we only have occasion meaning and no general understanding of an expression by which we know what its occasion meaning in a particular context is. Linguistic meaning is then completely particularist, and we don't know how to explain that two persons generally agree on what occasion meaning an expression has in a new context. But if radical contextualism is false, $\lambda e(\lambda c(\mu(e, c)))$ will (normally) be a meaning function mapping expressions on standing meanings. We can then ask about the relation between compositionality for standing meanings and e- and ec-compositionality for occasion meaning. The answer is that compositionality for occasion meaning, e- or ec-, implies compositionality for standing meaning, and that the converse does not hold (see Appendix 1).

[14] To prove independence, let L be the set of expressions $\{e_1, e_2, \sigma(e_1, e_1), \sigma(e_1, e_2), \sigma(e_2, e_1), \sigma(e_2, e_2)\}$. Let μ be such that $\mu(e_1, c_1) = \mu(e_1, c_2), \mu(e_2, c_1) = \mu(e_2, c_2), \mu(e_1, c_1) \neq \mu(e_2, c_1), \mu(e_1, c_2) \neq \mu(e_2, c_2), \mu(\sigma(e_1, e_2), c_1)) \neq \mu(\sigma(e_1, e_2), c_2))$. Then μ instantiates the schema of context shift failure but not the schema of substitution failure. For the other direction, let μ be such that $\mu(e_1, c_1) \neq \mu(e_1, c_2), \mu(e_2, c_1) \neq \mu(e_2, c_2), \mu(e_1, c_1) \neq \mu(e_2, c_2), \mu(e_2, c_1) \neq \mu(e_1, c_2), \mu(e_1, c_1) = \mu(e_2, c_1), \mu(\sigma(e_1, e_2), c_1)) \neq \mu(\sigma(e_2, e_2), c_1))$. Then μ instantiates the schema of substitution failure but not the schema of context shift failure.

'sleeps' is true of an object a at a time t iff a sleeps at t.

Following this pattern, we characterize the standing meaning of an expression by specifying its *extension* in a context c, or at a time t, for variable c and t, or the condition for belonging to this extension. A necessary and sufficient condition for belonging to the extension of 'sleeps' at a time t is that of sleeping at t.

We should now take account of the corresponding context sensitivity in the standing meaning of present tense 'rains'. For the purposes of the present discussion, let's first assume that the standing meaning of 'rains' is given by

(9) 'rains' is true of a time t iff it rains (somewhere) at t.

Let's say further simply that the standing meaning of impersonal 'it' is the identity function applied to contexts, that is

(10) for any context c, $(\mu(\text{'it'}))(c)=c$

(for a different treatment, see Appendix 2). The composition rule for impersonal 'it'+present tense feature placing verb phrase can then be given as

(11) 'it'⌢ Present(Φ) is true in a context c iff *mPhi* is true of all relevant elements of $(\mu(\text{'it'}))(c)$.

where 'Present' operates on a verb to give the present tense. Since by (9) the element of a context c that is relevant to 'rains' is just the time of c, (9), (10), and (11) combine to give

(12) 'it rains' is true in a context c iff it rains (somewhere) at the time of c,

or, after simplification,

(12') 'it rains' is true at a time t iff it rains (somewhere) at t.

With (12) we give the standing meaning of 'it rains' by specifying, for any time t, the condition for the sentence to be true at t. In order to complete the account, we need to provide a principle determining the content of an utterance of 'it rains'. So we add

(UC) The content of an utterance of a sentence s in a context c is given by specifying the conditions under which s is true in c.

(UC) is somewhat imprecise, since there is no mention of how the truth conditions should be specified, but I'll presently leave that difficulty aside, together with further questions about indirect speech acts and other complications.

Assuming that we can extract a time t from a context c as the time of that context, we combine (12) and (UC) to arrive at

> (13) the content of an utterance of 'it rains' in a context c is that it rains at the time of c,

or, simplifying with the assumption that the time of c is the time of utterance,

> (13′) the content of an utterance of 'it rains' at a time t is that it rains at t.

However, this brings us to a point parallel to Fodor's. For (13) and (13′) are obviously false. Uncontroversially, the correct clause is

> (14) the content of an utterance of 'it rains' in a context c is that it rains at the time of c at the location of c.

Assuming that (12) gives us the full *standing* meaning of 'it rains', it follows that the standing meaning is not enough to generate the utterance content, at least not by means of a principle like (UC). Again assuming (UC), we have to conclude that beside the standing meaning of 'it rains' there must be variable meanings to fill the gap. We will need one meaning for each location l, thus replacing (12) with

> (12_1) 'it rains'$_1$ is true at a time t iff it rains at l_1 at t
> (12_2) 'it rains'$_2$ is true at a time t iff it rains at l_2 at t
> .
> .
> .

Assuming that (9) and (10) are correct, that is, give us the standing meanings of impersonal 'it' and of 'rains', respectively, this again gives us a violation of *ec*-compositionality. For the occasion meaning of 'it rains' will be different at different locations, even though there is no change in occasion meanings of parts, nor of syntax.

In order to avoid this, we would need to get (14) with the help of (UC) while only relying on the standing meaning of 'it rains'.[15] And for this we would

---

[15] An alternative is to reject (UC), and replace it with a principle according to which there is a *pragmatic* addition to the content which brings in dependence on location. You can then keep (12). What is literally said by means of 'it rains', on this view, is that it rains somewhere at the time of utterance. It is implicated, and thus communicated, but not literally said, that

need as the standing meaning of 'it rains' something like Davidson proposed almost thirty years ago:

(15) 'it rains' is true as uttered by S at t iff it rains near S at t

(Davidson, 1967: 34; 1974: 135).[16] There are three obvious alternatives for deriving a clause like (15). The two first alternatives amount to replacing (9) as the clause for 'rains', and the third is to replace (11) as the compositional clause. Making the variables explicit, the first alternative gives us

(16) 'rains(x, y)' is true of a time t and a location l iff it rains at t at l

by which 'rains' is a two-place predicate with context sensitive standing meaning, true of times and locations. The second gives us

(17) 'rains(x)' is true of a time t at a location l iff it rains at t at l.

On this alternative 'rains' is a one-place predicate with context sensitive standing meaning, true of times *at* locations. The difference between being true *of* a location and being true *at* a location reflects the presence and absence, respectively, of a location argument in the predicate. Suppose we identify occasion meaning with occasion *extension*. That is, we assume that the extension of the predicate in a context is its occasion meaning in that context. We also assume that we get the occasion extension by assigning values to syntactic context variables. On these assumptions, the occasion meaning of 'rains(x,y)', according to (16), is a truth value (or something equivalent, like the universal or empty set of assignments), whereas the occasion meaning of 'rains(x)' according to (17) is a function from locations to truth values (or something equivalent). In both cases, the occasion meaning is context dependent. In the latter case, the occasion meaning *itself* (under the assumptions) is context sensitive, that is, yields a further value as applied to a context. If this description is right, we need three levels of meaning, where the first, standing meaning, is at most context sensitive, the second, occasion meaning, can be both context sensitive and context dependent, and the third, for which a name is wanting, is at most context dependent. Alternatively (and this is the view I shall settle for), one can take the view that the semantics of 'rains(x)' according to (17) is the same

it rains at the location of the speaker. This view is defended by Emma Borg (2004). Concerning my views on the semantics/pragmatics distinction, see s. 7.

[16] Davidson's clause simplifies matters by assuming that the contextually salient time and location of an utterance is the time and location of that utterance.

as that of 'rains(x,y)' according to (16), and that the difference is *only* syntactic.

The third alternative is to replace (11) by for example

(18) 'it'⁀Present (Φ) is true in a context c iff *mPhi* is true at l of all relevant elements of $(\mu(\text{'it'}))(c)$.

Here, the context sensitivity is introduced in the composition rule itself.

As it happens, none of these three alternatives is uncontroversial. The first method runs counter to pre-theoretic intuitions about syntax, for there does not seem to be anything in 'rains' that registers contextually salient location. The third method, to introduce context sensitivity in the composition rule, may be claimed to violate compositionality, the reason being that in a compositional semantics, the rules must not be context sensitive. Construed in one way, this claim is correct, construed in others incorrect.[17] But even in a framework where the claim is wrong, it is a problem that (18) relies on the assumption that what it is for Φ to be true *at* l is well-defined, and typically this is defined only in clauses like (17). Similarly, (17) requires that truth at l is an argument or a condition in the corresponding composition rule. Normally, then, (17) and (18) are applied together, which leaves us with only two alternatives. However, there is an argument in the recent literature, due to Jason Stanley (2000), that context sensitivity must be carried by an element in

---

[17] The rule (18) introduces an extra context dependence in the occasion meaning of an 'it'+verb compound. For instance, the truth value in a context of such a sentence will, because of this rule, depend on location. In virtue of this, (18) also introduces an extra context sensitivity in the standing meaning of sentences of this kind. Does such a rule violate compositionality? It does not violate compositionality for standing meaning, since standing meaning is allowed to be context sensitive and since the syntactic operation is an argument to the composition function anyway. Neither does it violate *e*-compositionality for occasion meaning, since according to (*e*-comp), the composition function does take an extra context argument, depending or not depending on the syntactic operation. However, it does violate *ec*-compositionality, since (*ec*-comp) does not allow the composition function to depend on context for more than what serves to determine the occasion meaning of the parts. That composition rules 'must not vary with context' is a condition stated in Stanley, 2000: 395. It is further claimed in Stanley and Szabo, 2001: 255–6 that a certain form of semantics for effecting quantifier domain restriction fails to meet this condition. That claim is rejected as incorrect in Pelletier, 2003: 153–6. However, since neither party of the debate clearly distinguishes between context dependence and context sensitivity, nor between different versions of compositionality for context dependence, it may well be that both are right in their way and that Pelletier misinterprets. On the other hand, Stanley and Szabo (2001: 255) incorrectly present the rule (43*b*) as context dependent; the real composition rule in that case is simply functional application, which itself is context invariant.

the syntax. In a weak sense, this is what is required by *ec*-compositionality: all context dependence must be traceable ultimately to lexical meaning of atomic parts. However, Stanley means this in a stronger sense: to each dependence on a context element there must correspond, in logical form, a unique syntactic variable. If Stanley's argument for this claim if successful, it rules out the second and third alternatives. The remainder of this chapter is concerned with this argument and its motivation.

4 Stanley on Unarticulated Constituents

In his paper 'Context and Logical Form', Jason Stanley presents three alternative ways of drawing a semantics/pragmatics distinction, or three different usages of the terms 'semantic' and 'pragmatic'. According to the first (Stanley, 2000: 393), semantics is the study of context invariant aspects of meaning. On this conception, the *semantic content* (Stanley's term) of two different utterances of a sentence like 'I am tired' is the same. According to the corresponding use of 'pragmatic', pragmatics is the study of those aspects of communication that depend on context, including the assignment of reference to indexicals.

According to the second usage (2000: 393–4), semantics is concerned both with context invariant meaning *plus* the assignment of denotations to elements of the logical form, including indexicals. Pragmatics is concerned with further aspects of utterance content, which an interpreter arrives at by way of applying conversational maxims.

On the third usage (2000: 394), semantics is concerned with the primary assignment of *truth conditions* to a sentence, relative to a context of utterance. Pragmatics is concerned with the further process of taking those truth conditions of a linguistic act as input, to yield other propositions implicated by that speech act as output.

Stanley himself favours the second way of drawing a semantics/pragmatics distinction. However, he also claims, as a positive thesis (2000: 395), that the second and the third distinctions *coincide*. That is, Stanley's thesis is that standing meaning plus assignment of reference to elements of logical form is both necessary and sufficient for determining the truth conditions of an utterance relative to a context. This thesis amounts to a wholesale rejection both of non-sentential utterances with truth-conditional content, and of so called *unarticulated constituents*.

The term 'unarticulated constituent' was introduced by John Perry (1986: 206), although a related idea can be found in Frege.[18] Perry was followed by Mark Crimmins (1992) and François Recanati (1993, 2002), among others. The definition, as given by Stanley (2000: 410) runs:

> x is an unarticulated constituent of an utterance u iff (1) x is an element supplied by the context to the truth-conditions of u, and (2) x is not the semantic value of any constituent of the logical form of the sentence uttered.

Although this formulation suggests that truth conditions are treated as structured entities with identifiable elements as constituents,[19] it seems not to be what Stanley has in mind, since he regards the following as a standard unarticulated constituent clause (2000: 415):

> R: "It is raining(t)" is true in a context c if and only if the denotation of "rains" takes $\langle t,l \rangle$ to the True, where l is the contextually salient location in c.

This indicates that for being an element supplied by the context to the truth conditions to an utterance, it is enough that reference to that element is required in *stating* the truth conditions. Clause R is taken to give the logical form of 'it is raining', making it explicit that there is a variable for time, but no variable for location. The relevant dependence on the contextally salient location is made explicit only in the meta-language, where there is both a

---

[18] In 'The Thought', Frege says 'If a time indication is needed by the present tense one must know when the sentence was uttered to apprehend the thought correctly. Therefore the time of utterance is part of the expression of the thought. If someone wants to say the same today as he expressed yesterday using the word "today", he must replace his word with "yesterday". Although the thought is the same its verbal expression must be different so that the sense, which would otherwise be affected by the differing times of utterance, is readjusted. The case is the same with words like "here" and "there". In all such cases the mere wording, as it is given in writing, is not the complete expression of the thought, but the knowledge of certain accompanying conditions of utterance, which are used as means of expressing the thought, are needed for its correct apprehension' (1918: 24). On a plausible interpretation, Frege is here arguing from (*ec*-) compositionality to a kind of non-linguistic articulation: the expression of the thought must include as much as is needed for avoiding to instantiate the schema of context shift failure.

[19] Perry's view in this connection is that propositions do have the objects, relations, etc. they are about as constituents. See Perry, 1986: 207. It should also be noted that Perry more recently (2001: 47–8) has distanced himself from Stanley's notion of an unarticulated constituent. As Perry explains it, unarticulated constituents are argument roles of relations that are not represented by explicit argument places or variables in the expressions of those relations.

time and a location variable. Davidson's clause (15) also counts as of the unarticulated constituent variety, provided that the object language sentence is given in logical form. In that case, assuming that in logical form context sensitivity is articulated by a variable, both time and location are unarticulated in Davidson's case.

Consistent with his general view, Stanley thinks that 'it rains' in logical form does have both a time and a location variable, so that, at least, it should be given as 'it rains(t, l)' (actually, as we shall see in section 7, it is more complex). Contrary to the time variable, which is reflected in the tense of the surface form, the location variable is unexpressed in the simple

(3) it rains

whereas it is made explicit in surface form by means of the indexical 'here' in

(4) it rains here

where the indexical fills the argument place. In both cases context supplies a location as a value to a syntactic element, visible in (4) but invisible in (3).

Moreover, Stanley has a general argument for this view and against semantic clauses of the unarticulated constituent kind, and he exemplifies it by means of (3). The argument turns on the phenomenon of *binding*. The sentence

(19) Every time John lights a cigarette, it rains

has, as Stanley points out (2001: 415–16), as one natural reading

(20) For every time t at which John lights a cigarette, it rains at t at the location in which John lights a cigarette at t.

The problem for an unarticulated constituent analysis, according to Stanley, is that this reading is unavailable. The only reading available on this analysis is (2001: 416):

(21) For every time t at which John lights a cigarette, the denotation of "rains" takes takes $\langle t,l \rangle$ to the True, where l is the contextually salient location in c.

This claim about clause R in relation to sentence (19) is correct, as far as I understand, and just about refutes it.

As Stanley points out, semantically, the location variable for 'it rains' is *bound* in (19). Stanley explains binding as follows (2001: 412): 'Let us say that α semantically binds β if and only if the interpretation of β systematically depends on the values introduced by α', which seems adequate for present purposes. Further, it is Stanley's view that an interpretation by which semantic binding takes place reflects the occurrence of *syntactic* binding, that is, the occurrence of variables and corresponding variable binding operators in the syntax. This seems to be the import of his *Binding Assumption* (2001: 412). As I understand it, Stanley takes this view to be confirmed by the failure of R to deliver the proper bound reading of (19).

However, in a brief passage, Stanley does concede the possibility of an account by which 'the semantic elements corresponding to bound variables can be supplied by the semantics, with no corresponding syntactic elements denoting them' (2001: 413), and credits Jeff King with the point. I am going to propose precisely such a semantic account. That is, I shall attempt to refute Stanley's *binding* argument against unarticulated constituent analyses by providing such an analysis that can deliver the desired reading of (19). This semantics will be somewhat more complex, allowing binding of context variables in the semantic meta-language.

The main ideas of this account will be presented in section 6, and the full semantics is given in Appendix 2. In section 7 I shall compare the proposed semantics with Stanley's own account, and also locate the issue in the broader setting of natural language compositionality and the semantics/pragmatics distinction. In the next section, however, I shall briefly discuss a response given to Stanley's argument from binding by Recanati.

5 Digression: Recanati on the Argument from Binding

In his response to Stanley, Recanati makes three major claims. First, Stanley, Perry, and others have concentrated on the wrong kind of examples: true unarticulated constituents are not required at all for expressing a complete proposition, but are optional. Second, Stanley's *binding* argument is fallacious, since as stated it will overgenerate variables, that is, prove that there must be variables in logical form where it is obvious that none is required. Third, even when properly restricted, the argument from binding doesn't work, which is demonstrated by Recanati's own semantic account of the binding phenomena.

In Recanati's first example (2002: 300), a speaker is asked whether he is hungry, and replies

(22) I've had a very large breakfast.

The conversational implicature is that the speaker is not hungry, and for that to come across the speaker must have stated, by means of (22), that he had a large breakfast on the day of utterance, even though no time is assigned to the breakfast event in the sentence itself. The time is then supplied by context, and it is a *true* unarticulated constituent, in Recanati's sense. The reason it qualifies is that the additional supply of time is a *free enrichment*, one that is not made obligatory by anything in the sentence. The sentence itself is adequate for expressing the less specific proposition that the speaker has had a large breakfast at some time or other.

Other examples involve sentences that *require* completion for the expression of a proposition, such as

(23) Gentlemen prefer blondes

(to *x*, for some *x*; the example, in Recanati (2002: 309) is taken over from Bach, 1994: 268–9). In cases like this, Recanati says, there is a sense in which the contextually provided element *is* articulated, namely in the sense that an expression in the sentence triggers the search for some completing entity.

That was also the case with Perry's original example, the sentence 'It is raining'. According to Perry, no proposition is expressed with this sentence, unless a location is contextually provided (Recanati, 2002: 309, 316; Perry, 1986: 206). In Recanati's sense, the location is on this view not a true unarticulated constituent, but 'is really the value of a hidden variable' (2002: 316). However, Recanati does think that 'It is raining' *can* be used for saying simply that it is raining somewhere or other, that is, for saying something true or false even if no location is provided, and imagines a context in which that will be natural (2002: 317).[20] On this view, the supply of location is optional, hence truly unarticulated. The example of 'it rains' can therefore still be used.

It is not completely clear whether Recanati wishes to change the *terminology*, so that something should (truly) be called 'articulated' just if it must be provided for the expressing of a proposition, whether or not there is a variable in the syntax that takes it as value, or whether he sticks with the accepted definition and pushes the *thesis* that whenever some value must be provided, then there in fact is a corresponding variable in the syntax. This question does not, however, matter for his further comments on Stanley.

---

[20] The story is that rain detectors have been installed all over a territory, or the whole Earth, such that each triggers a bell in some central Monitoring Room when detecting rain. Upon hearing the bell, the operator may say 'It is raining', meaning that it is raining at some place or other (2002: 317).

Recanati's second claim is that Stanley's binding criterion of articulatedness is misguided, for it can be applied also to cases where it is clear that there is no hidden argument. Recanati takes the sentence

(24) The policeman stopped the car

(2002: 325, taken over from Rumelhart, 1979: 78). There is a natural tendency to interpret an utterance of this sentence as meaning that the policeman stopped the car by means of a signal to the driver. However, with some additional contextual information, such as that the policeman was driving the car, we will assume that he stopped it in a different way. What we get from the sentence itself is only that the policeman stopped the car in some way or other. Recanati claims, plausibly, that any extra assumption about the manner of stopping interpreted as expressed by an utterance of it, is nothing but an optional pragmatic embellishment, corresponding to nothing in the semantics, and that this is quite uncontroversial. Yet, he says, if the argument from binding is valid, we will get the absurd consequence that (24) has a hidden variable for manner. For we can say

(25) However he did it, the policeman stopped the car

or

(26) In some way or other, the policeman stopped the car.

The meaning, in both cases, is that given by

(27) For some manner of stopping m, the policeman stopped the car in manner m.

This argument is elegant if correct, but it is not obviously correct. In a case of binding, when an argument place has been made explicit by means of a bindable indexical (such as 'he', 'she', 'it', 'that'), that indexical gets bound when made anaphoric on an appropriate quantifier. For instance, 'it' in

(28) Gizella smiles at it

gets bound in

(29) Whichever animal she encounters, Gizella smiles at it.

And 'that place' in

(30) It rains in that place

gets bound in

(31) Wherever I go, it rains in that place.

By contrast, 'that way' in

(32) The policeman stopped the car in that way

does not seem to get bound in

(33) However he did it, the policeman stopped the car in that way

or in

(34) In some way or other, the policeman stopped the car in that way.

Rather, (33) and (34) are odd, or at best interpreted as quantifying over sub-manners to a manner referred to by 'that way'.[21] It is therefore not obvious that the argument from binding works for manner *if* it works for location.[22]

Recanati's third claim is that, although binding indeed does occur in

(19) Every time John lights a cigarette, it rains

he has an unarticulated constituent analysis that accounts for it. The flaw in Stanley's argument, according to Recanati (2002: 328–9) is the assumption that it is the *same* sentence of the surface form 'it rains' that occurs in (19) as occurs isolated. On Recanati's account, there is an ambiguity: 'It rains' as occurring in (19) does have a location variable, whereas 'it rains' as occurring in isolation doesn't. Recanati compares this ambiguity with that between the transitive and the intransitive verb 'eat'. The intransitive verb is a one-place

---

[21] Unless I misrepresent her, I owe this argument to Elisabeth Engdahl, who used it much the same way against Ernie Lepore at the Stockholm–Rutgers conference of cognitive science, June 2003. Note that although 'For some manner, the policeman stopped the car in that manner' is well-formed, this is irrelevant. It would be relevant only if 'For some manner, the policeman stopped the car' were also well-formed, so that this latter sentence were a candidate for covert binding.

[22] A similar counter-argument is proposed by Cappelen and Lepore (2002: 273). According to Cappelen and Lepore, one could apply the same argument from binding to the sentence

(*) Everywhere I go, 2+2=4,

getting the reading 'For all places x, I go to x, 2+2=4 at x', demonstrating the existence of a hidden location variable in '2+2=4'. Since this is absurd, the binding argument is refuted, according to Cappelen and Lepore. The problem with this argument is that there is a crucial difference between (*) and Stanley's (19). In (19) the two interpretations, with a bound and with a free location variable, can have different truth values, confirming the hypothesis that the truth value depends on the value of the location parameter. In (*), this is not the case. Hence, although (*) is grammatical, it has not been shown that there is a semantic location dependence.

predicate true of eaters, whereas the transitive verb is a two-place predicate true of eaters and what is eaten.

On Recanati's account you can generate new predicates with an increased or decreased number of argument places by means of so-called *variadic functions*. In the increase case, this is represented by means of a family of operators called 'Circ'. It is exemplified (2002: 321) with the adding of a location argument to the intransitive 'eat':

$$\text{Circ}_{\text{location}}(\text{Eats}(x)) = \text{Eats\_in}(x, l)$$

The prepositional phrase 'in Paris' adds a location argument to the verb in this manner, but it also contributes Paris as the *value* of the location variable. This is represented as

$$\text{Circ}_{\text{location:Paris}}(\text{Eats}(\text{John})) = \text{Eats\_in}(\text{John}, \text{Paris})$$

In simplified notation this can be rendered as

⟨In Paris⟩ (John eats)

where the angular brackets indicate that the location assignment is optional (2002: 330).

In the case of binding, quantifier phrases can achieve the same as the prepositional phrase above. Thus 'everywhere I go' both contributes a location variable and *binds* that variable.

(35) Everywhere I go, it rains

is analyzed as

(36) [For every place l such that I go to l] (in l (it rains))

(2002: 330). On this analysis, 'it rains' as occurring in (35) corresponds to the formula '(in l (it rains))' in the logical form, and thus has a location variable. The simple sentence 'it rains', as used in isolation, corresponds to the proper constituent of that formula which does not contain the variable. This makes the ambiguity explicit.[23]

In Stanley's (19) it is more complex, since the location variable is not introduced by a location quantifier but as a function of time introduced by

---

[23] Recanati has commented (personal communication) that in the article he expressed himself misleadingly on this point. His real view is that the overt 'it rains' always corresponds to the proper part with the same wording in 'in l (it rains)'. His claim should then be rendered simply as the claim that the location variable is optional; i.e. 'it rains' sometimes occurs and sometimes does not occur with a location variable, whether overt or covert.

a time quantifier. The way to supply a location argument and the location value as a function of time is therefore

⟨ in location $f(t)$⟩ (it rains)

(2002: 333), and the full analysis comes out as

(37) [For every t such that John lights a cigarette at t] (at t ⟨in $\imath l$:John lights a cigarette in l at t⟩) (it rains)

(2002: 334, where '$\imath$' is a description operator; Recanati actually applies the analysis to 'Everywhere I sing, it rains', rather than to (19)).[24]

This is an interesting account, and when properly worked out might well result in a plausible semantics. However, this is not enough for Recanati's purpose, since there is a problem with the further claim that it saves the unarticulated constituent analysis. That claim depends on the positive thesis of ambiguity (or optionality), while the semantics itself is independent of this thesis, since it is possible that even isolated occurrences of 'it rains' should be analyzed as having the form '(in l (it rains)'. In fact, there is reason to think that this is the case (in Recanati's framework). For it seems that even when 'it rains' is used in the supposed non-locating sense (to boost your intuitions, consult n. 20), anaphoric reference to location is possible. In the examples

(38) It rains. John wants to go there.
(39) Whenever it rains, John wants to go there.

we seem to get exactly the same readings as in

(40) It rains somewhere. John wants to go there.
(41) Whenever it rains somewhere, John wants to go there.

(40) and (41) are straightforward cases of cross sentence and donkey anaphora, respectively, to be treated by your favorite account[25] as having the bound readings

(40′) There is a location l such that it rains in l and John wants to go to l.

---

[24] Recanati is seriously worried by the fact that a bound variable occurs in the representation of the unarticulated constituent, i.e. within the angular brackets, since 'a variable has got to be articulated . . . for variables are *linguistic expressions*' (2002: 335, italics in original). This I find hard to understand. Bound variables are part of our way to *represent* dependencies. Either Recanati has confused the representation of dependence with the dependence itself, or else there is more to the idea of an unarticulated constituent than I have understood so far.

[25] For instance, PFO. See Pagin and Westerståhl, 1993.

(41′) For any location l, whenever it rains in l, John wants to go to l.

Since Recanati's account does not offer any other way to supply the bound reading of 'there' than making it anaphoric on a noun phrase antecedent, his only option is to treat 'it rains' in (38) and (39) as elliptical for 'it rains somewhere'. On Recanati's account this is analyzed as

(42) [For some location l] (in l (it rains)).

Finally, it seems that such anaphoric back reference is always possible, and if this is true, then on Recanati's own account, all isolated occurrences of non-locating 'it rains' have the form of (42). Hence, the argument free version of 'it rains' is never actually encountered in natural English, but only the prefixed form '(in l (it rains))', with or without existential closure. Again, if this is right, Recanati's ambiguity claim (or optionality claim) is false. His account does not save the unarticulated constituent analysis.

6 Quantifying over Contexts

In this section I shall briefly set out the idea by which the bound readings of (19) and similar sentences can be produced by a semantics of the unarticulated constituent type. First, as was done in Kaplan (1989) and in Montague (1968, 1970a) we can model contexts as sequences of context elements, or equivalently as assignments of values to a set of context parameters. For any context c, the associated model will contain as elements, to begin with, the speaker of c, if any, the addressee, if any, the (contextually salient) time of c, the location. The context model must be so well-defined that projection functions can be applied to contexts. That is, we can have a function $\mathrm{Sp}(c)$ which returns the speaker of context c, and $\mathrm{Ad}(c)$ the addressee of c, if any. $\mathrm{T}(c)$ is the time of c, and $\mathrm{L}(c)$ is the location of c. One cannot take for granted that every context returns a value to every projection function. For instance, we may need, as David Kaplan has emphasized, to take account of contexts where no utterance is made, and so there is no speaker. The projection functions must therefore be partial.

What is supposed to be included in contexts? As I see it, the context includes anything over and above the sentence (actually or potentially) uttered that is available and may be employed for achieving communicative success. It is not likely that a definitive list of potentially relevant context features can be produced, and things will get much worse if we include in contexts what is needed for pragmatic phenomena like conversational implicature. For the the more limited concerns of the fragment treated in Appendix 2, we will still need more than what is suggested so far. For instance, we will need a function (call it 'TopMale$_i(c)$') that for a given context c delivers the i:th most salient male of c, intended to provide a referent to an occurrence of unbound 'he' or 'him'. Similarly for 'she' and 'her'. The appendix also suggests a function $D_i(c)$ for handling contextual quantifier domain restriction. Cf Appendix 2.[26]

A context variable 'c' is an individual variable of the semantic metalanguage. It can be bound by quantifiers in the meta-language, and this is used for handling expressions that quantify over context elements, such as 'every time'. At first we could try

(t) 'Everytime' $^\frown s$ is true iff for every context c s is true at $T(c)$.

This is okay, except that the original sentence, 'Everytime' $^\frown s$, might itself be context sensitive, and will in that case be evaluated relative to a context c. In that case, 'everytime' introduces quantification over contexts c' that differ from c with respect to time but not in other respects. This will make the treatment parallel to the handling of assignments in first-order semantics:

(tc) 'Everytime' $^\frown s$ is true at c iff for every context $c' \approx c/t$, s is true at c'

where '$c' \approx c/t$' is to be read as 'context c' differs from context c at most with respect to time'. In this case time will vary but, for example, location will be constant across the contexts c'.

However, to get the desired reading for Stanley's (19), we need to let location vary *together* with time. That is, we need to consider the location of each context c' where the embedded sentence is true, not just the time of c'. We can call this *concomitant* variation of context elements. Notationally, the change is small:

(tcl) 'Everytime' $^\frown s$ is true at c iff for every context $c' \approx c/t+l$, s is true at c'

where we consider all contexts c' differing from c at most with respect to time *and* location. The addition of the location variable simply reflects the

---

[26] It is a further interesting question whether contexts should be seen as subjective or intersubjective. Sometimes communication fails because of a mismatch in attention between speaker and hearer. A salience function like TopMale$_1(c)$ might then deliver a different value for the speaker and for the hearer, implying that the speaker context is different from the hearer context. At other times we might explain communicative success by reference to intersubjectively salient features of the environment.

availability of the corresponding reading of (19). Other variables may be added to the extent this is interpretationally adequate.

To get the bound reading of (19) we need a *locating* reading of its antecedent,

(43) John lights a cigarette

that is, the reading under which

(44) 'John lights a cigarette' is true at c iff John lights a cigarette at $T(c)$ at $L(c)$

as opposed to a non-locating reading where only $T(c)$ matters. Let's assume the locating reading and that (19) is to be interpreted as a quantified conditional:

(45) 'Everytime' ⌢ 'if John lights a cigarette, then it rains'

we get

(46) 'Everytime' ⌢ 'if John lights a cigarette, then it rains' is true at c iff for every context $c' \approx c/t+l$, 'if John lights a cigarette, then it rains' is true at c'.

With the locating reading we will get (after a number of recursive steps in the semantics)

'if John lights a cigarette, then it rains' is true at c' iff
(if John lights a cigarett at $T(c')$ at $L(c')$, then it rains at $T(c')$ at $L(c')$).

Making use of this equivalence in (46) we finally get

(47) 'Everytime' ⌢ 'if John lights a cigarette, then it rains' is true in c iff for every context $c' \approx c/t+l$, if John lights a cigarette at $T(c')$ at $L(c')$, then it rains at $T(c')$ at $L(c')$.

This seems to be (a semi-formal rendering of) the desired reading of (19). It *is* the desired reading provided we get the quantification over contexts right. But by (47) we only take into account contexts c' which share other features with c, such as perhaps that of having Elsa as the most salient female, a feature irrelevant to the interpretation of (19). This runs the risk of getting the truth conditions of (19) wrong, for the relation between rain and John's lightings of cigarettes is supposed to hold also in contexts where Elsa isn't the most salient female.

This complication parallels the situation in first-order truth definitions where we need to show that a particular assignment satisfies a closed sentence s iff *a*ll assignments satisfy s. More generally, an assignment f satisfies a formula φ iff *mphi* is satisified by any assignment f' differing from f at most with respect to variables not free in φ. Analogously, it will hold for *truth-in-a-context* that if the truth of s in c does *not* depend on some context element $P(c)$, then s is true in c iff s is true in any context c' differing from c at most with respect to P. Whether the truth of s *does* depend on P is determined by the semantic clauses. Where $I(s)$ is the set of context elements irrelevant to the evaluation of s, we will have in general

(I) s is true in c iff for all $c' \approx c/I(s)$, s is true in c'

Because (I) is true, we can be sure that if a statement like (47) is true of a particular context c, it will be true of all contexts c' differing from c at most with respect to $I(s)$. Hence the truth conditions will not be wrong.

For the complete outline of the context semantics, see Appendix 2.

7 Concluding Remarks

Since the context semantics proposed is of the unarticulated constituent variety, and since it does deliver the reading claimed by Stanley to be outside the reach of semantics of that kind, the claim is refuted. This does not, however, imply, that this context semantics is the right or best theory, or even better than Stanley's own proposal.

Stanley suggests that in logical form 'rain' is

(48) $\text{rain}(f(x), g(y))$

such that one argument gives time and the other location (Stanley, 2000: 416). Context supplies the values both to individual variables and function variables. In the normal case, the individual values are the salient time and location of the utterance, respectively, and the functions simply identity functions. For the bound reading of (19), Stanley suggests that the location argument gives the time as value to the individual variable and a function from times to locations to the function variable. Since the time variable will be bound by 'every time', the location value will be a function of the time introduced by that same expression, and thus bound by it. In the case of (19), the function is from a time t to the location of John at t.

Clearly, Stanley's proposal delivers the desired reading. The problem is that there is no clear limit to the readings that this framework delivers, since there is no clear limit to the possible values for the variables. Why not a function from a time t to the location where John's *mother* is at t, at least if she is contextually prominent in some way or other? Without a clear criterion of admissibility of values, especially function values, Stanley's account will over-generate readings, and no such criterion is offered.

But even if this objection is correct, some other articulated analysis may do better.[27] Is there in principle any reason to prefer the context semantics offered to any articulated competitor? I think there is a reason, in that speaker intuitions about syntax should count more than speaker intuitions about semantics, and I think speaker intuitions tell against treating 'rain' as a two-place predicate. Similarly, and maybe more obviously, it is strongly counter-intuitive to treat a predicate like 'red' as two-place, taking object and time arguments, even though in the semantics we must treat the corresponding concept as a relation between objects and times, or objects and contexts. I think that speaker intuitions about syntax are closer to how speakers consciously represent facts to themselves, while semantics should correspond to the real relation between the representation and what is represented. Still, even setting aside that I may simply be wrong about what speakers think, their intuitions can be overruled by strong theoretical concerns, and I don't want to place much emphasis on this reason against an articulated analysis. An articulated analysis that delivers the desired readings is on the whole acceptable.

My real concern is not really with the best analysis of (19) and sentences like it, but with the general phenomenon of context sensitivity in sentence meaning, even in case that sensitivity cannot be uniquely traced to particular syntactic constituents. Thus, I am concerned with the viability of the idea of unarticulated constituents, and therefore with the claim that it cannot be applied to 'rains' because of sentences like (19).

Why be concerned with unarticulated constituents? Part of the reason is that I find it extremely implausible that there is a fully articulated sentence, even if only in logical form, whenever a speaker successfully communicates a

---

[27] In fact you get one from the context semantics of Appendix 2 by simply adding a location argument to 'rains(t)' and adjusting the meaning of 'it$_i$' accordingly. Similarly, the time argument may be dropped. Clearly, from the semantic point of view, it does not matter whether time and location variables are in the syntax or not, as long as they are in the semantics. Note that on Stanley's preferred usage (cf. s. 4), the theory is fully semantic only if both variables are in the syntax, and partly pragmatic otherwise.

thought by linguistic means. This is one of Stanley's theses. He spends section 2 of his 2002 on arguing that prima-facie examples of thoughts communicated by means of non-sentential expressions are really examples of ellipsis, so that in each case there is a full sentence the speaker uses for expressing the thought, only that what he actually utters goes proxy for that sentence. I find some of Stanley's examples convincing but others unconvincing. In general, I think it is not too rare that a speaker manages to get across a thought with poor linguistic means, falling far short of what would be needed to get the thought across to an audience less in tune with the speaker. And this happens even in cases where the speaker would need much hard work to produce an adequate, fully articulated sentence. Since I don't have space to go into the matter in any detail, I'll simply assume here that such things happen. That is, I'll assume that pragmatic processes influence primary truth conditions, sometimes in compensation for poor linguistic articulation. This is what King and Stanley (2005) call 'strong pragmatic effects'. Strong pragmatic effects thus include inferential processes that influence primary truth conditions, as well as the presence of unarticulated constituents, for example, as in the context semantics of Appendix 2.

Now, if strong pragmatic effects occur, and if we accept two premises from Stanley, then the result is likely to be a failure of *ec*-compositionality. The first premise is that semantics is concerned with nothing else than context invariant meaning *and* the assignment of denotations to elements of the logical form, including indexicals (Stanley, 2000: 393–4), and the second that semantics is concerned with the primary assignment of truth conditions to a sentence, relative to a context of utterance (Stanley, 2000: 393–4). This does not go as far as the (Rad) thesis of section 3, according to which the (occasion) *meaning* of a sentence is the thought (proposition) it is used to express (since it stops short of conversational implicatures used for deriving secondary truth conditions). However, it goes far enough.

For *if* the occasion meaning of a sentence in a context of utterance is the primary truth condition of the utterance itself, and that results from combining standing part meanings with context dependent part meanings (like reference to indexicals), even though the sentence is too poor to fully articulate those truth conditions and might have been used for conveying a different thought even with the *same* part meanings, then we will have an instance of the schema of context shift failure (cf section 2). That is, the meanings of all the parts of a complex expression e will be the same in two different contexts c_1 and c_2, the mode of combination will be the same, and still e will have a different meaning in c_1 than in c_2. This is a violation of *ec*-compositionality for occasion meaning. It is not bound to happen, but it is likely that it will, given the three premises. We are almost back to Fodor's argument against compositionality of natural language.

What is needed to avoid this conclusion, if one believes in strong pragmatic effects, is a different view of the semantics/pragmatics distinction. I'll conclude with a few words about this. On my view, one major task of the general theory of language is to *explain* why linguistic communication succeeds so frequently, even when performed with new word combinations and between speakers with very little knowledge of each other and with very little help from the context. 'Pragmatics', in a wide sense, may be taken to stand for the general enterprise of understanding utterance content, both from the production side and from the interpretation side, for achieving such an explanation.

It is then, I think, a very plausible empirical *hypothesis* that a successful pragmatic theory, in this wide sense, will include as a proper part a *semantic* theory, that is, a theory relating syntactic parts to entities in a standing, context independent way, where these entities can be objects, properties, relations, functions, truth conditions, or yet something else, and including general principles for assigning some such entities to syntactically complex expressions, as depending on the mode of combination and on what is assigned to the parts. This will be a *semantic* theory provided it does have a uniform explanatory role within the wide pragmatic theory.

A pragmatic theory in the *narrow* sense will be roughly what fills the gap between the wide pragmatic theory and the semantic theory. That is, a narrow pragmatic theory will be concerned with those ingredients in—and factors determining—an utterance content that go beyond what is given by the semantics alone. It will be concerned with general features of communication, independent of any particular lexical or structural properties. It may be a Gricean account or a Relevance theoretic or Optimality theoretic account, or something yet further.

The present conception is closest to Stanley's first usage alternative, according to which semantics is concerned only with context independent meaning (but note that this includes the study of how occasion meaning depends on context). However, there is no assumption here that there must be something like a *semantic content*, in an intuitive sense of 'content', and for which semantics gives a full account. On the present conception, the semantics/pragmatics distinction is of a highly *theoretical* nature; a semantic value does not also have to belong to a phenomenologically real layer of content of an utterance. A claim that something *x* is 'strictly and literally said', or 'literally expressed', as opposed to something y that is implied or implicated in one way or other, does have a clear sense to the extent that x and y are *both* communicated, and y by means of x, but in case x is not itself communicated, the sense is not so clear. It *may* mean that we achieve the simplest overall theory when accounting for x by semantic methods and for y by a combination of semantic and pragmatic methods. But then one runs the risk that 'said' and 'expressed' are simply misnomers.[28]

APPENDIX 1

Assume that we have an e-compositional meaning function $\mu: L \times C \to K$, from expressions in a language L and contexts in a domain C to occasion meanings in a domain K. By functional abstraction over contexts and expressions, in that order, we arrive at a function $\mu' = \lambda e(\lambda c(\mu(e, c)))$. Applied to an expression e_i of L, we have

$$\mu'(e_i) = \lambda e(\lambda c(\mu(e, c)))(e_i) = \lambda c(\mu(e_i, c))$$

by λ-conversion. Assume that $\lambda c(\mu(e_i, c))$ is the standing meaning of e_i, and that for each $e \in L$ we get the standing meaning of e from μ this way. Then $\mu': L \to M$ is a meaning function from L to a domain M of standing meanings that are functions from C to K.

We want to show that if μ is e-compositional, then μ' is compositional. We need to show that there exists a composition function for μ'. By assumption there is one for μ, that is there is a function g such that for any (non-atomic) expression $e = \sigma(e_1, \ldots e_n)$ and any context c,

$$(+)\quad \mu(\sigma(e_1, \ldots e_n), c) = g(\sigma, \mu(e_1, c), \ldots, \mu(e_n, c), c).$$

Since $(+)$ holds for arbitrary c we can abstract over contexts to get

[28] I owe much to comments by readers of the first draft. I am grateful to Emma Borg, Kathrin Glüer, Ernie Lepore, Per Martin-Löf, François Recanati, and Jason Stanley. Ideas in the chapter have been discussed in seminars at the departments of philosophy, linguistics, and English at Stockholm University and the department of linguistics at Uppsala university. Many thanks to participants in those seminars, among others Maria Koptjevskaja-Tamm, Alan McMillion, Roussanka Loukanova, Claus Oetke, Dag Prawitz, Tor Sandqvist, Dag Wester-ståhl, and Åsa Wikforss. The work has been financially supported by the The Bank of Sweden Tercentenary Foundation, for the project *Mening, Kommunikation, Förklaring*.

$(++) \quad \lambda c(\mu(\sigma(e_1, \ldots e_n),c))=\lambda c(g(\sigma,\mu(e_1, c), \ldots ,\mu(e_n, c),c)).$

Note that

(i) $\lambda c(\mu(\sigma(e_1, \ldots e_n)),c))=\mu'(\sigma(e_1, \ldots e_n))$

Second, by λ-conversion it holds for each term '$\mu(e_i, c)$' that

(ii) $\mu(e_i, c)=\lambda c'(\mu(e_i, c'))(c)$

where $\lambda c'(\mu(e_i, c')$ is the standing meaning of e_i, that is,

(iii) $\mu(e_i, c)=\lambda c'(\mu(e_i, c'))(c)=\mu'(e_i)(c)$

Substituting in $(++)$ according to (i), (ii) and (iii) we get

(iv) $\mu'(\sigma(e_1, \ldots e_n)=\lambda c(g(\sigma,\mu'(e_1)(c), \ldots ,\mu'(e_n)(c),c))$

which is a form of (comp), with $\lambda c(g(c))$ as the composition function for μ'. Hence e-compositionality for occasion meaning implies compositionality for standing meaning. Since ec-compositionality implies e-compositionality it also implies compositionality.

The converse does not hold. To show this, let μ be such that

$\mu(e_1, c_1)=\mu(e_2, c_1), \mu(e_1, c_2)\neq\mu(e_2, c_2)$

$\mu(\sigma(e_1, e_2),c_1))\neq\mu(\sigma(e_2, e_2),c_1)).$

Then

$\mu'(e_1)=\lambda c(\mu(e_1, c')\neq\lambda c(\mu(e_2, c')=\mu'(e_2)$

and hence there is no substitution failure for μ'. μ' is therefore compositional. But there is substitution failure for μ, since

$\mu(e_1, c_1)=\mu(e_2, c_1) \quad$ but $\quad \mu(\sigma(e_1, e_2),c_1))\neq\mu(\sigma(e_2, e_2),c_1)).$

Hence compositionality for standing meaning does not imply e- or ec-compositionality for occasion meaning.[29]

Note: A context semantics need not take the standard form that every standing meaning is a function from contexts. For instance, assuming the the meaning of sentences are functions from contexts to truth values, and the meaning of singular terms are functions from contexts to objects, we have interrelated choices for the meaning of predicates and the composition function.

---

[29] These results were reported by Dag Westerståhl at the Stockholm–Rutgers conference on cognitive science, Stockholm June 2003, and the report is independently verified here.

In the standard version, the composition function is as in the proof above, that is, $\lambda c(g(c))$, built from functional application on occasion meanings and abstraction over contexts. The meanings of predicates are then functions from contexts to functions from objects to truth values.

The alternative is to take just functional application as the composition function for standing meanings, and let the meanings of predicates be functions from singular term meanings to sentence meanings. The net result for sentences is the same. On such a simpler approach, only expressions of the basic categories (usually terms and sentences) are of the standard form, that is, functions from contexts to occasion meanings, whereas standing meanings of other types are functions from standing meanings. The context semantics in Appendix 2 is of this simplified kind.

APPENDIX 2

I shall sketch a semantics for context sensitive expressions, whose distinctive feature is that object language quantifiers over context elements, such as 'everytime' or 'everywhere', whose effect is to reduce context sensitivity, are treated semantically by means of quantifying over the contexts themselves, rather than just over the corresponding *elements* of the contexts (time, location). We will then get different readings depending on which context elements are varied and which kept fixed.

Contexts are modelled as ordered *n*-tuples of context elements, as in Kaplan (1989) and as *indices* in Montague (1968, 1970a). Unlike in Kaplan's and Montague's pragmatics, possible worlds are not included as context elements. What is included is anything that is contextually available as guiding communicative efforts. It is assumed that contexts are sufficiently well-defined so that certain projection functions can apply to them: the function T as applied to a context c yields the time of c as value, L the location of c, and S the speaker of c.

What I shall here call 'the meaning' of a sentence is a function from contexts to sets of assignment functions. As the truth definition will show, it is the function which maps a context on the set of assignments under which the sentence is true. As a concept of meaning, this is very meager, since it is not designed to treat intensional phenomena such as modality or propositional attitudes. You can regard it either as a very poor notion of meaning, or as a very rich notion of extension, and in either case as in need of complementing for a full semantic theory. However, I shall also suggest a strengthened version, where the outputs of the meaning function are *structured* meanings.

Since this sketch is only intended to demonstrate the interpretive capacity of context binding, I shall try to keep everything else simple. The fragment will be minimal, and so will the syntax assumed. I shall not spell out the object language syntax more than what can be extracted from the semantic clauses. The theory is only supposed to handle the targeted phenomena of context sensitivity and the reduction of context sensitivity by binding.

Object Language Vocabulary and Syntax
proper names: 'John', 'Elsa'
singular indexicals: 'I', 'me', 'you', 'he', 'him', 'she', 'her', 'it'
impersonal pronoun: 'it'$_i$
intransitive present tense verbs: 'eats', 'sings'
transitive present tense verbs: 'sees', 'loves', 'lights'
feature placing verbs: 'rains', 'snows'
common nouns: 'dog', 'book', 'cigarette'
logical particles: 'and', 'or', 'if, then', 'it is not the case that'
determiners: 'a', 'the', 'every'
adverbial quantifiers: 'every time', 'some time', 'everywhere', 'somewhere'

The syntax is given by simple phrase structure rules in the obvious combinations. Impersonal 'it' only combines with feature placing verbs, and *vice versa.*

However, the semantic meta-language will apply to a *regimented* version of the object language, with individual variables ($x_1, x_2, \ldots$) and argument places for all expressions except singular terms. This will be referred to as 'L'. The feature placing verbs are given a time argument, thus 'rains(t)'. The relation between the regimented and the unregimented version is intuitively clear, and I shall not provide translation rules.

I shall give a denotation to each element of the regimented object language, including variables, so that the form of the semantics conforms to standard statements of compositionality. Syntactic combination will in each case consist in an argument expression's filling a slot in a matrix expression. The corresponding semantic function, that is, the composition function, is simply functional application. This is squarely in the Frege–Church–Montague tradition.

Finally, quantifier domain restriction will be implemented in the form of restrictions on assignments to variables. That is, in a contextually determined domain, variables will only be given values in the domain.

Elements of the Semantics

'[...]' will refer to the meaning function. In general, the meaning of a singular term will be a function from contexts to a function from assignment to objects. The meaning of an intransitive verb will be a function from such term meanings into formula meanings. Formula meanings will be functions from contexts to sets of assignments. And so on.

As usual, the lambda operator 'λ...' will be used for functional abstraction. I shall not set out a special application operator, but simply let the lambda abstracts double as both singular terms and functional expressions, since this will not cause any harm in practice. There is a universe U of individuals, a universe C of contexts, and a universe V of assignments of values in U to variables in L.

The meta-language will contain the following variables and parameters:

$a, a_1, \ldots$ ranging over individuals in U,
$c, c', c'', \ldots, c_1, c_2, \ldots$ ranging over contexts in C,
$t, t', t'', \ldots t_1, t_2, \ldots$ ranging over times in T(C),
$f, f', f'', \ldots, f_1, f_2, \ldots$ ranging over assignments in V,
$m_1, m_2, \ldots$ ranging over meanings of formulas in L,
$u, u_1, u_2, \ldots, v, v_1, v_2, \ldots$ ranging over meanings of singular terms in L,
$b, b_1, b_2, \ldots$ ranging over meanings of variables in L,
$r, r_1, r_2, \ldots$ ranging over meanings of feature placing predicates in L,
$\alpha, \alpha_1, \alpha_2, \ldots$ ranging over variables in L,
'X', 'X_1', 'X_2' ... ranging over sets of context elements,
'i' and 'j' ranging over natural numbers.

There will be some special functions:

Sp(c) gives the speaker of context c, and Ad(c) the addressee of c, if any. T(c) is the time of c, and L(c) is the location of c. C(S,t) is the context determined by speaker S and time t.

TopMale$_i$(c) is a function giving the i-th most salient male of context c. Similarly, we have TopFemale$_i$(c) and TopN$_i$(c) for reference of unbound feminine and neuter pronouns.

D$_i$(c) gives the i-th most salient domain of assignments of context c.

Ind(b) takes the meaning of a variable as input and delivers the index of that variable as output. Thus Ind(['x_1'])$= 1$.

Comp takes a set of assignments into its complement in V.

$f \approx f'/$Ind(b) holds iff assignments f and f' differ at most in what they assign to the variable with the index of b. $c \approx c'/l+X$ holds iff contexts c and c' differ at most with respect to location and the contextual elements of X

(i.e. differ at most with respect to location if $X=\varnothing$). Similarly, $c\approx c'/t+X$ holds iff contexts c and c' differ at most with respect to time and the contextual elements of X.

The meta-linguistic counterparts to lexical elements of the regimented object language will be italicized.

Semantic Clauses

1. $['John']=\lambda c(\lambda f\ (John))$
   $['Elsa']=\lambda c(\lambda f(Elsa))$

2. $['I']=\lambda c(\lambda f(Sp(c)))$ [same for 'me']
   $['you']=\lambda c(\lambda f(Ad(c)))$
   $['he']=\lambda c(\lambda f(\lambda i(TopMale_i(c))))$ [same for 'him']
   $['she']=\lambda c(\lambda f(\lambda i(TopFemale_i(c))))$ [same for 'her']
   $['it']=\lambda c(\lambda f(\lambda i(TopN_i(c))))$

3. $['it_i']=\lambda c(\lambda r(\ (r(c))(T(c))))$

4. $['eats\ (\ldots)']=\lambda u(\lambda c(\{f:eats(\ (u(f))(c),c)\}))$
   $['sings\ (\ldots)']=\lambda u(\lambda c(\{f:sings(\ (u(f))(c),c)\}))$

5. $['sees\ (\ldots,\ldots)']=\lambda u(\lambda v(\lambda c(\{f:sees(\ (u(f))(c),(v(f))(c),c)\})))$
   $['loves\ (\ldots,\ldots)']=\lambda u(\lambda v(\lambda c(\{f:loves(\ (u(f))(c),(v(f))(c),c)\})))$
   $['lights\ (\ldots,\ldots)']=\lambda u(\lambda v(\lambda c(\{f:lights(\ (u(f))(c),(v(f))(c),c)\})))$

6. $['rains(\ldots)']=\lambda c(\lambda t(\{f:rains(t,L(c))\}))$
   $['snows(\ldots)']=\lambda c(\lambda t(\{f:snows(t,L(c))\}))$

7. $['dog(\ldots)']=\lambda u(\lambda c(\{f:dog(\ (u(f))(c),c)\}))$
   $['book(\ldots)']=\lambda u(\lambda c(\{f:book(\ (u(f))(c),c)\}))$
   $['cigarette(\ldots)']=\lambda u(\lambda c(\{f:cig(\ (u(f))(c),c)\}))$

8. $[\ldots\ 'and'\ldots]=\lambda m_i(\lambda m_j(\lambda c(m_i(c)\cap m_j(c))))$
   $[\ldots\ 'or'\ldots]=\lambda m_i(\lambda m_j(\lambda c(m_i(c)\cup m_j(c))))$
   $['If'\ldots,\ 'then'\ldots]=\lambda m_i(\lambda m_j(\lambda c(Comp(m_i(c))\cup m_j(c))))$
   $['Not'\ldots]=\lambda m_i(\lambda c(Comp(m_i(c))))$

9. $\forall\alpha([\alpha]=\lambda c(\lambda f(f(\alpha))))$ [α ranging over object language variables]

10. $['a']=\lambda b(\lambda m_1(\lambda m_2(\lambda c(\lambda i(\{f:\exists f'(f'\in D_i(c)\ \&\ f\approx f'/Ind(b)\ \&$
    $f'\in(m_1\ (c)\cap m_2(c)))\})))))$

11. $['every']=\lambda b(\lambda m_1(\lambda m_2(\lambda c(\lambda i(\{f:\forall f'((f'\in D_i(c)\ \&\ f\approx f'/Ind(b))\rightarrow$
    $f'\in(Comp(m_1(c))\cup m_2(c)))\}))))))$

12. $[\text{'the'}]=\lambda b(\lambda m_1(\lambda m_2(\lambda c(\lambda i(\{f: \exists f'(f' \in D_i(c) \ \& \ f{\approx}f'/\text{Ind}(b) \ \&$
     $f' \in (m_1(c) \cap m_2(c)) \ \& \ \forall f''((f'' \in D_i(c) \ \& \ (f{\approx}f''/\text{Ind}(b) \ \& f'' \in (m_1(c))$
     $\rightarrow (b(f''))(c') = (b(f'))(c')))\})))))$

13. $[\text{'every time'}]=\lambda X(\lambda m(\lambda c(\{f: \forall c'(c'{\approx}c/t+X \rightarrow f \in m(c'))\})))$
     $[\text{'some time'}]=\lambda X(\lambda m(\lambda c(\{f: \exists c'(c'{\approx}c/t+X \ \& \ f \in m(c'))\})))$

14. $[\text{'everywhere'}]=\lambda X(\lambda m(\lambda c(\{f: \forall c'(c'{\approx}c/l+X \rightarrow f \in m(c'))\})))$
     $[\text{'somewhere'}]=\lambda X(\lambda m(\lambda c(\{f: \exists c'(c'{\approx}c/l+X \ \& \ f \in m(c'))\})))$

15. $\forall s$ (s is true as uttered by S at t iff $[s](C(S,t))=V$

16. $\{f:p\}=V$ iff p
     provided 'f' does not occur free in what replaces 'p'

Applications

We shall see how this semantics works in three examples, 'it rains', 'Elsa sees the book', and the Stanley sentence (19), 'Every time John lights a cigarette, it rains'.

(49) $[\text{' it rains' }]=[\text{'it}_i\text{'}]([\text{ 'rains }(\dots)\text{'}]) =$
      $\lambda r(\lambda c_1((r(c_1))(T(c_1)))(\lambda c(\lambda t(\{f: rains(t,\mathrm{L}(c))\})))) =$
      $\lambda c_1((\lambda c(\lambda t(\{f: rains(t,\mathrm{L}(c))\}))(c_1))(T(c_1)))$ (by λ-conversion on r)
      $\lambda c_1(\lambda t(\{f: rains(t,\mathrm{L}(c_1))\})(T(c_1))) =$ (by λ-conversion on c)
      $\lambda c_1(\{f: rains(T(c_1),\mathrm{L}(c_1))\})$ (by λ-conversion on t)

With the truth definition clause 15, this gives us

(50) 'it rains' is true as uttered by S at t iff
      $r b \lambda c_1)\{f: rains(T(c_1),\mathrm{L}(c_1))\}))(C(S,t))=V$, iff
      $f b f: rains \ (T(C(S,t)),\mathrm{L}(C(S,t)))\}=V$ (by λ-conversion on c_1)

With the additional axiom

17. it ϕ:s near S at t iff $mphi$ $(T(C(S,t)), \mathrm{L}(C(S,t)))$[30]

     we get

(51) 'it rains' is true as uttered by S at t iff $\{f{:}$it rains near S *at t*$\} = V$
      and finally, by axiom schema 16,

(52) 'it rains' is true as uttered by S at t iff it rains near S at t

that is, Davidson's (15).

---

[30] Same oversimplification as in s. 3. See n. 16.

Next, we shall look at contextual quantifier domain restriction in 'Elsa sees the book'. We have

(53) ['Elsa sees the book'] $=$ ['(the x_1)(book (x_1)')]([‘sees(Elsa, x_1)']) $=$
([‘the’]([‘x_1’]))([‘book(…)’]([‘x_1’]))(([‘sees(…,…)’]([‘x_1’]))([‘Elsa’]))

Taking the parts separately, we have

(54) ['the']([‘x_1’]) $=$
$\lambda b(\lambda m_1(\lambda m_2(\lambda c(\lambda i(\{f : \exists f'(f' \in D_i(c)$ & $f \approx f'/\text{Ind}(b)$ &
$f' \in (m_1(c) \cap m_2(c))$ & $\forall f''((f' \in D_i(c)$ &
$(f \approx f''/\text{Ind}(b)$ & $f'' \in (m_1(c)) \rightarrow$
$(b(f''))(c') = (b(f'))(c')))\})(1))))([‘x_1’]) =$

$\lambda m_1(\lambda m_2(\lambda c(\{f : \exists f'(f' \in D_1(c)$ & $f \approx f'/\text{Ind}([‘x_1’])$ &
$f' \in (m_1(c) \cap m_2(c))$ & $\forall f''((f'' \in D_1(c)$ & $f \approx f''/\text{Ind}([‘x_1’])$ &
$f'' \in m_1(c)) \rightarrow ([‘x_1’](f''))(c') = ([‘x_1’](f'))(c')))\}))) =$

$\lambda m_1(\lambda m_2(\lambda c(\{f : \exists f'(f' \in D_1(c)$ & $f \approx f'/1$ &
$f' \in (m_1(c') \cap m_2(c'))$ & $\forall f''((f'' \in D_1(c)$ & $f \approx f''/1$ &
$f'' \in m_i(c')) \rightarrow f''(‘x_1’) = f'(‘x_1’))\})))$

after λ-conversion on b and i (with argument 1) and applying axiom 9.

(55) [' book(…)']([‘x_1’]) $= \lambda u(\lambda c_2(\{f : book((u(f))(c_2),c_2)\}))([‘x_1’]) =$
$\lambda c_2(\{f : book(([‘x_1’](f))(c_2),c_2)\}) =$ (with λ-conversion on u)
$\lambda c_2(\{f : book(f(‘x_1’),c_2)\})$ (applying axiom 9)

(56) ([‘sees(…,…)’]([‘x_1’]))([‘Elsa’]) $=$
$(\lambda u(\lambda v(\lambda c_3(\{f : sees((u(f))(c_3),(v(f))(c_3),c_3)\}))))([‘x_1’]))([‘Elsa’]) =$
$(\lambda v(\lambda c_3(\{f : sees(([‘Elsa’](f))(c_3),(v(f))(c_3),c_3)\}))))([‘x_1’]) =$
$\lambda c_3(\{f : sees(([‘Elsa’](f))(c_3),([‘x_1’](f))(c_3),c_3)\}) =$
$\lambda c_3(\{f : sees(Elsa,f(‘x_1’),c_3)\})$

after λ-conversion on u and v and applying (axioms 1 and 9).

Applying (54) to (55), with λ-conversion on m_1 and c_2, we get

(57) $\lambda m_2(\lambda c(\{f : \exists f'(f' \in D_1(c)$ & $f \approx f'/1$ &
$f' \in (\{f : book(f(‘x_1’), c)\} \cap m_2(c))$ &
$\forall f''(f'' \in D_1(c)$ & $f'' \in \{f : book(f(‘x_1’), c)\} \rightarrow f''(‘x_1’) = f'(‘x_1’))\})) =$

$$\lambda m_2(\lambda c(\{f\colon \exists f'(f' \in D_1(c) \ \& \ f \approx f''/1 \ \&$$
$$book(f'(\text{`}x_1\text{'}), c) \ \& \ f' \in m_2(c) \ \&$$
$$\forall f''(f'' \in D_1(c) \ \& \ f \approx f'' \& \ book(f(\text{`}x_1\text{'}), c) \to f''(\text{`}x_1\text{'}) = f'(\text{`}x_1\text{'}))\}))$$

Applying (57) to (56), with λ-conversion on m_2 and c_3, we get

(58) $\lambda c(\{f\colon \exists f'(f' \in D_1(c\ ) \ \& \ book(f'(\text{`}x_1\text{'}),c) \ \& \ sees(Elsa, f'(\text{`}x_1\text{'}), c)) \ \& \\ \forall f''(f'' \in D_1(c) \ \& \ book(f''(\text{`}x_1\text{'}), c)\} \to f''(\text{`}x_1\text{'}) = f'(\text{`}x_1\text{'}))\})$

With some obvious axioms relating the existence of assignments to the existence of objects, from (58) we get, informally,

(59) λc ({f: there is an object a in the contextually most salient domain of c such that a is a book in c and Elsa sees a in c and any object b in the contextually most salient domain of c that is a book in c is identical with a})

which, with some overkill, yields the context-relative Russellian interpretation. Now to (19). With steps very similar to those above we get

(60) $\lambda c(\{f\colon \exists f'(f' \in D_1(c) \ \& \ f \approx f'/1 \ \& \ cig(f'(\text{`}x_1\text{'}),c) \\ \& \ lights(John, f'(\text{`}x_1\text{'}), c)\})$

as an interpretation of

(61) John lights a cigarette.

On this interpretation, John lights in c something that is a cigarette in c. That is, the lighting takes place at the location of c. However, there is also the non-locating reading, according to which John lights a cigarette at some location or other. We get that by applying the *somewhere* operation in the meta-language. There is no quantifier domain restriction of the intended interpretation ('a cigarette'):

(62) ['somewhere']$(\lambda c(\{f\colon \exists f'(f' \in D_1(c) \ \& \ f \approx f'/1 \ \& \\ cig(f'(\text{`}x_1\text{'}), c) \ \& \ lights(John, f'(\text{`}x_1\text{'}, c)\})) =$

$\lambda X(\lambda c(\{f\colon \exists c'(c' \approx c/l + X \ \& \ f \in (\lambda c(\{f\colon \exists f'(f \approx f'/1 \ \& \\ cig(f'(\text{`}x_1\text{'}, c) \ \& \ lights(John, f'(\text{`}x_1\text{'}), c)))\})(c'))\}) =$

$\lambda X(\lambda c\{f\colon \exists c'(c' \approx c/l + X \ \& \ \exists f'(f \approx f'/1 \ \& \\ cig(f'(\text{`}x_1\text{'}), c) \ \& \ lights(John, f'(\text{`}x_1\text{'}), c')))\})$

Since we are interested here only in the variation of location, we set $X = \emptyset$. We then get

(63) $\lambda c(\{f : \exists c'(c' \approx c/l \ \& \ \exists f'(f \approx f'/\text{I} \ \& \ cig(f'(\text{`}x_\text{I}\text{'}),c')$
   $\& \ lights \ (John, f'(\text{`}x_\text{I}\text{'}), c')\}))\})$

as the non-locating reading of (61). Similarly, we assume with Recanati that there is a non-locating reading of 'it rains':

(64) $\lambda c_\text{I}(\{f : \exists c'(c' \approx c_\text{I} \ /l \ \& \ rains \ (\text{T}(c'), \text{L}(c'))\}\})$

and since $c' \approx c \ / \ l$ we have $\text{T}(c') = \text{T}(c_\text{I})$, so (64) is the same as

(65) $\lambda c_\text{I}(\{f : \exists c'(c' \approx c_\text{I} \ / \ l \ \& \ rains \ (\text{T}(c_\text{I}), \text{L}(c'))\}\})$.

Now we shall apply the 'if, then' clause to the respective meanings of (3) and (61), and then apply the 'every time' clause to the results. We shall consider two applications of [every time], depending on whether $X = \emptyset$ or $X = \{l\}$, i.e. depending on whether it is only time, or time plus location that is varied. Then, since there are locating and non-locating readings of antecedent and consequent, we have three independent parameters, giving us the possibility of eight readings. If we just write 'here' for the contextually salient location, and 'there' for the bound location variable, we have, informally:

(a) Every time John lights a cigarette here, it rains then here
(b) Every time John lights a cigarette here, it rains then somewhere
(c) Every time John lights a cigarette somewhere, it rains then here
(d) Every time John lights a cigarette somewhere, it rains then somewhere
(e) Every time and place John lights a cigarette, it rains then there
(f) Every time and place John lights a cigarette, it rains then somewhere
(g) Every time and place John lights a cigarette somewhere, it rains then there
(h) Every time and place John lights a cigarette somewhere, it rains then somewhere

However, (d) is equivalent with both (f) and (h). The last but one reading, (g) (where 'there' is anaphoric on 'place', not on 'somewhere'), is odd, and should maybe be filtered out. It says that every time John lights a cigarette somewhere, it rains everywhere. What remains, then, is five or six admissible readings of (19).

Of these readings, (c) is what Stanley claims the unarticulated constituent analysis can deliver, and (e) is what he claims that analysis definitively cannot deliver. I shall therefore spell out the formal rendering of that reading. First, we have

(66) (['If ..., then ...']($\lambda c_1(f: rains(T(c_1), L(c_1)))$))
$$(\lambda c_2(\{f: \exists f' \in D_1(c) \& f \approx f'/1 \& cig(f'(`x_1`), c_2) \&$$
$$lights\ (John,\ f'(`x_1`),\ c_2)\})) =$$

$$\lambda c(\text{Comp}\{f: \exists f' \in D_1(c) \& f \approx f'/1 \& cig(f'(`x_1`), c) \&$$
$$lights\ (John,\ f'(`x_1`),\ c)\} \cup \{f: rains(T(c), L(c))\})$$

after λ-conversion on m_1, m_2, c_1, and c_2. Then, applying *every time*, with $X = \{l\}$, we get,

(67) (['every time']($\{\{l\}\}$))((66)) =

$$\lambda c(\{f: \forall c'(c' \approx c/t + l \to f \in \text{Comp}\{f: \exists f' \in D_1(c) \& f \approx f'/1 \&$$
$$cig\ (f'(`x_1`),\ c) \& lights\ (John,\ f'(`x_1`),\ c)\} \cup \{f: rains(T(c), L(c))\})$$

after λ-conversion on m and c.

Applying the truth definition and informally translating back, replacing talk of assignments with talk of objects, we get

(68) 'Every time John lights a cigarette, it rains'$_{(e)}$ is true as uttered by S at t_0 iff for any context c' differing from $C(S, t_0)$ at most in time and location, it holds that if there is an object a which is a cigarette in c' such that John lights a in c', then it rains at the time of c' at the location of c'.

which is the desired reading.

Comments

The semantics offered is inadequate in so far as it doesn't provide for the binding of pronouns, but lets that be handled by informal translation of pronouns into bound variables of the regimented object language. Moreover, even with this translation it doesn't deliver the donkey anaphora readings of some sentences that belong to the fragment (e.g. 'if John sees a dog, it eats'). In order to extend the theory to account for this we would need a dynamic machinery. For instance, one could use the PFO principle of variable binding and let the context variables c contain information about variables that have been quantified.[31] This would then amount to a dynamic setting in which contexts get updated after each clause of a sentence. In this respect the semantic would resemble other dynamic frameworks, such as DRT, or DPL.[32]

---

[31] See Pagin and Westerståhl (1993). Something like this would also be needed for an adequate treatment of sentences like (39) and (41).

[32] See Kamp and Reyle (1993) and Groenendijk and Stokhof (1991), respectively.

Another deficiency is that the semantics proposed only offers unstructured entities, functions from contexts to sets, as meanings, whereas there are reasons for thinking that structured meanings are required (cf. Pagin, 2003). However, this can easily be achieved. Instead of letting the function from meanings of parts to meaning of whole be function application, let it be pair formation. Thus, the meaning of 'it rains' would be simply $\langle['it'_i], ['rains(\ldots)']\rangle$. Meanings of complex expressions will then be tree structures: pairs of pairs, etc., where the leaves are the meanings of the simple expressions. The old unstructured meanings will then be returned by means of an evaluation function Eval. For each meaning w of a simple expression, Eval$(w)=w$, and for any well-formed meaning pair $\langle w_1, w_2\rangle$, it will hold that

$$Eval(\langle w_1,w_2\rangle)=(Eval(w_1))(Eval(w_2)),$$

that is, the old function application.

References

Bach, K. (1994). 'Semantic Slack: What is Said and More', in S. Tsohatzidis (ed.), *Foundations of Speech Act Theory* (London: Routledge), 267–91.

Borg, E. (2004). *Minimal Semantics* (Oxford: Oxford University Press).

Cappelen, H., and E. Lepore (2002). 'Indexicality, Binding, Anaphora and a Priori Truth', *Analysis*, 62: 271–81.

Chomsky, N. (1966). *Topics in the Theory of Generative Grammar (in Janua Linguarium)* (The Hague: Mouton & Co.). Partly reprinted in J. Searle (ed.), *The Philosophy of Language* (Oxford: Oxford University Press, 1971). Page references to the reprint.

—— (1980). *Rules and Representations* (Oxford: Basil Blackwell).

Crimmins, M. (1992). *Talk of Beliefs*, (Cambridge, Mass.: MIT Press).

—— and J. Perry (1989). 'The Prince and the Phone Booth: Reporting Puzzling Beliefs', *Journal of Philosophy*, 86: 685–711.

Davidson, D. (1967). 'Truth and Meaning', *Synthese*, 17: 304–23. Reprinted in Davidson, *Inquiries into Truth and Interpretation* (Oxford: Clarendon Press, 1984), 17–36. Page references to the reprint.

—— (1973). 'Radical Interpretation', *Dialectica*, 27: 313–28. Reprinted in Davidson, *Inquiries into Truth and Interpretation* (Oxford: Clarendon Press, 1984), 125–39. Page references to the reprint.

—— (1986). 'A Nice Derangement of Epitaphs', in E Lepore (ed.), *The Philosophy of Donald Davidson: Perspectives on Truth and Interpretation* (Oxford: Blackwell).

Fodor, J. (1987). *Psychosemantics*, (Cambridge, Mass.: MIT Press).

—— (2001). 'Language, Thought and Compositionality', *Mind and Language*, 16: 1–15.

Frege, G. (1918–19). 'Der Gedanke: Eine logische Untersuchung', *Beiträge zur deutschen Idealismus*, 2. 58–77. In English as 'The Thought. A Logical Inquiry', tr. A. M. and Marcelle Quinton, in P. F. Strawson (ed.), *Philosophical Logic*. (Oxford: Oxford University Press, 1967). Page references to the translation.

—— (1923). 'Gedankengefüge', *Beträge zur Philosophie des Deutschen Idealismus*, 36–51. Reprinted in Frege, *Logische Untersuchungen* (Göttingen: Vandenhoeck & Ruprecht, 1976). In English as 'Compound Thoughts', tr. R. Stoothoff, *Mind*, 72 (1963), 1–17. Page references to the translation.

Groenendijk, J. and M. Stokhof (1991). 'Dynamic Predicate Logic', *Linguistics and Philosophy*, 14: 39–100.

Hendriks, H. (2001). 'Compositionality and Model-Theoretic Interpretation', *Journal of Logic, Language and Information*, 10: 29–48.

Higginbotham, J. (1986). 'Linguistic Theory and Davidson's Program in Semantics', in E. Lepore (ed.), *The Philosophy of Donald Davidson: Perspecives on Truth and Interpretation* (Oxford: Blackwell).

Hintikka, J. and G. Sandu (1997). 'Game-Theoretical Semantics', in A. ter Meulen and J. van Benthem (eds.), *Handbook of Philosophical Logic* (Amsterdam: Elsevier).

Hodges, W. (1997). 'Compositional Semantics for a Language of Imperfect Information', *Journal of the IPGL*, 5: 539–63.

—— (1998). 'Compositionality is Not the Problem', *Logic and Logical Philosophy*, 6: 7–33.

—— (2001). 'Formal Features of Compositionality', *Journal of Logic, Language and Information*, 10: 7–28.

Janssen, T. (1984). *Foundations and Applications of Montague Grammar* (Amsterdam: Centre for Mathematics and Computer Science).

—— (1997). 'Compositionality', in J. van Benthem and A. ter Meulen (eds.), *Handbook of Logic and Language* (Amsterdam and Cambridge, Mass.: Elsevier and MIT Press), 417–73.

Kamp, H. and U. Reyle (1993). *From Discourse to Logic* (Dordrecht: Kluwer).

Kaplan, D. (1989). 'Demonstratives', in J. Almog, J. Perry, and H. Wettstein (eds.), *Themes from Kaplan* (Oxford: Oxford University Press), 481–563.

King, J. and J. Stanley (2005). 'Semantics, Pragmatics, and the Role of Semantic Content', in Z. Szabó (ed.), *Semantics vs. Pragmatics* (Oxford: Oxford University Press).

Montague, R. (1968). 'Pragmatics', in R. Klibansky (ed.), *Contemporary Philosophy: A Survey* (Florence). Reprinted in R. Thomason (ed.), *Formal Philosophy: Selected Papers of Richard Montague* (New Haven: Yale University Press, 1974), 95–118. Page references to the reprint.

—— (1970a). 'Pragmatics and Intensional Logic', *Synthese*, 22: 68–94. Reprinted in R. Thomason (ed.), *Formal Philosophy: Selected Papers of Richard Montague* (New Haven: Yale University Press, 1974), 119–47. Page references to the reprint.

Montague, R. (1970*b*). 'Universal Grammar', *Theoria*, 36: 373–98. Reprinted in R. Thomason (ed.), *Formal Philosophy: Selected Papers of Richard Montague* New Haven: Yale University Press, 1974). Page references to the reprint.

Pagin, P. (1999). 'Radical Interpretation and Compositional Structure', in U. Zeglen (ed.), *Discussions with Donald Davidson; Truth, Meaning and Knowledge* (London: Routledge).

—— (2002). 'Rule-Following, Compositionality and the Normativity of Meaning', in D. Prawitz (ed.), *Meaning and Interpretation* (Konferenser, 55; Stockholm: Kungl. Vitterhets Historie och Antikvitetsakademien).

—— (2003). 'Communication and Strong Compositionality', *Journal of Philosophical Logic*, 32: 287–322.

—— (n.d.), 'What is Communicative Success?', unpublished.

—— and D. Westerståhl (1993). 'Predicate Logic with Flexibly Binding Operators and Natural Language Semantics', *Journal of Logic, Language and Information*, 2: 89–128.

Partee, B. (1984). 'Compositionality', in F. Landman and F. Veltman (eds.), *Varieties of Formal Semantics: Proceedings of the Fourth Amsterdam Colloquium* (Dordrecht: Foris).

Pelletier, J. (1994). 'On an Argument against Semantic Compositionality', in D. Prawitz and D. Westerståhl (eds.), *Logic and Methodology of Science in Uppsala* (Dordrecht: Kluwer), 599–610.

—— (1994*b*). 'The Principle of Semantic Compositionality', *Topoi* 13: 11–24.

—— (2003). 'Context Dependence and Compositionality', *Mind and Language*, 2: 148–61.

Perry, J. (1986). 'Thought without Representation', *Supplementary Proceedings of the Aristotelian Society*, 60: 137–52. Reprinted in Perry, *The Problem of the Essential Indexical and Other Essays* (Oxford: Oxford University Press, 1993). Page references to the reprint.

—— (2001). *Reference and Reflexivity* (Stanford, Calif.: CSLI Publications).

Recanati, F. (1993). *Direct Reference: From Language to Thought*, (Oxford: Blackwell).

—— (2003). 'Unarticulated Constituents', *Linguistics and Philosophy*, 25: 299–345.

Rumelhart, D. (1979). 'Some Problems with the Notion of Literal Meanings', in A. Ortony (ed.), *Metaphor and Thought* (2nd edn., Cambridge: Cambridge University Press), 71–82.

Stanley, J. (2000). 'Context and Logical Form', *Linguistics and Philosophy*, 23: 391–434.

—— and Z. Szabó (2000). 'On Quantifier Domain Restriction', *Mind and Language*, 15: 219–61.

Westerståhl, D. (2002). 'On the Compositionality of Idioms: An Abstract Approach', in D. Barker-Plummer, D. Beaver, J. van Benthem, and P. Scotto di Luzio (eds.), *Words, Proofs and Diagrams* (Stanford, Calif.: CSLI Publications), 241–72.

—— (2004). 'On the Compositional Extension Problem', *Journal of Philosophical Logic*, 33: 549–82.

12

Presuppositions, Truth Values, and Expressing Propositions

M ICHAEL G LANZBERG

Philosophers like to talk about propositions. There are many reasons for this. Perhaps the most common is that philosophers are sometimes more interested in the content of a thought or utterance than in the particular sentence or utterance that might express it on some occasion. Propositions are offered as these contents.

Like many philosophical notions, this one has been the subject of extensive debate. For instance, it has been challenged on the basis of Quinean queasiness about intensional objects, and Chomskian qualms about the explanatory value of truth-conditional semantics. These are foundational worries about the notion of proposition. But there is another kind of worry about propositions, which leads to the topic of this chapter. The notion of proposition has been used to make some highly contentious *philosophical* claims. In particular, strong claims have been made by declaring that particular utterances, or whole classes of utterances, do not *express propositions*. Consider the following classes:

(1) *a.* M O R A L   E V A L U A T I O N : Torture is wrong.
     b. B O R D E R L I N E   C A S E S : John is bald.
     c. S E M A N T I C   P A R A D O X E S : This sentence does not express a true proposition.

Thanks to Lenny Clapp, Chris Gauker, Kent Johnson, Jeff King, Robert May, Roger Schwarzschild, Susanna Siegel, Mandy Simons, Jason Stanley, and an anonymous referee for helpful comments and discussions. Versions of the material were presented at the University of Cincinnati and the University of California, Irvine. Thanks to my audiences there for lively and valuable discussions.

    d. INDICATIVE CONDITIONALS: If the book is not here, it is at
    home.

For each of these, it has been claimed that no proposition is expressed by all
or some utterances of them.[1]

    The first of these runs us headlong into some substantial metaethics. The
rest display philosophical logic at its most contentious. At the very least, we
have gone far beyond the apparently innocuous idea that we can just talk
about the content of an utterance.

    Some have responded to such claims by suggesting that we should never
talk about failure to express a proposition, or at least never in any but the
most obvious of cases. At the very least, the questions surrounding these
examples demand that we provide some kind of explanation of just what it is
to express a proposition: an explanation sufficiently devoid of philosophical
suppositions that we could *apply* it to explain such philosophically contentious cases.

    The obvious place to look for such an explanation is linguistics. After all,
whether or not an utterance of some sentence expresses a proposition is
presumably a claim about natural language; one of which we might hope
linguistics offers an independent analysis. Now, linguists do not often talk
about expressing propositions the way philosophers do. But there is a phenomenon much discussed by linguists as well as philosophers of language
which appears to be closely related to what we are after: *presupposition.* For
instance, the recent textbook of Heim and Kratzer (1998) comes very close to
identifying presupposition failure with failure to express a proposition. They
say:

    If it is a contingent matter of fact that α is outside the domain of $[[\ \ ]]$,
    then α is a *presupposition failure.* (p. 81)

If we understand being "outside the domain of $[[\ \ ]]$" as the same as failing
to express a proposition, then we seem to have a proposal that comes close to
offering an analysis of expressing a proposition in terms of presupposition. Of
course Heim and Kratzer are not explicitly talking about the philosophical

---

[1] The first is, of course, a fairly crude form of emotivism. In pure form, it may be found in
Ayer (1946), though it has resonated with a great many more recent and refined expressivists.
The last is explicitly endorsed by Adams (1975). The idea that vague predicates with borderline
cases fail to express propositions is folklore. I discuss some reasons one might be driven towards
it in some unusual cases in my (2004). I am explicitly committed to the claim that some
utterances of Liar Sentences fail to express propositions (Glanzberg, 2001).

notion of proposition. But this would just make the analysis all the more useful, as it would be substantially philosophically neutral.

We should not, of course, ask too much of such an analysis. It is unlikely that it would directly resolve the sorts of philosophical issues we see in (1). Many of the contentious issues that are raised there go beyond firm linguistic judgments, or challenge the underpinnings of apparently firm judgments. Even so, I think that we would be much better equipped to approach these hard cases if we had a better understanding of the cases where there is good linguistic data. We would be better equipped to decide philosophically contentious cases of failing to express a proposition if we could spot it and explain it in uncontentious cases (and better equipped to reply to those who reject the very idea as well).

In this chapter, I shall try to come to such an understanding of the linguistic phenomenon of failing to express a proposition, how it may be identified, and what brings it about. Though this will not by itself explain the hard philosophical cases of (1), I do hope it will help us to understand what is at issue for these cases. The chapter has three linked goals. The first is to explain what it is to fail to express a proposition. Along with this goes the second goal of showing how failure to express a proposition may be recognized in natural language. This will lead to a discussion of *truth-value judgments*. Perhaps the most common idea about expression failure is that it can be recognized by judgments of lack of truth value. I shall argue that truth-value judgments are not a reliable test, and suggest some more refined discourse-based tests which I think do a better job of detecting failure to express a proposition. My third goal is to investigate how failure to express a proposition arises. As I mentioned, the natural place to look is to presupposition. It is a tempting idea, as the quote from Heim and Kratzer seemed to indicate, that failure to express a proposition is simply the effect of presupposition failure. This proposal, I shall show, is too strong. Once we consider the wide range of presuppositional phenomena, we see that some presupposition failures lead to expression failure, but some do not. To sort out what does lead to expression failure, we thus have to investigate in detail the sources of presuppositions. I shall show how presuppositions fall into two categories, corresponding to those that can lead to expression failure and those that cannot, and I shall offer an explanation of why we find this division within presuppositions.

The central thesis of this chapter is thus that we can make sense of the notion of failing to express a proposition, we can identify it by some reasonably reliable discourse tests, and we can explain how it arises in terms of a subspecies of the linguistic phenomenon of presupposition. The bulk of the chapter will be devoted to the last component. It will involve a detailed examination of a range of presuppositions and the effects of their failures. In doing this, I shall offer a unified analysis of the sources of these presuppositions. This analysis will allow us to trace the results of presupposition failure, and account for the difference in effect of different presuppositions. Though this is important for better understanding the philosophical idea of failure to express a proposition, there is also independent interest in understanding some of the details of how presuppositions work, and how and why they can have different effects.

This chapter will begin by looking at the notion of expressing a proposition itself in section I. Section II turns to the issue of how to identify expression failures, and offers an improvement on truth-value judgment tests. Section III introduces the notion of presupposition, and section IV surveys a wide range of presuppositional phenomena and shows that some lead to expression failure while some do not. An explanation of this is offered in the detailed analyses of elementary presuppositions in section V. The chapter ends with a brief conclusion, and an appendix offering some more technical development of the main idea from section V.

I Expressing Propositions

I shall begin, in this section, with some traditional, fairly abstract, philosophy of language. Before getting on to detailed analysis, we need to figure out what we are talking about when we talk about propositions and expressing propositions. I shall here propose an essentially Gricean analysis of these notions. This will frame the questions to be raised later, of when and how we succeed or fail in expressing propositions.

The key to a clear understanding of propositions, I believe, is to focus on the actual phenomena we might wish to discuss in terms of them. The primary example is the speech act of *assertion*.

I take it as a truism that the basic point of assertion is to convey information. In asserting *Snow is white* I tell you *that* snow is white, in asserting *The world is all that is the case* I tell you *that* the world is all that is the case.

Not any old rendering available of information amounts to successful assertion, however. For instance, my simply standing in front of an audience conveys huge amounts of information: that I am wearing a jacket, that I am slightly nervous, etc. But none of this is like the conveying of information by assertion. Of course, we normally expect assertions to involve the use of language. But the mere use of language is not enough. Suppose I say, with suitable winks and nudges:

(2) John . . . Jane . . .

I convey plenty of information, by using language, but hardly make an assertion.

What makes assertion different? For one thing, when I tell you that snow is white, I make a specific claim, which represents the world as being some way, and can be assessed as correct or incorrect. Successful assertions thus provide determinate truth conditions. Our cases so far, of conveying information but not being assertion, fail to do this. The utterance in (2) does not specify to most interpreters whether it is to convey, for instance, that John and Jane are having an affair, an illicit affair, or an illicit affair that could lead to Jane getting fired, etc. A sufficiently informed interpreter might be able to choose among these, but probably because she already had the information in question available.[2] Outside of this, the utterance is not specific enough to be determinately falsifiable by any given circumstance. Does evidence that Jane's job is secure amount to evidence that the claim is false? What of evidence that they are merely bridge partners? We are lacking, in an utterance like this, a specific claim with determinate content. We are lacking, at least, a determinate collection of truth conditions which correspond to the particular way the world is being represented as being.

Successful assertion must at least fix such determinate truth conditions. We may introduce *propositions* as the information conveyed in successful assertions. Hence, a proposition must at least encapsulate the determinate truth conditions of an assertion. For discussion purposes, I shall follow the familiar custom of taking the additional step of identifying a proposition with its truth conditions. In doing so, I put aside the question of whether or not propositions provide more fine-grained information than truth conditions. It will not matter for our purposes here.

I should also stress that though I shall talk about propositions as if they were objects, I am not here concerned with the ontological question of whether or not there really are such objects. What is important is that one

---

[2] Hence, in some contexts where a great deal of background information is available, this sort of case might satisfy the requirements for successful assertion I shall propose. The context I have in mind here is the 'water-cooler', in which not very much about John or Jane is known, but innuendos fly.

speaker conveys a specific content to another. Any way of describing this is fine with me.[3]

Merely requiring a proposition is not enough to describe successful assertion, however. If information is easy to find, so is *specific* information. (Sherlock Holmes, for instance, is portrayed as a master of gleaning highly specific information from non-assertoric situations.) What marks off assertion from any old way of finding specific information—of finding a proposition—is that assertions *convey* information. In assertion, the hearer is being *told* the specific information by the speaker, and this is something that is transparent to both of them. Sherlock Holmes's acumen is not required in such a case; only linguistic competence. As Grice observed, not only must information pass from one person to another, it must pass in virtue of both speaker and hearer recognizing that the information is to be transmitted by the making of the assertion. In the terms of Grice (1969), asserting that snow is white requires *meaning* that snow is white.

Grice's analysis of meaning in terms of intentions is notoriously complex, but for our purposes, we can replace the attempt at analysis with a more simple constraint, based on the notion of *common ground* (e.g. Stalnaker, 1978; essentially the same as the idea of *mutual knowledge* in Schiffer, 1972). Common ground information is information taken for granted among speakers at some point in a conversation. This is a strong notion: it requires not merely that each speaker accept a proposition (or at least, take it for granted for purposes of the current conversation), but that they recognize that all speakers do so, and that they recognize this to be the case, etc. Common ground is the commonly recognized background against which a conversation proceeds. (Common ground propositions need not be believed, as speakers can take something for granted within a conversation but not in fact believe it.)

With the notion of common ground, we can formulate the following constraint on successful assertion:

---

[3] As I have set up the issue, the brute ontological question of whether there are objects called 'propositions' is not of great interest. If we help ourselves to enough mathematical objects (as I think we should), we can find reasonable objects to bear the name.

What is an interesting question is whether or not the kinds of analyses I offer here *commit* me to the existence of propositions. Most of what I say about propositions can be easily paraphrased so as to avoid reference to the objects themselves, in favor of success conditions on acts of assertion. Whether or not all such talk can be paraphrased away is an open question. To the extend it cannot, we have a familiar kind of argument for an ontological commitment.

(3) For an assertion to be successful, the following must become common ground:

   a. The proposition encapsulating the information conveyed.

   b. That the information was to be conveyed by the assertion.

As both Grice (1975) and Stalnaker (1978) stress, assertion is a cooperative endeavor. It requires not just that speakers coordinate on what information is being conveyed, but on how it is being conveyed.[4]

I shall reserve the term *expressing a proposition* for circumstances in which the conditions of (3) are met. Spelling out the truism that the basic point of assertion is to convey information, we may now say that expressing a proposition is the *success condition* for assertion. It is what we are normally trying to do in making assertions. It is tempting to say, using the language of Austin (1975), that this gives the *felicity conditions* for assertion. However, as we will see below, this term is best reserved for a less demanding sort of condition.[5]

Expressing a proposition is a rather demanding task. How do we ever manage to do it at all? In most cases (and I suspect in virtually all cases), we rely upon language. To simplify, let us concentrate on what Grice would call

---

[4] The initial, much modified, proposal of Grice (1969) was U means something if U intended audience A to (*a*) produce response r, (*b*) recognize that U intends (*a*), (*c*) Fulfill (*a*) on the basis of (*b*).

[5] I have discussed the idea of the basic point of a speech act at length in my (2004). In that paper, I suggest that failure to express a proposition amounts to failure to make a genuine move in the practice of using language. A speaker is attempting to make a (genuine) assertion by some action, and if they fail to express a proposition, they fail to do so. As I stress there, this is not to say they have done nothing by their action, nor that they have done nothing intentional, but they have failed to make the specific act of assertion. For most of what I say in this chapter, it would be acceptable to describe the case of failing to express a proposition as involving a genuine assertion, but one that is defective in its basic structure (though I think that just amounts to failure to make a genuine assertion in the first place).

As an anonymous referee points out, the Grice-and-Stalnaker-inspired view I am proposing here does raise some difficult issues, related to speaker–hearer asymmetries, or different intentional states of different members of a conversation. For instance, consider a conversation in which one person utters some sentence, and some but not all members of the group thereby presuppose its content. The criterion given in (3) would count this as failure, though that may appear too strong.

These sorts of issue are interesting and important, but the common ground approach I have adopted here in effect idealizes away from them. It assumes that well-running conversations achieve more perfect exchange of information than they often do in real life. But, I think we can make progress in understanding the way information is conveyed in conversations by adopting this kind of idealization as a starting point.

the proposition *said* by an utterance. I express the proposition that snow is white—I convey it in the right way—by uttering the declarative sentence *Snow is white* with the right intonation. I chose the words whose linguistic meanings combine to fix the proposition that snow is white, and use them to express that very proposition. It is *expression*, as I may take it to be common ground what these words mean, and that used in the right way, with the right intonation, they are to convey that proposition. To stress, even when a proposition is encoded by the words uttered, it is still the Gricean idea of meaning and the restrictions of (3) that are fundamental to the account of expression.

Of course, this simple story is not often, if ever, applicable on its own. Most any sentence encodes a proposition only with the help of linguistic context. And since Grice pointed out the difference between what is said and what is implicated (both of which are part of what is meant), we cannot restrict ourselves even to linguistic encoding plus context. In what follows, I shall usually concentrate on what is *said* when looking for the proposition expressed by an assertion (though implicatures will become important for the discussion of factive presupposition triggers in section V).[6]

II Expression Failure and Truth-Value Judgments

If expressing a proposition is the success condition for assertion, then it should be unremarkable that there is such a thing as failing to express a proposition. Any failed assertion is an example.

However, expressing a proposition is a demanding task, and there is a lot that can go wrong in attempting to express a proposition. Failure to do so can come in more or less drastic forms. At the most extreme, one could attempt to say something, but start laughing instead, and fail to make an utterance at all. Or one might try to speak, but for whatever medical reason, manage to make only some odd croaking noises. Somewhat less extreme cases are those in which a performance error leads to uttering an ungrammatical sentence, and examples like (2). We will see others in a moment.

---

[6] There is a vigorous debate over whether what is said by an utterance can be read off the logical form of a sentence uttered, plus contextual contributions, or if autonomous pragmatic processes such as 'enrichment' are needed. I tend to operate as if the former holds, and am inclined towards this position, but nothing I say here relies on it. For the former position, see Stanley (2000). For the latter, among many authors, see Sperber and Wilson (1986), Carston (1988, 2004), and Recanati (1993) (as well as related work of Bach (e.g. 1994), though Bach takes a somewhat different view of what is said than I have been assuming here).

The kind of failure to express a proposition that is of interest here, which might be found in controversial examples like (1), is different. Cases like (1) do not involve an utterance which lacks an uttered sentence, or have a sentence which displays some gross defect or is incomplete. Rather, they are cases in which we have sentences that are fully well-formed syntactically, and we may assume they are properly produced in utterance. Yet, it is claimed, no proposition is expressed nonetheless. Let us reserve the term *expression failure* for this sort of case, where an act of assertion gets as far as producing a well-formed sentence, and yet still fails to express a proposition.

Though the examples of (1) are contentious, I believe there are some relatively uncontroversial examples of expression failure. The clearest come from failures of demonstratives. Suppose I say:

(4) That palm tree is going to fall.

Suppose I am pointing off into the distance, where there is no salient object, and certainly nothing like a palm tree. To be on the safe side, suppose also there are no grounds for treating this as shifted reference to some photograph of a palm tree, or as a report of my private sensory state. Suppose there is no salient candidate object available.[7]

I am going to take this as a paradigm case of expression failure. It fails to meet condition (3). It attempts to convey a proposition by way of the truth conditions determined from a sentence together with context. As no referent of *that palm tree* is available in the context, no such truth conditions are determined, and the attempt to convey information fails.

In this case, I think the judgment that there is something grossly wrong with the utterance is clear. And the fact that we cannot compute its truth conditions, as we do not have a value for the demonstrative phrase, supports the idea that we have failure to express a proposition. But most cases are not so clear. We need some way to spot expression failure more generally, and it turns out to be somewhat elusive.

The classic approach to this problem is based on *truth-value judgments*. The idea at least appears fairly straightforward. We are looking for cases in which an attempt to convey a truth-conditional proposition fails. We detect this by focusing on what would be potentially conveyed by an utterance, and

---

[7] I have discussed the specific case of complex demonstratives at greater length in work with Susanna Siegel (forthcoming). I should mention that we are not at all sure that complex demonstratives are devices of reference, and are inclined to follow King (2001) in treating them as quantifier phrases. However, this does not impugn their standing as sources of examples of expression failure.

asking if it is true or false. If, in cases where we are apprised of all the relevant facts, this fails to lead to a truth-value judgment, it appears the reason is that there are no truth conditions conveyed upon which to base those judgments. We fail to reach truth-value judgments because of expression failure.

As was pointed out by Strawson (1950), we are often in cases like (4) unwilling to give judgments of truth value. (As he later puts it (1964), we are "squeamish".) But there are some circumstances in which this tendency can be overridden. One fairly typical one is a pattern of what is sometimes called 'presupposition-canceling negation', such as replying to (5*a*) with (5*b*) in:

(5) *a.* That palm tree is going to fall. George said so.
    b. That palm tree is NOT going to fall—there is no palm tree.

Actually, for the demonstrative NP *that palm tree*, (5*b*) takes some effort. It is much easier to get with the definite description *the palm tree*. But with the right intonation pattern, with stress on the negation, and a kind of stress on each each word of the original sentence, it does seem we can say this.[8]

Another problematic case is what we might call 'repair-to-negation':

(6) *a.* Is that palm tree going to fall?
    b. Er...no..., there is no palm tree.

In cases like this, we note a defect in an utterance, and reach a negative judgment on the basis of it. In (6), it may be as much that we are rejecting some implication of the attempted claim, such as that we are in danger of being hit. But we can also get rejection of what may *look like* what is said itself. For instance, we have:

(7) *a.* This pen [*demonstrating a pen*] is in danger of being struck by that palm tree.
    b. Well, there is no palm tree, so I guess not.

The speaker here manages to reason from the defect in the utterance to its somehow not being able to be true, and gives a negative assessment.

It is not easy to decide exactly what these sorts of examples show. But they do present enough problem cases to cast doubt on the idea that our dispositions

---

[8] As Roger Schwarzschild suggested to me, the intonation pattern here does not seem to have much to do with focus. Rather, it seems to indicate that the words used are unacceptable, inviting us to see this sort of case as one of metalinguistic negation in the sense of Horn (1989). We do not need to decide now whether the phenomenon here is one of metalinguistic negation or not. We merely need to note that there is a kind of negative judgment available, which complicates the question of whether we have an assessment for truth value or something else.

to provide truth-value judgments form a good guide to whether a proposition is expressed. They are just not stable enough. In so far as there is no proposition expressed in (4), for instance, there is little reason to think there is a proposition expressed in (5) or (6); yet we are inclined to offer what look very much like truth-value judgments in the latter. Examples like (7) raise a number of questions about how closely our dispositions to give truth-value judgments are tied to subtle features of sentence structure. But still, they show enough plasticity in the availability of truth-value judgments to make us doubt how reliable these judgments can be as a test for successful expression.[9]

Even so, I believe these sorts of examples do point the way towards a better, more reliable test for expression. Examples like the repair-to-negation cases (6) and (7) display a common move in discourse, known as a conversational *repair*. This is a conversational move of correcting a defect in a discourse. The range of repair phenomena is quite large, and not by any means restricted to issues of proposition expression. But we tend to see some typical markers of repair, such as some discourse markers like the *er* particle I used above. This is characteristic of what conversational analysts call 'other-initiated repair', as are patterns of pausing between turns, and other markers.[10]. It appears that the intonation pattern in (5) also marks repair.

The notion of repair allows us to sharpen the Strawsonian test based on truth-value judgment into an empirically more robust set of diagnostics. We may think of truth-value judgments as occurring in discourse as responses to yes–no questions like (8a), or to tag questions, or corresponding queries about assertions like (8b):

(8) *a.* Is that palm tree going to fall?
     b. (i) That palm tree is going to fall.
          (ii) Is that right?

The Strawsonian idea about paradigm case of expression failure like (4) can be put that speakers cannot answer such queries. We have seen this is not quite right. They can, but in doing so, they must initiate a repair. They key mark of expression failure, I propose, is the need for repair in assessment.

Discourses are messy things, so it is not always that easy to detect this sort of need for repair. Speakers can sometimes talk around conversational defects rather than fix them. However, there are some discourse settings which bring

---

[9] Some of the issues surrounding cases like (7) are discussed in Von Fintel (2004) and in my (2002).

[10] See Schegloff *et al.* (1977) and Levinson (1983).

out the need for repair more clearly, and we may use these to construct some tests for expression failure.

One is what I shall call the *echo-assessment* test. In this, we ask speakers not only to make an assessment, but to attempt it with the same words as the initial assertion (or as close as we can come, modifying, for instance, occurrences of terms like *I* and *you*). So, for instance, we have no trouble with:

(9) *a.* Is Al Gore president?
     b. No, Al Gore is not president.

On other hand, what is correct about the Strawsonsian observation is that speakers will not offer:[11]

(10) *a.* Is that palm tree about to fall?
      b. # No, that palm tree is not about to fall.

In cases like this speakers will only give an assessment by initiating a repair, as in (5) or (6). When they do, they typically tend to avoid echoing the defective construction, as in (6), or at least use it only in a marked way, as in (5). We do not see:

(11) # Er... there is not palm tree, so I guess that palm tree is not about to fall.

In defective cases, the echo-assessment test asks speakers to do something which would reproduce the defect. If repair of the defect is required, speakers will not do this. Rather, if they make any assessment, they will initiate a repair and work around the defective construction. Thus, we can use the echo-assessment test to spot cases where repair is necessary.

A second diagnostic for the need for repair is the *indirect speech report test*. In cases like (4), speakers will be unwilling to provide *indirect* speech reports without initiating a repair. Normally, the repair is given by offering a direct quotation instead. Compare:

(12) *a.* # George said that that palm tree is going to fall.
      b. George uttered 'That palm tree is going to fall', but there is no palm tree.

As with the echo-assessment test, this test asks speakers to do something which would reproduce a defect. If the defect requires repair, speakers will not be willing to do so, or at least not unless they can do so in a way that also

---

[11] I mark discourse unacceptability by '#'.

makes the needed repair.[12] I shall group the echo-assessment and indirect speech report tests as the *repair tests*.

In canonical cases of expression failure, like (4), repair is required in order to report what was said, or to evaluate it. This is revealed in the repair tests, where we observe speakers unwilling to make echo-assessments or indirect speech reports. For shorthand, I shall call this status simply *repair obligatory*. In keeping with my usage of 'expression failure', I shall reserve this label for cases in which we have an acceptable utterance of a well-formed sentence, and yet still have obligatory repair.

Even when restricted to well-formed utterances of fully grammatical sentences, the status of repair obligatory contrasts with a much weaker kind of defect. Suppose we are discussing how well some contextually salient group of people did on an exam:

(13) *a.* How did the exam go?
    b. JOHN passed.

(Capitals indicate 'focal stress', or more properly, pitch accent.) In many contexts, this will generate the scalar implicature that no one other than John passed.[13] But suppose it is already established, and common ground in the context, that this situation cannot happen. We might respond with either (14*b*-i) or (14*b*-ii):

(14) *a.* How did the exam go?
    b. JOHN passed.
       (i) Yes, John passed.
       (ii) Yes, John passed ... but you don't mean the rest didn't, do you?

Likewise, in reporting, we could say either of (15*a*) or (15*b*):

(15) *a.* He said that John passed.
    b. He said that John passed, but he oddly seemed to suggest that the rest didn't which is not so.

---

[12] The repairs made by shifting to direct quotation are quite weak, amounting to marking what is defective about an utterance, and moving on. A more elaborate repair might be provided by the original speaker in the next turn. They might say something like 'oh, I meant ...'. But this does not appear to be required, once the initial repair is made.

[13] This example is modified from Rooth (1992). If the context provides us simply with a set of salient people, the implicature that no one else passed will be generated. But if the context provides other information, different implicatures are possible.

Options (14*b*-ii) and (15*b*) amount to initiating repairs, much as we saw before. But in these cases, unlike the previous ones, the repair appears to be optional. The (14*b*-i) and (15*a*) options, not making the repair, are acceptable as well.

Depending on the circumstances, we might or might not make repairs like these, perhaps depending on how central we think the generation of the unacceptable implicature might be for the wider purposes of the conversation, or what the premiums for repair in the conversation might be. In settings like the ones we see in courtroom dramas, where a witness is required to answer questions truthfully, but with no regard to implications, there would be a strong preference *not* to make the repairs. I shall refer to these sorts of cases as *repair optional* as opposed to *repair obligatory*. As usual, I reserve this term for optional repairs of well-formed utterances of fully grammatical sentences.

The mark of cases where no proposition is expressed, I propose, is the discourse status of *obligatory repair*. We have seen that the paradigmatic cases of expression failure, like (4), have this status. But moreover, obligatory repair is just what we should expect for cases of expression failure, by the standard for successful expression given by the conditions of (3). When these are not met, speakers either cannot identify a propositional content at all, or cannot identify it in a way that makes clear that it is the proposition being conveyed. Thus, without initiating a repair, they cannot assess the information conveyed, or report it as information conveyed. The result is repair obligatory status, as detected by the repair tests. Conversely, when we find repair obligatory by these tests, we are detecting a problem either in the providing of propositional content (the first clause of the expression condition 3), or in the conveying of that information (the second clause). The repair tests target the first clause, by asking a speaker to evaluate or report a specific content. They target the second clause, by asking the speaker as closely as possible to do so in the same way the content was to have been conveyed by the assertion in question. The repair tests, and the status of obligatory repair they detect, thus provide a good guide to when expression failure occurs.

The idea of repair-obligatory status, and the repair tests which detect it, improve upon the Strawsonian idea that expression failure corresponds to lack of truth value. It must be granted that the notion of repair is not as worked out as we might like, but I believe it is more empirically robust than the dispositions to make truth-value judgments with which we began, and it is better-targeted at the phenomenon described in the conditions of (3). At least, it is sufficiently refined to avoid the problems for truth-value judgment tests we saw in (5)–(7). It is important to stress that it is *obligatory* repair that marks expression failure. We have already seen that the weaker status of optional repair marks a lesser failing in an assertion, and this will become important in the discussion of presupposition to follow.[14]

The status of obligatory repair is quite specific. First of all, as I mentioned above, it is restricted to well-formed utterances of grammatical sentences. However, to see better the sense in which speakers can find a conversational repair to be obligatory, it will be useful to consider how repairs are applied when grammatical flaws are present. Consider some familiar cases:

(16) *a.* *John elapsed that Bill would come. (Subcategorization)
    b. *Poirot believes that himself is the best. (Binding)[15]

Now, consider applying the echo-assessment or indirect speech report tests to any of these. In each case, the speaker will not simply repeat the grammatical error, and so they will not give echo-assessments or indirect speech reports. In the binding error case, the repair is quite minor. Speakers will say:

(17) He said Poirot believes the *he* is the best.

This simply makes the repair without marking it, as it is quite clear what is happening.

A case like the subcategorization violation seems to require a more clearly marked repair. One might see:

(18) He said that John expected that Bill would come . . . at least, I think that's what he said, if he meant *expected* where he used *elapsed*.

What is important is that, in these cases, it is unacceptable to repeat the error in the sentence, and a repair is initiated to avoid it.

I reserved the term 'expression failure' for cases where we had no grammatical error, so these are not the cases we are interested in. But the normative force of obligatory repair is the same in both kinds of cases. Speakers are highly unwilling to repeat grammatical errors, and will not do so unless they are themselves making performance mistakes. Now, it should be mentioned

---

[14] Let me stress that many of the cases of obligatory repair we have looked at here are *interpretable*, in that a sympathetic interpreter in a situation of utterance could often come up with a plausible interpretation. But even when this can be done, there will be nothing *expressed* by the utterance. If an interpretation is available, it does not live up to the high demands on expressing a proposition given in (3).

[15] These are well-known. I draw the first from Chomsky (1965), and the second from the textbook of Haegeman (1994).

that it is not quite true that speakers will not repeat such defective sentences under any circumstances. If you really use brute force, you could get them to make all kinds of noises. But the norms of language use still preclude speakers from repeating grammatical errors. In the same way, they obligate repair in cases of expression failure.

Even so, applying the repair tests is not always so easy. Discourse is much more messy than, say, syntax, and speakers will quite often tolerate defective discourse, given the other demands placed on communicative exchanges. The norms of language use obligating repair compete with other norms. The repair tests are designed to screen off these competing demands as much as is possible, but they need to be handled carefully to do so effectively. For one thing, the tests should only be applied in cases where all speakers are apprised of all the relevant facts, including facts about what words the speaker used, about the context, and about whatever bears on the truth of the claim made. (Otherwise, we could see repair initiated not because of expression failure, but because the hearer simply did not hear the speaker properly, or did not know the value of an indexical.) To best screen off other norms of language use which might cloud the status of obligatory repair, it is best to imagine the tests applied in a 'courtroom' setting, where the person applying the tests is a witness on the stand. Here, the conversation places a premium on only accurate reporting and assessment, without regard for how useful or misleading that may be. The only norms that count are the ones relevant to obligatory versus optional repair.[16]

Though testing for a normative notion like obligatory repair can be difficult, the repair tests provide us with a better tool than either our direct intuitive judgments of whether a proposition is expressed, or the Strawsonsian truth-value judgment test. They are, I believe, empirically more substantial, and less philosophically biased.

---

[16] As comments by Gregory Ward made me appreciate, there are quite a number of delicate issues for applying the tests with ordinary speakers. For instance, different speakers will make different assumptions about the relative importance of assessing what was said versus any implicatures. Different speakers will also take the standard of assessment in echo-assessment somewhat differently. Some take it to be truth, as most philosophically trained readers will; but some take it to be a more epistemic notion. The precise *form* of denial used in the test is important for both issues.

Clearly, the tests, and especially, the protocols for testing, need to be refined to make them empirically more robust; though, as I say, I do think they already represent an improvement over direct intuitive judgments about expression, or the Strawsonian truth-value judgment tests. I hope to carry out these refinements, and add some more substantial data, in future work.

III Presupposition

So far, we have an abstract characterization of what it is to express a proposition, leading to the constraint (3). More concretely, we have identified a discourse status which corresponds to expression failure: that of obligatory repair. We also have some tests for detecting obligatory repair: the repair tests. But we still lack an explanation of how expression failure comes about, and of the conditions in which it comes about. We thus need a richer theory. To develop one, I shall begin by returning to the idea that I considered at the beginning, that an analysis of presupposition might provide the kinds of theory we need.

The analysis of presupposition that lends itself to an account of expression is that developed by Stalnaker (e.g. 1974). It has several components, which I shall discuss in turn.

The first component is an analysis of a *context* as a kind of information state: the context at a given point in a conversation consists of the information that is common ground among participants in the conversation at that point. A context may thus be represented as the set of propositions which are common ground, or as the set of possible worlds compatible with all the common ground propositions. If we think of propositions themselves as sets of worlds, the context is then the intersection of all the common ground propositions.[17]

In light of this model of context, we can recast the basic idea that the point of an assertion is to convey information. Conveying information is always done against a background of shared information. This is just the context in which an assertion is made. In conveying information, a successful assertion will make it the case that an additional proposition becomes common ground, and so is simply added to the context. Of course, the conditions of (3) still apply. It is not enough merely to add the proposition to the common ground; it must be done in the right way to count as conveying information. By (3), this requires adding to the context the additional information that the proposition was conveyed.

Thus, generally, the task of assertion is that of *updating* a context. For the most part, we are concerned with the content of an assertion itself, and may

---

[17] Stalnaker further analyzes a context in terms of the notion of *speaker presupposition*: the propositional attitude of taking for granted or presupposing. There are a number of issues that might be raised about whether speakers' individual presuppositions or the common ground is primary. However, for our purposes here, I shall suppress these, and simply work with the common ground.

suppress the additional common ground information that the proposition was conveyed by the assertion. Under this assumption, a context behaves as a record of the contents of assertions made in a conversation. Each successive proposition asserted is added to the record.

Let us introduce the notation $[[S]]^C$ for the semantic value of sentence S in context C: the semantically encoded information of S evaluated in C. We may then write the result of updating context C by an assertion of sentence S as $C + [[S]]^C$. In terms of possible worlds, $[[S]]^C$ is a set of worlds, and the result of updating the context is $\{w \mid w \in C + [[S]]^C\} = C \cap [[S]]^C$.

Against the background of information in C, the information conveyed by asserting S is what it adds to C. This is $C + [[S]]^C$. Thus, in accord with the discussion of section I, we can identify $S + [[S]]^C$ as the proposition expressed by the assertion of S in context C.[18]

Stalnaker's theory analyzes presupposition in terms of the context-as-information picture. It does so by way of the notion of *presuppositional requirements*. These are requirements a sentence places upon a context for the sentence to be *felicitous* in the context. Thus, presuppositional requirements are relations between a sentence S and a proposition p such that if S is felicitous in context C, C entails p. (If we think of contexts as sets of propositions, the requirement is simply that C includes p.[19])

A presuppositional requirement is a constraint on what an information state must be like for an assertion to be *felicitous*. Presupposition failure results in infelicitous utterance. We must be somewhat careful about just

---

[18] Thus, with Stalnaker (1978), and much of the subsequent work on dynamic semantics, I identify the proposition expressed with the information conveyed, $C + [S]^C$, rather then with $[[S]]^C$ itself.

[19] A similar idea was developed by Karttunen (1974). Generally, the Stalnaker–Karttunen approach to presupposition makes it a pragmatic notion; unlike, for instance, the semantic notion of presupposition deriving from Frege (1892) and Strawson (1952). The idea of implementing the Stalnaker–Karttunen approach in a dynamic context comes from Heim (1983). It has been developed extensively by a number of authors, as I shall discuss in section V.

It is common to see presuppositions identified by a test for implication under embedding in a family of environments, including negation, antecedents of conditionals, and interrogatives. This sort of test works in tandem with the characterization in terms of infelicity, as it is a diagnostic for what is presupposed by a given construction. This is a useful guide, but as Chierchia and McConnell-Ginet (1990) point out, it tends to over-generate. In their terms, it accepts implications that do not intuitively have presupposition status, or lead to infelicity. They give the example of nonrestrictive relative clauses. I am inclined to add selection restrictions as well, which seem to me to give very marginal judgments of infelicity. (This issue is discussed further by Kadmon, 2001.)

what presupposition failure is. It has been well-known since Lewis (1979) that, in many cases, presuppositions required by a sentence but not present in the context can be added to render an utterance of the sentence felicitous (the process Lewis dubbed *accommodation*). It is also known that many presuppositions are contextually defeasible. Infelicity only results if a presuppositional requirement is genuinely active, and so not defeated, and cannot be accommodated. Let us reserve the term *presupposition failure* for these cases.

This leaves the notion of felicity unanalyzed. As with the discourse notions I used in section II, it is taken for granted that it is clear enough in specific cases to make the characterization of presupposition useful. Especially when we leave felicity unanalyzed, it is tempting to make the generalization I mentioned at the outset, that presupposition failure and expression failure are one-and-the-same. In so far as the basic point of assertion is to express propositions—to convey information—is not the linguistically relevant notion of felicity that of expressing a proposition? If so, does not the notion of presupposition failure correspond exactly to that of expression failure (once we factor out cancelation and accommodation)? One half of this correspondence holds trivially. Any expression failure will be an infelicity of some kind. Hence, according to the characterization of presupposition I have sketched here, all expression failures are presupposition failures. It is the converse direction which is more problematic. The conjecture that all presupposition failures are expression failures is tempting, but I shall argue in the next section that it does not hold.

IV Presuppositional Phenomena

The characterization of presupposition given in the last section is highly abstract. To test the conjecture that all presupposition failures are expression failures, we need a better picture of the range of presuppositions to be found in natural language.

Linguists have identified a great many presuppositional phenomena. They are usually described in terms of *presupposition triggers*: constructions or lexical items whose presence generates, or at least usually generates, a presuppositional requirement. Presupposition triggers themselves come from many sources. Here is a sample of such requirements and their triggers and sources. Following common usage, I label the presuppositional requirements generated by each sentence simply as its presupposition:

(19) *a.* DEMONSTRATIVE NPs: That palm tree is about to fall.
- Presupposition: Contextually available value of *that palm tree.*
- Trigger: Demonstrative NP *that palm tree.*
- Source: Semantic value of trigger.

b. FACTIVES: John regrets voting for Bush.
- Presupposition: John voted for Bush.
- Trigger: Lexical item *regret.*
- Source: Conversational implicature.

c. CLEFTS: It was John who solved the problem
- Presupposition: Someone solved the problem.
- Trigger: Structure of cleft.
- Source: Linguistic rules (usually classified as conventional).

d. FOCUS-SENSITIVE PARTICLES: Even John solved the problem.
- Presupposition: Someone other than John solved the problem, and it was unlikely or unexpected that John did.
- Trigger: Lexical item *even.*
- Source: Conventional implicature (?).

e. ITERATIVES: John solved the problem too.
- Presupposition: Someone other than John solved the problem.
- Trigger, lexical item *too.*
- Source: Conventional implicature (?).

I shall discuss the sources of these presuppositions further in section V, and in the cases of conventional implicatures, I shall question the aptness of the label (though not really the basic point). This list is hardly exhaustive, or beyond controversy, but it does give a representative sample of the types of presuppositions.[20]

---

[20] Surveys of presuppositional phenomena, along with original references, may be found in van der Sandt (1988), Soames (1989), and Beaver (1997). Karttunen and Peters (1979) identify the presuppositions of *too* and *even* as conventional implicatures. Stalnaker (1974) argues that factive presuppositions are conversational. The argument is developed in Chierchia and McConnell-Ginet (1990). Related arguments are applied to other presupposition triggers in Levinson (1983) and Simons (2001*b*, n.d.). A survey of the issue of sources of presuppositions is given in Kadmon (2001).

There are a number of other commonly identified presuppositions, and some controversial ones. Demonstratives are usually classified as carrying referential presuppositions. Definite NPs more generally carry presuppositions, though there is controversy over exactly what the presuppositions are. The same holds for many quantificational NPs. Implicative verbs (e.g. *manage*) trigger presuppositions, presumably through their conventional implicatures.

We have already seen that demonstrative presupposition failure normally leads to expression failure. Applying the repair tests, we may ask about the rest of the presuppositions on the list. The failure of factive presuppositions appears to induce obligatory repair. Consider a context in which it is common ground that John did not vote for Bush, so the presupposition of *regret* (19*b*) cannot be accommodated. We see obligatory repair. The echo-assessment test yields:

(20) *a.* John regrets voting for Bush.
   b. Is that true?
   c. Er...John did not vote for Bush.

Applying the indirect discourse test we find:

(21) *a.* # John said he regrets voting for Bush.
   b. John said 'I regret voting for Bush', but he did NOT vote for Bush in the first place.

This gives failure for (19*b*) the same status as demonstrative failure (4). It counts by our tests as failure to express a proposition.[21]

I find the same results for clefts (19*c*). Thus, we have presupposition failure for the first three entries on the list leading to expression failure, as our conjecture predicted.

Sometimes one sees predicates with selectional restrictions counted as triggering presuppositions, though I think a Stalnaker-type analysis of presupposition makes this dubious. There is some controversy over whether focus generates presupposition, which we shall look at briefly in section V. The question of focal presupposition is addressed in Jackendoff (1972), Rooth (1999), Herburger (2000), and Kadmon (2001).

   [21] Mandy Simons suggested a case where *regret* may not appear to trigger obligatory repair:

(i) *a.* John doesn't regret voting for Bush.
   b. Yes, that's right, he didn't vote for him.

There are two points to make about this sort of case. In many contexts, the continuation of the answer is strongly required, and it seems to me to count as a repair. Hence, this need not present a counter-example. But perhaps more importantly, as I shall discuss at more length in section V.4, factive presuppositions are contextually cancelable. Much as Simons (2001*b*) herself argues for change-of-state verbs, factives appear to be canceled in contexts of total ignorance of the circumstances. Suppose we have:

(ii) *a.* I wonder what's going on with John.
   b. Well, he doesn't seem to regret voting for Bush.
   c. That's right (he didn't vote for him at all).

Here the continuation may be merely optional, but I am inclined to think the presupposition is simply canceled in this context, so we do not have presupposition failure at all.

However, quite a few presuppositions do not have this status. Instead, they have the status of repair *optional* discussed in section II. Representatives on our list are *even* (19*d*) and *too* (19*e*). Consider a context where the presupposition of (19*d*) cannot be accommodated. Suppose, for instance, that it is common ground that John is the most likely among relevant people to have solved the problem (and that this is not open for revision or discussion). We get:

(22) *a.* Even John solved the problem.
     b. Yes, John did . . . but why did you say 'even'?
     c. # That's NOT SO. He would have solved it if anyone did.

The indirect speech report test supports this:

(23) *a.* Even I solved the problem. (*said by John.*)
     b. John said that even he solved the problem . . . but of course, that's a bid odd, as he would have if anyone did.
     c. # John said 'Even I solved the problem', but that doesn't make sense, because he was most likely to have done it.

Our repair tests indicate that none of these amounts to expression failure; rather, they have the weaker failure marked by *optional* repair. I believe raw intuitions agree (for what they are worth). In the *even* case, the proposition expressed appears to be just that John solved the problem. We seem to get exactly the same proposition in the *too* case. The contrast with cases like (4) is strong. Though there is clearly *something* wrong with these utterances, neither intuition, nor the repair test, indicates expression failure.[22]

The breakdown appears to be this: our representatives of presuppositions triggered by semantic value requirements, structural positions, and conversational implicatures all appear to induce expression failure upon presupposition failure. For them, infelicity is expression failure. But our representatives of the presuppositions triggered by lexical items that carry conventional implicature appear to induce only the weaker status of repair optional. This is infelicity, as there is something wrong that is liable to be repaired, but it does not appear to be expression failure.[23]

---

[22] Observations along similar lines are found in Stalnaker (1973) and Karttunen and Peters (1979). Karttunen and Peters note that criticism of a speaker for a failed presupposition of *even* would "normally be rather mild" (p. 12).

[23] This bears out a distinction drawn by Soames (1989), between *expressive* and *pragmatic* presuppositions.

The conjecture that all presupposition failures are expression failures is thus false. A great many presuppositions do not lead to expression failure. This leaves us with a number of puzzles. First of all, we need an explanation of what does lead to expression failure, if not presupposition failure generally. We still need to understand how expression failure comes about, and what role presupposition plays when it does. To achieve this, we need a better understanding of the nature of the infelicity that arises when specific presuppositions fail. But moreover, we would like to explain the division among presuppositions this section has pointed out. It is not a simple conventional vs conversational division, for instance, as we find conventional elements on both sides.

V Analyzing Elementary Presuppositions

The only way to solve these puzzles is to look more closely at the details of some cases of presupposition. I started in section I with a highly abstract picture of what it is to express or fail to express a proposition. The subsequent sections began to fill in some details in this abstract picture. Section II offered some details on how expression failure may be identified. Sections III and IV began to fill in some details of how expression failure arises, by connecting it to presupposition and to the well-known range of presuppositional phenomena. But by the end of section IV we saw that the picture cannot be completed without a more thorough investigation of specific presuppositions.

I shall do this here for some of the key cases. The question we face is somewhat different from the usual one in the presupposition literature. I shall be almost entirely unconcerned with the projection of presupposition in complex sentences. Rather, we need to find out how specific triggers give rise to presuppositions in simple sentences, and what happens when these presuppositions fail. This is a task of analyzing *elementary* presuppositions.

V.1 More on Update Semantics

To analyze elementary presuppositions, I shall rely on the basic framework of assertion as context update described in section III. This has been applied to presupposition by a number of authors (e.g. Heim, 1983, 1992; van der Sandt, 1992; Zeevat, 1992; van Eijck, 1994; Krahmer, 1998; Beaver, 2001), mostly in connection with the projection problem. As I will not be concerned with projection, I need only some very basic features of the framework.

As we saw in section III above, the assertion of sentence S in context C conveys information by producing an update of C. Following the discussion of section I, we may assume it does so by way of some instructions linguistically encoded by S, which I shall call *update instructions*. As we may assume the encoding of these instructions, and the use of the sentence to convey that they are to be applied to C, are common ground, this ensures that the update of C by S amounts to the expression of a proposition, by the Gricean standard given in (3).

In the simplest case, as I discussed in section III, the update instruction encoded by S is simply to add the semantic value of S to C. The proposition expressed is then $S + [[S]]^C = C \cap [[S]]^C$. Where possible, I shall omit the double brackets. So, if S is an atomic sentence $F(t)$ displaying no context-dependence, then I indicate the update instruction encoded by S as:

(24) $C \mapsto C + [F(t)]$

However, it is known that there are other sorts of update instructions, which do more than simply adding a proposition to a context.

The kind of update instruction which will be of importance here involves setting up targets for inter-sentential anaphora. This is typical of indefinites (as in the treatments of Heim (1982) and Kamp (1984)) or so-called 'dynamic' existential quantifiers (as in the treatment of Groenendijk and Stokhof, 1991). To take a simple example (from Groenendijk and Stokhof, 1991), consider:

(25) A man walks in the park. He whistles.

The update instructions encoded by this discourse is:

(26) $C \mapsto C + [\exists x P(x)] + [W(x)]$

I shall for the most part skip the technical development of dynamic quantifiers (a brief presentation is given in the appendix). But informally, the first instruction sets up a discourse referent x which is taken to satisfy P. Subsequent occurrences of x are anaphoric on this discourse referent. Hence, x in the second instruction behaves as if 'dynamically bound' by the existential quantifier in the first instruction. (Of course, we then have to think of truth or falsehood as relative to both possible circumstances and assignments of values to discourse referents.)

Presuppositions can behave in ways similar to discourse anaphors, as was noted by Sandt (1992). Borrowing one of his examples, compare:

(27) *a.* A man walks in the park. He whistles.
b. John is ill. Mary regrets it.

The propositional anaphor *it* satisfies the presupposition of the factive, by finding the right proposition provided by previous discourse. I shall exploit a connection between presupposition and discourse anaphora, though a somewhat different one, as I develop an explanation of some elementary presuppositions.

Now that we have the basic framework of update semantics, I shall apply it to explain how elementary presuppositions arise, and what happens when they fail. I shall propose that a single dynamic operator creates presuppositional update instructions. Understanding how this operator relates to other update instructions will help explain why presupposition failures fall into two categories, and will, I believe, shed some light on how expression failure arises.[24]

I shall present my analysis in the course of examining one important presupposition trigger, the *cleft construction*, in section V.2. Then in sections V.3 and V.4, I shall show that the same analysis can be applied to other presuppositions mentioned in the list (19) of section IV.

V.2 Clefts

To see how elementary presuppositions relate to update instructions, we must look at individual cases of presupposition. It turns out to be useful to start with the cleft construction.

Clefts pattern with demonstratives and factives in inducing expression failure, according to the repair tests. As I noted in (19*c*), clefts carry an existential presupposition. Consider a context *C* in which this presupposition cannot be accommodated; for instance, one in which we are discussing the fact that no one has solved the problem. In such a context, we find repair obligatory:

---

[24] Much of the discussion of the relations between presupposition and anaphora, starting with van der Sandt (1992), have concentrated on how this might explain presupposition projection. As my interest here is not in projection, my discussion here will be somewhat different in focus.

I should also mention that many treatments of presupposition in dynamic frameworks dispense with 'static' meanings altogether, in favor of 'context-change potentials' as in Heim (1983). In section III, I offered a Stalnaker-inspired hybrid, with both dynamic and static elements. The rest of my discussion follows suit. I believe this is all that is needed to make the points I offer here, but all that I say can easily enough be converted into a fully dynamic framework. For critical comments on some of the motivations for such a framework, see Stalnaker (1998).

(28) *a.* The problem is unsolvable.
    b. It was John who solved the problem.
    c. Is that right?
    d. Err... no one solved the problem (as we all know).

No assessment or reporting of content seems possible until we repair the utterance. We have expression failure.[25]

The truth conditions of a cleft are plausibly that the clefted constituent (which immediately follows *it was*) gives an exhaustive list of what satisfies the following CP, where exhaustiveness is restricted to a contextually salient set of individuals I_C. Thus the truth conditions of (19*c*) are:

(29) *a.* It was John who solved the problem.
    b. $\forall x \in I_C(P(x) \longleftrightarrow x = j)$

I suggest we see the update instructions encoded by a cleft like (19*c* = 29) as looking like:

(30) Find an x such that $P(x)$ in the context. An exhaustive list of the contextually salient values x can take is given by j.

I shall first discuss how to represent these instructions, and then discuss how we get them from the cleft construction.

I shall write the instruction 'find an x in the context satisfying $P(x)$' as $\downarrow xP(x)$. As we must bear in mind accommodation, we can see successful processing of this instruction as occurring in one of two ways:

(31) $\downarrow xF(x) =$
    a. Find an x satisfying $F(x)$ in the context, or
    b. update the context to include an x satisfying $F(x)$, and proceed.

(Actually, I am unsure if we need to write the second clause explicitly into the semantics of $\downarrow$. As a kind of repair strategy, accommodation is always available, and the second clause simply describes how it would be carried out for the case of $\downarrow xF(x)$. But regardless, the second clause serves to remind us that accommodation is available.)

---

[25] There are some well-known complications about the discourse status of clefts. It is quite common to see clefts used to induce accommodation. The example I discuss has a pitch accent on the clefted constituent *John*. There is a distinct class of clefts that have a pitch accent on the CP (a focus?). These have notably different discourse properties, as discussed by Prince (1978) and Delin (1992).

On the proposal I shall make, it is the presence of $\downarrow$ that sets up a presupposition (and creates their anaphoric potentials). For the moment, I shall skip the formal development, as I think the intuitive idea of finding something in the context, and thereby making it salient in a way that allows for anaphoric reference, is clear enough.[26] (A brief and preliminary sketch of a more technical development of the semantics of $\downarrow x\phi(x)$ is given in the appendix.)

Using this notation, the update instruction for the cleft (29) is:

(32) $C \mapsto C + [\,\downarrow xP(x)\,] + [x = j]$

These instructions result in the truth conditions given in (29). They also provide for the existential presupposition. The instruction $[\,\downarrow xP(x)\,]$ can only be processed if the context entails $\exists xP(x)$.

Though these update instructions get the right truth conditions and presupposition, it still needs to be shown that they derive from the compositional semantics of the cleft. Unfortunately, a great deal about clefts—both their syntactic structure and many of their semantic properties—remains controversial. As I shall not be able to resolve these issues, I shall not be able to provide a compositional derivation of the update instructions. Even so, I do want to pause to note that an independently motivated analysis of clefts fits well with what I have proposed. I hope this at least makes my suggestion plausible.

Following Kiss (1998), let us suppose that the clefted constituent is marked for what she calls *identificational focus*. The function of identification focus, unlike the more familiar focus marked by pitch accent in English, is to mark a collection of values for which some predicate might hold as the exhaustive list of values for which it does hold. Identificational focus creates the truth conditions of exhaustive listing we saw in (29).

---

[26] There are a number of other proposals for how to account for presuppositions via a dynamic operator; notably, the ∂ operator (due primarily to Beaver (e.g. 2001), also discussed extensively in Krahmer, 1998). These proposals generally base presupposition on *partiality*, either by making the context-update function partial, or by making the update operation itself a partial operation in a many-valued or partial logic (cf. Heim, 1983; van Eijck, 1993, 1994; Krahmer, 1998; Beaver, 2001). Examples like (22), which show that we can have presupposition failure without expression failure, suggest that such an analysis is not refined enough. My analysis via $\downarrow$ seeks to uncover more details about how elementary presuppositions emerge, and what happens when they fail. In starting with a non-partial framework, and in exploiting connections with anaphora, my approach has some affinities with that of van der Sandt (1992), though the question of how closely they might be related is a complex one. (For some discussion of the relations between dynamic approaches to presupposition, see Zeevat, 1992.)

Structurally, this puts the clefted constituent in a syntactically marked position. We can think of this as looking something like:[27]

(33) [It was [John$_i$]$_{F^{ID}}$ [who$_i$ t$_i$ solved the problem]]

According to Kiss, the semantics of the F^{ID}-position provides the value of an operator expressing exhaustive listing. Writing this operator *EXH*, the relevant semantic structure looks like:

(34) *a.* [[John$_i$]$_{F^{ID}}$ [who$_i$ t$_i$ solved the problem]]
      b. John $= EXH_i$[t$_i$ solved the problem]

Semantically, we thus have the same structure in:

(35) *a.* It was John who solved the problem.
      b. John is the one who solved the problem.

Both have the truth conditions given in (29).

We get the update instructions of (32) by breaking up the processing of *EXH* into two steps, given informally in (36*b*) and more formally in (36*c*):

(36) *a.* $EXH_x(P(x)) = j$
      b. Find an x in the context. An exhaustive list of the values x can take is given by j.
      c. $[\downarrow xP(x)] + [EXH(x) = j]$

The first part of the processing of *EXH* is its presuppositional contribution. The second provides its asserted content, based on that presupposition.

More needs to be said to fully explain the mapping of LF to update instructions for clefts, but I hope this is enough to make the update instructions I have proposed plausible. I am more concerned now to point out that the update instructions explain both the presuppositions triggered by clefts, and their repair obligatory status.

First, executing the instruction $[\downarrow xP(x)]$ requires there to be a contextually salient x such that $P(x)$. Hence, the context must entail $\exists xP(x)$ for the execution of this instruction to be possible. For an utterance to be felicitous, it must be possible to carry out the update instructions it encodes (bearing in mind the possibility of accommodation). We thus find that for a cleft to be

---

[27] Kiss (1998) argues for a much more specific proposal on the structure of clefts. She proposes that the clefted constituent occupies the specifier position of a functional projection FP (focus phrase). Her analysis provides a structure like:

(i) [$_{IP}$ It was [$_{FP}$ John$_i$ [$_{CP}$ who$_i$ [$_{IP}$ t$_i$ solved the problem]]]]

Spec-FP is the F^{ID}-position.

felicitous, we must have $\exists x P(x)$ implied by the context. This is just the presuppositional requirement we saw above.[28]

Second, in this case, if the presupposition fails, we get expression failure. This may be explained by (32), together with the Gricean constraints on expression from (3). First of all, we should note that if the instruction $[\,\downarrow x P(x)\,]$ cannot be executed, neither can the instruction $[x = j]$. Hence, if the presupposition fails, none of the update instructions can be carried out. This is enough of a failure to violate the conditions of (3). The speaker is trying to convey a proposition by entering into the common ground that it is to be identified by executing a sequence of update instructions. The attempt to execute the instructions fails entirely, leaving the conversation no common ground information about what the speaker is trying to convey. Expression fails.

The failure to express a proposition has both semantic and Gricean factors. Semantically, it should be stressed that when the presuppositional instruction $[\,\downarrow x P(x)\,]$ fails, x is not set up as a discourse referent. As a result the subsequent instruction $[x = j]$ is not even defined. (As I discuss briefly in the appendix, this is already a stronger sort of failure than we see in the repair optional cases, where the relevant instructions are defined, but executing them leads to a failure state.) This sort of catastrophic failure of the update instructions creates a situation where no proposition can be the proposition conveyed, by the Gricean constraints of (3).

In repair optional cases, we will see that these factors can interact in other ways. In these cases, the update instructions fail in more innocuous ways, which allow for identification of a proposition expressed. To see how this may occur, we should turn our attention to the repair optional cases of *even* and *too*.

V.3 Presuppositions from 'Conventional Implicatures'

Many presupposition triggers appear to derive from conventional implicatures, including our examples of *even* (19d) and *too* (19e) (as was argued in the classic Karttunen and Peters, 1979).[29] We have also seen a marked difference in behavior between the presuppositions deriving from conventional

---

[28] I thus depart fairly dramatically from the classic discussion of Atlas and Levinson (1981). With Kiss, I am agreeing with Atlas and Levinson that the semantics of clefts includes exhaustiveness. For an opposing view, see Horn (1981).

[29] For further discussion see Kadmon (2001).

implicatures and others we have considered. Presupposition failure for pre-suppositions with sources in conventional implicature does not appear to induce expression failure. We get the status of *only* repair optional. I shall propose that we can see these presuppositions as having the same basic source as clefts: the presence of a ↓ operator. The difference in effects upon failure is the result of what happens when the update instructions are processed; not a difference in the basic nature of the presuppositions themselves. Indeed, I shall conclude this subsection by asking to what extent the category of conventional implicature might be subsumed under that of presuppos-ition—under that of the ↓ instruction.

Let us look more closely at the case of *even*, more or less following Rooth (1985). In (19*d*) I was not careful about where the focus (the 'focal stress' or pitch accent) falls. It is probably natural to read it as *Even JOHN solved the problem*. This might appear to have the structure:

(37) [[_{NP} Even JOHN] solved the problem]

One of the important points about *even* is that its semantics is sensitive to which constituent is in *focus*. Once we mark that, it will simplify our discussion, and not seriously effect the content of what I shall propose, to treat *even* as a sentential operator, giving:

(38) [[Even] [[John]_F solved the problem]]

The constituent marked F is in focus, realized in English by a pitch accent (the 'focal stress' indicated by capitals in (37)).

The interpretation of (38) is usually given in two parts:

(39) *a.* -
      $[[\text{Even John solved the problem}]]^C = [[\text{John solved the problem}]]^C$
      b. Presuppositions:
         (i) N solved the problem, for some contextually salient $N \neq$ John (the value of the focused constituent).
         (ii) For any contextually salient N such that N solved the prob-lem, it is more likely/expected that N solved the problem than that John solved the problem.

The presuppositional clause may be explained using the alternative semantics for focus (Rooth, 1985, 1992), in an appropriate form. For a sentence S with a focused constituent, let $Alt(S)$ be the set of propositions that result from replacing the focused constituent of S with each of its contextually salient alternatives. The presuppositional clauses then tell us that $Alt(S)$ is nonempty, and for any $p \in Alt(S)$, p is more likely than $[[S]]^C$. Let us abbreviate these conditions as $L_C(S)$. We can then abbreviate the semantic contribution of *even* as:

(40)   *a.* $[[Even\ S]]^C = [[S]]^C$
       b.   Presupposition: $L_C(S)$

There are quite a few ways this might be refined. For instance, the presupposition may require a context-dependent scale or measure of likelihood. This may or may not be a matter of probability *per se*. But we still have enough information in hand to begin to analyze the presupposition carried by *even*.[30]

We would like to offer the same sort of analysis as we gave for clefts, in terms of update instructions including $\downarrow$ instructions. It appears we can do so quite easily:

(41) $C \mapsto C + [\ \downarrow p(p = L_C(S))\ ] + [[S]]^C$

The presupposition here is conventionally attached to the lexical item *even*, by way of this update instruction. As usual, it generates the presuppositional requirement that $L_C(S)$ be implied by C, just as we expected.

Why then do we get only repair optional when we encounter failure of the instruction $[\ \downarrow p(p = L_C(S))\ ]$? After all, in the last case, we saw this sort of failure lead to obligatory repair.

The answer, I suggest, lies in the lack of connection between this instruction and anything else. In the cleft case, the $\downarrow$ instruction sets up a variable that is picked up by a later instruction. When the $\downarrow$ instruction fails, the variable is not set up, and the later instruction becomes undefined. This results in problems that interrupted the Gricean process of recognizing a proposition as conveyed, and so we have expression failure.

In the case of *even*, on the other hand, the $\downarrow$ instruction has no further effect. The semantics of *even* tells us what we are to look for in the context via $\downarrow$, but then provides no instructions relying on the context being that way. It makes no use of the variable $\downarrow$ sets up. Rather, it says simply: check to see if the context satisfies L_C, but then update by computing $[[S]]^C$.[31]

When this instruction cannot be executed, it is a defect. Hence, we have infelicity, and indeed we get repair optional status. But, it is not a defect that

---

[30] As I mentioned, I am more or less following Rooth here. His analysis builds on earlier work of Karttunen and Peters (1979).

[31] That the presuppositions and asserted content of *even* are independent (often called the phenomenon of 'presuppositional independence') was noted in Karttunen and Peters (1979).

interrupts the Gricean process. We can still determine the information content—the proposition—conveyed, by the subsequent instructions. These are well-defined, and are entered into the common ground by the utterance. Hence, we do meet the Gricean constrains of (3), even in spite of the failure to execute the $\downarrow$ instruction.

We see a similar result for iteratives like *too*. There we find something like:

(42) $C + \text{JOHN left too} = C + [\downarrow x(x \neq \text{John} \wedge \text{left}(x))] + [[\text{John left}]]^C$

This puts us in just the same situation as *even* when the presupposition fails.[32]

One moral of this situation is for the way we understand update computations. We have here an instance of a 'fault-tolerant' computation: one which is able to reach its end in spite of failure in one of its instructions. In the case of $\downarrow$ instructions, in particular, the semantics tells us something about where a fault-tolerant computation might be available. According to the semantics of the appendix, failures of $\downarrow$ instructions are not matters of the operation being undefined. As $\downarrow$ sets up discourse referents, it is always defined. Rather, failure of a $\downarrow$ instruction amounts to not finding what we need in the context. In the formal semantics, this results in the context being updated to the empty set. This is a violation of the Gricean norms of assertion (as in Stalnaker (1978)), and so an infelicity. But we have a natural fault-tolerant option when this happens. Simply rest to the prior context, and go on. In the cases of *even* and *too*, this process allows us to successfully compute the instructions that tell us what the asserted content of the sentence is to be, so we satisfy the Gricean constraints on expression as in (3). In the cases of clefts, however, the result of the fault-tolerant option is that the remaining update instructions become undefined entirely. We cannot even attempt to execute them. Thus, we violate the requirements of expression.

My analyses of *even* and *too* provide lexical entries which include $\downarrow$ instructions. These parts of the entries cover what is usually glossed as the conventional implicatures of these terms. Before leaving these examples, we should ask if this is the right result.

To a great extent, I am not sure if there is a substantial issue here. The lexical entries I have given make it the case that these terms conventionally carry information that is clearly separate from their propositional content

---

[32] Here again, the basic analysis of *too* comes from Karttunen and Peters (1979). The anaphoric aspect of *too* was noted by Kripke (reported in Soames, 1989), and is discussed in Heim (1992). For a treatment in DRT, which also explains the presuppositional independence of *too*, see van der Sandt and Geurts (2001).

(the update instructions that have any truth-conditional effect on context). Thus, we have the marks of conventional implicature. We could, if we wanted, replace my lexical entries with ones that had a special category of 'conventional implicature'. But if we did, we would then need to have a rule that made conventional implicatures affect update by being placed in the scope of a ↓ operator. The results would be exactly the same.

It thus seems simpler to me to treat these expressions as presuppositional, and not worry about the category of conventional implicature. I suspect that one reason for resisting this is the sense that the failure of a presupposition associated with a conventional implicature is different from that of demonstratives presuppositions or cleft presuppositions. But one of the virtues of my analysis is that this difference is explained directly, and so we do not need to appeal to the additional category of conventional implicature.

V.4 Factives

So far, we have seen how to account for some presuppositions by way of update instructions based on the ↓ operation. Moreover, these analyses offered us a way to explain the difference in expressive status of presuppositions like those of clefts, which lead to expression failure, and those of *even* and *too*, which do not. This is explained by the interaction of ↓ with other update instructions, and whether this leads to a sufficiently catastrophic crash of the update process to undermine the Gricean conditions on expression.

But so far, we have only looked at cases where a presupposition is conventionally encoded; by my analysis, encoded by a ↓ instruction. I have taken it for granted that there are some presuppositions whose sources are *conversational*. If the ↓-analysis of presupposition is to be adequate, we need to find a way of explaining such conversationally generated presuppositions in terms of it.

Above I offered factives (19*b*) as a typical case of a conversationally generated presupposition. This analysis is usually defended on the basis of the contextual defeasibility of these presuppositions, which comes close to the cancelability of conversational implicatures. Standard examples of contexts in which we do not have presuppositions for factives include:[33]

---

[33] Many authors have discussed these issues. The first example below is based on Stalnaker (1974), and the second on Levinson (1983). These sorts of examples are discussed at length in Chierchia and McConnell-Ginet (1990) and (somewhat critically) Kadmon (2001). Similar arguments for change-of-state verbs are given in Simons (2001*b*, n.d.).

(43) *a.* (i) If I discover that I left my bag in the restaurant, I'll be angry.
(ii) Context: looking for the bag (do not know where it is).
b. (i) At least John won't have to regret that he did a PhD.
(ii) Context: John dropped out of graduate school.

I shall assume these establish that factive presuppositions are conversational in nature, but they do not show just what the conversational source is, or how it works.

I noted in section IV that presupposition failure for factives leads to expression failure: we get obligatory repair. We could explain this if we found them to induce ↓ update instructions, and make further use of the variables these instructions set up (as we saw with clefts). This is what I shall propose. But in this case, due to the conversational nature of the presuppositions, no analysis which simply locates ↓ instructions in the meanings of factives can succeed. We need to explain how *conversational phenomena* can introduce ↓ instructions into the update procedures for factives.

An account of the generation of factive presuppositions, which I shall partially endorse, is found in Stalnaker (1974). It is based on the observation that factives *entail* their complements. *John knows p*, for instance, entails *p*. An entailment is not normally a presupposition: entailments do not normally survive under negation. Why should this entailment be different? Stalnaker argues as follows. Consider a typical utterance of *j knows p*:

[The speaker] would be leaving unclear whether his main point was to make a claim about the truth of [*p*], or to make a claim about the epistemic situation of [*j*] (the knower), and thus leaving unclear what direction he intended or expected the conversation to take. (Stalnaker, 1974: 55)

The story is basically Gricean. Speakers would be uncooperative if they failed to indicate which claim is primary. This can be remedied by making one claim presupposed rather than asserted.

There is a potential problem with this story: it might imply much too much. It seems as if it could be applied to *any entailment*. But many entailments do not carry presuppositions, even highly defeasible ones. We do not expect a conjunction $A \wedge B$ normally to presuppose one of its conjuncts, for instance. Consider:

(44) I voted for Bush and I don't like it.

In a setting in which I am well-known to have never even entertained voting for him, you will simply reply 'that is obviously not true'. Maybe this will tend to induce interpretations of irony, but not necessarily. If you overhear me trying to get in good with the lapsed Democrats club, you might just mutter under your breath 'liar'.

Indeed, we see this with the contents of factives themselves. Let us suppose that factives break down into two components: a fact component and an agent component. For *know*, this is given by the traditional analysis of knowledge, which breaks it down into an epistemic component (justified belief plus whatever else is required), and a factive component (the truth of the belief). We can likewise think of *regret* as being defined in terms of an agent component (the agent taking a negative propositional attitude—something like being sad) and a factive component.[34] Hence, we may suppose:

(45) *a.* know $(x,p)\longleftrightarrow E(x, p) \wedge^\vee p$
      b. regret $(x, p)\longleftrightarrow S(x, p)\wedge^\vee p$

(I do not want to make any particular claim about lexical decomposition here. Any way in which the meanings of these terms can be broken down into these components that makes the breakdown available to speakers for Gricean computations will suffice.)

The presupposition of *regret* would be nicely explained if its semantics generated an update instruction like:

(46) $C \mapsto C + [\ \downarrow x(x = p)] + [S(j, x)]$

(Cf. Beaver, 2001: ch. 6.) But this is not what the analysis of the meaning of *regret* in (45) gives us. Moreover, if it were, we would lose the conversational nature of the presupposition. What we need, it seems, is for there to be some conversational way to make the step from $S(j, p) \wedge^\vee p$ to $[\ \downarrow x(x = p)] + [S(j, x)]$. Moreover, this must occur in a way that does not require all entailments to undergo a similar transformation. I shall attempt to derive such a transformation along the lines Stalnaker suggests. But to avoid the over-generation of any old entailment turning into a presupposition, we will have to be much more careful with ideas about the ways that assertions relate to the direction of conversation.

First, I shall try to fill in the idea of direction in a conversation. The basic idea for doing so is one of coordinating on discourse topics. One way to set a discourse topic is to ask a question:

(47) Where is Bill?
      a. Bill is at the store.
      b. #Mary is at the store.

---

[34] *Sad* does not quite express what we want, as it itself appears to be factive. We need a non-factive negative propositional attitude.

Answering a question properly amounts to a kind of conversational relevance. Failing to do so is a kind of irrelevance. It is clear enough that this leads to some sort of conversational infelicity.

A similar constraint operates even when no explicit question has been asked. Compare:

(48) John did not come to work to day.
    a. He must be sick.
    b. # It might rain today.

The initial utterance, together with background circumstances, sets a discourse topic. This is so whether the utterance asks a question as in (47) or makes an assertion as in (48). The second utterance is only felicitous if it collaborates on the discourse topic.

This suggests a general principle:

(49) THE TOPIC COLLABORATION PRINCIPLE: A felicitous utterance must collaborate on the current discourse topic.

For most of what follows, this rough and informal statement will be clear enough. But I shall spend a moment discussing what would be involved in making it precise.

First, we might take more or less seriously the idea that a discourse topic is a question. Following Roberts (1996), we might develop this idea as follows. In the tradition of Hamblin, we can see the semantic value of a question as a set of propositions: those that count as answers to the question. For the wh-question *Who came to dinner?* asked in a context C with a contextually salient set of individuals I_C, this looks like $\{[[x \text{ came to dinner}]] | x \in I_C\}$.

Roberts defines a *partial answer* to a question in a context as any proposition that contextually implies an element of the semantic value of the question or the negation of one. A sufficient condition for collaborating on a discourse topic is then given by:

(50) If an assertion is a partial answer to the discourse topic of a context, it satisfies the Topic Collaboration Principle.

This is not anywhere near the whole story. I doubt it is even a genuine sufficient condition, as the range of contextually available implications will outstrip those that really make an answer count as appropriate. As I have argued elsewhere (2002), the topic structure of discourse is about as complicated as anything can be.[35] But for our purposes, we can work with (50) as a rough approximation of the felicity constraint we need.

Stalnaker's suggestion can be spelled out by looking at the behavior of conjunctions as answers to questions. Compare:

(51) *a.* What are we going to do today?
  b. We are going skiing and we are going to the museum.
(52) *a.* What are we going to have for dinner?
  b. #We are having pasta for dinner and it is raining outside.

The apparent generalization here is:

(53) A conjunction collaborates on a discourse topic only if each conjunct does.

This principle is reasonably well motivated, as it basically combines the Topic Collaboration Principle and the idea that each conjunct effects a separate update instruction, and so acts 'as if' a separate assertion. (I am putting aside the well-known fact that conjunctions generate implicatures, roughly of temporal or causal connection between the conjuncts.)

However, the principle is not sufficiently accurate. There are at least two ways a conjunction can collaborate on a topic: they can each partially address the topic, or the second conjunct can address a subtopic introduced by the first conjunct. Compare:

(54) *a.* Why is John a good baseball player?
  b. He runs fast and he throws far.
(55) *a.* What happened to John?
  b. His sister got sick, and she was taken to the hospital.

A more accurate principle seems to be:

(56) A conjunction $A \wedge B$ collaborates on a discourse topic Q only if either:
  a. A collaborates on Q and B collaborates on Q.
  b. A collaborates on Q and B collaborates on the topic of $Q + A$.

This is fairly close.[36] It is not perfect, as it does not fully reflect some rather delicate constraints on how topics may evolve in a discourse. For instance, it does not rule out:

---

[35] These issues have been discussed in a number of other places, including Carlson (1983) and van Kuppevelt (1995).

[36] A similar idea is developed for disjunction in Simons (2001*a*).

(57) *a.* What happened to John?
    b. ?? His mother died and he stubbed his toe.

However, I think we are close enough to try to address the behavior of factives.[37]

In light of this principle, let us consider again the case of *regret*. A fairly typical discourse topic for its appropriate use is something like:

(58) How is John feeling?
    a. # He voted for Bush.
    b. #/?? He feels sad about voting for Bush and he voted for Bush.
    c. He regrets voting for Bush.

Likewise we see:

(59) Can John pass the physics test?
    a. #$F = MA$.
    b. #/?? He believes $F = MA$ and $F = MA$.
    c. He knows/realizes that $F = MA$.

As these illustrate, in many cases where we would like to use terms like *regret*, the factive conjuncts of their meanings cannot collaborate on the discourse topic.

Now, any time we have a conversational rule like (56), and an utterance to which it applies, it is indicated conversationally that the utterance is in compliance with the rule. This is just a special case of Grice's general cooperative principle. And as with any application of this principle, conversational implicatures can be generated to preserve compliance with it.

In cases like (58) and (59), using the conjunction (*b*) would violate the conversational rule (56). This sets up the opportunity for an implicature which corrects the violation. In these cases, I suggest the implicature is that the factive component is to be put in the scope of a ↓ instruction. For the case of *regret*, for instance, this transforms the update instructions from $[S(j, p) \wedge^{\vee} p]$ into $[\downarrow x(x = p)] + [S(j, x)]$.

Now, instructions of the form $[\downarrow xF(x)]$ appear to be immune to the topic collaborating principle. We see this with more explicit directions as well:

(60) How is John feeling?
    a. #/?? He feels sad about voting for Bush and he voted for Bush.

---

[37] I examined constraints that might be relevant to cases like (57) in my (2002).

   b. Well, you already know he voted for Bush, and he feels really sad about it.[38]

   c. $[\downarrow x(x = [[\text{John voted for Bush}]])] + [S(j, x)]$

We can thus reconstruct the transformation as a typical kind of conversational reasoning:

   (i) The assertion of *John regrets voting for Bush* does not appear to be in accord with the conversational principle (56).
   (ii) It fails to be so because its content is in the form of a conjunction, where the conjunct $^{\vee}p$ does not collaborate on the discourse topic.
   (iii) The utterance would thus satisfy the principle if the conjunct $^{\vee}p$ were put in the scope of $\downarrow$.

The result is just the presuppositional requirement we have seen for factives. Successful execution of $[\downarrow x(x = p)]$ requires precisely that the context already imply p.

As with clefts, failure of this sort of presupposition results in expression failure. Again as with clefts, the update semantics, together with the Gricean constraint on expression, explains why. If the instruction $[\downarrow x(x = p)]$ fails, then the instruction $S(j,x)$ is undefined. As with clefts, this creates a situation where the constraint on expression (3) cannot be satisfied.

In this case, we might wonder why a different fault-tolerant strategy might not be available, which could reduce the infelicity to repair optional, rather than expression failure. When the $\downarrow$ instruction fails, why not just revert to computing $S(j,p)$, skipping the need for x and making the instruction well-defined? The reason, I suggest, is again basically Gricean. This process will not manage to provide a proposition *expressed*, by the conditions of (3). In cases where the presupposition is not contextually canceled, it is already in the common ground that to be cooperative, the utterance must be interpreted using the $\downarrow$-structure. For the speaker to succeed in what they are trying to accomplish, this instruction must be used. Hence, we can only recognize a proposition as having been conveyed by the speaker, by the lights of (3), in virtue of having been computed via this instruction. It is common ground that this cannot be done. Hence, no proposition can be expressed.

As a further test of the conversational account, we may verify that adding a $\downarrow$ instruction by way of the Gricean computation respects the accommodation

---

[38] The discourse marker *well* by itself is much more flexible than $\downarrow$. As Schiffrin (1985) documents, it can be used in many ways to mark points where some constraint on discourse coherence appears to be violated. *Well you already know* seems to mark deviation from (56) which $\downarrow$ simply avoids.

and cancelation behavior of factives. As I noted when I defined it, ↓ allows for accommodation if material is not already in the context. Hence, if we have no information about who John voted for, we can still have the presuppositional reading in:

(61)   a. What is going on with John?
         b. He regrets voting for Bush.

We find the presuppositions of factives to be canceled in those cases where we can see both conjuncts of the meaning analysis as collaborating on a topic. Here is a reasonably clear case:

(62)   a. What is likely to change your mood?
         b. If I discover that I left my bag in the restaurant, I'll be upset.

Here information about the bag is conversationally topical, and the presupposition is canceled. In contrast, we do get presuppositional readings in:

(63)   a. What's John's mental state like?
         b. If John discovers he left his bag in the restaurant, he'll be upset.
(64)   a. How are you feeling?
         b. ? If I discover that I left my bag in the restaurant, I'll be upset.

The first of these is fine; the location of the bag is not topical, and it has a presuppositional reading. The second is marginal. Indeed, it appears to violate a Q-maxim (Quantity) whether it is presuppositional or not, so it may not be a case where we even get to the Topic Collaboration Principle.

Now, assuming we can make sense of the conversational addition of ↓ instructions, we still have to clarify the difference in status between (58b) and (58c). The explicit conjunction is marginal to infelicitous, whereas the factive which should start out with the same content is fine. If we have an implicated instruction to add ↓, why should we not have it in both?

I believe there is a competing conversational principle that accounts for just the difference we see:

(65)   No felicitous utterance provides only update instructions in the scope of ↓.

An utterance that is entirely an instruction to find information in the background cannot be cooperative, as it cannot be informative. (This is thus an aspect of the informativeness principle of Stalnaker, 1978.) We can apply something like this to conjunctions as well. In update terms, we take each conjunct to count as a separate assertion, made in sequence. Thus, we should have:

(66) No felicitous utterance contains conjuncts which provide only update instructions in the scope of ↓.

This, of course, applies to explicitly uttered conjunctions, not to instructions encoded in the meaning of a single sentence.

We thus find (58*b*) to violate either (66) or (56). The impression I get upon hearing it is of attempting to satisfy (56) and getting only a marginal result, as in doing so we wind up violating (66). In contrast, we have no such problem with (58*c*).

To put the matter less formally, uttering *John regrets voting for Bush* threatens to violate the Topic Collaboration Principle by virtue of the content it provides. We can satisfy the Principle by reassigning some of that content to be found already in the context. In contrast, the explicit conjunction expli-citly offers a combination of two claims, one of which cannot satisfy the Principle. We could suppress it, by consigning it to the context, but then we violate the rule that one should not say something uninformative.

Let me conclude this section with a couple of remarks. I have offered a conversational account of the source of the presuppositions of factives. It must be noted, though, that a conversational instruction to put material in the scope of a ↓ operator is not an ordinary conversational implicature. Its content is something about the interpretation process itself, rather than more information about the world. There is one other clear example of this sort of process: the application of the diagonalization operator in Stalnaker (1978).

It might be best to think of the conversational process as more on par with the process of choosing readings of sentences. It amounts to showing that only one reading is available in a wide range of contexts. There are a few examples which tend to admit both presuppositional and non-presupposi-tional readings, such as:[39]

(67) She broke the camera before she took the picture.

This has a factive reading, where she took the picture, and a non-factive reading, where she did not. These can be bought out by:

(68) *a.* Did Sue take a picture?
b. She broke the camera before she took the picture (so I'm not sure if she was able to do it).

---

[39] Examples like this are discussed in Levinson (1983).

(69) *a.* Is Sue likely to break the computer?
      b. She broke the camera before she took the picture.

The second answer is presuppositional, the first is not.

Finally, let me say a word about the status of conversational principles like the Topic Collaboration Principle. These are instances of the general Gricean cooperative principle, but they also reflect the specific nature of discourse as a cooperative endeavor. I am sympathetic to the idea that they should be derivable from the cooperative principle, in the manner of the familiar Gricean maxims, perhaps together with a few more facts about discourse. But I do not have such a derivation, and I would not mind if they turned out to be special cooperative principles governing the rather special activity of communicating through discourse.

VI Conclusion

My goal in this chapter has been to shed some light on the phenomenon of expression failure. In section I, I examined in highly general terms what it is to express a proposition. This resulted in the Gricean constraint (3). I then turned to the question of how we may test for expression failure. I argued in section II that it corresponds to the discourse status of obligatory repair, which can be detected by the repair tests. In the remainder of the chapter, I turned to the issue of how expression failure arises. As I discussed in section III, the notion of presupposition provides a very general framework in which to investigate infelicities. This made inviting the conjecture that presupposition failure and expression failure are equivalent, and that to investigate the sources of expression failure, we simply need to catalog presupposition triggers. But we saw in section IV that this is not so. Some presuppositions lead to obligatory repair—to expression failure—upon failure, while some lead to the weaker status of repair optional. Explaining this difference led to a detailed examination of some elementary presuppositions in section V. This section showed how certain sequences of update instructions can interact with the Gricean constraint on expression to produce expression failure, while some can avoid expression failure even if they contain failing instructions.

The analyses I offered in section V were all based on the $\downarrow$-operator. Though I hardly began to analyze the full range of elementary presuppositions, I did consider some typical cases. This leads me to conjecture that all presuppositions can be explained in terms of ↓. Does this mean that all expression failure is derived from the kind of interaction between ↓-instructions, other update instructions, and the Gricean constraint we saw with clefts and factives?

Perhaps. At the very least, it does show us one fundamental way that expression failure can come about, even with a well-formed utterance of a grammatical sentence. Appreciating how this works, and how it differs from the situation in which the weaker status of repair optional emerges, gives us a richer understanding of the phenomenon of expression failure. It shows us not just how to test for expression failure in discourse, but how to explain what about the semantics and pragmatics of an utterance makes it fail to express a proposition.

APPENDIX: A TOY SEMANTICS FOR ↓

This is a sketch of some important parts of a highly simplified toy semantics for ↓ (using as a framework, a simplified version of Groenendijk *et al.*, 1996).

Start with a set W of worlds, and a domain of discourse D. D is the domain of contextually salient individuals, and we can pretend all worlds in W have universe D.

We can define a system of discourse referents r in D to be a (finite) partial function from the set of variables to D.

We then define $r[x/d]$ to be like r, but $dom(r[x/d]) = dom(r) \cup \{x\}$ and $r[x/d](x) = d$.

(The system of Groenendijk *et al.* (1996), like many systems of dynamic semantics, links variables (working as anaphors) first to discourse markers, and then interprets the discourse markers in D. But I will not make use of this feature here.)

A *possibility* based on D and W is a pair $\langle r,w \rangle$ where r is a system of discourse referents in D and $w \in W$.

An *information state* is a set of possibilities s such that if $i,i' \in s$, then i and i' have systems of discourse referents. Information states are sets of possibilities relative to a fixed system of discourse referents.

Let $i = \langle r,w \rangle, i' = \langle r',w' \rangle$. $i \leq i'$ iff $r \subseteq r'$ and $w = w'$. $s \leq s'$ iff *or all* $i' \in s' \; \exists i \in s (i \leq i')$.

Say s subsists in s' if $s \leq s'$ and every possibility in s has an extension in s'. If s subsists in s', s' changes s only by adding discourse referents.

Most context update clauses are standard. Update operations are applied to information states. For instance, writing $s[F(t)]$ for the update of information state s by $F(t)$, we have $s[F(t)] = \{i \in s \mid i \models F(t)\}$.

Genuine dynamic update is done by the existential quantifier $\exists$. Let $i[x/d] = \langle r[x/d], w \rangle$, and $s[x/d] = \{i[x/d] \mid i \in s\}$. The existential quantifier is then defined by:

$$s[\exists x \phi] = \cup_{d \in D}(s[x/d][\phi]).$$

$\exists$ can set up genuinely new discourse referents.

We now need to define the $\downarrow$-operator. $\downarrow x F(x)$ instructs us to find x such that $F(x)$ in the context if it is there. If it is, we set up x as a discourse referent, but otherwise, do nothing to the context. We are testing the context to see if it contains x such that $F(x)$, and the success of the test introduces the discourse referent but otherwise adds no content. The semantics of $\downarrow$ thus looks like

(70) $\quad \phi x \phi(x) = \begin{cases} \cup_{d \in D}(s[x/d][\phi]) & \text{if s subsists in} \cup d \in D \ (s\,[x\,/d\,]\,[\phi]) \\ \varnothing & \text{otherwise} \end{cases}$

This works like $\exists$, setting up a discourse referent which can take as value in the context anything which is F, so long as the context guarantees that something is F in every open possibility.

$\downarrow$ outputs $\varnothing$ when the presupposition it introduces fails. $\varnothing$ is one way to interpret a fail state in dynamic semantics. (Stalnakerian principles of assertion predict that any assertion updating the context to $\varnothing$ is infelicitous.[40]) Above, I suggested a kind of fault-tolerant computation process which would revert back to the prior information state if we reached this sort of failure.

But now consider a sequence of instructions like $s[\downarrow xF(x)][R(x)]$, much as we used in the cleft and factive cases above. Suppose the presupposition fails. In such a case, $s[\downarrow xF(x)]$ results in $\varnothing$. By the fault-tolerant strategy, we may reset the information state to s. But then we find that $s[R(x)]$ is *undefined* (so long as x is a new variable). This is a stronger sort of failure. It is not that the update reaches a failure state, but that the update instruction is undefined on the information state entirely.

There are many issues yet to be explored here. Many presuppositions, including some I discussed above, require propositional values of $\downarrow$. Work on

---

[40] More formal work with this sort of idea, see van Eijck (1993).

dynamic Montague grammars could be used to extend the proposal here to propositions. Certainly a more extensive discussion of the cross-categorial nature of presupposition is still needed.

REFERENCES

Adams, E. W. (1975). *The Logic of Conditionals* (Dordrecht: Reidel).

Atlas, D. J., and S. C. Levinson (1981). 'It-Clefts, Informativeness, and Logical Form: Radical Pragmatics (*Revised Standard Version*)', in P. Cole (ed.), *Radical Pragmatics* (New York: Academic Press), 1–61.

Austin, J. L. (1975). *How to Do Things with Words*, ed. J. O. Urmson and M. Sbisà (2nd edn. Cambridge, Mass.: Harvard University Press).

Ayer, A. J. (1946). *Language, Truth and Logic* (2nd edn. London: Victor Gollancz).

Bach, K. (1994). 'Conversational Impliciture', *Mind and Language*, 9: 124–62.

Beaver, D. I. (1997). 'Presupposition', in J. van Benthem and A. ter Meulen (eds.), *Handbook of Logic and Language* (Amsterdam: Elsevier), 939–1008.

—— (2001). *Presupposition and Assertion in Dynamic Semantics* (Stanford, Calif.: CSLI Publications).

Carlson, L. (1983). *Dialogue Games* (Dordrecht: Reidel).

Carston, R. (1988). 'Implicature, Explicature, and Truth-Theoretic Semantics', in R. M. Kempson (ed.), *Mental Representation* (Cambridge: Cambridge University Press), 155–81.

—— (2004). 'Explicature and Semantics', in S. Davis and B. Gillon (eds.), *Semantics: A Reader* (Oxford: Oxford University Press).

Chierchia, G. and S. McConnell-Ginet (1990). *Meaning and Grammar: An Introduction to Semantics* (Cambridge: MIT Press).

Chomsky, N. (1965). *Aspects of the Theory of Syntax* (Cambridge: MIT Press).

Davis, S. (1991). *Pragmatics* (Oxford: Oxford University Press).

Delin, J. (1992). 'Properties of It-Cleft Presupposition', *Journal of Semantics*, 9: 289–306.

Eijck, J. van (1993). 'The Dynamics of Descriptions', *Journal of Semantics*, 10: 239–67.

—— (1994). 'Presupposition Failure: A Comedy of Errors', *Formal Aspects of Computing*, 6A: 766–87.

Fintel, K. Von (2004). 'Would You Believe It? The King of France Is Back!', in A. Bezuidenhout and M. Reimer (eds.), *Descriptions and Beyond* (Oxford: Oxford University Press).

Frege, G. (1892). 'Über Sinn und Bedeutung', *Zeitschrift für Philosophie und philosophische Kritik*, 100: 25–50. References are to the translation as 'On Sense and Meaning' by M. Black, reprinted in Frege (1984).

Frege, G. (1984). *Collected Papers on Mathematics, Logic, and Philosophy*, ed. B. McGuinness (Oxford: Basil Blackwell).

Glanzberg, M. (2001). 'The Liar in Context', *Philosophical Studies*, 103: 217–51.

—— (2002). 'Context and Discourse', *Mind and Language*, 17: 333–75.

—— (2004). 'Against Truth-Value Gaps', in J. C. Beall (ed.), *Liars and Heaps: New Essays on Paradox* (Oxford: Oxford University Press), 151–94.

—— and S. Siegel (forthcoming). 'Presupposition and Policing in Complex Demonstratives', *Noûs*.

Grice, P. (1969). 'Utterer's Meaning and Intentions', *Philosophical Review*, 78: 147–77. Reprinted in Grice (1989).

—— (1975). 'Logic and Conversation', in P. Cole and J. L. Morgan (eds.), *Speech Acts*, vol. iii of *Syntax and Semantics* (New York: Academic Press), 41–58. Reprinted in Grice (1989).

—— (1989). *Studies in the Way of Words* (Cambridge, Mass.: Harvard University Press).

Groenendijk, J., and M. Stokhof (1991). 'Dynamic Predicate Logic', *Linguistics and Philosophy*, 14: 39–100.

—— M. Stokhof, and F. Veltman (1996). 'Coreference and Modality', in S. Lappin (ed.), *Handbook of Contemporary Semantic Theory* (Oxford: Blackwell), 179–213.

Haegeman, L. (1994). *Introduction to Government and Binding Theory* (2nd edn. Oxford: Blackwell).

Heim, I. (1982). 'The Semantics of Definite and Indefinite Noun Phrases', Ph.D. dissertation, University of Massachusetts at Amherst. Published New York, Garland, 1989.

—— (1983). 'On the Projection Problem for Presupposition', *Proceedings of the West Coast Conference on Formal Linguistics*, 2: 114–25. Reprinted in Davis (1991).

—— (1992). 'Presupposition Projection and the Semantics of Attitude Verbs', *Journal of Semantics*, 9: 183–221.

—— and A. Kratzer (1998). *Semantics in Generative Grammar* (Oxford: Blackwell).

Herburger, E. (2000). *What Counts: Focus and Quantification* (Cambridge Mass.: MIT Press).

Horn, L. R. (1981). 'Exhaustiveness and the Semantics of Clefts', *NELS* 11: 125–42.

—— (1989). *A Natural History of Negation* (Chicago: University of Chicago Press).

Jackendoff, R. S. (1972). *Semantic Interpretation in Generative Grammar* (Cambridge, Mass.: MIT Press).

Kadmon, N. (2001). *Formal Pragmatics* (Oxford: Blackwell).

Kamp, H. (1984). 'A Theory of Truth and Semantic Representation', in J. Groenendijk, T. Janssen, and M. Stokhof (eds.), *Truth, Interpretation, and Information* (Dordrecht: Foris), 1–41.

Karttunen, L. (1974). 'Presupposition and Linguistic Context', *Theoretical Linguistics*, 1: 181–94. Reprinted in Davis (1991).

—— and S. Peters (1979). 'Conventional Implicature', in C.-K. Oh and D. A. Dinneen (eds.), *Presupposition*, vol. xi of *Syntax and Semantics* (New York: Academic Press), 1–56.

King, J. C. (2001). *Complex Demonstratives* (Cambridge, Mass.: MIT Press).

Kiss, K. É. (1998). 'Identificational Focus versus Information Focus', *Language*, 74: 245–73.

Krahmer, E. (1998). *Presupposition and Anaphora* (Stanford, Calif.: CSLI Publications).

Kuppevelt, J. van (1995). 'Discourse Structure, Topicality and Questioning', *Journal of Linguistics*, 31: 109–47.

Levinson, S. C. (1983). *Pragmatics* (Cambridge: Cambridge University Press).

Lewis, D. (1979). 'Scorekeeping in a Language Game', *Journal of Philosophical Logic*, 8: 339–59. Reprinted in Lewis (1983).

—— (1983). *Philosophical Papers*, i (Oxford: Oxford University Press).

Prince, E. F. (1978). 'A Comparison of Wh-Clefts and It-Clefts in Discourse', *Language*, 54: 883–906.

Recanati, F. (1993). *Direct Reference* (Oxford: Blackwell).

Roberts, C. (1996). 'Information Structure in Discourse: Towards an Integrated Formal Theory of Pragmatics', *Ohio State University Working Papers in Linguistics*, 49: 91–136.

Rooth, M. (1985). '*Association with Focus*', Ph. D. dissertation, University of Massachusetts at Amherst.

—— (1992). 'A Theory of Focus Interpretation', *Natural Language Semantics*, 1: 75–116.

—— (1999). 'Association with Focus or Association with Presupposition?', in P. Bosch and R. A. van der Sandt (eds.), *Focus* (Cambridge: Cambridge University Press), 232–44.

Sandt, R. A. van der (1988). *Context and Presupposition* (London: Croom Helm).

—— (1992). 'Presupposition Projection as Anaphora Resolution', *Journal of Semantics*, 9: 333–77.

—— and B. Geurts (2001). 'Too', in *Proceedings of the 13th Amsterdam Colloquium* (Amsterdam: University of Amsterdam).

Schegloff, E. A., G. Jefferson, and H. Sacks (1977). 'The Preference for Self-Correction in the Organization of Repair in Conversation', *Language*, 53: 361–82.

Schiffer, S. (1972). *Meaning* (Oxford: Clarendon Press).

Schiffrin, D. (1985). 'Conversational Coherence: The Role of *Well*', *Language*, 61: 640–67.

Simons, M. (2001a). 'Disjunction and Alternatives', *Linguistics and Philosophy*, 24: 597–619.

—— (2001b). 'On the Conversational Basis of Some Presuppositions', *Semantics and Linguistic Theory*, 11: 431–48.

Simons, M. (n.d.), 'Why Some Presuppositions Are Conversational Implicatures', unpublished.

Soames, S. (1989). 'Presupposition', in D. Gabbay and F. Guenthner (eds.), *Handbook of Philosophical Logic* (Dordrecht: Kluwer), iv. 553–616.

Sperber, D., and D. Wilson (1986). *Relevance* (Cambridge, Mass.: Harvard University Press).

Stalnaker, R. C. (1973). 'Presuppositions', *Journal of Philosophical Logic*, 2: 447–57.

—— (1974). 'Pragmatic Presuppositions', in M. K. Munitz and P. K. Unger (eds.), *Semantics and Philosophy* (New York: New York University Press), 197–213. Reprinted in Stalnaker (1999).

—— (1978). 'Assertion', in P. Cole (ed.), *Pragmatics*, vol. ix of *Syntax and Semantics* (New York: Academic Press), 315–22. Reprinted in Stalnaker (1999).

—— (1998). 'On the Representation of Context', *Journal of Logic, Language, and Information*, 7: 3–19. Reprinted in Stalnaker (1999).

—— (1999). *Context and Content* (Oxford: Oxford University Press).

Stanley, J. (2000). 'Context and Logical Form', *Linguistics and Philosophy*, 23: 391–434.

Strawson, P. F. (1950). 'On Referring', *Mind*, 59: 320–344. Reprinted in Strawson (1971).

—— (1952). *Introduction to Logical Theory* (London: Methuen).

—— (1964). 'Identifying Reference and Truth-Values', *Theoria*, 30: 96–118. Reprinted in Strawson (1971).

—— (1971). *Logico-Linguistic Papers* (London: Methuen).

Zeevat, H. (1992). 'Presupposition and Accommodation in Update Semantics', *Journal of Semantics* 9: 379–412.

INDEX